COLLECTING COINS
for PLEASURE
& PROFIT

A comprehensive guide and handbook
for collectors and investors

BARRY KRAUSE

BETTERWAY PUBLICATIONS, INC.
WHITE HALL, VIRGINIA

Published by Betterway Publications, Inc.
P.O. Box 219
Crozet, VA 22932
(804) 823-5661

Cover design and photograph by Susan Riley
Photographs by Barry Krause
Typography by Park Lane Associates

Library of Congress Cataloging-in-Publication Data

Krause, Barry
    Collecting coins for pleasure & profit : a comprehensive guide and handbook for collectors and investors / Barry Krause.
        p. cm.
    Includes bibliographical references (p.) and index.
    ISBN 1-55870-207-5 (paperback) : $18.95
        1. Coins--Collectors and collecting--Handbooks, manuals, etc.
2. Coins as an investment--Handbooks, manuals, etc. I. Title.
II. Title: Collecting coins for pleasure and profit.
CJ81.J67 1991
737.4074--dc20   91-19493
                                                          CIP

Printed in the United States of America
0 9 8 7 6 5 4 3 2 1

Acknowledgments

Q. David Bowers (Company President) and Cathy Dumont (Company Photographer) of Bowers and Merena Galleries, Inc. of Wolfeboro, NH—for generously providing the black-and-white photos of so many wonderful rare U.S. coins that appear in this book (originally in recent Bowers and Merena auctions).

Dr. Arnold R. Saslow (Company President) of Rare Coins & Classical Arts Ltd. of South Orange, NJ—for generously allowing me to handle and photograph ancient coins from his stock, for use as illustrations in Chapter 1; and for giving me information on the ancient coin market.

The coin dealers in Chapter 13 — for providing information about their companies, with special thanks for personal replies from Q. David Bowers of Bowers and Merena Galleries, Inc.; Patrick Finn of Spink & Son Ltd.; Mark Goldberg of Superior Stamp & Coin Co., Inc.; Leon E. Hendrickson of Silver Towne Coin Co.; Dana Linett of Early American Numismatics; Dr. Arnold R. Saslow of Rare Coins & Classical Arts Ltd.; and Harvey G. Stack of Stack's.

Sanford J. Durst of Long Island City, NY—for permission to reprint a passage from his publication *Observations on the Practice of Counterfeiting Coins and Medals*, for use in Chapter 16.

The numismatic literature dealers in the Bibliography, namely: Charles Davis of Morristown, NJ;

Sanford J. Durst of Long Island City, NY; Orville J. Grady of Omaha, NE; George Frederick Kolbe of Crestline, CA; and Numismatic Arts of Santa Fe, NM—for providing price lists and catalogs of numismatic literature.

The American Numismatic Association of Colorado Springs, CO—for permission to publish ANA grading standards for U.S. coins and the use of ANA numerical grades; and for supplying a photograph of a coin bourse floor in action. Special thanks to Robert J. Leuver, Executive Director, ANA; and to Barbara Gregory, Editor/Publisher of *The Numismatist*.

The American Numismatic Society of New York City—for supplying Society information and photos for Chapter 18. Special thanks to Leslie A. Elam, Director of the ANS—for giving me a personal tour of the Society's building; to William E. Metcalf, Chief Curator of the ANS—for showing and explaining the Society's ancient coin collections to me; and to Roxanne Greenstein, Development Officer of the ANS—for supplying official Society photos and for answering my questions on ANS activities.

Coin grading services in Chapter 6 — for providing information about their companies. Specifically: American Numismatic Association Certification Service (ANACS, as it prefers) of Columbus, OH;

Numismatic Guaranty Corporation of America (NGC) of Parsippany, NJ; Photo-Certified Coin Institute (PCI) of Chattanooga, TN; and Professional Coin Grading Service (PCGS) of Newport Beach, CA.

Coin dealer organizations—for providing information for Chapter 13. Namely: Professional Numismatists Guild (PNG) of Van Nuys, CA; Canadian Association of Numismatic Dealers (CAND) of Ottawa, Canada; Industry Council for Tangible Assets (ICTA) of Washington, DC; British Numismatic Trade Association Ltd. (BNTA) of Coventry, England; and International Association of Professional Numismatists (IAPN) of Zürich, Switzerland.

Bernard Nagengast of E & T Kointainer Co. of Sidney, OH—for providing information for Chapter 5.

John Schwartz of Capital Plastics, Inc. of Massillon, OH—for providing information for Chapter 5.

Federal Bureau of Investigation, U.S. Department of Justice, Washington, DC—for providing information on the National Stolen Coin File for Chapter 5.

The Gold and Silver Institute of Washington, DC—for providing information for Chapter 15 and for allowing me to reproduce their graphs.

Ron Downing, Company President, *The Coin Dealer Newsletter* of Torrance, CA—for providing information on his publications for Chapter 15.

Federal Trade Commission of Washington, DC —for providing information for Chapter 15.

Los Angeles County Museum of Art, Los Angeles, CA—for providing a photograph of one of their paintings, and for permission to reproduce such in this book. Special thanks to Elliot M. Shirwo of the Museum's Photographic Services/Rights & Reproductions Department.

The United States Mint, U.S. Department of the Treasury, Washington, DC — for providing information on current U.S. coinage facilities; for providing official U.S. Mint photographs for use in this book; for providing historical data; and for making the coins that figure so prominently in this book. Special thanks to Hamilton Dix, Manager, Office of Public Information, U.S. Mint, Washington, DC; and to Eleanor McKelvey, Exhibits & Public Services, U.S. Mint, Philadelphia, PA; and to Olga K. Widnes, Administrator, Old Mint Museum,

San Francisco, CA; and to Melinda H. Hamm, Administrative Officer, U.S. Bullion Depository, Fort Knox, KY.

The United States Secret Service, U.S. Department of the Treasury—for information on counterfeit coins for use in Chapter 16. Special thanks to Robert R. Snow, Assistant Director, Office of Government Liaison and Public Affairs, U.S. Secret Service.

Western Publishing Co. of Racine, WI — for permission to quote coin prices from 1961, 1971, 1981, and 1991 editions of *A Guide Book of United States Coins*. Special thanks to Marge Hardy, Permissions and Contracts Administrator, Western Publishing Co.

The coin show promoters and societies of Chapter 14—for providing information on their shows.

The numismatic periodicals in Chapter 17—for providing me with up-to-date information for this book.

The corresponding secretaries of the numismatic societies in Chapter 18—for providing detailed information about their organizations.

The museums of Chapter 19, whose staffs provided detailed information about their coin displays and visitor rules; and whose staffs, in many instances, gave me personal museum tours of their coin exhibits.

The Wells Fargo History Museum, Bank of California's Museum of Money of the American West, and Old Mint Museum—all of San Francisco—for allowing me to take photographs of their museum exhibits.

The Nevada State Museum, Carson City, NV— for providing official photographs of the Carson City Mint building, and rights to publish them in this book. Special thanks to Gloria J. Harjes, Assistant Curator/Registrar, Nevada State Museum.

The staff of Santa Monica Public Library, Santa Monica, CA—for helping me with research.

The authors and publishers of the coin books listed in the Bibliography — which refreshed my memory on many things I discuss in this book.

KODALUX Processing Services of Hollywood, CA and Palo Alto, CA — for film processing for book photos.

Richard Photo Lab of Los Angeles, CA—for film processing for book photos.

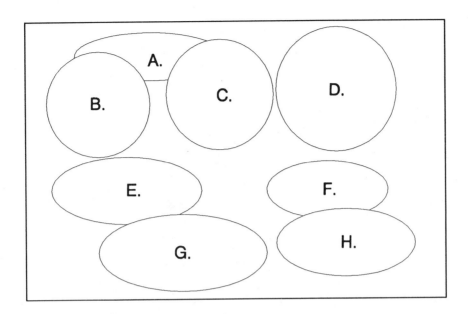

ABOUT THE COINS ON THE COVER

All coins pictured are from the author's collection.

A. Restrike of the silver Austrian *Maria Theresa Thaler.* All are dated 1780 but have been struck at many world mints up to the present day. The same design, including the date, was kept to please local populations of north and east Africa, who refused to accept other silver coinage in commerce. Contains about ³/₄ ounce of pure silver.

B. 1892 U.S. *Columbian Exposition Half Dollar* silver commemorative (same type for 1893). Sold for $1 each at the World's Columbian Exposition held in Chicago during the summer of 1893. About 2 ¹/₂ million total mintage of both dates combined—meaning that circulated examples are common and cheap. Flawless Uncirculated specimens command hefty prices. Struck in .900 fine silver, 30.6mm in diameter.

C. 1904 Philippines *50-Centavos* piece, large size variety, silver in Uncirculated condition. Struck under U.S. sovereignty. Listed in the *Red Book*®. 13.4784 grams when struck, .900 fine silver. 11,000 business strikes this year.

D. 1904 Philadelphia Mint *Double Eagle ($20 Gold Piece).* 34mm in diameter. Contains .9675 Troy ounce of pure gold, struck .900 fine. *Double Eagles* were the largest widely minted U.S. gold coins, struck from 1849 (the unique Smithsonian pattern) through 1933 (none legally placed in circulation for the last date).

E. 1878 San Francisco Mint *Morgan Dollar*, the first year of issue. Produced with the prodding of the Bland-Allison Act of 1878. Designed by George T. Morgan. 38.1mm in diameter, struck in .900 fine silver. When newly minted, each *Morgan Dollar* contained .77344 Troy ounce of pure silver. Produced 1878-1904, and 1921.

F. 1942 Philadelphia Mint *Liberty Walking Half Dollar*, struck in .900 fine silver, 30.6mm diameter. When newly minted, each *Liberty Walking Half Dollar* contained .36169 Troy ounce of pure silver. Designed by Adolph A. Weinman. Produced from 1916 through 1947.

G. *Eisenhower Bicentennial Dollar*, struck in 1975 and 1976, although all are "dual dated" 1776-1976. Struck in both copper-nickel clad and silver clad Proofs and business strikes. Obverse designed by Frank Gasparro. 38.1mm in diameter. Silver issue contains .3161 Troy ounce of pure silver.

H. 1826 U.S. *Half Dollar*, Capped Bust type with lettered edge. 32.5mm in diameter, struck at weight of 13.48 grams of .8924 fine silver, the *Bust Halves* are slightly larger in diameter, heavier, and with more silver than modern U.S. silver *Half Dollars*. Because they were stored and saved in banks at the time of issue, *Bust Half Dollars* of many dates and varieties are relatively easy to locate today, even in high grades.

1. "HISTORY INSTRUCTING YOUTH" medallion issued by the California State Numismatic Association (CSNA) for its 48th semi-annual convention, held in Fresno, CA on April 16-18, 1971. The design is adapted from the *One Dollar Silver Certificate* of 1896, created by Will H. Low and engraved by Charles Schlecht. The CSNA was organized February 22, 1947 and incorporated June 2, 1961. Bronze, 39mm in diameter. Author's collection.

Contents

Introduction

Take a coin out of your pocket or wallet. Look at the *obverse* (front side). Turn it over and study the *reverse* (back side). Run your finger along the *edge* (border) and tap the coin on a table or against another piece of metal—listen to it ring!

Hold this coin tightly in your closed hand and ponder what future generations of people will think of it when they gaze in puzzled awe on a rare monetary relic of the late 20th century!

COINS! Metal messengers from the remote past, buyers of the fleeting present, anticipators of the mysterious future!

COINS! Paying intrinsic homage to great nations and powerful leaders, to majestic animals and breathtaking landscapes, to stately buildings and graceful sailing ships!

COINS! Engraved with sovereign flags and patriotic slogans, with personifications of gods and goddesses, with laurel wreaths and dawning sunrises!

COINS for the piggy bank, coins for the vending machine, coins for the bus and subway, for parking meters and telephone booths, for sales tax and casino slot machines!

Do you have change for a dollar? Can I borrow a quarter? Should we tip the waiter with these coins? Is there a pot of gold at the end of your rainbow?

The ancient Greeks placed a coin in the mouth of a human corpse as payment to the ferryman Charon who rowed newly dead souls across the sacred River Styx.

Jesus held up a silver *denarius* of the Emperor Tiberius, and explained to the transfixed crowd: "Render unto Caesar the things that are Caesar's, and unto God the things that are God's."

Silver Crusader Pennies and medieval gold Florins. Chinese bronze "Cash" and Russian platinum Rubles. British Crowns and Germanic Thalers. COINS all!

Gold Doubloons and silver Pieces of Eight—pirate coins dug up on secluded coasts. Treasure chests retrieved from sunken shipwrecks on the Spanish Main!

George Washington threw a coin across the Potomac River, so numismatic legend says. Coins were placed on the eyelids of Abraham Lincoln as the martyred President lay dead by assassination.

Large Cents and Small Cents … Buffalo Nickels and Walking Liberty Halves … Silver Dollars and Double Eagles—the coins of collectors!

California Gold Rush coins, struck privately

from gold dust dumped on the assayer's desk by grizzled prospectors just in from the mother lode ... Civil War Tokens, brass testimony of a nation torn asunder ... Double Strikes and Doubled Dies, error coins for the specialist and scholar!

"Brother, can you spare a Dime?" queries the panhandler. And don't forget the formal fund-raisers such as the Infantile Paralysis charity solicitors in the days of the celebrated March of Dimes coin donations that paid for research that led to the poliomyelitis vaccine.

We are far from being the "cashless society" predicted by those who herald the extinction of circulating coinage. Coins have been with us for more than two and a half millenia, and will likely still be of some use for commerce as long as human beings endure on Earth.

Think about it! This coin that you are holding will quite likely outlive you!

But until you take your last glance at the wonders of this amazing world, continue to enjoy these metal creations of human ingenuity, these artistic servants of petty and noble endeavors, these precious little alloyed articles born in the fiery furnaces of the mintmasters' workshops, scattered to the ends of the Earth in the hands and purses of all who live and love the rare and the beautiful—the subjects of this book and the objects of your patient collecting and studying, these metallic symbols of glory and wealth—these COINS!

1

The Origin of Coins

The first coins were made in the 7th century B.C. in Lydia and Ionia in Asia Minor (what is now Turkey). Small lumps of *electrum*, a natural alloy of gold and silver, were stamped with merchants' punch marks as a guarantee of value. Size wasn't standardized at first, so for every business transaction with these "coins," the stamped metal ingots had to be reweighed. This problem quickly led to (1) standardized coin weights, guaranteed by government authorities, and (2) the use of obverse and reverse coinage dies, which caused the metal lump to flatten out into the circular shape that has been recognized for more than two and a half millenia as a "coin."

Barter was the original method of commerce, antedating the invention of coinage. For example, cattle, weapons, clothing, and food were freely bartered for needed goods. Obviously and unfortunately (for barterers, not for future coin collectors), barter was inefficient because you had to have a specific commodity that someone just happened to want in order to exchange it for what they possessed that you happened to want in return. You might have walked a long time with a couple of chickens before you found somebody with a nice spear to trade.

The word "money" is from the Latin *moneta* (from *moneo*, "to warn"). Juno was the Roman goddess of warning and guardian of finances, and as such she was known as *Juno Moneta*. The word "coin" is from the Latin *cuneus* ("wedge") because ancient coinage dies at that time looked like wedges. And coins themselves quickly became the medium of exchange in the ancient Greek world, replacing primitive barter with a monied coinage that was recognized and accepted at *intrinsic value* (actual metal value of the coin) by people far beyond the mere borders of the principality that made the coins. *Legal tender* means "lawful money," and governments from earliest times have declared their coinage to be legal tender; i.e., subject to compulsory acceptance by their citizens. *Fiat money*, which has little or no intrinsic value (like paper currency unbacked by precious metal), was to become commonplace as the centuries passed, due to government greed during inflation and at times when the royal treasuries were low on *specie* (precious metal bullion; e.g., gold or silver bars after they had been minted into circulating coins).

THE MINTING OF ANCIENT COINS

A *coinage die* is a piece of metal from which a coin

is struck. Usually there are two dies: (1) an *obverse die* for the front or "face" or "heads" side of a coin, and (2) a *reverse die* for the back or "tails" side of a coin. Dies in pre-machine age times were all hand-made by engraving the coin's design in reverse (a mirror image) on a soft piece of steel, which was then hardened by *annealing*, a process whereby metal is heated and then cooled slowly to prevent brittleness. Since every die in the ancient world was handmade, no two dies are exactly alike, creating endless fascinating coin varieties for the collector, as well as some refuge for the counterfeiter, who doesn't have to reproduce a coin exactly!

Every single ancient coin was individually hand-struck by hammering one die against another one, with the *flan* (blank piece of metal, to be the future coin) in between the dies. Usually the obverse die was placed in a depression on top of an anvil, a strong iron or steel block on which metal objects may be hammered and shaped. The reverse die was often a bronze punch that was placed on top of the flan. More care was generally allotted in the fashioning of the obverse die than the reverse die, because the obverse die contained (1) the *portrait* in high *relief* (the "raised" areas on the resultant coin), and (2) later on, vital lettering such as the emperor's name, etc.

When the dies were ready for action, a flan was heated in a furnace to soften the metal. Then the flan was picked up with iron or steel tongs and placed carefully on top of the obverse die nestled on the anvil. The reverse die on the underside of the punch was then positioned on top of the flan, and with a powerful whack of the hammer on the end of the punch (opposite the end where the reverse die was affixed), the reverse die was pounded into the soft flan. The flan simultaneously picked up the impression on its underside from the obverse die on the anvil. Then the newly struck coin was removed with tongs and allowed to cool and harden.

CHARACTERISTICS OF ANCIENT COINS

The resulting coin, from this laborious hand "minting" process, lacked uniform thickness and centering. Off-center ancient coins are common, and for some varieties a well-centered example on a wide, undamaged flan is the exception. Craftsmanship

standards of the "moneyer's art" have varied wildly from age to age, starting with the very first coins in ancient Greece. Ancient coins are often encountered with split flans, weakly struck designs, oversized and undersized flans (by diameter, not so much by weight — the weight was supposed to be uniform for a given denomination at a given time in history), and "edge" deformities—all caused by striking inconsistencies.

Coinage Metals

The use of the various coinage metals has hardly varied from ancient times through the Renaissance and even to our own day. Copper coins (abbreviated "CU" for "copper" in ancient coin collecting terminology) were used by the common people in daily business transactions. Many peasants on the farm, as well as poverty-stricken city dwellers, never saw anything but copper coins and were glad to get them when they did! Silver coins ("AG" = "silver") were paid to soldiers, especially during military campaigns, to keep them happy and less likely to mutiny. Silver was also used by tradesmen and town merchants, and occasionally by lower class people for major purchases, such as a horse or weapon. Gold coins ("AU") were used by governments, nobility, and wealthy merchants for serious transactions. The average peasant never saw a gold coin, and the average prince or international merchant wouldn't have wanted to see a copper coin. Fixed ratios of proportionate value, of course, existed for the various metals: so many copper pieces were worth one silver coin, and so many silver coins were equivalent to one gold. Highwaymen who robbed the lightly armed and unwary traveler were delighted to steal any coins they were able to get, and a rich person traveling with a heavy purse was prudent to arrange for an appropriate armed escort.

Coin Hoards

Burying coins was a common practice both in the ancient world and during the Middle Ages, especially during times of war. Newly discovered coin hoards all over Europe and the near east (Palestine, etc.) often yield whole handfuls of choice coins whose original owners hid them and never retrieved them for whatever reasons. Indeed, the reasonable market prices for many ancient coins ($25 for a cheap Roman bronze piece, $60 for a F-VF silver *denarius*) can, in part, be attributed to the fact that so many coin hoards have been unearthed. Another reason for the plentiful supply of ancient coins is something that we are apt to forget: many coins were made in the ancient world. The Roman Empire, at its height, had millions of people in it. Common varieties of ancient coins are not rare or valuable, and one of the first lessons we learn as serious coin collectors is that *age alone has little to do with a coin's market price.* Don't be impressed by a coin just because it is 2,000 years old. Is it beautiful and rare and desirable numismatically by those who know what is good? If it is, then it's worth spending money to obtain.

Patina (Toning)

One trait of many ancient coins is *patina*, the thin (or thick!) layer of chemical discoloration on the surface of a coin that has been oxidized over the passage of time. Copper and bronze coins show the most patination, silver the next most, while many gold pieces are dug up looking as brilliant as the day they were minted, centuries ago. Copper is the most chemically reactive of the metals commonly used in coinage. Copper passes from its shiny, metallic reddish-brown color to chocolate to black as it forms an oxidation crust. Many U.S. Large Cents minted in the first half of the 19th century are black from aging, so we can expect copper coins from the ancient world to show similar effects.

WARNING: *Do not try to clean the patina off a coin.* A coin that has been cleaned is almost universally hated by informed numismatists. A cleaned coin looks ugly because it looks "cleaned," artificially brightened up, tampered with, made to look newer or (supposedly) better than it really is. The exquisite green and brown patina on a genuine Roman *sestertius* that has never been cleaned helps to verify its authenticity and makes it look like what it actually is: an ancient coin. Some ancient silver coins *do* look better when they've been cleaned a little after being unearthed, but this is a job for experts, not for the beginning coin collector. So many coins have been forever ruined by amateur cleaning that a standard rule in coin collecting is: NEVER CLEAN A COIN! A cleaned coin won't fool an informed nu-

mismatist, and there's no point in trying to fool anybody else.

ANCIENT GREEK COINS

It is the opinion of virtually all serious admirers of coins that the most beautiful coins ever made are the coins of ancient Greece. Nothing coined since has surpassed the timeless sublime splendor of the finest numismatic productions by the artists and mintmasters of Greece before the Roman era.

Ancient Greek coins typically show the head of a mythological being like Athena or Hercules on the obverse, and animals or deities on the reverse. The "turtles" of Aegina, the "owls" of Athens, the "winged horses" of Corinth, and the "dolphins" of Syracuse form a zoological pantheon of wonderful creatures for a collection of ancient coin "animal topicals."

Early Greek coins with graceful animals, deities, and semi-human figures have been acclaimed for their beauty since they were created. The Corinthian silver and gold *staters*, with a helmeted Athena on the obverse and the winged horse Pegasus on the reverse, are handsome even when struck off-center; the epitome of simplicity and perfection when flawlessly struck and surviving down to our own time in Mint State (*"Fleur-de-Coin"* or "FDC"—the term for "Uncirculated" as used by ancient coin collectors). I like a lot of Greek coins, but the *Corinthian stater* is near the top of my list of favorites. For around $400 you can buy a high grade silver specimen that you will be proud to own.

The "owls" of Athens, introduced in the 6th century B.C., soon became legal tender throughout the Athenian colonial world. Athena, patron goddess of the city-state of Athens, appears on the obverse, while the stylized owl on the reverse characterizes this coin as Athenian. The owled *tetradrachms*, moderately heavy silver coins, are not rare today, but are in demand by collectors of ancients, hence their $300 to $500 retail price for a decent-looking specimen.

A word of collecting advice, usually ignored by beginners: *Buy quality rather than quantity.* One nice ancient coin in Extremely Fine to FDC condition is more worth having than half a dozen heavily worn coins for the same total purchase price. Quality sells itself, a fact you will be made very aware of when you go to sell some coins from your collection. I've never regretted buying an expensive coin.

If you desire to assemble a "chronological" collection of representative Greek pieces, you'll probably want a 7th century B.C. Lydian example as one of the earliest coins extant, perhaps something with character, such as a circa 630 B.C. electrum *stater* of Lydia, with an obverse showing a lion's head, symbol of the Mermnad dynasty of Lydia. These were among the very first coins that were guaranteed by an established government for weight, purity, and trade value.

The coins of Sicily, from 480 B.C. to 360 B.C., are considered by many to be the most beautiful coins of all time. One example is the large silver decadrachms of Syracuse, the famous "dolphin" coins. In the late 5th century B.C., the artist Euainetos engraved into dies a remarkable group of images, considering the primitive tools available then. The *decadrachm*'s obverse shows a profile of the nymph Artemis Arethusa surrounded by delicate swimming dolphins; the reverse pictures a four-horse chariot ready for battle or perhaps an Olympic race. These coins are not cheaply purchased; you'd better have a deep wallet to buy a choice *Syracusan decadrachm*!

Alexander the Great, the young man who looked and "acted" like a god, conquered the known world before dying at age thirty-three in 323 B.C. His coins, minted in a similar style even after his death, show the head of Hercules on the obverse, a seated Zeus on the reverse. Some say that the head of Hercules is really a portrait of Alexander, but no mintmaster would have admitted that when the coins were struck, because ancient Greek coins were made before it became popular to put real human beings' faces on circulating money.

The common designs of the coins of Alexander are not rare today. A F-VF Alexander silver *drachm* ("small" coin) can be bought for $100 or less. Choice specimens sell for a bit more. To give you an idea of the prolific output of some types of ancient coins, the Amphipolis Mint was the most productive mint in Alexander's empire. It is estimated that the Amphipolis Mint produced 13,000,000 coins using more than 2,000 obverse and reverse dies in an eighteen-year period in the 4th century B.C.!

ANCIENT ROMAN COINS

The first Roman coins were bronze and began to be produced in earnest circa 300 B.C. The collectors of Roman coins divide the coinage into two broad time periods: (1) Roman Republic coins from 269 B.C. to 30 B.C., the obverses of which typically portray a rather boring helmeted profile of *Roma*; and (2) Roman Empire coins from 30 B.C. to 476 A.D. Further collecting divisions can be made by separating the coinage of the Empire into early, middle, and late emperors.

The world record price for an ancient coin at auction was broken on November 29, 1990 in a New York coin auction conducted by Numismatic Fine Arts of Los Angeles (see Chapter 13 for dealer descriptions). A breathtakingly gorgeous gold *aureus* of M. Junius Brutus, one of Julius Caesar's assassins, was sold to the high bidder for $550,000, plus a 10% buyer's fee added on the hammer price, for a total of $605,000! The crowd in the auction room broke into congratulatory applause when the final price was reached.

The Romans had no qualms about honoring living people (something the modern United States frowns upon) of the Imperial family as portraits on coins. Roman women enjoyed this status as well as men, and the first coins to picture living women were Roman. Latin was used on Roman coins because it was the language spoken at the time in that area of the world. Roman coins bear an abbreviated form of the Latin words, so a little study is necessary before the collector of Roman coins can decipher and attribute (which emperor, when it was struck, etc.) an ancient Roman coin at random. The custom of using Latin on coins continues to the present. Take a coin from your pocket and look at it. Every United States coin currently in circulation has the motto "E Pluribus Unum," Latin for "One Out of Many" or "From Many, One."

The Roman writer Suetonius (c. 69 A.D. to 140 A.D.) wrote a group of biographies and histories entitled *De Vita Caesarum* (*On the Lives of the Caesars*) at the beginning of the 2nd century A.D. The book starts with Julius Caesar, who was murdered in 44 B.C., and ends with the Emperor Domitian, who died in 96 A.D. By custom, we have come to know Suetonius' work as *The Lives of the Twelve Caesars*, and coin collectors feel compelled to collect coins minted during the reigns of these rulers. Julius Caesar was part of the Roman Republic, while his successor Augustus bridged the historical gap between Republic and Empire. Some numismatists and all historians prefer to call Augustus the first real Roman Emperor, so sometimes you'll see the list of the "Twelve Caesars" including Nerva at the end and eliminating Julius at the beginning.

The "Twelve" Caesars And Their Reigns		
[Julius Caesar] 49 B.C. - 44 B.C.		[as Dictator]
Augustus	27 B.C. - 14 A.D.	[as Emperor]
Tiberius	14 - 37 A.D.	
Caligula	37 - 41 A.D.	
Claudius	41 - 54 A.D.	
Nero	54 - 68 A.D.	
Galba	68 - 69 A.D.	
Otho	69 A.D.	
Vitellius	69 A.D.	
Vespasian	69 - 79 A.D.	
Titus	79 - 81 A.D.	
Domitian	81 - 96 A.D.	
[Nerva]	96 - 98 A.D.	

A "complete" Roman Twelve Caesars "type set" would include a bronze *sestertius*, a silver *denarius*, and a gold *aureus* of each of these rulers; just a group of worn *denarii* for collectors on a tight budget, or everything in FDC for those with deep wallets. A *denarius* of one of these rulers will run from around $100 to $500 for a worn-to-choice specimen. *Sestertii*, to be worth collecting, should be fairly high grade coins; and for the Twelve Caesars, EF to FDC sestertii aren't cheap. A worn sestertius of one of these rulers can be purchased for $100 to $200. If it is at all nice and well-struck with minimal wear and pleasing toning, figure on spending $1,000 a coin. The gold *aurei* can sell for a couple of thousand dollars for a worn specimen to $10,000 and more for exquisite examples. I once saw, at the Long Beach Coin Show, a custom-made Lucite coin holder displaying genuine examples of gold *aurei* of the Twelve Caesars in what appeared to be FDC condition. It was marked "For Sale" but I don't remember the price.

Bible Coins

Bible students enjoy studying and collecting coins mentioned in the Bible or used by peoples during Biblical times. "Biblical coins" thus form a subspecialty of ancient coin collecting. *Judean shekels, the* "widow's mite" (probably a Greek copper *lepton*), and the "thirty pieces of silver" (possibly *tetradrachms* of Antioch and Tyre) that Judas received for betraying Jesus — all these are for sale from coin dealers who carry ancients. The most famous coin of the Bible is the "Tribute Penny," (Matthew 22:15-22) very likely (by informed numismatic consensus) a silver *denarius* of the Roman Emperor Tiberius (14 - 37 A.D.). A barely presentable Tribute Penny will cost you $200; a beautiful one, $500.

Some Roman Coin Characteristics

Realistic portraiture can be seen on many Roman coins. We know quite well what the emperors looked like because of their distinctive and constant appearance on coins of their reigns. The artisans who prepared the Imperial coinage dies did their best to show, in high relief (at least during the early Empire), an attractive but still realistic portrait of the rulers whose very words meant the life or death of thousands. The Roman public was shocked to see their Emperor Nero's head on their coins, showing his hair in wavy curls with points along his brow, in the style of Roman street gangs of that time.

Nero *debased* Rome's coins by increasing the number of gold *aurei* from 42 to 45 per pound, silver *denarii* from 84 to 96 per pound, and raising the base metal alloy percentage in silver coins from 5% to 10%. The Emperor Diocletian (reigned 284 - 305 A.D.) was fed up with the condition of Rome's currency, so he initiated his celebrated "monetary reform," which only temporarily checked the inflation and coin debasement that was to plague Rome until the end. A coin called the *follis* appeared in circulation. It was a bronze coin with a silver wash and fooled nobody who took the time to test it for bullion worth. Gold and silver tended to disappear from circulation, and the coins of the late Empire are rather pathetic, ghostly imitations of their former selves as they existed during the first century A.D.

Roman coinage paid for much of the political

and military administration of the Empire, but debasing the coinage brought discredit to the government. In the third century A.D., the Roman government insisted that its taxes be paid in bullion, not coins—they wouldn't even accept their own coins for tax payments!

The United States (and all other countries of the world) got away with debasing the circulating coinage in the mid-1960s because (1) the price of silver, which was totally removed from coins, was edging up beyond the point where the melt value equaled the face value; (2) because everybody knew the "faith and credit" of the U.S. government was the real backer of circulating money; and (3) because the citizens let the government get away with debasing the coinage.

MEDIEVAL COINS

The Middle Ages is defined as the period of European history from the fall of the Roman Empire (in 476 A.D.) to the beginning of the Renaissance and modern times (c. 1450 A.D., depending on the locality). Collectors of medieval coins usually include specimens from the Byzantine Empire, the Crusades, coinage of the Popes, and classic pieces like the gold *florins* of Florence and the gold *ducats* of Venice. Medieval coinage is not widely appreciated by Americans, because most American numismatists have traditionally believed that the history of the world's coinage began in 1652 with the first Massachusetts silver pieces. Also, medieval European history is not emphasized in U.S. school curricula as much as it is in the European countries where it happened. Also, medieval coins tend to be "cluttered" in appearance, with hard-to-decipher lettering. (There are specialized coin books for the Middle Ages that can help you learn to read it.) These coins are also the monetary product of a con-

fusing succession of many centuries of rulers. These factors are all to the good for the collectors of medieval coins because the market prices of such coins would go through the roof if *every* coin collector collected them.

MODERN COINS

Hammered coins were produced throughout the Middle Ages. The first coining machinery was invented in Europe in the mid-1500s. Such machinery greatly improved the standardization and perfection of the minting process but was bitterly opposed by the moneyers' guilds, who were afraid of losing their jobs due to the new "technology." *Machine-struck* coins were not widely made until the 1600s. *Punches* (for putting portraits, lettering, dates, etc., into coinage dies) became common in coin production in the 1700s, enabling rapid die preparation without having to engrave every detail of a coin every time a die was made. *Die varieties* of coins therefore become less common and more minuscule the closer we come to the present. With late 20th century technology and quality control, it is a wonder that we have any die varieties at all. With the tremendous numbers of coins made today with high speed coining machinery, something will occasionally go wrong. Another reason die varieties still exist in currently made coins is that die life is quickly exhausted, so new dies must continually be put into service, albeit supposedly made from the same master die (hub). Still another reason is that people make mistakes: human error, and nothing else, is to blame for the 1955 Doubled Die Lincoln Cent variety. At any rate, minor and major die varieties that achieve catalog status make for interesting hours spent by the specialist devoted to the thrill of the hunt. The greatest coins are never the ones already in our collections but the ones that remain to be found.

2. Lydia gold *stater* (lightweight variety) from the time of King Croesus, reigned 560-546 B.C., showing the foreparts of a lion confronting the forepart of a bull. About Mint State. Author's photo, taken from the stock and courtesy of Dr. Arnold R. Saslow.

3. Reverse of Lydian gold light *stater* from the previous photo, with oblong punch marks divided into two "squares." Such marks served as a guarantee of value on the world's first coins. Author's photo, taken from the stock and courtesy of Dr. Arnold R. Saslow.

4. Athens silver *tetradrachm* obverse, 479-393 B.C., with the head of Athena facing right. Grade: Choice Extremely Fine. Author's photo, taken from the stock and courtesy of Dr. Arnold R. Saslow.

5. Athenian silver *tetradrachm* reverse (from coin in previous photo), showing the Athenian owl. At the height of Athens' power in the fifth century B.C., these coins were accepted as legal tender throughout much of the Greek world. Author's photo, taken from the stock and courtesy of Dr. Arnold R. Saslow.

6. Corinth silver *stater* obverse, 415-387 B.C., with Athena wearing a Corinthian helmet. Grade: Mint State. Author's photo, taken from the stock and courtesy of Dr. Arnold R. Saslow.

7. Macedon silver *tetradrachm* from the reign of Alexander the Great, 336-323 B.C., minted during his lifetime. Obverse shows Herakles (the Greek equivalent of the Roman Hercules) facing right. Grade: Mint State. Author's photo, taken from the stock and courtesy of Dr. Arnold R. Saslow.

8. Reverse of the Macedonian silver *tetradrachm* from previous photo, showing a seated Zeus facing left. Unusually nice detail in a coin that is often encountered worn. Author's photo, taken from the stock and courtesy of Dr. Arnold R. Saslow.

9. Macedon gold *stater* from reign of Alexander the Great, 336-323 B.C., showing a helmeted Athena. Pella Mint. Grade: Mint State. Author's photo, taken from the stock and courtesy of Dr. Arnold R. Saslow.

10. Reverse of the Macedonian gold *stater* from previous photo, with a standing Nike (the winged goddess of victory). Called a "lifetime issue"; i.e., minted during the life of Alexander the Great, to distinguish it from the many coins of similar designs that appeared after his death. Author's photo, taken from the stock and courtesy of Dr. Arnold R. Saslow.

11. Silver *shekel* of Tyre, ancient Phoenicia, minted after 126 B.C., showing the head of Melqarth, a local Phoenician god (the equivalent of Hercules). Possibly one of the Biblically-described "thirty pieces of silver" that Judas received for betraying Jesus. Grade: Mint State. Author's photo, taken from the stock and courtesy of Dr. Arnold R. Saslow.

12. Reverse of the Tyrian silver *shekel* from the previous photo, showing an eagle standing "to left" on the prow of a galley. This coin was used to pay the temple tax of ½ *shekel* per year per adult male. Author's photo, taken from the stock and courtesy of Dr. Arnold R. Saslow.

13. Roman silver *denarius* from the reign of the Emperor Tiberius (14-37 A.D.). This is the "Tribute Penny" of the Bible. Obverse shows the bust of the Emperor facing right. Grade: Extremely Fine. Author's photo, taken from the stock and courtesy of Dr. Arnold R. Saslow.

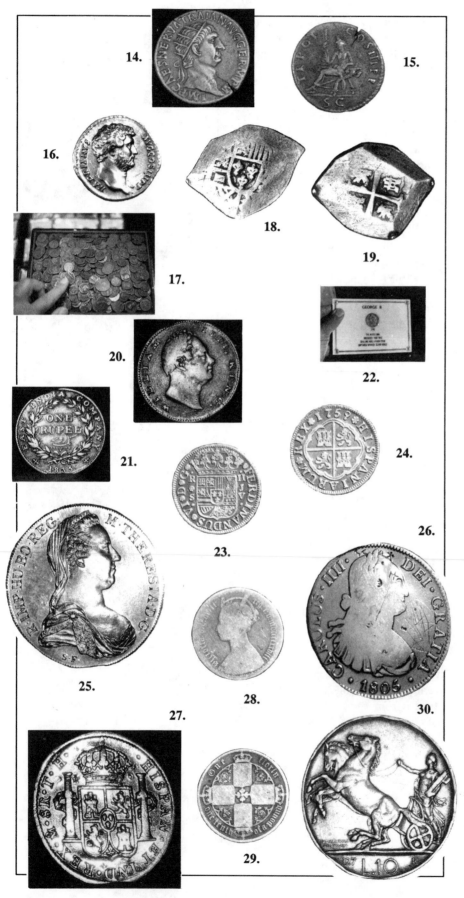

14. Roman bronze *dupondius* from the reign of the Emperor Trajan (98-117 A.D.), radiate head facing right. Grade: Choice Extremely Fine. Minted at Rome. Normal flan crack at lower right, caused by primitive handstruck coinage methods of the times. Author's photo, taken from the stock and courtesy of Dr. Arnold R. Saslow.

15. Reverse of the Roman bronze *dupondius* from previous photo, with Justicia (goddess of justice) seated to left. Coins of the Roman Empire typically had the living Emperor's portrait on the obverse and a diety on the reverse, and more care was taken to have a well-struck obverse than reverse, hence often weak-appearing reverse designs. Normal flan crack at top, continued from obverse side (see previous photo). Author's photo, taken from the stock and courtesy of Dr. Arnold R. Saslow.

16. Rome gold *aureus* of the Emperor Hadrian who reigned 117-138 A.D. Grade: About Mint State. Minted at Rome. One of the more "humane" emperors, Hadrian did much to improve his subjects' welfare. Gold *aurei*, like this one, are always in demand by collectors. Reverse shows Spes, the goddess of hope, walking to the left. Author's photo, taken from the stock and courtesy of Dr. Arnold R. Saslow.

17. Hoard of Roman Constantinian family bronzes, circa 300-360 A.D., consisting of *folles* and half *folles* (singular *follis*) of Constantine the Great and his sons. Ancient Roman coin hoards are still being discovered, evidence of people in the remote past who hid quantities of coins and, for some reason, never returned to retrieve them. Author's photo, taken from the stock and courtesy of Dr. Arnold R. Saslow.

18. *Cobs* are irregularly shaped silver (usually) coins made at Spanish Colonial mints in the New World. They date mostly from the 17th and 18th centuries, and were cut from bars of refined silver bullion, then trimmed to proper planchet weight, heated, and hammered between two dies. Many have been recovered from sunken Spanish treasure fleets that ran into hurricanes. Author's collection.

19. Other side of the *4-Reales* silver cob from the previous photo, showing quartered lions and castles quite worn. Sometimes so little of the design is visible on *cobs* that an exact date determination may be impossible. The word "*cob*" is derived from the Spanish *Cabo de barra* — "cut from a bar" — which is how the planchets were fashioned. Author's collection.

20. 1835 East India Company silver *One Rupee*, Colonial coinage from the reign of Britain's William IV. Struck on 11.66 grams .917 fine silver planchets. Circulated with pleasant gray toning. Author's collection.

21. Reverse of 1835 East India Company *One Rupee*. British India coins were struck from 1835 to 1947 when British rule ended with the partitioning of the country into India and Pakistan. Bilingual coins are common in countries where several dominant languages are used. Author's collection.

22. 1745 Great Britain silver *Shilling* in custom-made plastic display holder. Below the portrait of George II is the word LIMA, indicating that this *Shilling* was struck from captured Spanish silver coins. Pirate history embodied in a piece of metal. Author's collection.

23. 1759 Spain silver *2-Reales* piece from the reign of Ferdinand VI. Spain was the most powerful European country in the 16th century, but by the time this coin was struck her former glory had faded. Author's collection.

24. 1759 Spanish *2-Reales* piece from the previous photo, showing the quartered lions and castles characteristic of Spanish coins of the period. Lovely light gray field toning provides nice contrast for "whitish" devices and legend. Circulated but pleasant. Author's collection.

25. 1780 Austrian *Maria Theresa Thaler* silver restrike. All these coins are dated 1780, although many were struck at a variety of mints much later. A magnificent coin appears even more elegant when it is enlarged. Author's collection and photo.

26. 1805 silver *8-Reales* struck in Mexico City, under Spanish Colonial ruler Charles IV (ruled 1788-1808). Such coins circulated heavily in the young United States, until the mid-19th century when the U.S.

Mints began to address the coinage needs of the growing nation. This specimen has been cleaned and scratched. Author's collection and photo.

27. Reverse of the 1805 silver *8-Reales* piece from the previous photo. Circulated and cleaned, the author has used reflected sunlight to make this specimen more beautiful than it deserves to be! Struck on 27.07 grams .903 fine silver planchets. Author's collection and photo.

28. 1878 Great Britain silver *Florin* (equivalent to 2 Shillings). Heavily circulated, has been cleaned. Struck on 11.3104 grams .925 fine (Sterling) silver planchets. Author's collection.

29. Reverse of the 1878 British silver *Florin* from the previous photo. Has been cleaned at one time, and retoned. Coins are generally most popular (per capita of population) in their country of origin. British coins, naturally, have their most appreciative audience in Great Britain, although keen American collectors sometimes venture into British numismatics with intense investigation. Author's collection.

30. Reverse of Italian *10-Lire* piece of 1927, circulated but still presentable. Struck on 10 grams .835 fine silver planchets. Obverse bears the portrait of Vittorio Emanuele III. Author's collection and photo.

2

History of U.S. Coinage

In the earliest Colonial days, there existed no locally produced coins in America. Permanent settlements of transplanted Europeans began to be established along the Atlantic seaboard of what is now the United States in the early 1600s. Colonial governments derived their just powers from the mother countries in Europe: the French in the north (Canada), the English in the central region (New England through the Carolinas and Georgia), and the Spanish in the south (Florida and the Caribbean and into Mexico and beyond).

The first coins to circulate in the New World were British, Spanish, and French. We speak English now in the United States because the British settled what is now our eastern seaboard, and the culture spread westward as the nation grew. Eastern Canada, specifically Quebec, still has a strong French influence. And, of course, Spanish is the native tongue of inhabitants of most areas in the Western Hemisphere south of the United States, with Portuguese-speaking Brazil the prime exception.

The European governments were opposed to supplying their overseas colonies with coins. The philosophy of mercantilism ran rampant in the courts of Europe as medieval feudalism declined and as the Age of Exploration flowered in the 15th and 16th centuries. Mercantilism held that a mother country's economic interest is best served by fostering strong home-based industries protected by tariffs, monopolies, and exploitation of Colonial natural resources to tilt the balance of trade always in the direction of the mother country, with the resultant amassing of huge quantities of precious metal bullion in the royal treasuries. In other words, the American Colonies (French, English, and Spanish) existed solely for the mother countries' benefit. Colonial settlers were supposed to produce raw materials, such as lumber, metal bullion, furs, and spices, which were shipped to Europe in exchange for manufactured goods like house furniture and farm tools.

Barter was the method of commerce in the early American Colonies, not by choice but by default. The Colonial governments in Europe were afraid to give coins to the Colonists because the Colonists could thereby become more independent financially. No mints were established by Britain in her American Colonies, and any coins that the American Colonists happened to come by were quickly sent back to Europe to pay for manufactured goods, taxes, and "hard currency" debts. In 1642, tobacco was declared legal currency in Virginia; tobacco was also used in extensive bartering in the Carolinas. Beaver skins and Indian wampum (stringed shell "beads") were ubiquitous Colonial "money."

FOREIGN COINS IN THE COLONIES

So it was that British, Spanish, and French coins circulated as money in the British Colonies in America. Official currency in the British American Colonies was British, and financial documents were written up in pounds, shillings, and pence. Practical currency, however, consisted of whatever foreign coins could be obtained, along with barter.

Huge quantities of silver were pouring out of Spanish America, and the *Spanish Milled Dollar* (also known as a "piece of eight," "pillar dollar," "8 Reales piece," or "Silver Dollar") rapidly became the most commonly seen large silver coin in the British American Colonies. It was used as the basis of contracts and financial obligations, superseding the British currency notations on documents. In other words, when you owed someone money, the debt was converted to its equivalent of *Spanish Milled Dollars* when it was discharged.

The *Spanish Milled Dollar* features two globes between the Pillars of Hercules on the obverse; the Spanish coat of arms on the reverse. More than ten million pieces of eight were captured by the British from Spanish treasure ships at the Battle of Vigo Bay in 1702. The coin is called a piece of eight because of the custom of cutting the dollar into halves, quarters, and eighths to make change. Each eighth was known as a "bit," so a quarter of a dollar was "two bits"—the origin of our nickname for a U.S. 25¢ piece. One Spanish gold *doubloon* equaled sixteen *Spanish Milled Dollars* in exchange value. Because so many of these dollars were struck at Spanish Colonial mints in Mexico and South America, they are plentiful today, and for $100 you can buy a worn but discernible specimen. Because they circulated extensively, they are so "old," and many of them have been retrieved from the ravages of the sea in sunken treasure, *Spanish Milled Dollars* in top condition are a little scarce and can run many hundreds of dollars. Beware of counterfeits.

COLONIAL COINAGE PRODUCED IN AMERICA

Foreign silver and gold coins were kept legal tender from 1793 to 1857 in the United States, by act of Congress. The first U.S. Mint of the new United States nation was established at Philadelphia in 1792, but before that date, state and private "mints" produced coins to supplement whatever could be gotten from Europe. Many of these "Colonial coins" were copper pieces, some were silver, and a very few were gold, like the gold *Brasher Doubloon* of 1787, one of which sold at the 1979 Garrett Sale auction for $725,000.

The beauty of Colonial American coins lies in their romance. Often crudely struck on irregular *planchets* (flans), Colonial coins have a special appeal to numismatists who find the coins' origins in pre-Revolutionary America to be a fact that makes their "imperfect" appearance of secondary importance. Uncirculated examples of many Colonial coins do not exist. A rare variety of Connecticut "copper" may have a Very Fine specimen as the finest known.

The first mint established in the British American Colonies was in Boston in 1652. It was an illegal mint, born of necessity because the British government in London wouldn't allow the Colonists to import coins from England. The Massachusetts General Court appointed John Hull as Master of the Mint and ordered him to coin *shillings*, *sixpences*, and *three-penny pieces* from silver. Hull was a Boston silversmith, and he was paid 1 shilling and 3 pence for every 20 shillings he coined (6% of the money he made) for Massachusetts Bay Colony. He kept his contract for making coins for thirty years, but all of Hull's coins except the *Oak Tree Twopence* of "1662" were dated 1652 to make the British government think that the coins were made before the present London authorities were in power.

The most affordable of Hull's coins today are the "*Oak Tree*" coins of 1660-1667 and the "*Pine Tree*" coins of 1667-1682 (but all dated 1652). For a couple of hundred dollars you can buy a worn piece; $1,000 will purchase a fine specimen. At the Garrett Sale auction of 1980, a John Hull "*New England*" *sixpence* (of which eight are known to exist, the most recently discovered specimen having been found in February 1990, by a Long Island woman searching through an old potato field in East Hampton, New York) of 1652, with the simple "NE" and "VI" design, sold for $75,000.

These first Massachusetts silver coins were criminally "clipped" along the edges to secure silver shavings, which could be sold as bullion at a free profit to the clipper. Such petty larceny was counteracted by new coin designs wherein the designs more or less filled the planchet on both sides so clipping would be noticeable. The "reeded" (grooved, like U.S. dimes, quarters, and halves today) edges and lettered edges of early U.S. mint coinage would later serve the same anti-clipping purpose. Clipping has been done since ancient times. Some of John Hull's *Pine Tree shillings* are found bent today, possibly evidence of a practice used in those times to keep witches away.

The non-money uses of coins would itself fill a book as large as this one. Coins were worn around Colonial children's necks to repel witches. Coins were carried as good-luck pieces, tossed into fountains and wishing wells, and placed on the eyes of corpses or in the mouths of the dead—a carryover from ancient Greece when a coin was placed in a dead person's mouth to pay the ferryman Charon for passage across the River Styx into the underworld regions. Coins have been used as unreliable poison detectors when cooked with mushrooms. And many human events and choices have been decided by the flip of a coin.

Some popular Colonial coins among collectors today are: Connecticut, Massachusetts, New Jersey, New York, and Vermont *coppers*; the *"Rosa Americana" coppers* of 1722-1733 (struck in England); the Carolina and New England *"Elephant Tokens"*; the *"Nova Constellatio" coppers* of 1783 and 1785 (and a few silver pieces, one of which sold in the 1979 Garrett Sale for $190,000); the *Continental Dollars* of 1776 in pewter and silver; the *"Talbot, Allum and Lee"* cents of 1794-1795 (struck in England); and the *"Washington" tokens*, of which many varieties exist.

THE ESTABLISHMENT OF THE U.S. MINT

In 1784, a year after the American Revolution ended, Thomas Jefferson proposed a *decimal monetary system* for America, to replace the pounds,

shillings, pence British system. Decimalization spread around the world, starting officially with the United States in 1792 (when one dollar became equal to 100 cents) and France in 1794 (when one franc became equal to 10 décimes or 100 centimes).

The word "cent" comes from the Latin *centum*, meaning "one hundredth" or $1/100$ of a dollar in the newly established U.S. currency. The word "dime" is from the Latin *decimus*, meaning "tenth," i.e., $1/10$ of a dollar in U.S. money.

In the April 6, 1792 resolution by Congress, the U.S. Mint was established, and specifications were given for the legends and devices on the new coins:

Upon one side of each of the coins there shall be an impression emblematic of Liberty with an inscription of the word "Liberty" and the year of coinage; upon the reverse of each of the gold and silver coins there shall be the figure of representation of an eagle, with the inscription "United States of America"; and upon the reverse of the copper coins there shall be an inscription which shall express the denomination of the piece, namely, cent, or half cent, as the case may require.

President George Washington was opposed to having his portrait on the new U.S. coins, hence the symbolic portrait of the goddess of "Liberty." Thus, the first official U.S. coins were allegorical, like the ancient Greek coins, without living persons portrayed.

David Rittenhouse was appointed by President Washington in 1792 to be the first Director of the Mint. Construction of a Mint building began in Philadelphia in late summer 1792. The first coins struck under U.S. Mint auspices (although the new Mint building wasn't yet built) were silver *Half Disme*, inscribed "HALF DISME" on the coins' reverse. Fifteen hundred of these coins were made, and George Washington supplied some of his own silver plate for the coinage of these *Half Dismes*. When they come on the market, you can expect to pay several thousand dollars for even a worn specimen. Other coins struck in 1792, as patterns for proposed coinage, were the *"DISME"* in silver and copper (a copper specimen selling in the 1981 Garrett Sale for $54,000) and the famous *"Birch Cent"* in copper (an Uncirculated specimen selling in the

1981 Garrett Sale for $200,000).

Regular U.S. Mint coinage commenced in 1793 for copper *Half Cents* and *Large Cents*; 1794 for silver *Half Dollars* and *Dollars*; 1795 for silver *Half Dimes* (some of which were dated 1794) after completely changing the design of the 1792 *HALF DISME*, and for gold *Half Eagles* ($5 pieces) and gold *Eagles* ($10 pieces); and 1796 for silver *Dimes* and *Quarter Dollars*, and for *Quarter Eagles* ($2.50 gold pieces). All of these first U.S. Mint coins are scarce, especially in good states of preservation, so beware of counterfeits and altered dates (see Chapter 16).

Mint Mintage Records

Mintage records of the Mint don't tell the whole story of a coin. Mintage quantities alone are unreliable in estimating how many coins of a given series and date still exist for several reasons: (1) Coins were often struck in years other than the date on them because early 19th century U.S. Mint dies were used until they wore out, so coins carried on the Mint ledgers as having been minted in a given year may in reality have included coins struck from obverse dies of earlier dates. (2) Coins have been remelted either by the Mint itself (and the quantities melted not deducted from the quantities minted in the original mintage records) or by private parties after the coins have left the Mint into circulation. (3) Coins have been hoarded, both at the Mint in storage and in the hands of private citizens, resulting in a disproportionate quantity of hoarded coins surviving in "mint state" into the future, when compared with non-hoarded coins of similar mintages of the same denomination and time period. (4) The Mint records themselves may be in error, either by fault or design by Mint employees (for example, the U.S. Mint insisted that no *1913 Liberty Head Nickels* were ever made, yet five of them exist due to their apparently having been deliberately struck by a Mint employee without official authorization).

This accounts for the coin market price discrepancy between two coins of apparently equal mintages. For example, the *1909 VDB Lincoln Cent* struck at the Philadelphia Mint in a quantity of 27,995,000 currently sells for half as much in Uncirculated condition as a *1927-D Cent* from the Den-

ver Branch Mint (27,170,000 minted). The mintages are almost identical, yet the uncirculated price of the *1909 Cent* is cheaper because many of them were hoarded by the public at the time of issue, a common practice when a new coinage design is released by the government. However, circulated specimens of the *1909 VDB Cent* will now cost a collector a couple of dollars each, while circulated *1927-D Cents* can be purchased retail at less than a dollar. This clearly indicates that the *1909 VDB* coin is scarcer in circulated condition than the *1927-D* coin, which saw wide circulation immediately when it was released in the economic boom times of the late 1920s, and undoubtedly continued to circulate during the Great Depression of the 1930s when people couldn't afford to hoard money.

Adjustment Marks

Adjustment marks are often seen on coins made in the early days of our Mint, especially on silver coins. Adjustment marks are places on a coin where thin slivers of metal were filed off before striking to make an overweight planchet the correct weight. Don't confuse adjustment marks with collector-induced defects such as cleaning striations, cabinet friction from sliding a coin around in its storage containers, and accidental scratches.

U.S. MINTS

Mint Location	Years of Operation	Mintmark
Philadelphia, PA	1792 to date	none or P
Charlotte, NC	1838-1861	C
Dahlonega, GA	1838-1861	D
New Orleans, LA	1838-1909	O
San Francisco, CA	1854 to date (with interruptions as an "Assay Office")	S
Carson City, NV	1870-1893	CC
Denver, CO	1906 to date	D
West Point, NY	1984 to date	W

While the Philadelphia Mint served the people of the young United States well for almost half a century, the need arose for opening Branch Mints as the population spread westward, particularly in areas where large quantities of gold or silver were being mined, causing explosive population growth with "instant" massive immigration of fortune seekers. Above is a list of the U.S. Mints, past and present, their years of operation, and the mintmark letter that appears on the coin design to indicate where the coin was made.

The Denver Mint was an Assay Office from 1863 to 1906 when it achieved full Branch Mint status. The difference between an Assay Office and a Mint was that a Mint could legally make coins. Miners brought gold nuggets and native silver to an Assay Office, which melted the bullion, assayed it (determined the percentage of pure precious metal in the sample), and poured it into bars stamped with their weight and fineness (purity). The bars were then returned to the people who deposited the raw bullion. A Mint took unrefined bullion from depositors, then returned minted coins in equivalent exchange value. Private "mints" and "assay offices" sprung up wherever gold was discovered in quantity, and the *private* or *territorial* coins produced by these private businesses, while much in demand by collectors today because of their scarcity and gold rush romance, were often suspect at the time of issue because private gold coins were sometimes underweight; i.e., the stated denomination stamped on the coin ($5, $10, etc.) was greater than the actual bullion value of the precious metal contained therein. Thus, some private gold coins circulated at a discount off face value; others were refused outright by a business public that demanded full value in its circulating coinage. The establishment of a U.S. government Assay Office or Mint was welcomed; either could be depended upon to return honest value for customers depositing unrefined bullion.

Pre-Civil War U.S. Mint Coinage

I remember my high school U.S. history teacher telling our class that we would feel out of place in *pre*-Civil War United States. He pointed out that after the Civil War, with increasing urbanization and industrialization, the cities of this country began to look and "act" more as they do at the present. But imagine a primarily rural nation, with widely scattered small communities accessible mostly by horse travel, with slavery a government-approved practice, without the modern conveniences of telephones, electric light, indoor bathrooms, and food refrigeration, and *without a uniform currency in circulation*, and you'll have some idea of what it was like to stroll down the street of an American town in the time of Abraham Lincoln's youth. Low wages (a dollar a day was a nice income before the Civil War), child labor, runaway disease epidemics, minimal grammar school education for most, little social mobility, no voting rights for women, no deposit insurance to protect customers from bank failures, primitive fire protection, and constant threat of robbery by highwaymen or murder at the hands of a gun-toting populace—the good old days don't seem so good anymore!

But for the people living then, it was the modern world, the only reality they could possibly know. And the slowly trickling output of coins from the U.S. Mints was making citizens more aware that someday they might be able to dispense with foreign coins and the lingering vestiges of the barter system, to do business entirely with the minted monies of their new and proud nation.

Copper *Half Cents* and *Large Cents* were made by the Philadelphia Mint from 1793 to 1857, with several "breaks" in the yearly sequence for *Half Cents*, and only 1815 being omitted for *Large Cents*. United States *Cents* have been coined every year, from 1793 (1792, including the rare *Birch Cent*) to date, with the exception of 1815 because of a copper planchet shortage due to the War of 1812. During that War, the U.S. imposed an embargo on Britain, which supplied copper planchets in the early days of the U.S. Mint. Counterfeit and altered date *Large Cents* exist with the year 1815, but no knowledgeable collector would ever buy one, except for curiosity value.

Silver *Half Dimes* were minted from 1794 (actually made in 1795) to 1873, with several gaps in the date sequence. After they were established, the Branch Mints of New Orleans and San Francisco coined many *Half Dimes* also. *Dimes*, weighing double the weight of *Half Dimes*, were started at the Philadelphia Mint in 1796 and have been produced up to the present day, with a few "year" exceptions. The *Dimes* were of the same alloy composition as the first *Half Dimes*: .8924 silver and .1076 copper or 89.24% silver, and 10.76% copper by weight. The same composition was used for the *Quarters* and *Halves* of the Mint.

Silver *Quarter Dollars* were started in 1796 and were produced irregularly until the 1830s. Silver *Half Dollars* began in 1794 and, after skipping a few years, have been continued into the 20th century, as have the *quarters*. The screw press was used to mint the first U.S. coins, then horse-powered presses, then (in 1836) steam-powered presses. Twentieth century U.S. coins are struck on high-speed electric coinage presses.

Silver Dollars were produced from 1794 to 1803, then from 1836 onward. The celebrated *1804 U.S. Silver Dollar*, of which fifteen specimens are known, was struck in 1834-1835 for proof set presentation purposes, and in 1859 for coin collectors. Philadelphia Mint records show that 19,750 *Silver Dollars* were struck in 1804, but undoubtedly all of these were dated 1803, as *Dollars* dated 1804 are among the great rarities of U.S. coinage.

In 1795, gold *Half Eagles* ($5 gold pieces) and *Eagles* ($10 gold pieces) were begun, followed by *Quarter Eagles* ($2.50 gold pieces) in 1796. Until 1850, when *Double Eagles* ($20 gold pieces) were initiated for circulation (the 1849 $20 piece was a "pattern"), the $10 gold piece was the highest denomination U.S. coin.

Nineteenth century U.S. coin designs include an allegorical representation of the Goddess of Liberty, the coin's date, and a constellation of stars (usually thirteen, for the original number of American Colonies) on the obverse, and the words "UNITED STATES OF AMERICA" and (usually) the denomination on the reverse, along with an eagle for silver and gold coins or a wreath for copper coins, as prescribed by Congress on April 6, 1792. The "Phrygian Cap" ("Liberty Cap" coinage) on the head of the Goddess of Liberty, as portrayed on early U.S. coins, was the symbol of free men in ancient Rome.

The original U.S. Mint gold coins of 1795-1796 were .9167 fine gold and .0833 copper, or 91.67% pure gold by weight. In 1834, *Quarter Eagles* and *Half Eagles* were redesigned in appearance, and reduced in both diameter and weight (and in gold content to .8992 fine) because the old-style coins were worth more for bullion value than their face

value. In 1837-1838 silver U.S. coins were standardized at a new alloy ratio: .900 silver, .100 copper, or 90% silver.

The financial Panic of 1837 was due to overspeculation in land sales and banking, with a resultant collapse of local banks when specie payments were suspended (as they had been in 1814-1817, and were again to be suspended in 1861), and the public began hoarding coins. *Hard Times Tokens* of the 1830s were privately minted, mostly in copper, to supply the urgent need for small change (which the Mint wasn't doing very well) and to make a political statement. Many of these *Half Cent* and *Large Cent*-sized tokens dealt with President Andrew Jackson's battles with the Bank of the United States. *Hard Times Tokens* often carry slogans such as "MILLIONS FOR DEFENSE, NOT ONE CENT FOR TRIBUTE" or "I TAKE THE RESPONSIBILITY." These tokens, depending on the variety's scarcity, can be purchased now from dealers for prices ranging from a few dollars up.

Overdates are common on 1800-1850 U.S. coins because dies were used until they were no longer serviceable, and it was more convenient for Mint workers to punch a new date slug into last year's die than to hand-engrave an entirely new die.

Bust Half Dollars of 1807-1839 were minted in large quantities (for the time) and stored in banks in Mint bags as a concentration of silver bullion value to back paper currency and to serve as a financial reserve. Thus, such coins are common today in high grades (EF to UNC) because many of these half dollars didn't circulate.

THE CALIFORNIA GOLD RUSH

Although it had been found before, like Columbus' "discovery" of the New World, James Marshall's "discovery" of California gold was the discovery that counted! Marshall was walking along the mill race at John Sutter's mill on the south fork of the American River (near present-day Coloma, California), when suddenly he saw something yellow and shiny at his feet. He picked the tiny nugget up, carried it back to show his buddies, and announced: "Boys, I think I've found a gold mine." After subjecting the specimen to specific gravity tests (it was about 19 times as heavy as water) and a nitric acid test (no effect on gold metal), they finally concluded that it was indeed gold. The date was January 24, 1848.

Then the world rushed in. So many would-be prospectors came to California in the next two and a half years that California's population exploded to the point of justifying statehood, and on September 9, 1850, California became a state of the Union. Nicknamed the "Golden State," with the motto "Eureka" ("I have found it"), California captured the public's imagination as few things have before or since the Gold Rush.

Ship captains lost their crews as soon as they docked in San Francisco harbor—everyone fled for the gold fields, and San Francisco Bay was littered with abandoned ships, some of which were converted into hotels with rooms at exorbitant prices. Everything was expensive. Fresh eggs were $6 a dozen. Goods had to be shipped over land or by way of Panama or around the tip of South America to San Francisco, where shiploads of merchandise were sold before they were even unloaded on the docks. In 1849, a dollar a day was a normal factory worker's or farm laborer's wage. Yet Delmonico's Restaurant in San Francisco did a thriving business with a menu that included: "Boiled Salmon $1.75, Filet of Beef $1.75, Lobster Salad $2.00, Sirloin of Venison $1.50."

The "Forty-niners" were the people who came to California in 1849, a label they proudly kept as the years passed. "I was here in '49—when it all began!" they would tell their grandchildren. At first, finding gold was so easy that you could pry it out of a quartz boulder on the surface of the ground, using a steel pocket knife. Stories were spun of how some prospectors got a dozen ounces of gold dust with a single pan of stream sediment! Boomtowns grew overnight in the Sierra Nevada gold country (now a picturesque auto tour on California Highway 49), and gamblers, gunslingers, and other assorted riff-raff made their way to the gold mining camps where human life was as cheap as gold was valuable. Merchants posted store prices in terms of pinches or ounces of gold dust.

The severe shortage of money hampered commerce all over California during the Gold Rush era. Private assayers and bankers partially filled the currency demand by minting "private gold coins," some of which were slightly underweight to cheat the miners who deposited bullion in exchange for the more readily recognized value of coins. Moffat & Company, Miner's Bank, and Pacific Company set up in the coin-making business in San Francisco in 1849. Firms like Baldwin & Co.; Wass, Molitor & Co.; and Kellogg & Co. soon followed. The "Pioneer" gold coins of these firms are eagerly collected by numismatists today. Prices range from slightly under $1,000 to many thousands of dollars per piece. A handsome Uncirculated $10 gold coin of Miner's Bank (issued 1849) sold for $135,000 in the 1980 Garrett Sale. A Proof $50 gold coin (slug) of Kellogg & Co., dated 1855, sold for $154,000 in the 1984 Carter Sale. *Beware of counterfeit California Pioneer gold coins.* They may have the right weight and gold content but be totally spurious, thus separating the gullible collector from the numismatic cash "premium" paid over the bullion value of the forged coin.

With the establishment of the U.S. Branch Mint at San Francisco in 1854, a gradually increasing output of San Francisco-minted U.S. coins slowly began to alleviate the coin shortage in bullion-rich, coin-deficient California. Silver *Quarters* and *Half Dollars* were first made at the San Francisco Mint in 1855. Gold, in $1, $2.50, $5, $10, and $20 coins was struck first at that Mint in 1854. *Three-dollar* gold pieces started in 1855 at San Francisco. Some San Francisco-minted gold coins are scarce and valuable. Beware of altered dates and faked mintmarks. The *Double Eagle* ($20 gold piece) was inaugurated by the Philadelphia Mint in 1850 (the single 1849 example in the Smithsonian is a "pattern") directly due to the huge influx of gold shipped east from the California Gold Rush.

CIVIL WAR MONETARY PROBLEMS

On the eve of the Civil War, *Half Cents* and *Large Cents* were discontinued and replaced by small copper *Flying Eagle Cents*, as per the Act of Congress, February 21, 1857. This Act also took away the legal tender status of foreign coins. America was finally about to get serious about providing a circulating coinage sufficient for its citizens' needs. The first *Indian Head Cents* were made in 1859 and replaced the short-lived *Flying Eagle Cents*. I remember the first time I saw an *Indian Cent*. I was eight or nine years old and one of my classmates from school was visiting with me in my parents' backyard. Suddenly he took out an *Indian Head Cent* from his wallet and let me handle it. I remember thinking to myself: "I've never seen this coin before. What is it worth? Do more of them exist? I want one. What is its story?"

By the summer of 1862, silver coins had vanished from circulation due to widespread hoarding. The outcome of the War was very much in doubt, and nervous citizens enacted Gresham's Law in a textbook manner. Gresham's Law states that when two coins (or "monies") of equal face value are simultaneously circulating, the one with the base metal content will drive the one with precious metal content out of circulation. Silver and gold coins were quickly hoarded during the Civil War, then copper coins, so that only paper currency circulated in both the North and South. Coins of the various denominations were minted by the U.S. during the War, but these coins were immediately withdrawn from circulation when people got hold of them.

Business was in chaos because shopkeepers couldn't make change. Some ingenious schemes were devised to deliver small circulating "change" to the public. *Civil War Tokens* of mostly copper and brass were privately struck to pass as one-cent pieces, being the size and roughly the same composition as the new *Indian Head Cents*. Postage stamps and currency that looked like stamps were used in place of real coins. Encased postage stamps—metal- and mica-encased stamps, which are now worth $100 and up if genuine—appeared in different denominations.

The romantic *1861-O Half Dollar* minted at the New Orleans Mint was struck from the same type of dies under three different governments: (1) the United States, (2) the state of Louisiana after secession, and (3) as Confederate States' authorized coinage. More than two and a half million total *1861-O Half Dollars* were minted, but they cannot be distinguished as to one of these three issuing authorities.

The Confederacy itself produced several "pattern" coins—a *Cent* and a *Half Dollar*, of which only a few specimens were made. The Confederacy didn't have the bullion to make coins in quantity. When Rhett Butler bid $150 in gold for a dance with Scarlett O'Hara in *Gone With the Wind*, it was understood that bullion raised for the "glorious cause" of the Confederacy would most likely be shipped to Europe to buy desperately needed manufactured goods that might be slipped past the Union blockade.

By Act of Congress, April 22, 1864, the 88% copper/12% nickel *Indian Head Cents* were changed to 95% copper/5% zinc and tin, and the weight of the Cent was reduced from 4.67 grams to 3.11 grams. That's why bronze *Indian Cents* (from 1864 on) look thinner and feel lighter than the earlier *Flying Eagle Cents* and copper-nickel *Indian Cents* (also called "*White Cents*" due to their grayish nickel-alloy color).

The 1864 Act that changed the Cent composition also provided for the creation of a *Two-Cent Piece* in bronze. Appearing later that year, the *Two-Cent Piece* was unpopular with the public, who preferred to use two one-cent pieces. Scarce in Proof and truly Uncirculated condition, the U.S. *Two-Cent Piece* of 1864-1873 is an example of our "obsolete coinage" — coin denominations that no longer exist in currently minted coins. Deep religious feelings were widespread during the Civil War, so the motto "IN GOD WE TRUST" was placed on the *Two-Cent Piece*, the first U.S. coin with such a legend.

"*Liberty Seated*" *Silver Dollars* (of the 1840-1866 "No Motto" design) were minted every year of the 1861-1865 Civil War, but none circulated until after the War, due to hoarding. The same can be said for U.S. gold pieces of that time period.

LATE 19TH CENTURY U.S. COINS

Three-Cent Pieces in silver were made by the Philadelphia Mint from 1851 to 1873 (and at New Orleans in 1851 alone). Nickel *Three-Cent Pieces* were struck only at Philadelphia, from 1865 to 1889. *Three-Cent Pieces* were unpopular with the public, and the quantities minted dwindled as time went on. In glittering Proof, such coins are quite desirable to coin collectors today.

Silver *Half Dimes* were continued up to 1873, and denominationally overlap the production of nickel *Five-Cent Pieces*, commonly called "*Nickels*," which were inaugurated in 1866 as per the Act of May 16, 1866. These *"Nickels"* have been made from 1866 to the present day and haven't changed at all in weight (5 grams) or composition (75% copper, 25% nickel) in all that time. Their diameter (21.2 millimeters) has been constant since 1883.

"Nickels" have been popular from their beginning in 1866, probably because 5-cent coins are easy to make change with in a decimal monetary system with dimes, quarters, and dollars. Also, *"Nickels"* are larger than *Cents, Dimes, Half Dimes,* or *Three-Cent Pieces,* and the public seems to favor larger coins if it wants coins at all (witness the near-"quarter"-sized *Susan B. Anthony Dollar* fiasco of the early 1980s). I put the word *"Nickel"* in quotes because there is no such thing as a *"Nickel"* officially, just as there is no United States coin called the *"Penny."* These are slang terms for what the U.S. Mint calls *"Five-Cent Pieces"* and *"Cents."* The *"Penny"* is a carryover word from when America was part of the British Empire.

Frank Woolworth opened his first "five and ten cent store" in Lancaster, Pennsylvania on June 21, 1879. The first day's sales were $127.65. Woolworth and his "cheaply priced department store" competitors stimulated demand for small change so much that in 1882 more than 11 million nickel *Five-Cent Pieces* were minted. *"Nickel"* production averaged more than 13 million per year for the rest of the 19th century, and more than 27 million per year for the first decade of the 20th century. (At present, more than 1 billion *"Nickels"* are minted per year!) By 1912, Woolworth had 611 stores with a total gross of more than $60 million in annual sales—not bad for a store chain that advertised "All merchandise at 5¢ or 10¢ per item."

The ill-fated U.S. *Twenty-Cent Piece* of 1875-1878 had just two years of serious production followed by two years of Proof-only issues. The public didn't like the *Twenty-Cent Piece* because it looked like, and was similar in size to, a *Quarter Dollar.* The U.S. silver *3¢ Pieces* and *20¢ Pieces* are the only U.S. Mint silver coins that don't have a reeded (or lettered) edge; *3¢ Pieces* and *20¢ Pieces* have "smooth" edges like *"Nickels"* and *Cents.*

The U.S. *Trade Dollars* of 1873-1885 were authorized for U.S. trade with China and Japan. Oriental merchants were suspicious of and choosy about the types of silver coins they accepted in business transactions. When the Mexican silver "dollar" had more silver (by weight) in it than the American silver *Dollar,* the Orientals demanded Mexican dollars in payment from American businessmen. The U.S. government countered by coining the *Trade Dollar* expressly to compete with the Mexican dollar. The *Trade Dollar* had more silver in it than the Mexican dollar, and many U.S. *Trade Dollars* have survived with "chop marks" counterstamped on them — punch marks of Oriental merchants who thus guaranteed and accepted the *Trade Dollars* at par in business deals. Ten *Trade Dollars* were coined in 1884, five in 1885, obviously by Mint employees, but officially these coins don't exist because they aren't noted in Mint records.

The Bland-Allison Act of February 28, 1878 authorized the unlimited production of U.S. *Silver Dollars* from 2 million to 4 million dollars' worth of silver bullion, to be purchased each month for *Silver Dollar* coinage. The resulting coins, the *Morgan* type *Liberty Head Silver Dollars* of 1878-1921, flooded the government's vaults with so many *Silver Dollars* that there they remained for years until they were gradually dispersed to the public in the 20th century, some being melted under the terms of the Pittman Act in 1918. The Panic of 1893 and the general economic depression that characterized its effects on the public was in part caused by overproduction of silver coins and rejection of silver by international trade.

Charles E. Barber, Chief Engraver of the U.S. Mint, designed the *"Barber" Liberty Head Dimes, Quarters,* and *Half Dollars* of 1892-1916 (the *Halves* being minted through 1915)—a new design in the U.S. coinage. Barber lacked creative talent and was jealous of others who wanted to meddle in his function of designing the nation's coins. Nevertheless, the *"Barber"* coins, although lacking the dramatic varieties of early 19th century U.S. coins due to better quality control and better equipment by 1892, are popular among numismatists who appreciate well-struck silver coins. They are also hard coins to find without "bag marks" all over in Uncirculated condition.

Three-Dollar Gold Pieces were made from 1854 to 1889 by the Mint and its branches. The story is told about how the *$3 Gold Piece* was issued to make it easy for the public to pay for a full pane of

100 3-cent stamps at the post office. More likely this coin was issued to absorb the increasing amounts of gold pouring into the U.S. Treasury from California. *Three-Dollar Gold Pieces* currently sell for high premiums over bullion value because of their low mintages, and they have been extensively counterfeited to defraud collectors and investors.

20TH CENTURY U.S. COINS

New U.S. coin designs were introduced in the 20th century: the *Lincoln Cent* in 1909, the *Buffalo "Nickel"* in 1913, the *"Mercury" Dime* in 1916, the *Liberty Standing Quarter Dollar* in 1916, the *Liberty Walking Half Dollar* in 1916, and the *Peace Dollar* in 1921. *Indian Head* U.S. gold coins began with the *Eagles* ($10 pieces) in 1907, followed by (with different obverses) *Quarter Eagles* ($2.50 pieces) and *Half Eagles* ($5 pieces) in 1908. The beautiful *Saint-Gaudens Double Eagles* ($20 gold coins) appeared in 1907.

Then, of course, designs were further changed with the introduction of the *Washington Quarter Dollar* in 1932 (intended as a one-year commemorative of the 200th anniversary of George Washington's birth, we use the same design on our 25-cent pieces today); the *Jefferson "Nickel"* in 1938; the *Roosevelt Dime* in 1946; the *Franklin Half Dollar* in 1948, replaced by the *Kennedy Half Dollar* in 1964; the new *Lincoln Memorial* reverse to the *Lincoln Cent* in 1959; and finally, the *Eisenhower Dollars* in 1971, and the ill-fated *Susan B. Anthony Dollars* in 1979.

The *Lincoln Cent* replaced the *Indian Head Cent* in 1909, the centennial of Abraham Lincoln's birth. Designed by Victor D. Brenner, the *Lincoln Cent* was loved by the public from the beginning. The August 1909 issue of *The Numismatist* (journal of the American Numismatic Association, still current) reported the public reception of the Lincoln Cent:

No new coin type has ever commanded the interest of the public and editorial reference and news space in the general press as has the Lincoln cent. Heralded long in advance, it was issued to an expectant populace on August 2nd. About 25,000,000 had been coined and distributed to various Sub-Treasuries and banks throughout the country so

that the distribution could commence in all parts on the same day. As soon as it became known that a new coin had been issued places of distribution were besieged, particularly in New York, Boston, Philadelphia, Chicago, and St. Louis, where long lines formed leading to Sub-Treasuries, and continued each day with increased interest until August 5th, when the sign was displayed "No More Lincoln Pennies."

Those not content to stand in line and obtain a supply at face value (one hundred was the most that would be supplied an individual) offered to purchase at a premium, and for a few days newsboys, messengers and street fakirs had a harvest in selling the new coins at two or three for five cents. When no more were obtainable at Government supply places, stories in explanation were invented, "going to be called in," etc., and prices soared in different sections, as much as a dollar each being paid for specimens.

Popular *Lincoln Cent* varieties, among collectors, are the scarce *1909-SVBD*, *1914-D*, *1922-plain*, *1943 steel cents* (made out of zinc-coated steel due to a copper shortage during World War II), exceedingly rare *1943 copper cent* errors, and *1955 Doubled Die Cents*.

A severe shortage of cents in circulation in 1974 led many banks to give a 5 to 10% "reward" over face value for anyone turning in rolls of cents. Mint Director at the time, Mary Brooks, commented, "... there are plenty of 'pennies', but they're in the wrong places. Somewhere in this vast country of ours, however, in excess of 30 billion 'pennies' are in hiding."

President Theodore Roosevelt had the renowned sculptor Augustus Saint-Gaudens redesign the *Eagle* and *Double Eagle* U.S. gold coins. Saint-Gaudens was also supposed to design a new cent, but it was never finished, as he died of cancer in August 1907. The *Saint-Gaudens Double Eagle* ($20 gold piece) is considered by many numismatists to be the most beautiful American coin ever minted, with a face-view of a striding Goddess of Liberty on the obverse, and a majestic eagle in flight on the coin's reverse.

President Franklin D. Roosevelt's March 9, 1933 Act prohibited gold hoarding by the public, and required all gold coin, bullion, and gold certificates (gold-backed paper currency) to be delivered to a bank by May 1, 1933. This Act permitted $100 of numismatic gold to be held by each coin collector in the country. After the gold was turned in, Roosevelt immediately raised the official price of gold, forever making himself hated by "hard money" advocates who maintain that citizens should prefer precious metal coinage over "worthless" paper currency. It is numismatically fortunate that many people in America disobeyed Roosevelt's gold confiscation order, or we wouldn't have the wonderful selection of old gold coins and gold certificates that grace so many of the collections of private coin collectors today.

Then there are the silver and gold U.S. *commemorative coins* issued in the 20th century (see Chapter 7). Of many designs and minting qualities, these coins have been all but forgotten in the minds of the general public, except for coin collectors and museum curators who keep their memory alive.

At present in the United States (as, indeed, in most of the world), coins are mainly used for small change; paper money has evolved as a substitute for coinage as the primary medium of currency; and credit cards and checks threaten to make even paper currency obsolete. Because of the rising price of silver on the commodity markets (see Chapter 15), silver was removed from circulating U.S. coinage as of 1965, and replaced with the ugly copper-nickel clad U.S. coins of 10¢, 25¢, 50¢, and (when they've been struck) $1 denominations (ignoring the silver ones issued specifically for collectors).

Take a *Quarter* out of your pocket or wallet. Look at its poorly struck features, as compared to its silver cousins of pre-1965 vintage. Look at the pure copper (and essentially worthless) core peeking out at you along the coin's edge. Study, for a minute, the durable but "difficult to make a striking impression in" cupronickel outer surfaces that sandwich the coin's copper core between them. We now use copper for our coins because it is cheap, and we use a nickel-alloy outer surface because it is resistant to wear. More *Quarter Dollars* were minted in 1965 (the first year of "clad" coinage, when U.S. circulating coins truly became "debased") than in any other year in U.S. Mint history since its founding in 1792. The grand total is 1,819,717,540 coins, according to Mint records, which is why you still see 1965 *Quarters* in circulation, where they will undoubtedly continue to serve the public well into the 21st century—mere metallic ghosts of their former glorious silver selves.

U.S. MINTS

There are four U.S. Mints currently striking coins: Philadelphia, San Francisco, Denver, and West Point. The U.S. Bullion Depository at Fort Knox, KY stores much of the U.S. government's gold in standard Mint bars of about 400 troy ounces each. No visitors are allowed at Fort Knox or at the West Point Mint. The current Philadelphia Mint and Denver Mint can be toured, as can the old San Francisco Mint (but not the new San Francisco Mint).

The Charlotte, NC Mint, although reconstructed, can be visited, as can the Carson City Mint. Both of these are now museums (see Chapter 19). The Dahlonega, GA Mint was destroyed by fire in 1878, but coin exhibits can be seen there (Chapter 19). The New Orleans Mint has been restored, and parts of the building can be visited.

The current Philadelphia Mint is the fourth building to bear that title, opened August 14, 1969. The new San Francisco Mint is the third building to bear that title, opened in the summer of 1937. The Denver Mint has had only one facility under full Branch Mint status, opened for business in February 1906, although a previous structure was used as an Assay Office before full Branch Mint authorization.

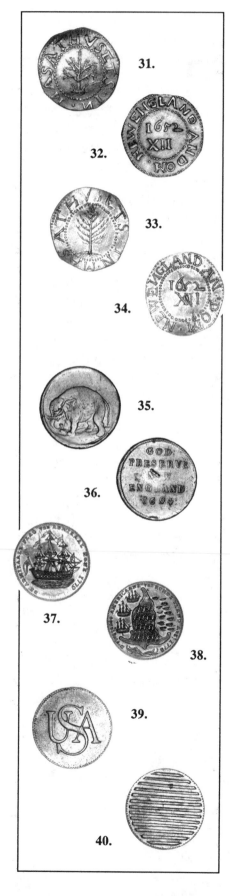

31.
32.
33.
34.
35.
36.
37.
38.
39.
40.

31. 1652 Massachusetts Bay Colony silver *Oak Tree Shilling*. Struck by John Hull sometime in the 1660-1667 period, although all coins bear the 1652 date to evade English laws against local American Colonial coinage. 73 grains, 27.5mm. Lot #1173 of the Bowers and Merena *Norweb* sale of October 13, 1987, described in the catalog as "Clear and bright surfaces, an attractive golden gray in color. No signs of any mishandling whatsoever ..." Realized a hammer price of $18,700 (including 10% buyer's fee). Graded "AU-50" in the catalog. Courtesy Bowers and Merena, Inc.

32. Reverse of *Oak Tree Shilling* of previous photo. Courtesy Bowers and Merena, Inc.

33. 1652 Massachusetts Bay Colony silver *Pine Tree Shilling*. Lot #1196 of the Bowers and Merena *Norweb* sale of October 13, 1987, listed in the catalog as "MS-60, among the finest known ... 72.4 grains, 28.6mm ... An outstanding specimen, with breathtaking iridescent gold and blue toning. Fully struck tree ..." Realized $26,400 (including 10% buyer's fee). Courtesy Bowers and Merena, Inc.

34. Reverse of *Pine Tree Shilling* of previous photo. Catalog description includes: "Usual reverse die state seen, with diagonal break running from A, through the date and denomination, and reaching M in the legend below. Exceptionally sharp reverse. Full root structure!" Courtesy Bowers and Merena, Inc.

35. 1694 *New England Elephant Token*. Believed to have been struck in England to promote her American Colonies. Lot #1237 of the Bowers and Merena *Norweb* sale of October 13, 1987, listed in the catalog as "VF-30. Rarity 8. 240.9 grains. 28.5mm ... Dark chocolate brown ... Second finest of the three known

..." Realized $25,300 (including 10% buyer's fee). Courtesy Bowers and Merena, Inc.

36. Reverse of *New England Elephant Token* of the previous photo. Catalog description includes: "Old nick in the center of the reverse, a few edge dents noticeable, as well. Soft in the reverse center, but only E too faint to be legible ..." When exceedingly rare coins come up for auction, though they may be damaged, they attract spirited bidding! Courtesy Bowers and Merena, Inc.

37. 1779 *Rhode Island Ship Token* struck in brass. Lot #1259 of the Bowers and Merena *Norweb* sale of October 13, 1987, described in the catalog as "MS-60, among the finest known ... appears to have been struck in England ... for distribution in the Dutch market, in an attempt to persuade the Dutch to remain neutral and nonbelligerent during the American Revolutionary War ..." Realized $6,600 (including 10% buyer's fee). Courtesy Bowers and Merena, Inc.

38. Reverse of the *Rhode Island Ship Token* from the previous photo. Catalog description includes: "Brass, or yellow bronze, Rarity-4. 147.7 grains. 32.3mm ... Deeply toned, in gorgeous iridescent gold, purple, and rose shades. More sharply struck than any this cataloguer can remember seeing ..." Courtesy Bowers and Merena, Inc.

39. The *Bar "Copper"* of circa 1785, believed to have been struck in England for circulation in America, first seen in New York in November 1785. The design may have been copied from a Continental uniform button. Obverse has three interlocking letters "USA." Lot #1413, the last lot in the Bowers and Merena *Norweb* sale of October 13, 1987, listed in the catalog as "AU-50. Copper. 87.3 grains. 24.5mm.

Medium orange brown, with some surface pitting ..." Realized $2,310 (including 10% buyer's fee). Courtesy Bowers and Merena, Inc. This is the author's favorite Colonial coin.

40. The reverse of the *Bar "Copper"* (also called *Bar "Cent"*) of the previous photo, showing thirteen bars symbolizing the original thirteen American colonies. Small "spur" off the right of the second bar, and "die spine" between sixth and seventh bar, as characteristic of originals. Cheaper-costing (to the modern collector) copies were made by Bolen in 1862; on the copies, the obverse "S" passes over, rather than under, the "A". When the author asked Walter Breen about this coin, Mr. Breen stated that maybe 8,000 to 9,000 originals were made in 1785 in Birmingham, England, and that more counterfeits exist of this than of any other American Colonial coin! Photo courtesy Bowers and Merena, Inc.

41. 1786 *Immunis Columbia/New Jersey Shield* copper, second finest known. Lot #1551 of the Bowers and Merena *Saccone* sale of November 7, 1989. Catalog description includes: "15 examples traced. A newly discovered specimen. 154.4 grains, heavy planchet. 28.8mm ... AU-55 to 58 ... Fully struck, centered, and round, with a full border of denticles on both sides ..." Realized $33,000 (including 10% buyer's fee). Courtesy Bowers and Merena, Inc.

42. Reverse of *Immunis Columbia/ New Jersey Shield* copper from previous photo. Catalog description includes: "... the horizontal and vertical lines in the shield on the reverse are sharp and separated ... Rare, and always popular with sophisticated collectors of early American issues. For example, Carl Wurtzbach, who owned the Parmelee specimen, exhibited it at the 1912 ANA Convention, held that year in Rochester,

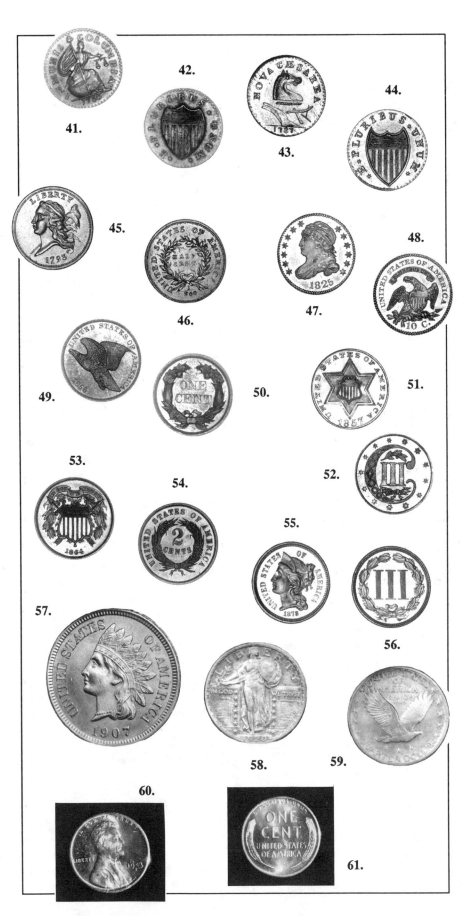

New York." *Immunis Columbia* coins were made after the American Revolution, but before adoption of the U.S. Constitution and subsequent official federal coinage. Has been attributed by some researchers to William Wyon's mint in Birmingham, England. Courtesy Bowers and Merena, Inc.

43. 1787 *New Jersey* copper (Maris 48-g), Lot #1353 of the Bowers and Merena *Norweb* sale of October 13, 1987. Catalog description includes: "MS-60, mint red. Tied for finest known. Rarity-1. 143.9 grains 28mm ... Sharply struck and perfectly centered ... Pronounced clash marks on the obverse around the horse's head; doubtless the cause for the reverse break ..." Struck by private mint under contract to the state of New Jersey. Realized $24,200 (including 10% buyer's fee). Courtesy Bowers and Merena, Inc.

44. Reverse of *New Jersey* copper from previous photo. Attributed as type M48-g as per the definitive catalog by Dr. Edward Maris. Bowers and Merena auction catalog description states, in part: "Early reverse state, the diagonal break almost imperceptible ..." Courtesy Bowers and Merena, Inc.

45. 1793 *Half Cent* struck by the new U.S. Mint on Seventh Street near Arch in Philadelphia. A "one year" type coin, with Liberty facing left, and cap and pole behind her head. The cap symbolizes freedom, derived from ancient Rome where newly freed slaves were given a cap. In early America, a cap on a pole in the town square was sometimes erected to proclaim liberty and independence. Lot #1 of the Bowers and Merena *Norweb* sale of November 12, 1987. Catalog description states, in part: "111.2 grains. AU-50. Rich, smooth, glossy brown surfaces. Superbly struck ..." Realized $13,200 (including 10%

buyer's fee). Courtesy Bowers and Merena, Inc.

46. Reverse of 1793 *Half Cent* from previous photo. Bowers and Merena catalog description states, in part: "Walter Breen theorizes that the obverse was the work of Robert Birch, possibly with the aid of Joseph Wright ... It is believed that Adam Eckfeldt and Robert Birch cut the reverse dies this year, using punches prepared by one Jacob Bay. The edge is lettered TWO HUNDRED FOR A DOLLAR, thus giving the coin two indications of denomination, on the reverse and on the edge ..." Mint records state that 35,334 *Half Cents* were minted in 1793, the first regular year of Mint operation. Walter Breen told Mrs. R. Henry Norweb that this coin is, in his opinion, the second finest known of its type. Courtesy Bowers and Merena, Inc.

47. 1825 Proof *Dime*. Lot #429 of the Bowers and Merena *Norweb* sale of October 12, 1987. Catalog description includes: "Proof-65. Rarity-2. Finest known, finer than any other 1825 dime recorded ... Its surfaces are an attractive medium gray with faint iridescent blue highlights ... Presumably struck at least twice to bring up detail and create the sharpness necessary for a presentation strike." Realized $7,425 (including 10% buyer's fee). Courtesy Bowers and Merena, Inc.

48. Reverse of 1825 Proof *Dime* from previous photo. Bowers and Merena catalog description includes: "Centers somewhat soft, but peripheries sharply struck. Full denticulation, and perfectly centered. Brilliant, Proof surfaces ..." Courtesy Bowers and Merena, Inc. The *Capped Bust* type *Dimes* were minted at Philadelphia intermittently from 1809 to 1837. Unlisted as Proofs in the *Red Book*, such gem quality *Dimes* as this one always at-

tract spirited bidding at auction.

49. 1856 *Flying Eagle Cent*, Proof. Lot #25 of the Bowers and Merena *Saccone* sale of November 6, 1989. Catalog description includes: "Proof -65. A blazing, sharply struck, beautifully centered gem ... we are inclined to the view that the presently offered coin is in the upper echelon of the finest 1% of all those extant ..." Realized $13,200 (including the 10% buyer's fee). Courtesy Bowers and Merena, Inc. The author asked Walter Breen his opinion of the issuing status of this coin, and Mr. Breen stated that the whole issue consists of patterns and restrikes of the duly adopted design of this coin.

50. Reverse of Proof 1856 *Flying Eagle Cent* from previous photo. Courtesy Bowers and Merena, Inc. Designed by James B. Longacre, who also created the *Indian Head Cent* that replaced the *Flying Eagle Cents* in 1859. It is believed that between 1,000 and 2,000 *Flying Eagle Cents* were struck with the 1856 date. Beware of altered dates and outright counterfeits, which abound.

51. 1857 *Silver Three-Cent Piece* in Proof. Also called a "*Trime*", the *Silver Three-Cent Piece* was minted from 1851 to 1873, but was decidedly unpopular with the public, undoubtedly due to its small size and competition with the *Half Dime* and (later) *Nickel Five-Cent Pieces*. Thus, from initial mintages of over 6 million in 1851, over 18 million in 1852, and over 11 million in 1853, *Silver Three-Cent Piece* production gradually declined to essentially Proof and collector pieces during the last ten years of production. This specimen was Lot #270 of the Bowers and Merena *Norweb* sale of October 12, 1987. Realized $4,180 (including the 10% buyer's fee). Courtesy Bowers and Merena, Inc.

52. The reverse of the 1857 *Silver Three-Cent Piece* from the previous photo. Described in the Bowers and Merena catalog as "Proof-64. Deep mirrored surfaces heavily toned gold, indigo blue, lime green, and charcoal gray. Very sharply struck. Heavy die polish marks are visible beneath the toning. Probably fewer than 20 Proofs exist, of which this is one of the finest." Courtesy Bowers and Merena, Inc. The specimen illustrated is Variety 2, with three lines bordering the obverse star. Supposedly issued to make it easy to buy 3-cent stamps at the post office, as effective July 1, 1851, the domestic U.S. letter rate became 3¢ per ½ oz. up to a distance of 3,000 miles, but some researchers dispute this justification for a new circulating coin denomination.

53. 1864 Proof Small Motto *Two-Cent Piece*. Lot #233 of the Bowers and Merena *Norweb* sale of October 12, 1987. Catalog description states, in part: "Proof-64 to 65. Possibly the second finest of fewer than two dozen known specimens ... Deep mirrored surfaces beneath magnificent magenta, fiery orange, and indigo blue toning. Razor sharp strike. Virtually immaculate surfaces ... completely free of carbon spots ..." Realized $16,500 (including the 10% buyer's fee). Courtesy Bowers and Merena, Inc.

The first U.S. coin with the motto "IN GOD WE TRUST," which was inspired by a November 13, 1861 letter by the Reverend M.R. Watkinson of Ridleyville, PA, written to the Secretary of the Treasury. Watkinson's letter stated, in part: "One fact touching our currency has hitherto been seriously overlooked. I mean the recognition of the Almighty God in some form on our coins ... What if our Republic were now shattered beyond reconstruction? Would not the antiquaries of succeeding centuries rightly reason from our past

that we were a heathen nation? ..." By Act of April 22, 1864, Congress authorized the *Two-Cent Piece*, expressly for relieving the national coin shortage caused by hoarding during the Civil War; and IN GOD WE TRUST appeared on the 1864 *Two-Cent Pieces* for the first time in U.S. coinage history.

54. Reverse of 1864 Proof *Two-Cent Piece* from the previous photo. Like the *Three-Cent Pieces* (both silver and nickel) of which there is overlapping contemporaneity, the U.S. *Two-Cent Piece* was unpopular with the public, such that for every single year of its issue, 1864 to 1873, there was a decline in total mintage from the previous year. Mint records show that 19,847,500 *Two-Cent Pieces* were struck in 1864, and only 65,000 in 1872, the last year of business strikes. The fact that *Two-Cent Pieces* are readily found in heavily worn condition indicates that they saw extensive circulation, in spite of public and government disenchantment with the issue. Designed by James B. Longacre, the same designer of the *Indian Head Cent,* the *Two-Cent Piece's* 95% copper, 5% tin and zinc composition has been cruel to its preservation over the years — uncleaned, unspotted, undamaged high grade (AU to UNC) *Two-Cent Pieces* with original color and pleasant appearance are becoming quite difficult to find, and sell for a well-deserved premium when encountered. Photo courtesy Bowers and Merena, Inc.

55. 1878 Proof *Nickel Three-Cent Piece*. Lot #58 of the Bowers and Merena *Saccone* sale of November 6, 1989. Described in the catalog as "Proof-65 ... Both the obverse and reverse are brilliant with rich frosted devices and deeply mirrored fields ..." Realized $1,650 (including the 10% buyer's fee). Courtesy Bowers and Merena, Inc.

56. Reverse of the 1878 Proof *Nickel Three-Cent Piece* from the previous photo. A Proof-only year for these coins, with just 2,350 minted. Designed by James B. Longacre. The *Nickel Three-Cent Pieces* were intended to replace the *Silver Three-Cent Pieces*, but were likewise rejected by a monetarily fickle public, partly due to the popularity of the Nickel *Five-Cent Pieces*, which were introduced in 1866, a year after the *Nickel Three-Cent Pieces* (1865). Photo courtesy Bowers and Merena, Inc.

57. 1907 *Indian Head Cent*, Uncirculated with "bag marks." Designed by James B. Longacre, the *Indian Head Cent* was produced by the millions for every year from 1859 to 1909 (with the exception of 1877, when 852,500 were struck). Uncirculated specimens generally show no wear on the strands of hair above the ear of the Indian Princess, or on the four "diamonds" on the ribbon along the back of her neck. Reverses sometimes look "better" than the obverses. A coin that is notorious for being tarnished, cleaned, and artificially colored to mimic original Mint State. Look at a lot of *Indian Cents* before you buy an expensive one. This particular business strike specimen has a wire rim, visible at right edge of coin, indicative of high striking pressure. Author's collection.

58. 1920 San Francisco Mint *Standing Liberty Quarter Dollar*. Circulated, with obvious wear on the date due to its high relief, a problem that was addressed in *Quarters* dated 1925-1930, which bore a recessed date to inhibit wear. Designed by Hermon A. MacNeil, the *Standing Liberty Quarter* is often seen with beautiful toning, although Uncirculated specimens with sharply struck heads and shields are scarce. Mintmark "S" is just to the upper left of the date. Author's collection.

59. Reverse of the *Standing Liberty Quarter* of the previous photo. The 1920-S had a mintage of 6,380,000. Scarcest coin in this series is the often-counterfeited 1916 Variety 1, which should be purchased only from the most reputable sources. Author's collection.

60. 1943 San Francisco Mint Steel *Lincoln Cent*. Due to a shortage of copper in World War II, the *Cents* for 1943 (with the exception of rare copper errors) were struck on zinc-coated steel planchets. Although over 1 billion 1943 *Cents* were produced in the combined mintages of Philadelphia, Denver, and San Francisco, these steel *Cents* are getting harder to find in pristine unrusted original color Mint State. Author's collection.

61. Reverse of the 1943-S *Lincoln Cent* of the previous photo. When buying AU-BU *Lincoln Cents*, insist on well-struck details as evident on this specimen. Also note that any hairline scratches or bag marks will be definitely observed when you go to sell your coins, even though you may think little of such flaws on the day you're buying them. Author's collection.

62. 1945 San Francisco Mint *Winged Liberty Head Dime* (more popularly called *"Mercury" Dime*). Minted most years from 1916 through 1945. Designed by Adolph A. Weinman, who stated in 1916, regarding Liberty's portrait: "... the wings crowning her cap are intended to symbolize liberty of thought." It is a small coin, often overlooked by investors and rich collectors, but scarce in "flawless" struck-up mark-free Mint State examples for some dates. Author's collection.

63. Reverse of the 1945-S *"Mercury" Dime* from the previous photo. Not a clipped planchet, but the author's left fingers holding the coin while

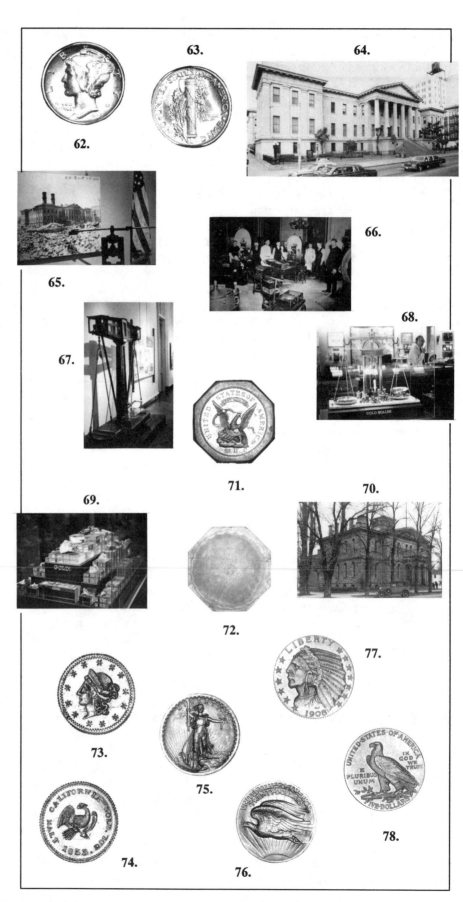

his right hand snaps the shutter on a handheld camera. Notice the mint-mark "S" to the right of the "E" in the word "ONE," and the not quite "split bands" of the horizontal strands around the fasces bundle. In designer Weinman's own words, the fasces (ancient Roman authority symbol) show "the strength which lies in unity, while the battle-ax stands for preparedness to defend the Union. The branch of olive is symbolical of our love of peace." Author's collection.

64. The "Old Mint" at Fifth and Mission Streets in San Francisco as it appears today. This building was the second U.S. Mint at San Francisco, and was operational from 1874 to 1937. Nicknamed the "Granite Lady" by San Franciscans, the building is now a museum of Mint history (see Chapter 19 for visiting data). Official U.S. Mint Photograph, courtesy U.S. Department of the Treasury.

65. Photograph of the "Old Mint" standing amid the rubble of the 1906 San Francisco earthquake and fire, with a model of an 18th century coinage screw press in the foreground. Author's photo of exhibit at the Old Mint. One of the few large buildings to withstand the destruction of the earthquake. The Mint had its own groundwater supply, which employees pumped from the central courtyard to wet down the roof; they closed the bulletproof cast iron shutters after the windows melted in the heat of the fire, to keep out the smoke. San Francisco's citizens came to the Mint to get water immediately after the earthquake. Courtesy U.S. Department of the Treasury.

66. Mint employees on duty at the Old San Francisco Mint, with several "oval" coinage presses in the background. Author's photo of photo on exhibit at the Old Mint. Courtesy

U.S. Department of the Treasury.

67. Large original Mint scales for weighing bullion, on display at the Old Mint in San Francisco. The scales are taller than the author's height of 5 feet, 6 inches! Author's photo of exhibit at the Old Mint, San Francisco. Courtesy U.S. Treasury Department.

68. Gold scales of polished brass, manufactured by Howard & Davis of Boston, MA, on display at the Wells Fargo History Museum on Montgomery Street in San Francisco. Private express companies, like Wells Fargo, carried gold dust and refined bars and coins during the Western mining era of the last half of the 19th century. Extremely accurate scales were in demand throughout Gold Rush territory because of the huge sums of money that constantly changed hands in the bullion trade. Author's photograph of Museum exhibit. Courtesy Wells Fargo History Museum, San Francisco.

69. Exhibit of raw nuggets and gold dust at the Wells Fargo History Museum, San Francisco. Naive prospectors were often cheated out of the fair value of their gold findings by small upstart merchants and private assay offices. Hence the demand for the establishment of a U.S. government assay office and subsequent San Francisco Mint. From such bullion, often painfully extracted in hard prospecting work, came the privately minted and U.S. Mint gold coins of the 1850s. Author's photo of Museum exhibit. Courtesy Wells Fargo History Museum, San Francisco.

70. Carson City Mint building, Carson City, NV, where U.S. coins were struck from 1870 to 1893. It is now a museum, owned and operated by the state of Nevada (see Chapter 19). Silver from the nearby Comstock Lode helped to build San

Francisco and to finance the Union side of the Civil War. Nevada miners found it convenient to have a Branch Mint in Carson City, ready and able to receive bullion for exchange into coinage. Carson City-minted coins have a romantic appeal and consequent premium value for coin collectors. Official photograph, courtesy Nevada State Museum, Carson City, NV.

71. 1851 Augustus Humbert *$50 Gold Piece* (also called a "slug," "ingot," or "quintuple eagle"). Humbert was appointed U.S. Assayer in 1851 in San Francisco, under contract with Moffat & Co., which opened the U.S. Assay Office there on January 29, 1851, and continued in operation until December 14, 1853 when the first San Francisco Mint was being established. Lot #821 of the Bowers and Merena *Saccone* sale of November 6, 1989. Realized $15,400 (including the 10% buyer's fee). Courtesy Bowers and Merena, Inc.

72. Reverse of 1851 Augustus Humbert *$50 gold slug* from previous photo, showing "engine turnings" as an anti-counterfeiting design, and the numeral "50" in the center. Described in the Bowers and Merena auction catalog as "AU-50 ... 1,309.7 grains. 887 THOUS... ." (and from the Garrett Collection, sold in 1980). Courtesy Bowers and Merena, Inc.

73. 1853 California *Half Dollar* fractional gold piece. Privately-issued gold pieces in denominations of 25¢, 50¢, and $1 appeared in California in 1852 to help alleviate the severe shortage of small change. Octagonal or round, with either a Liberty or an Indian Head on the obverse, they have been imitated and counterfeited in later years of the 19th century. Issued primarily by San Francisco jewelers in 1852-1853, all genuine specimens bear a denomination

on the reverse, or abbreviation, such as: CENTS, DOLL., DOLLAR. This piece was Lot #1027 of the Bowers and Merena *Norweb* sale of October 13, 1987. Realized $12,100 (including 10% buyer's fee). Courtesy Bowers and Merena.

74. Reverse of 1853 California *Half Dollar* fractional gold piece of the previous photo. Bowers and Merena catalog description includes: "MS-60 and prooflike ... evenly toned and sharply struck ... two specimens are accounted for with this being the finer of the two examples ..." Courtesy Bowers and Merena, Inc.

75. Saint-Gaudens *$20 Gold Piece* of 1907 (with Roman numerals MCMVII), in High Relief. The design of Augustus Saint-Gaudens, who was commissioned by President Theodore Roosevelt to redesign American coinage. Considered by many to be the most beautiful American coin of all time. 11,250 struck, and several dozen struck in extremely high relief. Beware of counterfeits. Lot #668 in the Bowers and Merena *Saccone* sale of November 6, 1989. Realized $12,100 (including the 10% buyer's fee). Courtesy Bowers and Merena, Inc.

76. The reverse of the 1907 High Relief *$20 Gold Piece* from the previous photo. The high relief made the coins difficult to stack, and supposedly the Roman numerals confused some people, so later in 1907 the date was changed to Arabic numerals, and the coin's relief lowered. Struck in low relief from 1907 to 1933. Courtesy Bowers and Merena, Inc.

77. 1908 Indian Head *$5 Gold Piece* in Matte Proof. Designed by Bela Lyon Pratt, and issued 1908-1916, 1929. Lot #973 of the Bowers and Merena *Norweb* sale of October 13, 1987. Catalog description includes: "Matte Proof-64 ... a tiny line extending downward from the sixth star. Otherwise the piece is virtual perfection ..." Realized $16,500 (including the 10% buyer's fee). Courtesy Bowers and Merena, Inc.

78. 1908 Indian Head *$5 Gold Piece* reverse. Unique in American coinage, the Indian Head *Quarter Eagles ($2.50 Gold Pieces)* and *Half Eagles ($5 Gold Pieces)* have their designs incuse — recessed into the field of the coins rather than in relief as exists on all other U.S. coins. Beware of counterfeits and altered mintmarks. At the time of issue, the coin was criticized as being a receptacle for dirt and disease, as well as being easy to counterfeit. Courtesy Bowers and Merena, Inc.

3

Making Modern U.S. Coins

More U.S. coins are minted in *one day* today than were minted during an entire year of the Civil War (on the average). More than 20 billion coins are produced by the U.S. Mints on an annual basis.

The primitive early 19th century techniques for making coins have been replaced by high speed sophisticated machines that would make an early U.S. Mintmaster gasp in awe if he could take a tour (as you can today; see the end of this chapter) of one of our Mints in operation.

This chapter explains how current U.S. coins are made, from the design stage to the finished product available at your neighborhood bank. I decided to make the procedure easy to follow (and review) by numbering each part of the process. Variations occur, of course, depending on what kinds of coins are being made, and production problems are dealt with as they arise, but in general this is how coins (like the ones in your pocket) are made: die preparation, planchet preparation, coining, and then distribution.

DIE PREPARATION

1. Design for a new coin is selected by the Director of the Mint, and approved by the U.S. Secretary of the Treasury. By tradition, the Mint Director is a woman, and the Treasury Secretary is a man. The design may come from "in-house" artists at the Mint (such as the Chief Engraver) or from open competition from entries submitted by private citizens.

2. An original sketch of both obverse and reverse of a proposed coin is prepared by the Mint's Chief Engraver and approved by the Mint Director.

3. A wax model (actually made of "plastilene") of the approved sketch is prepared, showing the coin's features in bas-relief. This wax model is generally three to twelve times larger than the finished coin will be. The wax model looks like an enlarged version of the coin, with a positive image.

4. A plaster "negative" is cast from the wax model, incorporating detail work. A negative is a reverse image of the final coin.

5. A plaster "positive" is made from the plaster negative and submitted to Mint Headquarters and interested parties for approval.

6. A rubber mold negative is made from the plaster positive.

7. An epoxy model positive is made by pouring

epoxy into the rubber mold negative. This epoxy model has an extremely hard surface, necessary for the transfer process that comes next. The epoxy model looks like the coin, only larger.

8. A Janvier "pantographic" (transfer) lathe transfers the enlarged design image of the epoxy model positive to a metal hub, which will have the positive image of the finished coin size. The epoxy model positive is mounted on one end of the Janvier transfer engraving machine (as it is also called). A tracing tool at one end of the machine traces the large epoxy model, while at the other end a stylus cuts the design in miniature into a soft steel blank directly to the size of the finished coin, producing a positive replica, or *hub*. This Janvier transfer lathe is a brilliant invention, allowing coin designs to be drawn by artists who are unskilled at making small, coin-sized sketches. Hand-to-die engraving, which is how coin dies were prepared for most of coinage history, was basically eliminated at the U.S. Mint by the adoption of the portrait lathe in 1836 (for mechanically producing master dies from original models). The Hill reducing machine in 1867 further improved this process. And in 1907 the Janvier lathe more or less perfected the process of transferring tiny details from model to die.

9. The hub positive is the first metallic rendition of the coin's design, and the first to be the actual size of the coin, produced from a reduction of the larger epoxy model via the Janvier lathe. As the hub is the original reduced image of the coin, it is annealed (heat treated, then slowly cooled) to harden it, and guarded with care and security. The hub is made of steel.

10. The master die negative is made from the hardened hub on a hydraulic press. The master die is then hardened and used to make a ...

11. Working hub positive, which is extracted by a cold-forging process. The working hub is now used to prepare ...

12. Working dies negative; i.e., many working dies with a reversed image of the coin. Actual coins are struck from the working dies. When a working die wears out or breaks, a new working die is put into service, as long as the coin design is authorized to be struck. The working die is what makes the coin

by stamping a blank piece of circular metal. In the old days (before the Civil War), mintmarks and dates were hand-punched into each working die, resulting in numerous die varieties for U.S. *Large Cents* and *Bust Half Dollars*, for example. The original hub is carefully stored in a safe place to ensure against loss of the original reduction (item #9 above).

PLANCHET PREPARATION

Planchets (also called blanks or flans) are the little circular, flat, smooth pieces of metal that are struck into coins by the action of the dies.

1. Alloy ingots are purified metal bars that are made by refining, assaying, melting, mixing, and hardening metal that has been extracted from metal ore.

2. Rolling the ingots through a rolling mill results in metal strips of uniform thickness. The ingots are squeezed through the rolling machine and are of the proper alloy (metals mixture, e.g., silver and copper) for the specific coins to be struck. For post-1964 U.S. clad coinage, two outer sheets of 75% copper and 25% nickel are bonded under explosive pressure to an inner core sheet of pure (100%) copper, to result in a clad strip that is ready for blanking (see below). In the old days of the Mint, alloying and rolling were done there; at present, the metal coinage strip is purchased from private manufacturers.

3. Blanking occurs when a multipunch blanking press punches out circular metal planchets from the rolled strip. The strip is fed into high speed automatic punch presses that cut planchets of the proper diameter. The U.S. Mint buys metal coinage strips that are about 13 inches wide by 1,500 feet long and weighing 6,000 to 8,000 pounds, in coil roll form. The leftover strip, after planchet punching, is called webbing, and it is shredded and returned to the factory for reprocessing into more strip.

4. Annealing of planchets softens them by heating in a special furnace.

5. Riddling of the planchets occurs in a riddling machine, which screens out blanks of the wrong size and shape.

6. Polishing of planchets occurs in a tumbler filled with a chemical bath that washes them and cleans them, then ...

7. Drying of planchets (after washing) is done with forced hot air.

8. Upsetting of planchets in an upsetting mill occurs when the blanks are rolled on their edges with just enough pressure to raise a rim around them. This makes the blank easier to stamp into a coin, and it lengthens the life of the finished coin. During the upsetting process, the planchets' edges harden, thereby preventing soft metal from squirting between the collar and the dies during the coining process. Upsetting also removes any metal burrs and smooths the blanks' edges, thereby making it easier to feed the blanks automatically into high speed coinage presses. It is hard to believe that in the early days of the U.S. Mint, coins were struck one by one, by hand!

9. Weighing and inspection of finished planchets is now done to be sure that the planchets are properly made for the coining process.

COINING

That special day has arrived! One of the most ingenious feats of human beings, the making of coins, occurs with almost magical sophistication in the coining rooms of the U.S. Mints. Whoever condemns the machine age and technological progress of humanity should examine a primitive screw press (which laboriously handmade one coin at a time) in a museum exhibit, then go and watch the near-miraculous robotics of a modern electric coinage press in operation.

1. The coinage press is set with the working dies, one showing the obverse negative, the other showing the reverse negative images of the coin's design. The obverse and reverse dies are anchored firmly, one above the other vertically, and between the collar that will limit the lateral movement of planchet metal from the coin's edge as it is being struck.

2. Feeding of the planchets into the coinage press is done automatically from feeder tubes, which stack the planchets and feed them individually into the coining press. Metal "fingers" of the press firmly grab

each blank and place it perfectly between the dies.

3. Striking (or coining) the planchet in the coining press is done with a single stroke in which both obverse and reverse dies strike opposite sides of the planchet at the same time that they force metal from the planchet's edge against the restraining collar. (This may be a collar "die" in itself, adding *reeding*—the grooves along the edges of U.S. dimes, quarters, half dollars, and dollar coins—and in pre-Civil War times, maybe a "lettered edge.") The blank is stamped (coining is also called stamping) with the designs and inscriptions that make it a genuine United States coin of the realm! Most of the U.S. Mint's presses are equipped to strike four coins simultaneously; others are dual-operation, striking two. At the Denver Mint, for instance, approximately 40 tons of pressure is used in the coinage press to strike a *Cent* or a *Dime*; 60 tons for a "*Nickel*"; 80 tons for a *Quarter*; and 110 tons for a *Half Dollar*.

4. Ejection of the newly made coins from the coinage dies in the coinage press is done automatically into a bin or hopper at the bottom of each press. This is where "bag marks" (minute scratches on Uncirculated coins) begin, and this is why Proof coins are still handstruck and not "bounced" against other coins after being made.

5. Inspection of the newly minted coins gathering in the bin at the bottom of the coinage press is done periodically by the Press Operator who uses a magnifying glass to spot check each batch of coins. Undamaged coins are sent to the counting machines; defective coins are melted in the Mint furnaces. Of course, defective coins occasionally escape the watchful eyes of Mint employees; otherwise we would never have any modern "Mint errors" in coin collections.

6. Counting of the shiny new coins is done by automatic counting machines, which receive the coins after they have been conveyed from the drop bins at the coinage presses. This is the FIRST CHECKING PROCEDURE to keep track of how many coins have been made. From the counting machine the coins fall into open canvas bags for bagging.

7. Bagging of the counted coins is done by denomination and total dollar value. When the bags are full, they are sewn shut using a small, hand-held sewing machine. Each bag is preprinted with identifying

information about its contents; e.g., "U.S. MINT, DIMES, $1,000." One Mint bag will hold a specific number of coins: 5,000 *cents* ($50); 4,000 *"nickels"* ($200); 10,000 *dimes* ($1,000); 4,000 *quarters* ($1,000); 2,000 *half dollars* ($1,000); and 2,000 *dollars* ($2,000). The Philadelphia Mint formerly made all canvas bags used to ship coins; now these bags are purchased from commercial suppliers.

8. Weighing of the bagged coins is the SECOND CHECKING PROCEDURE to verify quantities of coins minted. A bag of given denomination and total value should have a fixed weight. Security is always tight at the Mint, and needless to say, Mint employees have reputations for honesty.

9. Storage of the freshly bagged coins is done at the Mint where they were made. The sealed bags are neatly piled on pallets (portable warehouse platforms). The heavy pallets loaded with coins are moved by forklift to storage vaults, which are guarded by security officers. In these vaults the coins remain until they are sent to Federal Reserve Banks for distribution.

DISTRIBUTION

1. Federal Reserve Banks (of which there are twelve scattered around the country) receive the coins from the Mint:

District Numbers & Letter Symbols	Federal Reserve Banks
1-A	Boston, MA
2-B	New York, NY
3-C	Philadelphia, PA
4-D	Cleveland, OH
5-E	Richmond, VA
6-F	Atlanta, GA
7-G	Chicago, IL
8-H	St. Louis, MO
9-I	Minneapolis, MN
10-J	Kansas City, MO
11-K	Dallas, TX
12-L	San Francisco, CA

You would think that Federal Reserve District 10 (Kansas City), which includes all of Colorado, would be more logically headquartered in Denver where a Branch Mint actually is, but this District also includes Nebraska, Kansas, and much of Oklahoma. I suppose when the Federal Reserve system was set up, they figured that Kansas City would better serve the whole District, even though it is close to St. Louis, another Federal Reserve District Bank.

Stocks of Mint coins are shipped directly to the Federal Reserve Banks. Huge tractor-trailer trucks (some measuring 55 feet long and 13½ feet high) are used to transport the 1¢ and 5¢ coins. *Dimes, quarters*, and *half dollars* are transported by armored carrier.

2. Counting occurs again at the Federal Reserve Bank where the Mint bagged coins are opened and counted for the THIRD CHECKING PROCEDURE to verify the coin count.

3. Wrapping and boxing of the coins is done at the Federal Reserve Bank, where the coins are rolled with common coin rolling papers (unless member banks specify otherwise). A charge is made for this rolling service, which is the FOURTH CHECKING PROCEDURE. The rolled coins are placed in cartons for delivery to member banks. Each carton has identifying data on it, such as: "Federal Reserve Bank of Atlanta, $500, Quarters."

4. Shipment to member banks of coins from the District Federal Reserve Bank is done by armored car, registered mail, or express. National banks are part of the Federal Reserve system and get their coins from the District Bank directly. State banks are not Federal Reserve system banks and usually get their coins from a national bank.

Bank coin orders are filled without regard to date or mintmark. If a commercial bank has excess cash on hand, circulated coins may be returned to the Federal Reserve Banks. Here, the coins are sorted for "fitness"; badly worn or bent coins are removed and returned to the Mint for recoinage. The Federal Reserve says that around 20 billion coins valued at well over $2 billion pass through their coin processing units each year. Foreign and counterfeit coins are removed as they are encountered.

And that's the story of how new coins get to your neighborhood bank!

MINT TOURS

PHILADELPHIA MINT
5th and Arch Streets (at Independence Mall)
Philadelphia, PA 19106
(215) 597-7350

The U.S. Mint at Philadelphia is open to the public from 9:00 A.M. to 3:30 P.M., but the days vary, so call ahead to make sure that the Mint will be open on the day you plan to arrive. Admission is free.

Philadelphia Mint tours are self-guided and start immediately when you enter. When you walk in the front door, go up the escalator two flights and turn left for the Visitors Gallery. The exhibit numbers in the Gallery match the numbered explanations in your free brochure. Use the pushbuttons in the Gallery to hear recorded information. The entire coinage operations may be viewed from the glass-enclosed Gallery, which has been designed to accommodate 2,500 visitors per hour. Coin production lines are shut down on weekends and federal holidays.

This is the fourth Philadelphia Mint, and this modern building was opened August 14, 1969. Be certain to visit the David Rittenhouse Room on the mezzanine, where Mint relics and historical coins and medals are on display. A sales area is in the lobby downstairs, where current Mint-made U.S. commemorative coins, medals, and souvenirs may be purchased.

DENVER MINT
320 West Colfax Avenue
Denver, CO 80204
(303) 844-3582

The U.S. Mint at Denver is open for guided tours for the public on Monday, Tuesday, Thursday, and Friday from 8:10 A.M. to 3:00 P.M.; and on Wednesday from 9:10 A.M. to 3:00 P.M., but it is closed for a couple of weeks for "Settlement" each year, so call in advance to confirm that tours will be given on the day you arrive. Admission is free. Closed weekends and federal holidays.

All tours are guided, taking about 20 minutes; the Mint can handle 25 to 55 tour visitors every 15 minutes. The Mint is located in the middle of downtown Denver. When I visited the Mint I parked on a side street, but wherever you park, allow enough time for the Mint tour and visiting the coin exhibits and sales area. You can also stamp your own Denver Mint medal (for $1) on an authentic coin press.

ORDERING MINT PRODUCTS

CUSTOMER SERVICES
U.S. Mint
10001 Aerospace Road
Lanham, MD 20706
(301) 436-7400

To add your name and address to the customer mailing list of the U.S. Mint, write to the above address. You will be notified of future offerings of Mint-made products for sale, such as *Proof Sets, Mint Sets*, and *Commemorative coins. Proof Sets* are specially made coins from polished dies, hand-struck, then packaged (lately) in a plastic case for sale to collectors. *Mint Sets* are business strikes of the current year's coins. You can also request a list of medals for sale, and a brochure describing *American Eagle* gold and silver bullion "coins."

The Mint is slow when dealing with the public, so be patient when ordering or requesting information.

79.

80.

81.

82.

83.

84.

85.

86.

79. The "third" San Francisco Mint, operational since 1937, deactivated in 1955, reactivated in 1965 as the San Francisco Assay Office, to help alleviate the coin shortage then, and officially regaining Mint status in 1988. Not open to visitors. Specializes in Proof coin production. Official U.S. Mint photograph, courtesy U.S. Department of the Treasury.

80. The Denver Mint at West Colfax and Evans Streets began producing coins in 1906. A refinery was installed in 1906 to refine gold and silver. Additions and remodeling have occurred over the years. Guided public tours available. Official U.S. Mint photograph, courtesy U.S. Department of the Treasury.

81. The "fourth" Philadelphia Mint, at Fifth Street and Independence Mall, opened for business in 1969. Self-guided tours are conducted on the glass-enclosed elevated visitor's gallery during business hours. Be sure to walk across the street and see the original Liberty Bell when you visit the Mint and, if you have time, see Independence Hall where the Declaration of Independence was adopted. Official U.S. Mint photograph, courtesy U.S. Department of the Treasury.

82. The West Point Mint at West Point, NY was completed in 1938 as the West Point Silver Bullion Depository, produced coins in the 1970s and 1980s, and achieved official Mint status in 1988. Among other things, U.S. gold commemorative coins and gold Eagle bullion coins are struck at the West Point Mint. No visitors allowed. Official U.S. Mint photograph, courtesy U.S. Department of the Treasury.

83. 1884 Pattern U.S. *Five-Cent Piece*, struck in nickel. Lot #835 of the Bowers and Merena *Saccone*

sale of November 6, 1989. Catalog description states: "Proof-66 (PCGS). Nickel. Sharply struck and largely brilliant with some faint blushes of champagne iridescence. The fields are virtually perfect save for a single minute fleck noted beneath the star under M in AMERICA." Realized $3,850 (including 10% buyer's fee). Courtesy Bowers and Merena, Inc.

84. Reverse of 1884 Pattern U.S. nickel *Five-Cent Piece* of the previous photo. Patterns are coins officially produced by the Mint as new coinage designs for consideration by the proper authorities. If the design is not subsequently adopted for general coinage, the coin remains a "Pattern" in numismatic terminology. Many Patterns are extremely scarce and of great beauty, and would be even more costly if more collectors appreciated them. Cataloged in the Judd reference (see Bibliography). Courtesy Bowers and Merena, Inc.

85. A "blank"—also called a "planchet" or "flan"—for a bronze U.S. *Lincoln Cent*. This piece has been out of the Mint for a while, but smooth, clean blanks (like this one once was) are used by rapid-feed automatic electronic coinage presses at the U.S. Mint coinage rooms. For one reason or another, such blanks "escape" from the Mint, and are worth a moderate value in the coin market. From the author's collection.

86. A "mini-bag" (as distinguished from "official" Mint bags of $2,000, for *Dollar* coins) of 100 *Susan B. Anthony* clad *Dollars* from the Denver Mint, freshly opened and being studied for striking characteristics and any potential "errors." From the author's collection.

4

Starting a Coin Collection

Coin collecting is an ancient hobby. Educated Romans in the time of Julius Caesar collected Greek coins that were already centuries old. According to Suetonius, the Roman Emperor Augustus would have foreign coins and old coins distributed during the celebrations of *Saturnalia*, undoubtedly to impress the recipients, who then gazed with fascination on these ancient objects in their hands.

Thirteenth and 14th century Popes were avid coin collectors. The 14th century Florentine poet, Petrarch, loved the ancient coins he purchased from peasants when he was in Rome; he even made a present of some old silver and gold coins to Emperor Charles IV. Sixteenth century Dutch scholar Hubert Goltzius wrote an encyclopedia of Roman coins that was the standard reference on the subject for more than two centuries. In order to research this monumental project, Goltzius traveled all over Europe to examine the collections of more than 700 wealthy coin collectors. Commenting on this time period, Bimard de La Bastille said, "There was no prince or lord who did not pride himself in owning coins, although there still were many among them who could not even read."

In the 16th century, Catherine de Médicis (wife of Henry II of France) collected coins, as did the famous Flemish painter Peter Paul Rubens, who once bought and sold a collection of 18,000 coins! The 18th century Abbot Joseph Hilarius Eckhel, Director of the Imperial Coin Cabinet at Vienna, spent his whole life studying ancient coins and published eight volumes summarizing what he learned. The 18th century Dukes of Tuscany valued coins as much as art.

So many famous collectors and scholars of coins are known from the 19th century that it would take a book larger than this one to discuss their accomplishments, to say nothing of our own century's numismatists. A founder of the Numismatic and Antiquarian Society of Philadelphia in 1858 remarked: "The mania for coin collecting was then raging fiercely, and desires had arisen with very many persons to become better acquainted with the science." In the 19th century John Quincy Adams collected coins, as did J.P. Morgan. In our own century, Victor Emmanuel III of Italy and King Farouk of Egypt were famous coin collectors.

REASONS TO COLLECT COINS

Coin collecting is fun! You learn history, geography, politics, and economics from studying the coins of a nation. The fame and fortunes of the most prominent people to have ever lived are displayed "forever" on durable metal coins.

There are six main types of involvement in the "coin hobby": accumulators, hoarders, collectors, numismatists, dealers, and investors.

The Accumulator

The *accumulator* is a person who likes to take a coin that's "pretty" or "different" and toss it in a cigar box (a collectible item in itself!) or desk drawer. The accumulator has no plan or long-range strategy in assembling these coins. And if the coins are locally legal tender, they may be quickly spent when cash is needed!

The Hoarder

The *hoarder* keeps every coin of a given type; say, every *cent* encountered, or every *Kennedy Half Dollar*. The hoarder is more systematic than the accumulator. The hoarder hoards coins out of (1) obsessive compulsion, (2) boredom, (3) a wish to avoid carrying around ever-increasing amounts of small change (the pickle jar full of "pennies"), or (4) hope that the hoarded coins will increase in value.

All coins were hoarded during the American Civil War; gold coins were hoarded during the Depression in the 1930s; *Kennedy Half Dollars* were hoarded in 1964-65—so much so that the U.S. Mint struck more than 400 million silver *Kennedy Halves* with the 1964 date, and continued to mint 1964-dated halves into 1966 in a futile attempt to discourage hoarding.

The Collector

The *collector* has definite (although maybe constantly changing) goals in the acquisition and subsequent arrangement and storage of coins. A collector may want to get one of every date of a given coin type, for example, or three different coins from every foreign country visited. Collectors store their coins in special holders and albums. Collectors read coin magazines and buy and sell coins at coin dealerships. (See "Types of Coin Collections" below.)

My advice to a beginning collector is to collect a little of everything so that one can familiarize oneself with many aspects of coins before deciding on a narrow collecting specialty. (1) Save coins from circulation, housing them in a coin folder or album (e.g., a "series" such as *Lincoln Cents* by date and mintmark); (2) bring back foreign coins from travels; and (3) purchase cheaper *Proof Sets, Mint Sets,* old obsolete U.S. and foreign coins (like *U.S. 2-Cent Pieces* and British *Half Pennies*), tokens, cheap medals, and maybe a few coin errors.

When I was in high school in the early 1960s, my classmate buddies and I (like the kids in the movie, *Stand By Me*) would walk or bicycle to banks and shopping center department stores, where we would buy rolls of circulated *Lincoln Cents* at face value, then take them somewhere to break open and sort through, hoping to find scarce dates for our collections. Then we would reroll the "leftovers" into full-sized papered rolls of fifty coins, and cash them in for more *cents* (and get some strange stares from cashiers or tellers) or for paper dollars. This was the early 1960s, the calm before the numismatic storm, the last years of innocent coin collecting when you always had the chance of finding something rare in circulating coinage. It was a time when I would spend silver *Morgan Dollars* and *Liberty Walking Halves* at face value for comic books or bubble gum because I didn't want to carry around a lot of heavy silver coins in my pants pocket! When I was playing poker with my buddies during one of our ritual weekend card game sessions, I needed some gambling money, so I sold an *1882-O (New Orleans Mint) Silver Dollar* across the card table in the basement of my parents' house—for $1.10, ten cents over face, which I thought was a little cheap, considering that the coin looked truly Uncirculated to me. How sad that kids today may never know the thrill of receiving an old and rare coin in store change!

One thing a collector does is upgrade the collection, by buying and selling coins, trading them, or (when possible) finding better ones in circulation—the *condition quality of the collection is continually improved.* You "sell your junk and you buy good stuff." But when you sell coins, you never misrepresent them — honesty and a good reputation are worth more than all of the coin collections in the world.

The Numismatist

The *numismatist* is a student and scholar of

coins, medals, and related objects. Walter Breen is perhaps the finest example of a living numismatic expert on U.S. coins. In my article "Striking the issues" in the December 12, 1990 edition of *Coin World*, I pointed out that Walter Breen has forgotten more about U.S. coins than most big-time coin dealers will ever know! A numismatist does original research. A numismatist may or may not also be a coin collector. You can do research with someone else's coins, especially if you can't afford to buy them!

In coin collecting slang, just about everybody calls himself or herself a "numismatist," especially coin dealers who (whether they are knowledgeable or not) like to bill themselves as "Professional Numismatists." Anyone can buy and sell coins. But it takes years and years of experience to know a lot about those same coins. True numismatists, like real specialists of any kind, tend to be rather humble about their knowledge, and after fifty years of intensely studying coins, they will often be heard to say, "Gee, I'm pretty ignorant about coins. But I'm hoping to learn a few things about them this week!"

The numismatist researches (1) the origins and purposes of the coin's designers and producers, (2) the historical significance, (3) the artistic and manufacturing problems involved in making the coin, and (4) how the coin was accepted and used by the public. The numismatist investigates all varieties of the coin. The numismatist reads all available references on the types of coins being studied, and is a member of appropriate numismatic societies, often contributing newly discovered information for everyone's benefit.

The Dealer

The *dealer* is a person who buys and sells coins with the expectation of making steady profits overall (not necessarily on every single transaction). The dealer is a businessperson, either part-time or full-time. Just as other people have *their* jobs that provide their money income, coin dealers earn a living (or try to) by buying coins at wholesale prices and selling them at retail prices.

There is some overlap in these definitions. A dealer may also be a collector (although they tend *not* to be, to avoid a conflict of interest in paying more than they should pay as dealers, in order to

buy a coin for a personal collection) or a numismatist as well as a dealer. The best dealers are numismatists (like Q. David Bowers, whose love of coins shows clearly in the many informative books he has written on coins). The worst dealers are those who know less about coins than their customers do.

It isn't easy being a dealer; the apprenticeship requires more time and energy than most would-be dealers are willing to devote, in order to advance in their new profession. Every year, a number of coin dealers go broke, and during coin market crashes (like 1990), legions of coin dealers go broke, or their businesses are at least seriously damaged. Some of the more successful coin dealers are discussed in Chapter 13.

The Investor

The *investor* tries to make big money from buying and selling coins over the long term (say, five or ten years). Investing in coins is the most difficult of all endeavors in the coin hobby (except for "speculating"—see Chapter 15), because serious coin investing involves trying to predict future mass human behavior based on a bewildering array of known and unknown factors, which are only partially understood today. See Chapter 15 for "tips" on coin investing, should you be considering entering that risky country!

TYPES OF COIN COLLECTIONS

There are many ways to collect coins: U.S. vs. foreign coins, Uncirculated vs. circulated, regular issues vs. commemoratives, copper vs. silver vs. gold coins, *Proof* and *Mint Sets* vs. business strikes, singles vs. rolls, expensive vs. cheap, rare vs. common, new vs. old, type vs. series, "slabbed" vs. "raw" (late 1980s grading slang), normal strikes vs. errors, numismatic value vs. bullion value, patterns vs. accepted designs, etc.

We may collect foreign coins by:

☐ country or region
☐ date (such as birth year) or century
☐ size ("minors" vs. large silver "crowns")
☐ rulers (coins issued during a given monarch's reign, for example)
☐ topic (or "thematic" in British terminology),

such as coins showing animals or ships
❑ event, such as war siege money, Olympics commemoratives

Many foreign coins are cheaper than U.S. coins due to lower face values at current exchange rates, the use of aluminum or other base metal, and particularly less collector demand than for U.S. coins. Cheap aluminum and zinc alloy foreign "junk" coins of the last forty years are sold in sacks by the pound (weight unit, not monetary unit!).

Tobacco, salt in ancient Rome (the origin of our word "salary"), seashells on South Sea islands, ivory in Africa, strung beads (wampum) by North American Indians, beaver skins in Canada, and metal rings of the ancient Egyptians and Celts—all these have been used as money in the past, and some numismatists enjoy studying such "odd and primitive" monies as a collateral hobby to coin collecting.

The stone money of Yap, Swedish plate money, leper colony coins, prison money and military currency, and the "gun money" of Ireland (made by James II from cannon and cannon balls), the leather money of Germany, and the wire money of Mexico and Russia are interesting sidelines in the story of how money has evolved in different places at different times.

Chinese "cash" are old Chinese coins with square holes in their centers. Platinum was used to mint coins in Russia when that metal was thought to be more common than it is.

Foreign coins can be collected by time period: ancient Greek or Roman pieces, Byzantine coinage, coins of the Dark Ages in Europe, Medieval coins, Renaissance medals (if you can afford them), and coins of Modern period nation-states of the 20th century. If you were born on October 13, maybe you should collect the coins of Edward the Confessor, King of England from 1042 to 1066; he was canonized and that is his "day."

United States coins can be collected by:

❑ series (e.g., a date set of *Indian Head Cents*, 1859-1909)
❑ type (e.g., one coin of each major design, such as one *Morgan Dollar*, one *Liberty Walking Half*, etc.)
❑ pattern or trial pieces (these can be very expensive)
❑ commemoratives — silver or gold U.S. commemorative coins

❑ year (e.g., one of each coin type made during your birth year)
❑ sets like *Proof sets* or *Mint sets*
❑ private or territorial issue (like *Pioneer* gold coins)
❑ errors—faulty coins, due to mint-caused mistakes
❑ denomination (e.g., $20 gold pieces of all types)
❑ certification—only buying coins that have been certified genuine and (maybe) graded by a grading service
❑ topical design (e.g., California-related coins, coins with women on them, coins showing assassinated Presidents, coins showing animals, mountains, flags, monuments, etc.)

"Short set" collecting is popular for collectors on a tight budget: e.g., *1940-1947 Half Dollars,* instead of all of them from the first in 1916; U.S. *Proof sets* 1960 to date (ignoring the expensive ones from 1936 through the early 1950s); *Indian Cents* 1900-1909, etc.

Bullion collecting is popular. For example, you can buy old circulated U.S. silver coins at close to bullion melt value to limit the "downside" financial risk. Or you can buy bullion-tied coins like South African *Krugerrands,* English *Sovereigns,* Canadian *Maple Leafs* for foreign issues; American "*Eagles*" for U.S.-produced bullion "coins."

And then there are *tokens* and *medals* and related items (see Chapter 10 for details) for those who want to branch out from coins proper.

TERMINOLOGY OF A COIN'S "PARTS"

Knowing the names of the "parts" of a coin is absolutely essential for a coin collector, so that you can talk to other collectors and dealers in an intelligent and informed manner.

OBVERSE—The front of a coin, the "heads" side.
REVERSE—The back of a coin, the "tails" side.
DEVICE—The major part of a coin's design; subdivided into "main device" (usually the obverse portrait), "secondary device" (e.g., an eagle on the reverse, etc.) Devices are raised (usually), non-lettered, and non-numeraled design areas of a coin.

EDGE — The thin external curved (usually, since most coins are circular) surface of a coin; the edge is oriented vertically when a coin is lying flat on a table; edges may be smooth, reeded, lettered, etc.

RIM — The slightly raised border, just inside the edge limit of a coin's "body," visible from the front or back of a coin; often confused with the *edge*.

FIELD — The flat surface of a coin, the area between the rim and the devices.

LEGEND (or INSCRIPTION) — The lettering on a coin.

EXERGUE — Area at the bottom (usually) of a coin for the value or date (e.g., "FIVE CENTS" is in the exergue on a *Buffalo Nickel*, separated by a horizontal line from the rest of the coin's design).

MOTTO — Patriotic and/or state-sanctioned religious phrase on a coin (e.g., "IN GOD WE TRUST" or "E PLURIBUS UNUM").

MINT MARK (also MINTMARK) — Letter(s) or other symbol showing where a coin was made.

DATE — The year, usually in numerals, on a coin. May not always be the year when, in fact, the coin was struck.

DESIGNER'S INITIALS — An optional inscription on a coin, indicating who designed it.

In addition to the above numismatic terms for a coin's parts, *Right* (or "R") and *Left* (or "L") refer to the direction a face or animal, etc., is "looking" on a coin's design. For example, on the *Lincoln Cent* the head faces towards the viewer's right, so *Lincoln Cents* are said to have *Bust Right* (or *Bust R*).

Relief refers to the "raised" markings on a coin, those parts of the design higher than the field. All current U.S. coins are struck in relief. *Incuse* refers to recessed markings in a coin's design (or die); for example, the *Quarter Eagle* ($2.50 gold piece) of 1908-1929 and the *Half Eagle* ($5 gold piece) of 1908-1929 have their entire designs incuse, below the surface of the coin's obverse and reverse fields, the only U.S. coins to be so struck.

BUDGET FOR COIN COLLECTING

Few beginning coin collectors think much about their hobby budget's effects on the long-range direction of their collection. But if you have $5 or $10 per month to spend on coins, you'll not be collecting gold pieces, for example. I have found, during many years of collecting many things (coins and otherwise), that beginners almost universally are attracted to quantity over quality. They feel better having a large collection of average or mediocre pieces than a small high-grade collection. And on a tight budget, you can't afford many high-priced coins, so to have a collection increase in size, such a collector chooses to buy many lower grade coins *or* cheap common coins in nice condition.

There is a lot to be said for buying and handling a lot of coins. You get experience that way. For a beginner to blow the entire year's collecting budget on a single "gem-quality" coin might be a sound choice investment-wise but a poor choice knowledge-wise. The trick is to select a coin collecting specialty that allows you to purchase nice-looking coins within your budget. I would rather see a beginner start with Uncirculated *Lincoln Cents* (the recent dates, since World War II, being quite cheap, most less than $1 each for pristine Uncirculated specimens) than with Good-Very Good *Barber Half Dollars*, although both collections would be fun to build. The old saying, "Buy the best quality you can afford" applies to coins as well as to everything else in life—if you want to salvage a substantial amount of your "investment" when you decide to sell your collection.

On the other hand, buying low grade silver coins (like Good-Very Good *Barber Halves*) when silver is cheap on the commodity exchanges may yield handsome profits for bullion value alone when silver increases in price, as it did in the late 1970s. I think you should consider your first coin collecting expenditures as a necessary "learning period," if you're young enough to expect to be around for a few years; then you can afford to make mistakes by buying and handling a lot of coins to study and learn about them. Later on you can always spend serious money on expensive coins — after you've learned enough so that you don't get ripped off in bad coin deals!

And you should read about coins. "Buy the book before the coin" has been sound coin collecting advice since coin books were first written. Every public library in the United States has coin collecting books, usually filed under the 737 call numbers of the Dewey Decimal System. The first thing I did when I began coin collecting was go to the Joliet Public Library (in my hometown of Joliet, Illinois) and check out every book they had on coin collecting, in both the children's and adult book sections. I read the books, returned them, then checked them out again and read them again. At that time I couldn't afford to buy books as I can now. See the Bibliography at the end of this book for outstanding coin books, most of which are for sale by coin dealers; some of which may be waiting in your own public library, waiting for you to strip away the veil of ignorance in your quest to become an informed coin collector! How do you think I learned enough to write this book? By spending thirty-five years *reading* about coins, and *talking* about coins with dealers and other coin collectors, and by *buying*, *studying*, and *selling* coins as my interest in them waxed and waned.

SOURCES OF COINS

Circulation

Circulation is the most convenient source of coins for your collection. Pre-1965 U.S. *dimes*, *quarters*, and *halves* don't circulate anymore because their silver content (intrinsic or bullion value) is worth more than their face value (fiat value). "*Wheat Cents*," those *Lincoln Cents* made before 1959, are rarely seen in circulation also, but many billions exist, and the hoarding of common date worn *Lincoln Cents* is not rational.

I recommend that a new collector start coin collecting by assembling an album full of *Lincoln Cents* by date and mintmark, from circulation, starting with 1959 coins. It is the cheapest U.S. "short set" coin collection series that it is possible to assemble from currently circulating coins, and you'll start to learn a bit about coins as you examine them every day in your pocket change.

Other Collectors

Other collectors are an excellent source of coins for your collection, if you can find such people. If you work or go to school, let your fellow employees or classmates know that you are a new coin collector; they may be willing to trade coins with you and

help you learn about the hobby. Of course, you always run the risk of being taken advantage of financially by more experienced collectors, but that problem will fade in direct proportion to your increasing knowledge of coins.

Coin Dealers

Coin dealers are the primary source of coins for the most serious coin collectors. Dealers have (1) the coin stock, (2) the experience to guide you, and (3) the knowledge of what coins are really worth. A coin dealer who has worked full-time for twenty years at his profession is in a unique position to help a new coin collector. Realize, of course, that most dealers will probably try to sell you coins that they already have in stock, regardless of what you ask for, so don't feel obligated to buy or collect what they suggest. There are a lot of coin dealers in the world; if you feel uncomfortable doing business with one, try another.

Listed under "Coins for Collectors" in the telephone book Yellow Pages, you can track down local coin shops near where you live. If the nearest dealers are far away, you may have to do business by mail or visit *coin bourses* (places where many dealers gather for doing weekend business with the public) in a larger town. (See Chapter 17 for publications that list these coin dealers and coin shows.)

Unwritten "rules" for doing business with coin dealers: (1) Don't lie, (2) say what's on your mind regarding the coins being discussed so that the dealer can help you, (3) be up-front about your hobby budget, (4) ask a lot of questions, (5) handle all of the dealer's coins with the utmost care, and (6) don't be afraid to ask for a small discount if the coin is expensive for your budget. (It is tacky to ask for a discount off a $1 priced coin; it is normal to request a cheaper price for a $500 coin.) And it is considered bad manners to take up an hour or more of a dealer's time (at his shop or at a bourse) and not do any business. If you're looking at expensive coins, you don't have to buy one. But if you sort through a box of cheap coins for a couple of hours, then buy none of them, most dealers will have trouble controlling their blood pressure, unless, of course, you're a kid, and the dealer knows you're on a tight budget, and the dealer has the time and space for you to paw through his stock.

One more thing: coins almost always look better at a dealer's shop than they do when you get them home! Part of it is the lousy fluorescent lighting in many coin stores and coin shows; part of it is psychological—the plush "showroom atmosphere" distorts our judgment when we are buying coins; and part of it is that you have the leisure to study a coin endlessly in the comfort of your home and to notice defects that seemed invisible yesterday at the coin store.

Support your local coin store, if possible. Your neighborhood coin dealer will get to know you and your collection, may offer you discounts because you're a valued customer, will sell you what you need in the line of collecting accessories (coin holders, coin albums, coin books, magnifiers, etc.), may put aside and save coins for you that he knows you may need for your collection, will offer priceless "free" advice based on his years of experience as a professional coin retailer, stands ready to give you immediate answers (by phone or at the coin shop) to your coin collecting questions, and (VERY IMPORTANT) may buy back coins from you when you get tired of them. A friendly dealer who knows you may even be willing to buy cheap coins (that he'll have a hard time selling) from you just to keep your business.

Imagine the convenience of having a coin store a few minutes away from your home!

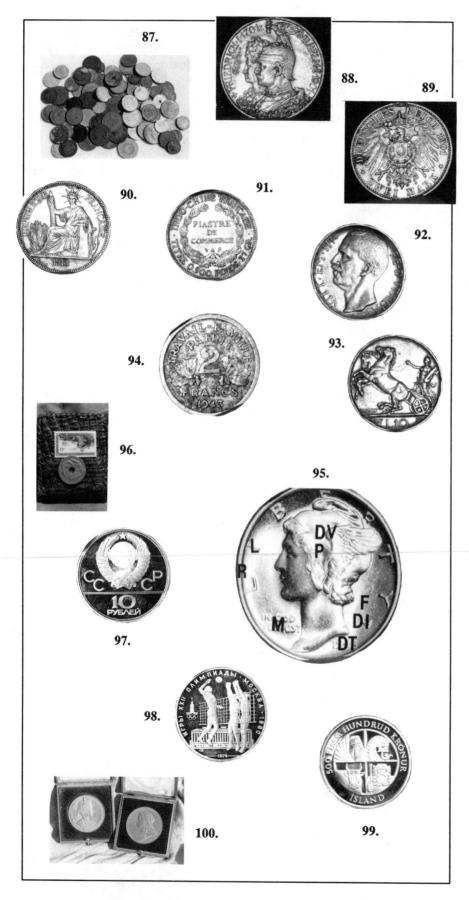

87.
88.
89.
90.
91.
92.
94.
93.
96.
95.
97.
98.
100.
99.

87. There is something to be said for a beginner in coin collecting, who enjoys searching through and studying a mixture of cheap foreign coins. The cash expenditure is small (some dealers have them in boxes, "your pick" at 5¢ or 10¢ apiece); the risk of damaging an expensive coin is irrelevant; and you get to handle and examine many different types of coins, thus training your powers of observation, as well as picking up some foreign language vocabulary. From the author's "collection."

88. Prussia: silver *2-Mark* piece of 1901, celebrating 200 years of the Kingdom of Prussia. 2,600,000 minted, also in Proof. Circulated, but nice contrasting details and toning. Some collectors specialize in "dual portrait" obverses. Author's collection. 11.111 grams, .900 fine silver.

89. Reverse of the 1901 Prussian *2-Mark* piece from the previous photo. There are sixty-one German States listed in Krause & Mishler's *Standard Catalog of World Coins* (see Bibliography). You could easily spend a lifetime collecting and learning about just the extensive German States coinage; in fact, some numismatists have done exactly that! Author's collection.

90. 1913 French Indo-China silver *Piastre*. Circulated, but with "character"; interesting toning and no grossly distracting blemishes. The author purchased this coin specifically for photographing for this book, from a coin dealer at a Reno, NV coin show. The dealer was an American soldier in Vietnam and bought this coin from a fellow soldier, who told him that these older large silver coins were quite popular there. Author's collection.

91. Reverse of the 1913 French Indo-China *Piastre* from the previous photo. Coin weighs 27 grams and is of .900 (90%) fine silver.

Mintmark "A" below the word "COMMERCE" ... for the Paris Mint. French Indo-China, of course, comprised what are now the separate nations of Vietnam, Cambodia, and Laos. Undoubtedly the present inhabitants of those countries retain some French Colonial coins to this day, either as family mementos or as serious bullion hoarding. Author's collection.

92. Kingdom of Italy silver *10-Lire* piece of 1927, with obverse portrait of Vittorio Emanuele III (ruled 1900-1946). 44,801,000 minted in 1927. 10 grams, .835 fine silver. Circulated with even wear. Author's collection.

93. Reverse of Italian *10-Lire* piece from previous photo. A country proud of its history and heritage will often put reminders of such into its coinage designs, hence the Roman chariot on this coin. Some modern Greek and Italian coins recall the splendor that was their civilization in ancient times. Author's collection.

94. An aluminum coin: 1943 French *2-Francs*, a Vichy French State issue, struck in Paris (without mintmark). Instead of the traditional inscription on French coins: LIBERTÉ. EGAL-ITÉ. FRATERNITÉ (LIBERTY, EQUALITY, FRATERNITY), the legend reads: TRAVAIL . FAMIL-LE . PATRIE (WORK, FAMILY, COUNTRY). European coins of World War II are often crudely made of cheap base metal and shallow striking, evidence that something more important than beautiful coinage was occupying people's thoughts. Author's collection.

95. Major "parts" of a coin's design (see text for explanation): Device (DV), Portrait (P), Legend (L), Rim(R), Motto (M), Field (F), Designer's Initials (DI), Date (DT). And on the reverse of this particular coin: Denomination, Country's Name, Mintmark (if any), another Motto.

96. Topical (thematic) coin collections can be built around a certain subject: animals, ships, buildings, etc. The author collects coins, stamps, and billfolds related to crocodiles and alligators (with due respect for conservation laws). Author's collections.

97. 1979 U.S.S.R. silver *10-Roubles* commemorative coin for the 1980 Moscow Olympics. Proof. Evidence of a lot of die polish in the fields; unlikely to have been "whizzed" (artifi-cially brushed to make it look shiny) because the field striations do not extend onto the devices or lettering. Author's collection. 33.3 grams, .900 fine silver.

98. Reverse of 1979 U.S.S.R. silver *10-Roubles* Olympic commemorative coin, with volleyball players and 1980 Moscow Olympics logo. Extensive die polish in the fields. Proof. Sports enthusiasts often specialize in Olympics-related coins and medals of the world, combining numismatics with their interest in international sport. Notice how carefully the author is holding this coin by its edges. Author's collection.

99. Obverse of Iceland *500-Kronur* piece of 1974, Proof, 20 grams, .925 silver. Iceland has only 250,000 inhabitants, but its 20th century coinage includes interesting specimens of moderate cost to the collector on a tight budget. Author's collection.

100. Perhaps medals will become your next area of numismatic specialization. Maybe a pair of turn-of-the-century British bronze medals, in their original presentation cases, or some other aspect of exonumia, like transportation tokens, gaming counters, or military awards. Author's collection.

5

Handling and Preserving Coins

Being made of metal, coins are more durable than rare stamps, oil paintings, antique furniture, and other "perishable" collectibles. But don't let the apparent timeless strength of a coin's substance make you neglect the care and respect that you should give your coin collection, when handling and storing these enchanting little circular bits of historical money. The number of coins that have been permanently damaged by careless handling and poor storage would easily fill many rooms the size of the one in which you are now reading this book.

This chapter discusses handling coins, coin holders and albums, "collecting tools," and how to report a coin theft.

HANDLING COINS

1. *Always handle coins by their edges*, never by their "flat" surfaces.

2. Handle coins over clean, soft surfaces (like a jeweler's felt pad, for sale for a few dollars at any lapidary [rock collector's] shop) in case they should fall. Expect them to roll when they do fall.

3. Put coins in protective holders, either soft plastic "flips" or hard plastic display holders, for frequent handling or long-term storage.

4. Handle expensive Uncirculated and any nice Proof coins with protective gloves. I like clean latex/vinyl surgical gloves, but soft cotton gloves (for sale by coin dealers) are what most coin collectors use, if they use gloves at all.

5. Handle one coin at a time, preferably slowly and carefully, especially if the coin doesn't belong to you.

6. Don't cough or breathe heavily on Uncirculated/Proof coins to avoid tarnishing immaculate surfaces.

7. Never clean a coin. You can break this rule when you're an expert. For every coin that has been "improved" by cleaning, probably a thousand have been permanently damaged, at least in the eyes of veteran collectors who prefer original surfaces to cleaned surfaces of aging coins. An eighty-year-old coin that has been cleaned looks like an eighty-year-old person pretending to be a teenager—a little comical because of the pretense.

8. For long-term storage, keep coins away from heat and excessive humidity. A kitchen or bathroom is usually a bad place to hide a coin collection (burglars look everywhere). Coins may oxidize (tarnish) faster when stored by a heater or in direct sunlight, and plastic coin holders may react chemically and

damage coins that are subjected to too much heat.

9. Keep coins away from foreign chemicals that could permanently discolor the coins: dust, food and drink (eat *away* from your coin collection), household cleaners, medicines, fingerprint oil, and dirt. I wash my hands before I handle my nice coins. Keep coins away from contact with: rubber bands, adhesive tapes of any kind, other metals (including staples, paper clips, and other coins), wood, paint (fresh or otherwise), and smoke.

10. Don't rub anything across a coin's surface, including towels, erasers, brushes, and the clear plastic sliding "windows" on coin albums. A scratch on a coin is there forever (or at least for your lifetime). Minute "hairline" scratches on coins are sometimes called *cabinet friction*, from the days when serious numismatists stored their coins on trays in wooden cabinets, and the coins would get lightly scratched as they slid around.

COIN HOLDERS

There are a number of different hard and soft plastic coin holders for sale to protect coins and permit their safe handling when not in storage. Valuable coins should never be stored in paper envelopes (like the 2" x 2" brown or white opaque coin envelopes), because the paper's sulfur content may discolor the coins; the same is true for cardboard holders and folders. When you buy a coin in a paper or cardboard holder (especially if it is stapled shut), carefully remove the coin and transfer it to a plastic flip. The cardboard holders with soft plastic windows "are unsafe because they are swarming with microscopic paper dust, which has been known to cause carbon spots" on coins, in the words of Bernard Nagengast, environmental engineer and President of E & T Kointainer Company (see below). Also there is the risk of rust transferring from the staples in such holders to a coin's metal surface, and the extreme danger of scratching an enclosed coin on one of the staple points when the coin is removed from the holder. Remove all staples *before* removing a coin from a stapled cardboard holder. Never use polyvinyl chloride (PVC) plastic or cellulose acetate coin holders. Such chemicals were common for coin holders years ago, but experiments and long experience have shown that vinyl

and acetate plastics can discolor and harm coins.

SOURCES FOR COIN HOLDERS

Two companies that I recommend, as sources of the safest coin holders that we know of at the present time, are E & T Kointainer Company and Capital Plastics, Inc. The products of both companies are described below; any coin dealer can supply you with these products, or you can order them directly from the companies. Of course, I have no financial interest in these companies, or in any other firm I ever recommend in print.

E & T Kointainer Company

E & T KOINTAINER COMPANY
P.O. Box 103
Sidney, OH 45365
(513) 492-1027

Written specifically for publication in this book, Bernard Nagengast, President of E & T Kointainer Company, sent me a handwritten letter, which reads, in part:

Our company was started in 1950. During the mid 1940's, Dr. Francis Epps (who became president and secretary of the Central States Numismatic Society) noticed that a proof Indian cent he owned had gotten spots on it. He had a friend who was a research chemist and together they analyzed all forms of coin storage and came to the conclusion that none in use at the time was suitable, so Dr. Epps invented the KOINTAIN and began E & T KOINTAINER in 1950 to manufacture and sell them. Dr. Epps was the first to recommend use of a neutral solvent to remove contaminants from coins, and was the first to advocate use of polyethylene sleeves, instead of cellophane, for coins. Since that time we have never sold any product which could harm coins (which is why we NEVER sold vinyl holders).

I acquired the company in 1979, and in 1981 expanded the product line by inventing a double pocket flip made of MYLAR® to replace vinyl flips. We were also the first, in 1979, to apply vapor corrosion technology used in industry and medicine to the numismatic area.

Flips

Flips are little soft plastic coin holders, usually 2" x 2", with two pockets—one for the coin and the other for a card insert on which identifying data may be written. The flips "open" towards their middle fold (between the pockets), and are folded with their open sides within the fold between the pockets so that coins have a hard time falling out.

E & T Kointainer Company Products

SAFLIP® is a good quality flip for coins. It is made of Mylar® (chemically known as polyethylene terephthalate), the same inert plastic material used by museums and archivists to protect valuable documents. SAFLIPs have been used by prominent coin dealers, like Bowers and Merena, Littleton Stamp and Coin Co., and Heritage Rare Coin Galleries. SAFLIPs are for sale by E & T Kointainer Co. at about $14 per hundred, plus shipping. Write to the address above for the latest prices.

KOINTAIN® coin holders are also sold by E & T Kointainer Co., and consist of two convex clear plastic "sides" that fit snugly around a coin and touch only the coin's "edges." KOINTAINs are used by the Smithsonian Institution, the Carnegie Museum, and the ANA Museum for their coins. KOINTAIN prices vary, depending on the size; write for a price list.

DISSOLVE®, a neutral coin cleaning solvent (chemically: trichlorotrifluoroethane), is also sold by E & T Kointainer Co. DISSOLVE is a non-flammable solvent that can be used to remove oil, grease, and dust from a coin before inserting it in a coin holder. It isn't cheap, priced around $9.60 (including federal excise tax) for an 8-ounce can, plus shipping, but it can be reserved for your better coins, and has been recommended by coin dealers for removing PVC residues.

Capital Plastics, Inc.

CAPITAL PLASTICS, INC.
628 North Erie Street
P.O. Box 543
Massillon, OH 44648
(216) 832-4287

John Schwartz, of Capital® Plastics, was kind enough to send me information about the company for publication in this book.

In 1952 the company got its start in a basement workshop where coin holders were made and sold to coin collectors. Today, Capital Plastics, Inc. has three divisions and three plants with more than 27,000 square feet and a professional staff of experts. The Capital Collector Plastics division sells holders and albums for collectors of coins, paper money, stamps, and baseball cards.

Capital Plastics coin holders are made from inert Plexiglas® acrylic hard plastic. The holders consist of three plastic panels, the center panel containing an opening to the coin, which is then sandwiched between the clear outer panels, and secured with plastic screws and posts. The middle panel comes in a choice of several colors, black and white being the most handsome and most common. The middle panel can be bought with identifying data for the coin, such as type, date, etc.

Capital Plastics' holders are made in many different sizes, for one coin or a set (such as a Proof Set holder for five coins). The cheapest holder, and the one most commonly seen at coin show dealers' tables, is the single coin holder (stock #144), which is made for denominations of *Half Cents* through *$20 gold pieces*. These holders sell for around $2.29 each. They aren't cheap, but they're the nicest coin holders made today, and collectors usually display their best (and most expensive) coins in them. The company also offers custom-made holders, in case you can't find what you want in its 16-page catalog ($2 from above address).

Any coin dealer will sell you a Capital holder or can order it for you if the dealer is set up for selling collecting supplies.

COIN ALBUMS

"Coin Boards" became popular in the 1930s for collecting coins by date. Dealers such as Wayte Raymond popularized these cardboard boards with printed dates and "holes" for insertion of the appropriate coins. Who hasn't seen the blue cardboard Whitman® coin folders, usually three "pages" with dates and mintmarks for coins of a given denomination? I collected *Lincoln Cents* from circulation with these coin folders when I was a kid in the late

1950s. At that time you could still find rare *Lincoln Cents* in circulation, all the way back to the first ones dated 1909. The Whitman folders exist today, for sale at any coin shop.

A more elaborate kind of cardboard coin folder has been and is being made with sliding plastic panels to cover both sides of the coins, so they can be examined with obverses showing on one side of the page, reverses on the other side. These folders are great for a beginning collector or one who collects circulated coins, because the folders are cheap and fun to use. The major disadvantages are: (1) the coins might fall out, (2) you have to be careful that you don't scratch a coin when manipulating it inside of the sliding "windows," and (3) there is always the chance that the cardboard chemicals, especially sulfur, will discolor the coins over time. Actually, some beautifully toned silver coins have been extracted from cardboard holders where they rested for many years, acquiring a "patina" from the cardboard that makes them desirable to many collectors today. But I don't recommend deliberately storing coins in cardboard to tone them!

The better coin albums today (and the more expensive) have all plastic pages and inserts. They're a little bulky, but coins look nice in them. Any coin dealer will help you get one of these albums.

I recommend that you use cheap albums and holders for your cheap coins, expensive holders and albums for your expensive coins, and inert plastic flips for any coins. Special plastic boxes can be purchased to store a row of flips standing upright, and these boxes have an added advantage of being able to fit inside some bank safe deposit boxes.

Finally, be extra careful when handling the coin collection of another person. Don't assume that the coin holders and albums are sturdy. Rapidly turning the pages of an album may send a coin flying! And *always ask permission* before you take someone else's coin out of its protective holder. When the coin is out, be nicer to it than if it was your own. Coin dealer Joseph Coffin once said that an old-timer will feel justified to commit murder if a beginning collector grabs his prized Proof coin carelessly.

OTHER COLLECTING TOOLS

Besides nice coin holders and albums, the following "tools" and accessories will prove useful from time to time.

1. Screw-top clear plastic coin tubes. These come in standard sizes, e.g., for 50 *one-cent* coins, for 40 "*Nickels,*" etc. Don't put your expensive coins in these tubes as they may scratch against each other. These are great for storing rolls of heavily circulated coins, like *Indian Cents* or *Buffalo Nickels* grading "Good." They cost around 25¢ or 30¢ each.

2. Magnifying glass. Absolutely essential for the serious collector. Any kind will do for a beginner, but the advanced collector will want a good 10 power handheld magnifying lens to see detail on a coin. I use a Bausch & Lomb 10X triplet ($25 to $40 retail), and have used lower power jeweler's loupes as well. A cheap magnifier may be worse than none at all. Cheap lenses have inferior optics, causing distortions and color aberrations. Remember, unless you lose it or break it, a magnifying glass can last a lifetime!

For the sophisticated affluent collector, a stereomicroscope (like the dissecting 3-D microscopes in biology labs), with a 30 power magnification, allows explor-ing for evidence of coin tampering and counterfeiting. These microscopes cost hundreds of dollars for a good one. Cheaper ones may give you distorted images.

3. Cotton gloves are convenient for handling Proofs and Brilliant Uncirculated coins. They are for sale at any coin shop. Surgical gloves and medical "examination" gloves make acceptable substitutes. These are $1 a pair or less.

4. Coin trays with felt pad inserts make it safer to handle rare coins. If you drop them, they land gently on the soft pad. I use jeweler's felt pads in black, white, and purple. (I photographed a lot of the coins in this book on these pads.) These can be found at any lapidary ("rock collecting") supply store for a couple of dollars. Add a couple dollars for the hard tray. I like the 7½" x 14" jeweler's felt pads.

5. Cheap 2" x 2" plastic coin holders. Besides the nice holders described earlier in this chapter, buy some of the cheap "snap together" holders for around 25¢ each for your cheaper coins, or for selling coins so encased.

6. Coin wallet. This is a handy little thing for carrying around your coins at a coin show, or taking them to and from a coin shop, etc. They are made of plastic, they come in different sizes and numbers of pages, and cost $2 and up. Be careful that coins don't slide out as you carry the wallet.

7. Caliper. This is used for accurately measuring the diameter of coins. A clear "see-through" plastic millimeter ruler is an acceptable substitute. Calipers cost $5 and up.

8. Gram scale or balance. These get expensive, costing several hundred dollars and up for a nice one. They are used for weighing coins accurately. If you work in a science lab or have access to one, ask permission to weigh your coins there.

9. Plastic storage boxes for 2" x 2" coin holders, including flips. These are around $3 each. They are convenient for inserting in some bank safe deposit boxes. Plastic is better than cardboard boxes, because cardboard may harm the coins chemically.

THE NATIONAL STOLEN COIN FILE

In November 1988, the Federal Bureau of Investigation of the U.S. Department of Justice formed the National Stolen Coin File (NSCF) to help combat theft of rare coins from public and private victims. The services of the NSCF are available to law enforcement agencies for official use in criminal investigations of alleged coin theft. Private citizens who have had coins stolen from them should report the theft to their local police department having jurisdiction over the crime. The local police will, in turn, decide if the case warrants help from the FBI.

Why Thieves Steal Coins

Burglars, robbers, pickpockets, embezzlers, and other assorted thieves like to steal coins because:

1. Coins are highly liquid (easy to sell due to their universally recognized value). An endless selection of pawn shops, coin dealers, and bullion brokers await the visit of anyone with rare coins to sell. And these buyers generally don't embarrass you by accusing you of thievery (unless they've been alerted by the police or the numismatic community about specific coin thefts).

2. Coins are concealable. They can easily be hidden and transported. You can even mix a rare coin with your pocket change and get it through a metal detector security check at an airport!

3. Coins may be hard to identify and trace. Keep photographs of rare coins—in a place away from where the coins themselves are stored—so that law enforcement authorities can compare any coins they recover with alleged stolen ones. In reality, there are so many *Morgan Dollars* and gold coins in the world that without a photo identifying the rare coin's particular surface blemishes, the chances of proving that it was your coin that was stolen are slim. Smart thieves quickly discard incriminating coin holders, "personalized" coin albums, etc., before they try to sell their coin loot. And they may travel to another state to unload stolen coins.

4. Coins are often of great value, hence they make tempting targets for people with larceny in mind. Cases are on record of burglars carefully extracting the valuable coins from home-stored collections and leaving the cheap coins behind—showing that even some bandits acquire a degree of numismatic good taste! Hide your coins well at home, in different locations so that the burglar doesn't get them all with one lucky "find." Better yet, *store all expensive rare coins in a bank safe deposit box.* And insure them.

Reporting Stolen Coins to the FBI

All reporting of stolen coins should be done via your local police department. The detective who investigates your case should be made aware (if he or she isn't already) of the National Stolen Coin File, which handles stolen coin reports on form FD-763 (on which at least one valuable coin *must* be fully described). An official police communication, the National Stolen Coin File Data Sheet (form FD-763) and photographs of the stolen coins should be submitted by local police to:

DIRECTOR
Federal Bureau of Investigation
Attn: National Stolen Coin File
9th and Pennsylvania Avenues, NW
Washington, DC 20535
(202) 324-4434

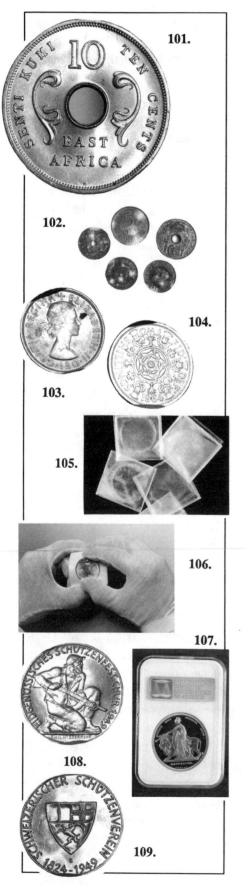

101.

102.

104.

103.

105.

106.

107.

108.

109.

101. Coins should always be held by their *edges*, not by their obverse and reverse "flat" surfaces. Handle valuable coins over a soft surface in case they fall. A jeweler's felt pad is ideal; a clean towel or piece of clothing can be an acceptable substitute. Expect coins to roll if you drop them. And wash your hands before handling valuable coins outside of their protective holders. 1964 East African copper-nickel *Ten-Cent piece.* Author's collection.

102. These zinc coins and tokens have been tarnished and corroded with oxidation mottling. Zinc coins must be kept away from dirt and moisture, and the same applies to copper. Such metals are highly reactive chemically; i.e., merely breathing on them makes them seem to tarnish in front of your eyes. Don't let such coins touch each other, and keep Uncirculated specimens in inert plastic flips. Author's "collection."

103. 1964 Great Britain copper-nickel *2-Shillings* piece, with several distracting tarnish spots, the worst being in one of the worst possible locations aesthetically, on the coin: directly in front of the portrait's "line of vision." Mishandling coins can result in such blemishes, and trying to clean them usually creates more damage. Be nice to your coins and they'll be nice to you! Author's collection.

104. The reverse of the 1964 Great Britain *2-Shillings* piece from the previous photo. The reverse looks OK, but the tarnished obverse destroys the collector value of this piece. Author's collection.

105. None of these soft plastic "flips" has a coin still in it, but you can see

where the coins once were: covered with dust, scratches, and coin "impressions." These dangerously soiled flips should be thrown away. If a coin is worth placing inside a flip, it is worth placing inside a clean one. New flips at your local coin shop cost a few cents apiece. What do your coins cost?

106. Before being sealed in a grading service holder, a coin is first placed in the central insert. The interior section of the holder grips the coin by its entire rim, applying pressure evenly, and does not damage the coin in any way. Photo courtesy Numismatic Guaranty Corporation of America.

107. Although you can't touch it or examine its edge, a coin encapsulated ("slabbed") inside a grading service plastic coin holder may be protected from careless handling. Some collectors like to have their rarest and most valuable coins encapsulated in such holders. Photo courtesy Numismatic Guaranty Corporation of America.

108. 1949 Switzerland *Shooting Medal,* actually a commemorative issue, not one of the rarer and more expensive so-called "Swiss Shooting Thalers" struck in silver from 1855 to date. Still, a legitimate numismatic collectible, perhaps for someone born in 1949? Author's collection.

109. Reverse of the Swiss *Shooting Medal,* struck in silver, from the previous photo. With 125th anniversary "dual date" common to many commemorative medals and even some coins. A mark on a coin may very well stay there "forever," so HANDLE YOUR COINS AND MEDALS CAREFULLY! Author's collection.

6

Coin Grading

Grade is a coin's *condition*, a measure of the wear and surface marks that a coin has received since the moment it was struck.

Grading is important because it determines both the selling price and the numismatic desirability of a coin. Slight differences in grade can mean a huge difference in price when the coin is looked up in a standard pricing catalog. Absolute fortunes have been won and lost in the coin market when (1) the buyers or sellers are ignorant of grades, or (2) somebody outright lies about a coin's grade in order to make money, or (3) grading standards change over time.

Grading is the most controversial aspect of numismatics. Long before you were born, coin collectors and dealers were arguing about grading. And long after you and I pass on, numismatists will undoubtedly still be locked in passionate debates over which grade to assign this or that particular coin!

BAD COIN GRADING EXPERIENCES

Unfortunately, a lot of disheartening melancholy seems to persist in the minds of those who believe they have been "burned" in coin grading transactions. It is common for collectors to quit their coin hobby after they've lost money due to what they honestly think are the grading misrepresentations of people with whom they have done business. Part of this is because of the natural human tendency to be a bit biased towards one's own possessions: if you're buying the coin, it looks Fine ... if you're selling the coin, it suddenly looks Extremely Fine! It is remarkable just how much the grades of coins improve merely by lying around in our albums for a while!

The coin business is much like the used car business — you can make some great deals, but you have to do your homework. Nobody will ever walk up to you and offer you the best car or coin in town — you have to go searching for it. To a true collector, the thrill of the chase is always more exciting than the idle possession of things of value; the best coin is never the one we already own, it is the magnificent gem that we will unexpectedly find next week or maybe next year!

Don't be turned off to coins because of a few bad experiences with "grading sharks." You don't quit buying cars or clothes because you got a bad deal on one of them twenty years ago. You learn from experience and become a wiser consumer.

And don't waste your time carrying long-term

grudges against people who once gave you a bad coin deal: life is too short to spend it walking around mad at everybody. When I was a little boy, I read a magazine article about how residents in some southern U.S. town were welcoming northern investors and northern immigrants, for helping them to develop apartment buildings, stores, and parking lots near the sites where some bloody Civil War battles took place between their ancestors just a couple of generations ago. The article went on to describe how much fun the northerners and southerners were having by working and playing together, and ended with this sentence, which impressed me when I read it: "Even the bitterest of hatreds eventually dissolve in liquid Time."

EVOLUTION OF COIN GRADING

It is hard to believe, from the perspective of the late 20th century, that many mid-19th century coin collectors classified their coins with only *two* grades: *new* or *used*! In the February 1892 issue of *The Numismatist*, author J. Hopper listed *twelve* coin grades: Very Poor, Poor, Fair, Very Fair, Good, Very Good, Fine, Very Fine, Extremely Fine, Uncirculated, Mint Proof, and Mint Brilliant Proof.

In the late 1930s, *The Standard Catalogue of United States Coins and Tokens* by Wayte Raymond (the "authoritative" U.S. coin catalog in its day) listed *seven* grades: Fair, Good, Very Good, Fine, Very Fine, Uncirculated, and Proof.

In the 1969 (5th edition) of *A Guide to the Grading of United States Coins* by Martin R. Brown and John W. Dunn (nicknamed the "*Brown & Dunn*" or the "*B&D*" grading guide) there are *eight* grades for the diagrams of *circulated* coin conditions: Fair, About Good, Good, Very Good, Fine, Very Fine, Extremely Fine, About Uncirculated. First published in 1958, the *B&D Guide* was the standard U.S. coin grading reference until 1970.

In 1970, the book *Photograde* by long-time coin dealer James F. Ruddy was published. The black-and-white actual photos of coin grades in *Photograde* were an improvement over the line sketches of coins in the Brown & Dunn book. *Photograde* listed *seven* circulated grades for its coin photos: About Good, Good, Very Good, Fine, Very Fine, Extremely Fine, About Uncirculated. *Photograde*

was designated as an "Official Grading Guide" by the ANA in 1972. *Photograde* was the most sophisticated U.S. coin grading book from 1970 to 1977, although many collectors (including me) enjoyed using both *Photograde* and the *Brown & Dunn Guide* simultaneously when trying to figure out the grade of a circulated coin, during the 1970-1977 collecting years.

In 1977, *The Official American Numismatic Association Grading Standards for United States Coins*, compiled and edited by Ken Bressett and Abe Kosoff, appeared and more or less replaced all previous grading guides. Dubbed the *ANA Grading* book, my copy of the original 1977 edition lists *ten* circulated grades and *three* Uncirculated (and three Proof) grades by words and numbers adapted from Dr. William H. Sheldon's numerical grading system for the *Large Cents* of 1793-1814 (explained in his 1949 book, *Early American Cents*, later titled *Penny Whimsy*). The *ANA Grading* book had line sketches of coin grades (like the *B&D* book does) and was the first "numerical grading" guide book for general U.S. coin types. The 1977 edition lists the coin grades shown on the next page.

In the 1981 edition of the *ANA Grading* book, two more Uncirculated grades were added: MS-63 and MS-67. "MS" means "Mint State" (i.e., Uncirculated).

The ANA Certification Service (ANACS), founded by the ANA in 1972 to *authenticate* coins with certificates provided to the coins' owners, started to *grade* coins also in March 1979. In February 1986, the Professional Coin Grading Service (PCGS) was formed privately by a group of dealers and quickly took away some of the coin grading business from the ANACS by offering *eleven* different Mint State Grades (MS-60, -61, -62, -63, -64, -65, -66, -67, -68, -69, and MS-70), among other "improvements" over the ANACS.

Other commercial (privately owned, in contrast to the non-profit ANACS) coin grading services sprang up to cash in on the profits to be had from the new fad of certified coin grading, and some grading companies withered in the face of fierce competition for the coin collectors'/investors' grading service dollars. Those that survived the 1980s include (1) ANACS (sold in the summer of 1990 to Amos Press, the private hobby publishers of *Coin*

Uncirculated Coins	Proof Coins	Circulated Coins
MS-70 (Perfect Uncirculated) MS-65 (Choice Uncirculated) MS-60 (Uncirculated)	Proof-70 (Perfect Proof) Proof-65 (Choice Proof) Proof-60 (Proof) Impaired Proofs (i.e., less than MS-60 grade)	AU-55 (Choice About Uncirculated-55) AU-50 (About Uncirculated-50) EF-45 (Choice Extremely Fine-45) EF-40 (Extremely Fine-40) VF-30 (Choice Very Fine-30) VF-20 (Very Fine-20) F-12 (Fine-12) VG-8 (Very Good-8) G-4 (Good-4) AG-3 (About Good-3)

World), (2) Numismatic Guaranty Corporation of America (NGC), (3) Photo-Certified Coin Institute (PCI), and (4) Professional Coin Grading Service (PCGS), with PCGS dominating the certification business in the late 1980s (see below for addresses of these grading services).

Encapsulation—"Slabbing"

PCGS started *encapsulating* coins in February 1986. This means sealing coins in inert plastic rectangular holders, after authentication and grading. These holders were quickly named "slabs" and the process of submitting a coin to be slabbed was called "slabbing." Other grading services followed suit and slabbed coins for their patrons. "Raw" coins are unslabbed coins.

Advantages of slabs include: (1) the coin is protected from damage; (2) the coin's grade is somewhat substantiated, reducing gross errors in overgrading or undergrading (helpful to semi-knowledgeable buyers or sellers); (3) the coin comes with a ready-made storage holder, suitable for filing in a bank safe deposit box; (4) the coin's market value may be increased just by virtue of its being slabbed, which some collectors feel adds to the coin's "salability"; and (5) the coin's authenticity is "guaranteed" by the grading service, which will refuse to encapsulate a coin that is counterfeit (as many gold coins are) or that has been tampered with (cleaned, plugged, falsely toned, etc.).

Disadvantages of slabs include (1) you can't touch the coin (I like to touch my coins), (2) you

can't examine the coin's edge very well because it is "hidden" in the plastic, (3) the printed grade on the slab may be false or questionable (services get a reputation for being conservative or liberal graders), especially from less prestigious grading services, (4) you run the risk of damaging the coin if you decide to break it out of the slab, (5) slabs take up more storage space than thin plastic flips, and (6) scratches and other flaws on the plastic holder may look like they're on the coin (and vice versa), (7) you can't precisely weigh a coin that is sealed in a holder; weighing is useful in counterfeit evaluation (you're trusting the grading service's opinion that it isn't a counterfeit coin), and (8) it is impossible to remove contaminants from slabbed coins. Coins can "age" in a slab. These last two objections (7 & 8) were pointed out to me by Walter Breen when I discussed slabs with him at a recent coin show.

Some Coin Grading Services

Here are four coin grading services that survived the 1980s "grading wars." Other services exist, but these are the ones I'm going to discuss. These four services take prominent display ads in the coin periodicals (see Chapter 17). I have no financial interest in any of these companies, nor do I guarantee their grading expertise; after all, coin grading is somewhat subjective.

As I write this, only one of these companies (PCI) allows coin submissions by individual collectors. The others (ANACS, NGC, and PCGS) have "authorized submission centers" (coin dealers) where collectors may send their coins to be forwarded to the grading service headquarters. Write to the grading service for a list of these submission agents, as well as for the latest prices for certification and encapsulation services, by sending a self-addressed stamped business-sized (No. 10) envelope to:

AMERICAN NUMISMATIC ASSOCIATION
CERTIFICATION SERVICE (ANACS)
P.O. Box 182141
Columbus, OH 43218
(800) 888-1861

Originally begun by the ANA in 1972, the ANACS (as it prefers to call itself today) was sold to privately-owned Amos Press of Sidney, OH during the summer of 1990. Handles U.S. and foreign coins. Write for list of authorized submission dealers.

NUMISMATIC GUARANTY CORPORA-
TION OF AMERICA (NGC)
P.O. Box 1776
Parsippany, NJ 07054
(201) 984-6222

The first grading service to introduce a security hologram on its coin holders. NGC prohibits its management from buying, selling, or trading coins for commercial profit, thus avoiding conflict of interest. Certifies U.S. and foreign coins. Write for list of authorized submission dealers.

PHOTO-CERTIFIED COIN INSTITUTE
(PCI)
3952 Brainerd Road, Box 80096
Chattanooga, TN 37411
(615) 622-3856

Anyone may submit coins to PCI (send for submission forms). All PCI graders are coin dealer professionals, with from fifteen to twenty-five years experience in the coin business. Certifies all U.S. coins and selected foreign coins.

PROFESSIONAL COIN GRADING SER-
VICE (PCGS)
P.O. Box 9458
Newport Beach, CA 92658

The company that originated "slabs" in 1986. Grades U.S. and foreign coins. Publishes monthly *Population Report*, which summarizes the numbers of coins in each grade that have been certified by PCGS. As of the company's fifth year of operation (1991), PCGS had graded a total of 2,446,283 coins with a cumulative declared value of $2,846,511,120.00.

The capsules of all the grading companies have similarities, but I'll describe the PCGS "coin slab". It has (1) Inert, Optical Grade Plastic, (2) a Certification Tag, (3) a Hologram and Emblem, (4) a Retention Ring, (5) a Bar Code, (6) a Tamper-Evident Seal, and (7) a Stackable Edge. A company brochure states:

PCGS has a policy of prohibiting the encapsulation of coins with problems such as artificial toning, cleaning, environmental damage, PVC damage, major scratches, or planchet flaws … PCGS does not refund its grading fee on coins which must be rejected, since the coin must be examined to determine its status.

PCGS accepts coins for authentication and grading through a network of 620 PCGS authorized dealers throughout the United States and Canada; also in London, Zürich, and Tokyo. Write the company for a list of dealers and schedule of encapsulation fees.

THE MEANING OF COIN GRADES

It depends on the coin type, and it depends on who is doing the grading, but here are some general guidelines for assigning a grade to a coin (modified from the *ANA Grading* book):

1. UNCIRCULATED (UNC) — Shows no wear on the highest points of a coin's design. May have "bag marks," also known as "contact marks" or "hair lines," which are scratches and nicks from being jostled against other new coins in Mint bags. May be brilliant or toned. The many degrees of Uncirculated grades—popularized in the 1980s—are quite subjective, as the *identical coin* has received different Mint State grades when submitted to different grading services, and even when the same coin is submitted to the same grading service! Astronomical price differences exist between MS-63 and MS-65 grades for many coins. MS-60 is the lowest UNC grade, also called "Commercial Grade UNC," and is

characterized by many unsightly bag marks. MS-70 is a perfect coin, without visible flaws, the highest grade possible. Few coins, including modern Proofs, can claim to be MS-70. Highly lustrous coins are Brilliant Uncirculated (BU). Tarnished or heavily bag-marked coins are Uncirculated (UNC).

2. PROOF (PR or PF)—Proof is not a grade; it refers to how a coin is manufactured (hand-struck on polished dies, polished blanks, etc.). Proof coins may have any numerical grade like UNC coins if they show no wear (e.g., Proof-65, Proof-60). Proof coins don't technically circulate because they were never made for circulation, but in effect they can show wear (from circulation or otherwise), and as such are called IMPAIRED PROOF and are properly designated with a number like Proof-58 or Proof-45, referring to the degree of "wear" just as if it was a business strike circulated coin. May be brilliant or toned. PL means "PROOF-LIKE"—a business-strike UNC coin with highly reflective fields; PL is not a proof.

3. ABOUT UNCIRCULATED (AU) — Only a tiny bit of wear on the highest points of a coin's design. Much original Mint luster should be present. Toned or untoned. Sold by crooked dealers as UNC, more AU coins have masqueraded as UNC than any other adjacent grade misrepresentations. Sold by honest dealers as "Borderline Uncirculated" or "Slider" grade. Common AU grades, from worst to best: AU-50, AU-55, AU-58. It is a fact that many Premium Quality (PQ, also called "High End," i.e., unusually nice for the grade) AU coins are actually more desirable and should be priced higher than many UNC coins that have heavy bag marks or ugly toning. The price difference between AU and BU coins is often immense; if the coin shows any wear, it is not UNC.

4. EXTREMELY FINE (EX or XF) — More wear than AU coins; high parts of design show easily noticeable wear. Usually some Mint luster remains. A highly collectible grade for rare coins. Common grades are EF-40 and EF-45.

5. VERY FINE (VF)—All lettering and major features of coin's design are sharp but with more wear than EF. No Mint luster usually present. Common grades are VF-20 and VF-30.

6. FINE (F)—Major design parts are sharp but coin shows moderate wear all over. All letters of the word "LIBERTY" show on 19th century U.S. coins. The lowest collectible grade for "common" coins, unless your budget is very small. High parts of design have worn off. Commonly called F-12. If you have an imagination you can see some Mint luster.

7. VERY GOOD (VG) — More wear than F. Finer details have almost worn off. The word "LIBERTY" is only partly visible on 19th century U.S. coins. Called VG-8.

8. GOOD (G)—Shows heavy wear. Major design features still visible. The word "LIBERTY" not visible on 19th century U.S. coins. The lowest collectible grade of a coin unless it is quite rare. Called G-4.

9. ABOUT GOOD (AG)—Very heavy wear, with parts of the lettering and date worn smooth. Date may be hard to read. No "defects," just extremely heavy wear. Not a desirable coin unless it is a rarity (and even then, I'd hesitate to buy it). Called AG-3.

SPLIT GRADES

A coin may appear to be between two grades. For example: F-VF means that the *whole coin* grades between FINE and VERY FINE. When one side grades higher than the other side, the obverse is stated first and is separated by a diagonal line from the reverse grade: VF/F means the obverse is VERY FINE, but the reverse is FINE.

Split grades can also be stated with numbers—AU/EF can also be written AU-50/EF-45 or simply 50/45. Split grades are more commonly used with ancient coins than with U.S. coins.

Split grades tend to be sold at their highest grade but purchased at their lowest grade!

GRADING QUALIFICATIONS

It isn't enough to state a coin's technical (or numerical) grade. You have to say something else about how the coin "ranks" with others of the same grade.

Average (AV or AVG) means typical for the grade; AVF means "Average VERY FINE."

Premium Quality (PQ) or "*High End*" means

unusually nice for the grade. An immaculate AU coin (AU-PQ) may be more desirable than a UNC coin covered with contact marks or ugly tarnish.

Low End means just barely making the grade.

Problem-free coins show "honest wear" but no discernible defects such as rim nicks or unsightly field marks. Problem-free coins in high grades are always in demand. Problem-free coins have never been cleaned.

UPGRADING

A collector is constantly *upgrading* a collection; i.e., replacing lower grade coins with higher grade ones of the same type, date, etc. A *filler* is a coin of poor quality, often damaged, grading FAIR or POOR, and used to "fill" a space in a coin album until the collector can find (and afford!) a better specimen.

LUSTER

Luster is the natural sheen or reflectivity of a coin as minted. It is also known as "Mint Frost" or "Mint Bloom." Cleaned coins show faked luster, which appears dull and abnormally uniform compared with the real thing. Experience in viewing many coins teaches the numismatist what genuine luster looks like. Take a pencil eraser and rub across a worn brown *Lincoln Cent* and you'll see what faked luster looks like. Original color 19th century copper coins attract spirited bidding at auction.

TONING

Toning is the natural oxidation of a coin's surface, resulting in color changes. Toning is different from luster. Luster is how a coin shines. Toning is the new colors that have been added to the coin's original color. When toning is unattractive, it is called *tarnish*. "When they buy a coin they call it tarnish, when they sell a coin they call it toning!"

An Uncirculated coin may be *brilliant* (shiny) or *toned* (discolored). "Original cabinet toning" means colors naturally derived from the trays or albums in which the coins were housed for many years. Toning beauty is highly subjective. Toning is often faked by heating or chemically treating a coin.

PLANCHET QUALITY AND STRIKE

More so with older coins than coins made today, the uniform quality of the planchet (unstruck coinage blank) and the "strength" and "centering" of the striking dies affect the beauty and value of a coin. Ancient coins are notorious for being irregularly struck, especially with weak reverses. U.S. clad coinage (since 1965) tends to be weakly struck when compared with pre-1965 silver U.S. coins.

SURFACE MARKS

It makes an enormous difference *where* the surface marks (contact marks, bag marks) are on a coin's design. A scratch across the date numerals renders a coin uncollectible in the eyes of most collectors. A dozen tiny marks hidden within the eagle's feathers on the reverse may not be nearly as distracting as one prominent mark across Liberty's cheek on the obverse of big coins like the *Morgan Dollar* or *Barber Half Dollar*.

I don't like marks on a coin's rim or edge (called rim "dings"). I also am irritated by what looks like an "artificial" scratch across the field (as though it were caused by a pin, which it may have been), as compared with a more "natural" contact mark that looks as though it came from circulation.

EYE APPEAL

Some coins are said to have "eye appeal"—they just look nice, regardless of grade. I've seen some awful-looking coins proudly displayed in slabs on a coin bourse dealer's table — right next to unslabbed ("raw") coins with breathtaking eye appeal. Just because someone else says that a coin is pretty doesn't obligate you to agree. Do *you* think the coin is pretty?

111.

110.

112.

113.

114.

116.

115.

117.

118.

119.

120.

121.

123.

122.

110. The author grades this coin About Good because the lettering on the right is partly worn away. Liberal graders might try to sell this coin as Good. Author's collection.

111. The reverse of the 1881 *Indian Head Cent* from the previous photo. The reverse grades Good. *Indian Cent* reverses are often better "preserved" than their respective obverses. Author's collection.

112. This coin grades Good: all lettering is delineated, and the major features and coin's rim are evident. The author finds the wear on the numeral "9" and the little scratch near the base of the last numeral "1" to be particularly disturbing "defects" — any damage to the all-important date on a coin should lower the coin's market value. Author's collection.

113. Reverse of the 1901 *Indian Head Cent* from the previous photo. Reverse grades Very Good, as wreath details are beginning to show, and the lines in the shield are fairly evident. Some distracting nicks on the "N" of the word "CENTS." Author's collection.

114. This *Indian Cent* grades Very Good because some of the lettering in the word "LIBERTY" on the headband is visible. Traditionally, *Indian Cents* are graded Very Good if any three letters (or two full letters and two "halves," etc.) of LIBERTY are visible, but *Indian Cents* don't all wear alike, so some flexibility in grading is necessary. When you can't see any letters of LIBERTY, the coin grades Good at best. 1870 is a "better" date *Cent*, with 5,275,000 struck. Author's collection.

115. Reverse of 1870 *Indian Cent* from the previous photo. Reverse grades a strong Very Good in the author's opinion. The wreath and shield still show considerable wear,

although not enough to reduce the grade to Good. A liberal grader would call this Fine. The author finds the small scratches on both "N" letters to be distracting. "Honest wear" with no conspicuous scratches and original color makes a desirable collectible coin, regardless of grade. Author's collection.

116. This *Indian Cent* grades Very Fine in the author's opinion. All letters of "LIBERTY" on the headband are clear. The headdress feathers show wear on their tips. Some of the "diamonds" are becoming visible on the ribbon at the back of the neck of the Indian Princess. Definite wear on the hair strands above the ear. Surface marks and toning as expected for the grade. The author does not like the tiny rim nick above the letter "E" of the word "STATES." Author's collection.

117. The reverse of the 1905 *Indian Head Cent* from the previous photo. This surface grades Very Fine, in the author's opinion, because the lettering, shield, and wreath all show more wear than should be evident in a sharply struck Extremely Fine coin. The reverse has claims to being Extremely Fine, but the author grades conservatively. Author's collection.

118. Extremely Fine to About Uncirculated. Cynics would grade this 1901 *Indian Cent* "EF" if they were buying it, "AU" if selling it.

Traces of wear on the high points of the coin: the strands of hair above the ear, some of the hair immediately behind the ribbon, and on the ribbon itself (although wear on the "diamonds" can vary in high grade *Indian Cents*). Shows much original mint luster, not obvious in a black-and-white photo. Some surface toning and field marks, the most disturbing of which are the "fingerprint" lines on the right side of the coin—permanent evidence of some long ago "touch" by a person who never dreamt that his fingerprint would be immortalized in this coin book. *Indian Cents* are notorious for tarnishing even as they rest in your collection! Handle all copper coins with great care. Author's collection.

119. An Uncirculated specimen of *Indian Cent*, of the minimum quality acceptable to serious collectors with deep wallets. No wear evidence, even on the highest points of the design: the strands of hair above the ear, the lock of hair behind the ribbon, the diamonds on the ribbon. A few surface bag marks, the most obvious being one on the cheek of the Indian Princess, and one in the field in front of her upper lip. Note the wire rim at right, indicative of strong striking pressure in the coinage press. Full original Mint luster and color. Author's collection.

120. Reverse of the 1907 *Indian Cent* from the previous photo. Uncirculated, with all details struck up nicely. Apparent wear is actually re-

flected light from the lustrous surfaces. Hand-held (both coin and camera) and shot in the late afternoon Los Angeles sunlight in the author's back yard. Author's collection.

121. Edge nicks and rim nicks (also called "dings") may be common on pre-1850 copper coins, but they should be avoided if possible. Lazy and/or crooked coin dealers often don't mention edge nicks in their coin descriptions in price lists. You may not think much of an edge scratch when you are buying a coin, but be assured that it will definitely be noticed when you go to sell the coin. A major problem with "slabbed" (sealed encapsulated) numismatic items is that you can't see their edges. Author's photo and "collection."

122. Part of the author's "grading set" of *Morgan Dollars*, arranged in increasing grade from left to right. Top row could be called: Fair, About Good, Good, Fine. Bottom row: Very Fine, Extremely Fine-About Uncirculated, Uncirculated. Or do you disagree? Author's collection.

123. Reverses of the *Morgan Dollar* "grading set" from the previous photo. Notice how the eagle shows increasing definition and "brilliance" as the grade increases. Author's collection.

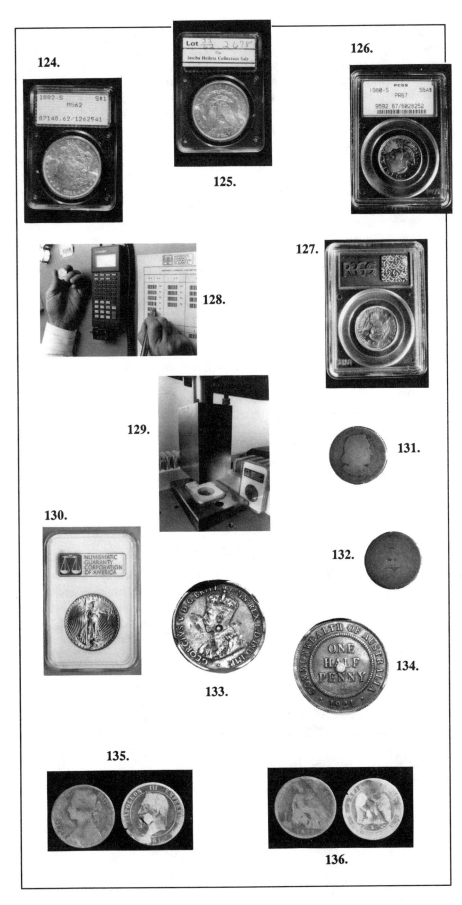

124.

125.

126.

127.

128.

129.

130.

131.

132.

133.

134.

135.

136.

124. An "early" Professional Coin Grading Service (PCGS) "slab" that predates the bar code and hologram security features. An 1882 San Francisco Mint *Morgan Dollar* graded MS62—"Mint State 62"—showing full original luster, no wear on the high points (strands of hair above the eye and ear), and small bag marks that are not too deleterious. Author's collection.

125. Reverse of the 1882-S *Morgan Dollar* in its vintage PCGS holder, with the auction lot sticker still attached. The eagle's breast feathers and wingtips show the definition required for Uncirculated classification. From the Jascha Heifetz Collection, now in the author's collection.

126. Just exactly why anyone would want to "slab" a modern U.S. Proof coin that was struck in the quantity of 3,554,806—virtually all of which were choice specimens when they left the Mint — is beyond the author's comprehension. Even more amazing is that anyone would pay a hefty premium for the privilege of owning a coin that is not rare in the highest states of preservation, merely because it is "slabbed." So it grades Proof-67—big deal! A 1980 San Francisco Mint Proof *Susan B. Anthony Dollar* in its PCGS holder. Author's collection.

127. The reverse of the 1980-S Proof *Anthony Dollar* from the previous photo. When the author saw this coin in its slab on a dealer's table at a Glendale, CA coin show, the dealer wanted $18 for it. The author offered $17, whereupon the dealer lifted a heavily worn early 19th century U.S. *Silver Dollar* from his display table and said, "Let's flip for the difference. If you win, you get it for $17; if I win, you pay $20." The author agreed, the dealer flipped the *Bust Dollar*(!), the author was wrong on the call (and can't remember if it

was heads or tails), and paid $20 for this slabbed modern wonder. With PCGS hologram security imprint. Author's collection (although he doesn't advise flipping *Bust Dollars* when negotiating prices with a dealer!).

128. The Numismatic Guaranty Corporation of America (NGC) "Grading Room" is one of the most modern and well-equipped in the industry. Lighting has been scientifically installed to give true readings of the coins' color and luster. Photo courtesy Numismatic Guaranty Corporation of America.

129. At the grading service, the coin is first authenticated and graded, then goes to the "Encapsulation Room" where, in a dust-free atmosphere, the coin and its label are sonically sealed in what is purported to be a relatively tamper-proof plastic holder. The coin in its holder is then packed in a protective foam package for shipment back to the submitting dealer and, ultimately, the coin's owner. Photo courtesy Numismatic Guaranty Corporation of America.

130. Advantages of hard plastic, sonically sealed, tamper-proof hologram holders that encapsulate coins include: (1) a third party "guarantee" of authenticity; (2) a third party "opinion" on grade; (3) the coin can be dropped without the owner's blood turning to ice; (4) the coin can probably be safely stored for a long time in this holder; and (5) when the owner decides to sell, the "slab" provides some assurance to a suspicious buyer who is not an

expert in the series. Major disadvantages are: (1) you can't touch the coin; (2) you can't see its edge; (3) there is always the chance that the coin is in fact fake or overgraded; and (4) many slabs do get bulky in small storage places. Photo courtesy Numismatic Guaranty Corporation of America.

131. The "WORST KNOWN EXAMPLE" of a silver commemorative U.S. *Columbian Half Dollar*, in its stapled cardboard holder, as purchased across a dealer's table (by the author) at a San Jose, CA coin show. A dealer watching the transaction commented that he's seen worse examples of this coin. No "damage"— just excessive wear. Author's "collection."

132. The reverse of the "WORST KNOWN EXAMPLE" of the *Columbian Half Dollar* from the previous photo. You can actually still see parts of the hull and sail rigging of Columbus' flagship *Santa Maria*, and portions of the two Earth hemispheres below. Why did the author buy this coin? To photograph for this book. When you lose your sense of humor, you lose one of the precious things that make you human. Proudly resting in the author's "collection"!

133. Because there are photos in this book of many rarities costing many thousands of dollars each, the author feels justified in including illustrations of cheap coins and even damaged coins, to make the book a numismatic education and entertaining volume as well as a semischolarly summary of some aspects of coin collecting in the late 20th

century. This Australian bronze *Half Penny* of 1921 had its market value destroyed when someone drilled a hole through its center, possibly to carry on a chain or string, to wear as jewelry, etc. Author's collection.

134. The reverse of the 1921 Australian *Half Penny* from the previous photo, with hole drilled through center (still showing a metal "spur" from the drilling process). Market value is thus destroyed, but the coin may be collected as a curiosity. 5,280,000 minted. Purchased by the author from a dealer's "5¢ box" of cheap foreign coins. Who says that coin collecting has to be expensive? Author's collection.

135. 1875 Great Britain bronze *One Penny* piece, heavily worn and scratched, with portrait of Queen Victoria (ruled 1837-1901). And 1861 French bronze *10-Centimes* piece, worn, edge cut, and pitted on the beard of Napoleon III (ruled 1852-1870). Of no market value, but great for a beginner who wants to touch coins more than a century old, that can be purchased for 5¢ each from a dealer's "5¢ box." Author's collection.

136. Reverses of the British 1875 *One Penny* piece and French 1861 *10-Centimes* piece from the previous photo. French piece has a "K" mintmark for Bordeaux. Worn and damaged, but a lot of history for 5¢ each from a dealer's "5¢ box." If these coins could talk, they'd tell us some interesting stories of where they've been, who handled them and why, and what human joys and sorrows they've seen. Author's collection.

7

Popular U.S. Coins

Popularly collected U.S. coins are discussed in this chapter: *Large Cents, Indian Cents, Lincoln Cents, Buffalo "Nickels," "Mercury Dimes," Bust* and *Liberty Seated* and *Barber* coinage, *Liberty Walking Half Dollars,* silver *Dollars* of all types, gold coins, and commemorative coins. Advantages and disadvantages of specializing in each, past and current collecting fads, and trends for the beginner and intermediate collector are explained in plain words for you to enjoy!

Whole volumes have been written on each of these coin series, so this chapter doesn't pretend to have the entire story of any of these coins. But if you like United States coins, why not collect one of these popular series? Their popularity and the fact that published references on them exist guarantees that somebody will be waiting to buy these coins should you ever decide to sell them.

LARGE CENTS: 1793-1857

When I was a little boy in the 1950s, I sent in a dollar for a *Star Rare Coin Encyclopedia* from the famous coin dealer B. Max Mehl in Fort Worth, Texas. It was a wholesale (dealer buying) price list, with entertaining stories and comments interspersed with the prices. I read it over and over again until the cover became frayed, then I sent for the company's retail list and pondered a long time on how to spend my $1.50 coin collecting budget (which I saved up from my 25¢ a week allowance). Finally, I ordered an *1817 Large Cent* with 13 stars, in Good condition, from the Mehl firm for $1.50. When the package arrived, I opened it up and there it was: an *1817 Large Cent*, worn and blackish, as beautiful a thing as I had ever held in my hands up until that moment, not counting the pet dogs at my grandma's house!

U.S. *Large Cents* (and *Half Cents*) were made of pure copper, hence their extreme tendency to oxidize into the black tarnish that was on my first *Large Cent.* (Described above — guess why I selected it? Because it was the oldest coin in the catalog that I could buy with my $1.50!) Copper tones faster than any other common coinage metal. Uncirculated *Large Cents* with original Mint *red* color are scarce and in high demand. *Red* cents have the color of a newly minted Lincoln "penny." As *Large Cents* age, they go through a *Red-Brown* phase, then *Brown,* then *Black* (the least desirable color). Copper coin colors are abbreviated as follows:

Red—RD
Red & Brown—RB or R & B
Brown—BN or BRN
Black—Blk or "Dark"

So you might see a *Large Cent* advertised for sale as: 1848 1¢ RB UNC $250 (translation: 1848 U.S. *Large Cent*, Red and Brown Uncirculated, $250). Unscrupulous individuals will clean the blackish-brown tarnish off a *Large Cent*, "recolor" it, and sell it as "Uncirculated," when, in fact, it may be honestly called a cleaned AU coin, of far less value than a real Uncirculated specimen. Uniform chocolate brown coloring is normal on *Large Cents*, even for many Uncirculated pieces, and a knowledgeable collector will not pass up an undamaged high grade brown *Large Cent*.

1808-1814 *Large Cents* were made from "soft" copper, which wore away quickly, hence most surviving specimens are heavily worn. Genuine Uncirculated specimens would attract lively bidding at auction. Pre-1800 dates in high grades are very expensive: four and five figure retail prices, and beware of forgeries. Uncirculated *Large Cents* after 1840 are cheaper than the earlier dates.

Large Cents and *Half Cents* were not legal tender when issued; they filled the necessity for small change, but couldn't be deposited in a bank, and were unpopular with the public because of their heavy weight and moderate purchasing power. Hoards have been found in Uncirculated condition, the sources of such handsome coins for collectors today.

Go to a coin show and look at nice *Large Cents*. The best color is subdued *Red*; the worst is *Blackish-Brown* corrosion. But be careful if you buy one of these pre-Civil War U.S. *Cents*: you might get addicted to them!

INDIAN HEAD CENTS: 1859-1909

I love *Indian Head Cents*. Simple, American design; seen in an endless variety of colors; cheap (when heavily worn) for a beginner, exquisite (when Uncirculated) for the advanced collector; bridging history from before the Civil War to the first decade of the 20th century; the coin of the common people, the smallest denomination when issued (and still!); a non-bullion numismatic coin for those who appreciate such. It makes me wonder why everyone doesn't collect *Indian Head Cents*!

The *Flying Eagle Cents* of 1856-58 are often collected along with *Indian Cents*, by custom and because they were, in effect, forerunners of the *Indian Cents*. The *1856 Flying Eagle Cent* is called a "pattern" by some numismatists because of the small quantities struck (about 600 in 1856, then maybe 1,200 to 1,500 restrikes in the next few years). It is called a "business strike" by others because many circulated specimens are found, proving that it did indeed circulate. I asked Walter Breen, who told me that the 1856 *Flying Eagle Cent* is a pattern in his opinion.

Legend has it that when James B. Longacre was designing the *Indian Head Cent* in 1859, his young daughter and a visiting Indian Chief happened to be in the room. Longacre supposedly took the feathered headdress from the Chief and placed it on the little girl's head, and from this "model" he sketched the "Indian Princess" as the portrait for the new *Cent* coin. Like many legends, this one is based more in romance than in fact. The "Indian" head is in reality "Liberty" with an American Indian headdress.

It isn't a large coin, so look it over well when you buy it. *Indian Cents* are sometimes sold with unmentioned rim and edge nicks, field scratches, and carbon spots. The coin has a notorious habit of tarnishing, so never touch the flat surfaces of a nice one. Many otherwise gorgeous *Indian Cents* have ugly fingerprints or spots on them, evidence of an encounter with foreign chemicals in the past. Lazy (or nervous!) collectors may avoid collecting copper coins like the *Indian Cent* because they're afraid the coins will tarnish rapidly and lose their value; they will if you abuse them. Wear cotton gloves when handling immaculate Uncirculated specimens.

Indian Cents (and *Lincoln Cents*, for that matter) are common in grades less than VF-XF. Because double digit millions (e.g., 28,075,000 for the 1862 issue, etc.) were coined for most dates, Uncirculated *Indian Cents* are not exceedingly scarce, although flawless bright red ones are. The 1877 is the *Key Date*, often altered or forged to bilk unwary collectors; expect to pay several hundred dollars for a worn one, several thousand dollars for a pristine Uncirculated example.

Proofs were made for every year of the *Indian Cents*. For similar quality, Proofs always sell for more money than business-strike Uncirculated *Indian Cents*. Scarce minting varieties, like the 1888/7 overdate, are not strictly necessary to complete a "basic" series set of *Indian Cents*.

Because they were made principally of copper, *Indian Cents* exhibit a riot of rainbow colors, depending on the individual coin's "circulation" history. Uncirculated specimens show all shades of toning, including: gold, rose, violet, tan, sky blue, fiery orange, etc. My favorites are pastel hues overlying brilliant reflective Mint luster in Proof examples. Circulated *Indian Cents* show every shade of brown conceivable (and even a few that might not be conceivable!), as is the case with most old copper coins of any type. A "matched set" of similarly-toned near-flawless Proof *Indian Cents* of the full date run (1859-1909) would be worthy of national exhibition.

Be unusually cautious when buying the two San Francisco mintmarked *Indian Cents*: the 1908-S and the 1909-S—the "S" mintmarks may be soldered or glued on the cheaper Philadelphia mintmarkless versions of these dates, or a fabricated "S" mintmark may be "chased" out of field metal in the appropriate place on the coin—forgery skills that would have honest applications in legitimate industry, if the forger had a conscience to match his dexterity.

LINCOLN CENTS: 1909 TO DATE

Much of what I said about *Indian Cents* also applies to *Lincoln Cents*. They're copper coins, so be careful when handling them and be fussy about their appearance when paying good money for them!

The *Lincoln Cent* has the first President and the first real person to appear on a regular issue U.S. coin (previous series had an allegorical "Goddess of Liberty" or a generalized "Indian" as the coin portrait).

Lincoln Cents are ideal coins with which to begin coin collecting because (1) the design has been current longer than any other U.S. coin (at least for the obverse), (2) their total mintage exceeds any other U.S. coin, making them reasonably priced, (3) they have many cheap as well as rare varieties to suit all budgets, (4) a lot of people collect *Lincoln Cents*, so you have lots of sources and potential buyers for

your collection, and (5) as a minor coin, these cents have no intrinsic value, so all of their market value is strictly numismatic, a factor that tends to stabilize their prices during wild fluctuations of gold and silver bullion prices.

As the centennial of Abraham Lincoln's birth (in 1809) approached (1909), there was a suggestion to redesign the U.S. *one-cent piece* in his honor. The task of designing the new *Lincoln Cent* fell to an immigrant artist, Victor David Brenner, and design it he did, with all of the simple elegance and harmonious distinction by which Lincoln himself merited immortality in the annals of human history.

When Secretary of War Edwin M. Stanton was told that President Lincoln had just died from his assassination head wound, Stanton remarked: "Now he belongs to the ages!" And as long as any of the already-struck several hundred billion specimens of the *Lincoln Cent* endure into the future, just so long will the material evidence remain that there was a person whose physical presence has been symbolically preserved on this coin.

Coin designers have often signed their work (in the dies, translated into "initials" on their finished coins). So the uproar that arose in condemnation of Victor D. Brenner's following antique custom by inserting his initials "V.D.B." on the reverse of his *Lincoln Cent* was as theoretically unjustified as it was successful in having the "offending" initials removed, but not before 27,995,000 of these coins were struck at the Philadelphia Mint, and only 484,000 at the San Francisco Mint. This made the San Francisco-struck "V.D.B." *Cents* (or "*1909-S VDB*" in numismatic slang) scarce and marketable.

Key Lincoln Cents and roughly what you might expect to pay for a "lower grade" Uncirculated specimen:

1909-S VDB	$500
1914-D	$1,000 (beware of forgeries)
1922-"Plain"	$3,500 (be *sure* it is UNC when paying this much money)
1955 Doubled Die	$800 (unnecessary for a "basic" date set)

The *1909-S VDB* is worth buying just because it is perennially popular. "Everybody" wants it, and (if they get the money to spend) "everybody" buys it eventually, so collector demand is always strong.

Beware of altered dates to appear as though they are *1914-D Cents*. These cents have also been counterfeited, or have had "D" mintmarks stuck on cheap 1914 Philadelphia versions.

The *1922 "plain" Lincoln Cents* were produced when foreign matter (probably metal) in the "D" mintmark portion of the die made it difficult to strike up the mintmark on the planchet. All *1922 "plain" Cents* were struck at Denver. It is not strictly necessary for a "complete" set of Lincolns. This is a perfect coin to buy with certification when purchasing it (insist on it); watch out for *1922-D Cents* with mintmark removed, masquerading as *1922-plains*.

I like the looks of a *1955 Doubled Die Cent*. The double image was caused by a slight turn during the hubbing of a working die; i.e., the hub (master die) was turned a little when reentering the impression in an obverse working die. These are not to be confused with *double struck* coins that are made by two strikings from a normal die (to make it all confusing, *doubled die* and *double struck* coins are both sometimes called "double impressions"). Dangerous *1955 Doubled Die* counterfeits exist; buy from a reliable dealer. Other *Doubled Die Lincoln Cents* are known, with the 1972 being the most popular (and less expensive than the 1955 error). Red UNC *1955 Doubled Die Cents* now retail at four figure sales prices.

While not expensive (Uncirculated specimens are a few dollars each), 1943 zinc-coated steel cents are romantic reminders of the copper shortage during World War II. These steel cents were too light in weight and weren't accepted by all vending machines. Pristine Mint specimens carry a premium when offered for sale. Many *1943 Cents* are rusted and discolored, and truly "perfect" examples are getting scarcer every day. It is a challenge to locate exquisite original colored *1943 Cents* with no obvious surface flaws. These are $5 to $10 each.

"BUFFALO NICKELS": 1913-1938

First of all, it's not a *nickel*, and secondly, it's not a *buffalo*! It's an *Indian Head Five-Cent Piece* but few collectors call it that. It has long been affectionately known as a *Buffalo "Nickel"*, and if you ever mention it, every coin collector will know what you're talking about. This is a coin that is known by its reverse design: the "buffalo" is, of course, an American bison. And what could be more American than the Indian and "buffalo" on this coin?

Designed in 1913 by James E. Fraser, the Buffalo Nickel has a 75% copper and 25% nickel alloy. The nickel makes it durable, the copper gives it the pretty range of toning colors seen on many specimens. Living Indians served as models for the obverse portrait, while the bison "Black Diamond" in the New York Zoological Gardens was used by Fraser for the reverse.

Buffalo Nickels are often found weakly struck, especially the earlier dates, 1913-1927. This was due to the difficulty of striking a high relief coin in nickel. Coins dated 1928-1938 tend to have better strikes. The Branch Mints (Denver and San Francisco) of early *Buffalo Nickels* tend to have worse strikes than Philadelphia coins.

While many look similar in color to the *Jefferson "Nickels"* (1938 to date) that replaced them, *Buffalo "Nickels"* are found in a variety of colors. I like golden tones the best. Dark gray and bluish-gray look ugliest to me. Extremely beautiful, but always suspicious (for possible artificially toned specimens) are rainbow effects. Still, a riot of colors all over an Uncirculated toned *Buffalo Nickel* is certainly worth thinking about!

Buffalo Nickels (and *Liberty Standing Quarters*: 1916-1930) are often found with their dates worn off because the date numerals were high on the designs. Such coins are worth only double face value for the *Buffaloes*, silver bullion value for the *Quarters*.

Buffalo Nickels get expensive for truly Uncirculated coins, and sharply struck early dates may be rare. Choice UNC 1921-S, 1924-S, and 1926-S examples will run over $1,000 each, and make sure they're Uncirculated and genuine! The full horn and shoulders should be struck up on the bison on UNC specimens.

MERCURY DIMES: 1916-1945

Their official name is *Winged Liberty Head Dimes*, but everybody (almost) calls them *"Mercury" Dimes*. The wings on Liberty's cap are meant to represent freedom of thought. Mercury in mythology, the messenger of the gods, wore a winged cap (*petasus*) or winged sandals (*talaria*) or both, as depicted in classical ancient art.

Mercury Dimes are reasonable in price from 1934 to 1945, except for the 1942/1 overdates, which cost a couple of hundred dollars each just for a worn one. UNC specimens of all dates are available, but UNC Branch Mints (Denver and San Francisco) of the earlier dates will cost you $100 to $300 apiece for many of them. The *Mercury Dime* was designed by Adolf A. Weinman in 1916, the same year he also designed the *Liberty Walking Half Dollar*.

Key dates in *Mercury Dimes* and their retail prices for "lower grade" Uncirculated coins:

1916-D	$3,000 (buy it certified)
1921	$800
1921-D	$900
1926-S	$700

BUST, LIBERTY SEATED, AND BARBER COINS

The silver coins of *Bust*, *Liberty Seated*, and *Barber* series have these issue dates:

Type	10¢	25¢	50¢
Bust designs	1796-1837	1796-1838	1794-1839
Liberty Seated designs	1837-1891	1838-1891	1839-1891
Barber designs	1892-1916	1892-1916	1892-1915

Early *Bust* silver coins tend to be expensive: four *Liberty* and five figure prices for high grade specimens. Later *Bust* coins are cheaper. Many varieties exist.

Liberty Seated silver coins span fifty-four years and cover a wide range of scarcities. If your collecting budget is low, you collect them circulated. Cleaned *Liberty Seated* coins are epidemic, so be sure that you get what you pay for. Uncirculated *Liberty Seated* coins have a wide range of toning colors.

Barber coins have a uniform design with few real varieties. Uncirculated *Barber Half Dollars* are underrated; get them with unblemished cheeks on Liberty's face. Worn *Barber* coins are cheap. Scarce dates exist, but they can be avoided by a "type set" collector.

WALKING LIBERTY HALF DOLLARS: 1916-1947

Considered one of the most beautiful of all American coins, the *Walking Liberty Half Dollar* is also tremendously popular with coin collectors. Designed by Adolf A. Weinman, this coin replaced the Barber design in 1916. *Liberty Walking Halves* dated from 1916 to 1929 tend to be less well struck than later issues; the earlier ones are also more scarce (and more expensive) in Uncirculated state. Coins dated 1933 to 1940 were struck from dies made with a new master hub, and the details of Liberty's head, gown, and hand are usually more visible than for the 1916-1929 coins. "*Short Set*" 1941-1947 *Liberty Walking Halves* are the cheapest of all, but well-struck Uncirculated specimens without bag marks command nice three figure prices.

You'll pay several thousand dollars apiece for choice Uncirculated examples of many of the 1916-1929 dates. In heavily circulated grades (Good to Very Good), none of the *Liberty Walkers* is outrageously expensive, and many collectors enjoy the challenge of completing a "matched set" of these coins in lower grades. Problem-free AU coins are always saleable. The earlier dates are often toned, either handsomely or poorly. "If you're selling it you call it toning, if you're buying it you call it tarnish!"

Overpromoted by dealers in the 1980s, the market prices for UNC *Liberty Walkers* skyrocketed, then crashed. Don't pay UNC prices for AU coins! And a heavily bag-marked (lightly scratched) UNC *Liberty Walker* isn't a nice coin. I'd rather have an unmarked AU with natural golden toning for the same money. Millions of these coins were made, so take your time in selecting them. With a total mintage of well over 400 million, there are a lot of *Liberty Walking Half Dollars* extant—don't feel that you have to buy the first one you see!

U.S. SILVER DOLLARS

As the largest silver coin made by the U.S. Mints, *Silver Dollars* are always lovely and saleable. The

Bust Dollars of 1794-1803 and the *Gobrecht Dollars* of 1836-1839 are expensive in higher grades and aren't worth collecting (in my opinion) in low grades, except for the rarities. These early U.S. *Silver Dollars* are often encountered *cleaned*; buy them with original color and with a minimum of surface marks. It will cost you a couple of thousand dollars for a decent specimen (VF-AU) of most dates.

The *Liberty Seated Silver Dollars* of 1840-1873 are $100 apiece in Good-Very Good; $2,000 apiece for truly Mint State coins with nice appearance with most dates. Cleaning these *Dollars* has been epidemic, and many have "retoned" after a long-ago cleaning session. Look at a lot of them to learn how to distinguish natural color from "cleaned" color. These are underpriced in the *Red Book* in high grades.

Trade Dollars of 1873-1885 were not legal tender at the time of issue: banks, post offices, and railroad ticket agents wouldn't take them. Small businessmen took them and sold them at a discount off face value to get rid of them. Truly Uncirculated *Trade Dollars* are a bit scarce, costing $1,000 and up. Chop marks, applied by Oriental merchants, are common and drastically reduce the coins' value. *Trade Dollars* of 1884 and 1885 were unofficially struck (like the *1913 Liberty Nickel*) and aren't needed for a basic "complete" set. Many *Trade Dollars* tend to look awful, with scratches all over their broad fields, aging tarnish and irregular discoloration, and the all-too-frequent chopmarks. A "perfect" specimen always attracts brisk bidding at auction. Buy them high grade; don't waste your time with junk.

The Morgan Dollar

Morgan Silver Dollars of 1878-1904, 1921 are collected by more collectors than any other coin, except maybe the *Lincoln Cent*. Criminally overpromoted by high pressure salesmen in telemarketing scams, as well as by advertisements of fly-by-night companies in the 1980s, it was little wonder that the UNC *Morgan Dollar* market crashed in 1990 (along with a lot of other coin series). At the start of 1991, you could buy slabbed *Morgan Dollars* cheaper than at any time since 1986. Most dates are common, and they are worth not much more than bullion value for heavily worn coins; UNC specimens may be

overpriced if they look unusually nice. Just remember, millions were minted for most dates; this coin is great to collect, but it isn't "rare" ... as evidenced by the fact that every coin dealer in the country has quantities of them in stock. The Key Date *Morgan* is 1895, costing $10,000 to $20,000 in high grade Proof; beware of forgeries and altered dates/mintmarks.

The Peace Dollar: 1921-1935

The *Peace Dollar* is similar to the *Morgan Dollar* in price and availability. *Peace Dollars* are usually poorly struck, however, and well-defined ones *without* bag marks but *with* original toning are scarce. A *Peace Dollar* set would be a great series to assemble in any grade: Good-Fine for tight budgets, pristine Uncirculated for rich connoisseurs. In fact, I have started a set myself, as a result of buying a 1922 specimen with light golden toning to photograph for this book!

U.S. GOLD COINS

They're expensive and they're beautiful. And they're extensively counterfeited. If you know everything in this book and have a deep wallet, *maybe* you're ready to think about gold coin collecting. Gold coins are for sale at $150 and up at any high class coin shop. Get a book on them and start reading. Buy *Pioneer* gold coins from reliable dealers.

U.S. COMMEMORATIVE COINS

Listed individually in the *Red Book*, it would take a couple of chapters the size of this one merely to touch on the different types. The many different types of 20th century U.S. silver and gold commemorative coins have a popularity that comes and goes with collectors. A high grade UNC set of all the types is a joy to behold, and I just hope that you don't overpay to assemble such. No U.S. silver Commemorative Half Dollar is worth $50,000, even if it is the finest known specimen of the issue, in my opinion.

U.S. PROOF COINS

A great way to collect U.S. coins is in *Proof*. Proofs

are coins made with carefully cleaned blanks and highly polished dies, handstruck on hydraulic presses (these days). The commonly-seen high rims are due to the metal under extra pressure being pressed against the collar aligning the obverse and reverse dies and the blank.

U.S. Proof coins of 1858 to 1915 usually had *frosted devices* and a *mirror-like field*. Proofs from 1936 on are usually mirror-like all over because the whole die was polished, not just the fields. Post-World War II U.S. Proofs are sometimes frosted.

Many collectors start with the latest *Proof Sets*, available directly from the U.S. Mint or from dealers, and work backwards, obtaining the scarcer sets as finances permit. A *Proof Set* is a group of coins, one of each denomination struck for that year in Proof. *Proof Sets* cost around $10 and up for average recent sets (since 1960). The 1936 Set costs several thousand dollars. Nineteenth century sets (including gold) will require you to mortgage your house.

Proof is not a grade. Proof is a method of striking coins. An "impaired proof" is a Proof coin that escaped into circulation and has some wear. Proof coins are graded UNC Proof, AU Proof, XF Proof, and with numerical grades as well. Insist on examining *all* surfaces, including the edge, of expensive Proof coins before you buy them. Scratches anywhere on Proof coins annoy most collectors, although the retail market price may not reflect this.

UNITED STATES COINS—TYPE SET

A *Type Set* of United States coins should include one example of each of the major design changes. But what exactly distinguishes a major from a minor design change in coinage is sometimes open to debate.

When I studied taxonomy (the scientific classification of plants and animals) in college, my biology professors would say: "There are two kinds of people in the world: *groupers* and *dividers*. Groupers like to make big categories. Dividers like to make many small categories. So there are differences of opinion about whether to separate or join certain species in one taxonomical subdivision."

And the same applies to coins: a type set can be widely or narrowly defined, depending on your numismatic conviction and the depth of your wallet. A beginning collector on a tight budget would sensibly choose few coin types. A veteran collector with unlimited funds would be justified in collecting everything by date; i.e., every coin available.

The following charts show what I think should be included in a basic U.S. coinage type set. I've named the coins and their varieties with customary numismatic terminology. Feel free to use this listing as a guide for collecting U.S. coins and modify it to suit your needs.

UNITED STATES COINS—TYPE SET

Denomination	Metal	"Variety"	Dates of Issue
HALF CENTS	Copper	Liberty Cap—Head Left	1793
		Liberty Cap—Head Right	1794-1797
		Draped Bust	1800-1808
		Classic Head (Turban Head)	1809-1836
		Coronet (Braided Hair)	1840-1857
LARGE CENTS	Copper	Flowing Hair—Chain Reverse	1793
		Flowing Hair—Wreath Reverse	1793
		Liberty Cap	1793-1796
		Draped Bust	1796-1807
		Classic Head (Turban Head)	1808-1814
		Coronet—Matron Head	1816-1835
		Coronet—Young Head	1835-1857
SMALL CENTS	Copper-Nickel	Flying Eagle	1856-1858
	Copper-Nickel	Indian Head—Laurel Wreath	1859
	Copper-Nickel	Indian Head—Oak Wreath and Shield	1860-1864
	Bronze	Indian Head—Oak Wreath and Shield	1864-1909
	Bronze, except for Zinc-coated Steel in 1943 (and wrong metal planchet errors) Bronze 1959-1982;	Lincoln Head—Wheat Reverse	1909-1958
	Copper-plated Zinc 1982 to date	Lincoln Head—Memorial Reverse	1959 to date
TWO-CENT PIECES	Bronze	One major variety; Small Motto and Large Motto types in 1864	1864-1873
THREE-CENT PIECES	Silver	No lines bordering star, No Olive Sprig, No Arrows	1851-1853
		Three lines bordering star, With Olive Sprig, With Arrows	1854-1858
		Two lines bordering star, With Olive Sprig, With Arrows	1859-1873
THREE-CENT PIECES	Nickel	One major variety	1865-1889

Denomination	Metal	"Variety"	Dates of Issue
HALF DIMES	Silver	Flowing Hair	1794-1795
		Draped Bust—Small Eagle	1796-1797
		Draped Bust—Heraldic Eagle	1800-1805
		Capped Bust	1829-1837
		Liberty Seated—No Stars	1837-1838
		Liberty Seated—With Stars, No Arrows	1838-1853; 1856-1859
		Liberty Seated—With Arrows	1853-1855
		Liberty Seated—Obverse Legend	1860-1873
FIVE-CENT PIECES	Nickel	Shield—With Rays	1866-1867
		Shield—Without Rays	1867-1883
		Liberty Head—Without CENTS	1883
		Liberty Head—With CENTS	1883-1913
		"Buffalo" (Indian Head)—Type 1—On Mound	1913
		"Buffalo" (Indian Head)—Type 2—On "Line"	1913-1938
		Jefferson	1938-1942; 1946 to date
	Silver	Jefferson	1942-1945
DIMES	Silver	Draped Bust—Small Eagle	1796-1797
		Draped Bust—Heraldic Eagle	1798-1807
		Capped Bust—Open Collar	1809-1827
		Capped Bust—Closed Collar	1828-1837
		Liberty Seated—No Stars	1837-1838
		Liberty Seated—With Stars, No Elbow Drapery	1838-1840
		Liberty Seated—With Stars, With Drapery, No Arrows	1853-1855
		Liberty Seated—With Stars, With Arrows	1853-1855
		Liberty Seated—With Legend, No Arrows	1860-1873; 1875-1891
		Liberty Seated—With Legend, With Arrows	1873-1874
		Barber (Liberty Head)	1892-1916
		"Mercury" (Winged Liberty Head)	1916-1945
		Roosevelt	1946-1964
	Copper-Nickel Clad	Roosevelt	1965 to date
TWENTY-CENT PIECES	Silver	One major variety	1875-1878
QUARTER DOLLARS 1796	Silver	Draped Bust—Small	
Eagle		Draped Bust—Heraldic Eagle	1804-1807

Denomination	Metal	"Variety"	Dates of Issue
		Capped Bust With Motto	1815-1828
		Capped Bust—No Motto	1831-1836
		Liberty Seated—No Motto, No Elbow Drapery	1838-1853
		Liberty Seated—With Arrows, With Rays	1853
		Liberty Seated—With Arrows, No Rays	1854-1855
		Liberty Seated—No Arrows, No Rays	1856-1865
		Liberty Seated—With Motto, No Arrows	1866-1873; 1875-1891
		Liberty Seated—With Motto, With Arrows	1873-1874
		Barber (Liberty Head)	1892-1916
		Liberty Standing—Type 1	1916-1917
		Liberty Standing—Type 2	1917-1924
		Liberty Standing—Type 2, Recessed Date	1925-1930
		Washington	1932-1964
	Copper-Nickel Clad	Washington	1965 to date
	Copper-Nickel Clad and Silver Clad	Washington—Bicentennial Reverse	1976
HALF DOLLARS	Silver	Flowing Hair	1794-1795
		Draped Bust—Small Eagle	1796-1797
		Draped Bust—Heraldic Eagle	1801-1807
		Capped Bust—Lettered Edge	1807-1836
		Capped Bust—Reeded Edge, "50 CENTS" Reverse	1836-1837
		Capped Bust—Reeded Edge, "HALF DOL." Reverse	1838-1839
		Liberty Seated—No Motto, No Elbow Drapery	1839
		Liberty Seated—No Motto, With Drapery, Small Lettered Reverse	1839-1842
		Liberty Seated—No Motto, With Drapery, Large Lettered Reverse, No Arrows, No Rays	1842-1853; 1856-1866
		Liberty Seated—No Motto, With Arrows, With Rays	1853
		Liberty Seated—No Motto, With Arrows, No Rays	1854-1855
		Liberty Seated—With Motto, No Arrows	1866-1873; 1875-1891
		Liberty Seated—With Motto, With Arrows	1873-1874
		Barber (Liberty Head)	1892-1915
		Liberty Walking	1916-1947
		Franklin	1948-1963
		Kennedy	1964
	Silver Clad	Kennedy—Eagle Reverse	1965-1970
	Copper-Nickel Clad	Kennedy—Eagle Reverse	1971-1974; 1977 to date

Denomination	Metal	"Variety"	Dates of Issue
SILVER DOLLARS	Copper-Nickel Clad and Silver Clad	Kennedy—Bicentennial Reverse	1976
	Silver	Flowing Hair	1794-1795
		Draped Bust—Small Eagle	1795-1798
		Draped Bust—Heraldic Eagle	1798-1804
		Gobrecht Dollars (Liberty Seated, Flying Eagle)—several types	1836-1839
		Liberty Seated—Spread Eagle, No Motto	1840-1866
		Liberty Seated—Spread Eagle, With Motto	1866-1873
		Trade Dollars	1873-1885
		Morgan (Liberty Head)	1878-1904, 1921
		Peace—High Relief	1921
		Peace—Low Relief	1922-1935
	Copper-Nickel Clad and Silver Clad	Eisenhower—Eagle Reverse	1971-1974
	Copper-Nickel Clad and Silver Clad	Eisenhower—Bicentennial Reverse	1976
	Copper-Nickel Clad	Eisenhower—Eagle Reverse	1977-1978
	Copper-Nickel Clad	Anthony	1979-1981
GOLD DOLLARS	Gold	Liberty Head (Type 1)	1849-1854
		Indian Head—Small Head (Type 2)	1854-1856
		Indian Head—Large Head (Type 3)	1856-1889
QUARTER EAGLES ($2.50 Gold Pieces)	Gold	Capped Bust—Head Right, No Stars	1796
		Capped Bust—Head Right, With Stars	1796-1807
		Capped Bust—Head Left	1808
		Capped Head—Wide Planchet	1821-1827
		Capped Head—Narrow Planchet	1829-1834
		Classic Head (Ribbon)	1834-1839
		Coronet	1840-1907
		Indian Head	1908-1929
THREE-DOLLAR GOLD PIECES	Gold	Indian Head—Small Letters in "DOLLARS" (Type 1)	1854
		Indian Head—Large Letters in "DOLLARS" (Type 2)	1855-1889
FOUR-DOLLAR GOLD PIECES (STELLAS)	Gold	Flowing Hair and Coiled Hair varieties in each year	1879-1880

Denomination	Metal	"Variety"	Dates of Issue
HALF EAGLES (*$5 Gold Pieces*)	Gold	Capped Bust—Head Right, Small Eagle	1795-1798
		Capped Bust—Head Right, Heraldic Eagle	1795-1807
		Capped Bust—Head Left	1807-1812
		Capped Head—Head Left, Wide Planchet	1813-1829
		Capped Head—Head Left, Narrow Planchet	1829-1834
		Classic Head	1834-1838
		Coronet—No Motto	1839-1866
		Coronet—With Motto	1866-1908
		Indian Head	1908-1929
EAGLES (*$10 Gold Pieces*)	Gold	Capped Bust—Head Right, Small Eagle	1795-1797
		Capped Bust—Head Right, Heraldic Eagle	1797-1804
		Coronet—No Motto, Type 1 Head, Large Letters	1838-1839
		Coronet—No Motto, Type 2 Head, Small Letters	1839-1866
		Coronet—With Motto	1866-1907
		Indian Head—No Motto	1907-1908
		Indian Head—With Motto	1908-1933
DOUBLE EAGLES (*$20 Gold Pieces*)	Gold	Coronet—No Motto	1849-1866
		Coronet—No Motto, Paquet Reverse	1861
		Coronet—With Motto, "TWENTY D." Reverse	1866-1876
		Coronet—With Motto, "TWENTY DOLLARS" Reverse	1877-1907
		Saint-Gaudens—No Motto, High Relief	1907
		Saint-Gaudens—No Motto, Low Relief	1907-1908
		Saint-Gaudens—With Motto	1908-1933
COMMEMORATIVE COINAGE	Gold and Silver	Many types, with silver commemorative half dollars of 1892-1954 being the most popular	1892 to date

137. 1794 *Half Cent*, Normal Head, *Cent* Type wreath. Lot #9 of the Bowers and Merena *Norweb* sale of October 12, 1987. Catalog description includes: "107.7 grains. Uncirculated, MS-60 to 63, with much original mint red still remaining ..." Realized $15,400 (including 10% buyer's fee). Copper *Half Cents* and *Large Cents* of 1793-1857 are wonderful coins that teach us much about the early years of the U.S. Mint at Philadelphia. Courtesy Bowers and Merena, Inc.

138. Reverse of the 1794 *Half Cent* of the previous photo. Early U.S. copper coins in this superior state of preservation are so rare that they are only seen at auction or in the inventories of major dealers who can afford the capital to keep them in stock. Courtesy Bowers and Merena, Inc.

139. 1843 Proof *Dime. Liberty Seated*, with stars, elbow drapery, upright shield (Variety 2). Auction catalog states, in part: "Proof-63 or finer. A splendid specimen ... Walter Breen lists five pieces definitely known to him ..." Realized $6,325 (including 10% buyer's fee) as Lot #469 at the October 12, 1987 session of Bowers and Merena's *Norweb* sale. Courtesy Bowers and Merena, Inc.

140. Reverse of the 1843 Proof *Dime* from the previous photo. *Liberty Seated* coinage spanned some of the most fascinating and turbulent years in U.S. history. The *Dimes*, for example, ran from 1837 to 1891, replacing the earlier *Bust* design, and being replaced themselves by the *Barber* type. Photo courtesy Bowers and Merena, Inc.

141. The fabulous 1894 San Francisco Mint *Barber Dime*. Lot #584 of Bowers and Merena's *Norweb* sale of October 12, 1987. Catalog description includes: "Proof-65. Light gold-

en and lilac surfaces. Extremely sharply struck. One of the finest of about a dozen known specimens ... At the time of issue in 1894, the 1894-S dime escaped the notice of numismatists. It did not escape the notice of Superintendent Daggett, who apparently set aside a few examples for his own use, at least two of which subsequently passed to his daughter, Hallie Daggett ..." Realized $77,000 (including 10% buyer's fee). Courtesy Bowers and Merena, Inc.

142. Reverse of the 1894-S *Barber Dime*. Supposedly 24 specimens were struck in Proof, of which 14 "escaped" from the Mint, and 10 were probably remelted. The Bowers and Merena catalog states, in part: "In 1928 Farran Zerbe was quoted as stating that in 1905 he was told by the Mint that $2.40 was needed to balance Mint accounts at the end of the fiscal year (June 30, 1894). So they struck 24 dimes, of which all but two or three went into circulation ... Another version has it that when the dies for the 1894-S dime were received at San Francisco, 24 pieces were struck. It was anticipated that an additional coinage would occur, but none did, leaving the total mintage for the year at just 24 pieces ..." Courtesy Bowers and Merena, Inc.

143. The *Indian Head Cent* of 1859-1909 served as the lowest denomination U.S. coin struck in those years (as indeed the Lincoln *Cent* still is). Three main varieties exist: the one-year-only copper-nickel laurel wreath reverse of 1859, the copper-nickel ("white cent") oak wreath and shield reverse of 1860-1864, and the bronze alloy of 1864-1909. One of the author's favorite coins, it is a challenge to find choice nice-looking, problem-free *Indian Cents* in any grade. The specimen pictured is Uncirculated with a few bag marks. Author's collection.

137.

138.

139.

140.

141.

142.

143.

144.

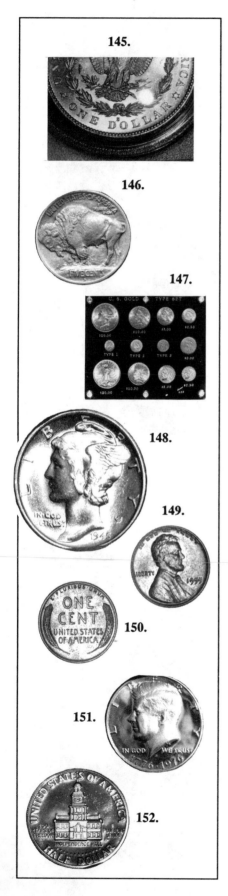

145.

146.

147.

148.

149.

150.

151.

152.

144. The silver *Morgan Dollar* of 1878-1904, 1921 is one of the most collected U.S. coins, along with the *Lincoln Cent*. Millions and millions of *Morgan Dollars* were made, and many rested in storage, either at the Mints themselves or in bank vaults, so these coins are not rare today, even in high grade, *except* for some years/mintmarks. Be patient and selective when buying *Morgan Dollars*. Every coin dealer in the country has some, but it is up to you to find nice-looking coins at a price you're willing to pay. Don't buy coins with distracting marks on Liberty's cheek or in the fields. Author's collection and photo.

145. A San Francisco Mint *Morgan Dollar*, as can be readily verified by the small "S" mintmark on the reverse side just below the wreath. Beware of removed mintmarks, added-on mintmarks, and altered dates, as well as coins that are outright counterfeits. Author's collection and photo. The small circular white area below the arrowheads is light reflecting off the plastic coin holder, not a hole in the coin!

146. A *"Buffalo Nickel"* of 1913, Denver Mint, Type 1—with the bison standing on a raised "mound." This mound was reduced to a "line" during 1913, the first year of mintage, and for all following years (until 1938) — Type 2 in collector terminology. Designed by James E. Fraser, the bison on the reverse side was modeled from "Black Diamond," a bison in the New York Zoological Gardens. Having no intrinsic bullion value, all *Buffalo Nickels* would be worth their face value of 5¢ each … if there were no coin collectors. Author's collection.

147. A type set of U.S. gold coins, mounted in a Capital® plastic display holder. Coins graded EF-45 to MS-60, mostly, as Lot #803 of the Bowers and Merena *Saccone* sale of

November 6, 1989. Realized $3,520 (including 10% buyer's fee). Since gold coins are expensive for a collector on a moderate budget, many such collectors (if they buy gold at all) assemble a "type set" of major design types of U.S. gold coins. Even purchased at the rate of one coin a year, a handsome set like this one would be "finished" at the end of only a dozen years. Courtesy Bowers and Merena, Inc.

148. A *"Mercury" Dime*, officially known as (and preferred by Walter Breen as) a *Winged Liberty Head Dime*. The author likes the name *"Mercury" Dime* because (1) custom dictates its use, (2) it is not a "bad" name, and (3) it is easier and shorter to say and write than *Winged Liberty Head Dime*. A lovely little silver coin, minted from 1916 to 1945. Author's collection and photo.

149. 1955 "Doubled Die" *Lincoln Cent* in Uncirculated condition. Getting harder to find Uncirculated. Lot #54 of the Bowers and Merena *Saccone* sale of November 6, 1989. Catalog description states, in part: "MS-63. Frosty and about 95% mint red. Here is one of the nicest original color Doubled Die cents we've had the opportunity to handle in recent years!" Realized $1,760 (including 10% buyer's fee). Caused by inadvertent "doubling" in the obverse working die, about 20,000 of these errors were struck, many of which escaped into circulation, hence the existence of EF and AU specimens. Beware of counterfeits. Courtesy Bowers and Merena, Inc.

150. Reverse of the celebrated 1955 "Doubled Die" *Lincoln Cent* (doubling is only on the obverse), with the "Wheat Ears" design of 1909-1958. *Lincoln Cents* and *Morgan Dollars* are the most widely collected U.S. coin types. Because they have no intrinsic bullion value, every U.S. *Cent* ever made (including *Large*

Cents and the 1955 "Doubled Die" *Lincoln Cent*!) would be worth merely face value of one cent each … if there were no coin collectors. Photo courtesy Bowers and Merena, Inc.

151. 1976 *Kennedy Half Dollar*, Proof copper-nickel clad, with Bicentennial design (dual date on the obverse). An amazing quantity of *Kennedy Half Dollars* has been made — Mint records show that 433,460,212 were struck in 1964 (the first year of issue) alone! The fact that *Kennedy Halves* don't circulate doesn't mean that they're rare. The public prefers *Quarters*, and current *Kennedy Halves* are just sitting around in bank vaults and in private hoards. Author's collection.

152. The Bicentennial reverse of the 1976 *Kennedy Half Dollar* from the previous photo. If more vending machines accepted *Half Dollars*, they might circulate. As it is, the American public prefers paper money to a pocketful or walletful of heavy, high denomination coins like *Half Dollars* or *Dollars* (*Anthony* or otherwise). Author's collection.

8

Rare U.S. Coins

This chapter tells about some famous and rare U.S. coins. I have selected them for their lofty market prices also—but not because high cost is always coincident with scarcity of a coin. Many "rare" coins (e.g., obscure foreign issues unpopular with collectors, U.S. "minor" one-of-a-kind "flyspeck" varieties with no market demand) are in fact cheap to buy because collector demand is nonexistent. But we normally associate rare U.S. coins with high sales prices, and the following coins play that numismatic market role with a flair that can only be generated by the complete synthesis of romance, history, rarity, and collector obsession as embodied in a small piece of metal.

1804 SILVER DOLLAR

Called the "King of American Coins," the *1804 Silver Dollar* separates the collectors with "affluent" budgets from the truly wealthy. Fifteen specimens are known, and every one of them is a *restrike* (a coin that was struck with a date of an earlier year), as none were made before the year 1834. Generally, restrikes are a little more cheaply priced than original date coins, but the *1804 Dollar* is an exception, and no originals were made in 1804 for comparison

with the restrikes. It is the most famous U.S. restrike.

U.S. Mint records state that almost 20,000 *Silver Dollars* were made in 1804, but these were almost definitely "restrikes" themselves, i.e., dated 1803. In the early years of the Mint, dies were kept in service for as long as possible, and it was standard procedure to use an old die long after the date on it had passed.

In the years 1834-1835, some 1804 Dollars were struck as presentation pieces for proof sets. This was the origin of the "King of Siam Proof Set" containing the 1804 Dollar (the set sold at the Superior Auction Galleries May 28, 1990 sale in Beverly Hills, CA for $3,190,000 including the 10% buyer's premium).

Specimens of the *1804 Dollar* were later made at the Mint for collectors, some of them being struck in 1859, a curiosity that might be termed a "restrike of a pseudostrike" (since none were actually made in the year 1804 to begin with). The *1804 Dollars* made in the 1834-1835 period have slightly different reverses than later-struck pieces.

B. Max Mehl, the legendary Fort Worth, Texas coin dealer of the first half of the 20th century, described this coin:

In all the history of numismatics of the entire world there is not today and there never has been a single coin which was and is the subject of so much romance, history, comment, and upon which so much has been written and so much talked about and discussed as the United States silver dollar of 1804.

Whenever an *1804 Dollar* comes up at auction, bidding is feverish and accompanied by news media and a crowd of dealer and collector observers. Some auction records for the *U.S. 1804 Silver Dollar*:

Year of Auction	Coin Pedigree	Sale Price
1950	Dexter Specimen	$10,000
1961	Idler Specimen	$29,000
1970	Appleton Specimen	$77,500
1972	Idler Specimen	$80,000
1974	Appleton Specimen	$150,000
1980	Garrett Specimen	$400,000
1981	Dexter Specimen	$280,000
1985	Idler-Buss Specimen	$308,000
1989	Adams Specimen (with second reverse)	$220,000
1989	Dexter Specimen (with first reverse)	$990,000

1792 BIRCH CENT

The first U.S. copper cent is known as the *Birch Cent*, supposedly named after the man who designed it. A "Flowing Hair" Liberty Head adorns the obverse, along with the date "1792" and the inscription "LIBERTY PARENT OF SCIENCE & INDUSTRY." A variety exists with the edge inscribed "TO BE ESTEEMED BE USEFUL." Several reverses are known on the *Birch Cent*, one having "1/100" under the laurel wreath encircling the words "ONE CENT," the other having the letters "G*W.Pt."(for "George Washington President"). The "Washington" variety is considered the earlier design, and his initials were removed in deference to the republican anti-authoritarian mood of the young nation.

An Uncirculated copper *Birch Cent* sold at the 1981 Garrett Sale for $200,000. A unique (only one known) white metal *Birch Cent* sold at the same auction for $90,000.

1848 "CALIFORNIA GOLD" QUARTER EAGLE

While not the rarest coin imaginable, the *1848 California Gold Quarter Eagle* ($2.50 gold piece) is one of my favorites. More than 200 ounces of gold from the first discoveries in the California gold fields were sent east by Col. R.B. Mason, Military Governor of California to U.S. Secretary of War William L. Marcy. Much of this gold was used to make *$2.50 gold pieces* at the Mint. Each coin was counterstamped with the mark "CAL." above the eagle's head on the reverse side *as each coin rested in the obverse die* on the coinage press. Genuine specimens should show no "damage" or flattening on the obverse side, but beware of complete counterfeits also.

Of these special "*California Gold*" Quarter *Eagles*, 1,389 were struck, and because many are encountered worn, it is obvious that they circulated. At the Philadelphia Mint in 1848, 7,497 "normal" *Quarter Eagles* were minted, but these regular issue coins tend to be reddish due to the copper alloy. The *1848 "CAL."* Quarter Eagles are more "brassy" in color because the California gold bullion contained some silver.

A rather worn specimen of the "CAL." variety retails for around $5,000. An Uncirculated coin goes for upwards of $30,000. If it's genuine, you have California gold rush history in your hands. If it's counterfeit, you have about an eighth of an ounce of gold, if it even has any gold. Get this coin certified before purchase!

BRASHER DOUBLOON

New York goldsmith Ephraim Brasher produced several gold "*Doubloons*" in 1787, possibly to serve as patterns for a copper coinage contract that Brasher and his partner, John Bailey, wanted from the new United States government. The crudely fashioned eagle on the coin has "EB" (Brasher's initials) countermarked on its design. Fewer than ten specimens of the coin are known, one selling for $725,000 in the Garrett Sale of 1979, another selling for $625,000 at the 1981 Garrett Sale. The coin gets its name "*Doubloon*" because it weighed about as much as a Spanish gold *Doubloon* of the time.

1849 DOUBLE EAGLE

Because of the gold flowing out of California to the U.S. Mint, it was decided to increase the production of gold coins, hence the introduction of the *$20 gold piece* (or *Double Eagle*). In 1849 a pattern *Double Eagle* was struck, followed by an *1850 Double Eagle* mintage of 1,170,261 Philadelphia Mint and 141,000 New Orleans Mint coins. However, the *1849 Double Eagle* is unique; there is only one known specimen and it resides in the Smithsonian Collection. Of course, it is not for sale! You may inspect it, though, on your next Smithsonian visit (see Chapter 19).

1861 CONFEDERATE HALF DOLLAR

In 1861, at the start of the Civil War, the Confederate Treasury Secretary Christopher G. Memminger ordered the New Orleans Mint to strike Proof patterns for a *Confederate Half Dollar*. Only four of these coins were made, showing a normal 1861-dated federal *Half Dollar* obverse, with a specially designed Confederate die on the other side of the coin with the legend "CONFEDERATE STATES OF AMERICA, HALF DOL." and a shield topped by a Liberty Cap, with a sprig of cotton to the left and rice to the right. These original four *Confederate Half Dollars* have passed through private collections over the years, with one — the "Taylor-Saltus" specimen — being donated to the American Numismatic Society (the ANS, not the ANA; see Chapter 18).

Five hundred Restrikes were made of the *Confederate Half Dollar*, now selling for several thousand dollars each in UNC. J.W. Scott & Co. of New York City struck 500 more "*Scott Tokens*" (as they are called) with the original Confederate die reverse, and a "Scott Obverse" reading: "4 ORIGINALS STRUCK BY ORDER OF C.S.A. IN NEW ORLEANS 1861 ******* REV. SAME AS U.S. (FROM ORIGINAL DIE SCOTT)." These Scott Tokens sell for around $500 UNC.

The reason the Confederates never coined more *Half Dollars* is they were short of bullion and short of everything else as the Civil War progressed. Of the *1861-O U.S. Half Dollars* 1,240,000 were struck at New Orleans under a Louisiana secessionist government, and another 962,633 of these federal designs were minted after Louisiana became a Confederate State. These coins, however, are indistinguishable from the 330,000 *1861-O Half Dollars* made before secession. Confederate pattern "*cents*" are known, produced by Robert Lovett of Philadelphia. They are priced at several thousand dollars and up, depending on condition and the metal in which they are coined.

1870-S $3 GOLD PIECE

Only one *1870 $3 Gold Piece* is known from the San Francisco Mint. It grades VF-EF, showing that it indeed circulated at a time when people didn't collect gold coins by date. It was sold in the 1982 U.S. Gold Sale for $687,500.

1894-S DIME

San Francisco Mint Superintendent J. Daggett had twenty-four *Dimes* struck at his Mint with the 1894 date — expressly for distribution to friends. It is thought that less than half survive today. Beware of forgeries and altered mintmarks from the relatively common Philadelphia and New Orleans 1894 *Dimes*. An Uncirculated *1894-S Dime* sold at a Stack's 1990 auction for $275,000.

1895 MORGAN DOLLAR

It's not the rarest coin in this chapter, but because so many people collect *Morgan Dollars* and see the 1895 issue being offered with great advertising fanfare, I thought I would include it here alongside other rare U.S. coins.

U.S. Mint records state that 12,000 business *strikes* (for circulation) and 880 *Proofs* were made of the *1895 Morgan Dollar* of the Philadelphia Mint. But none of the business strikes has ever turned up, so it has been surmised that every one of the 12,000 business strikes was melted under provisions of the Pittman Act of 1918. Of the original Proof mintage of 880, maybe fewer than 500 survive, mostly in various AU to UNC grades. A handsome Proof

1895 Dollar sold for $33,000 in the 1988 Norweb Sale. Beware of forgeries and removed mintmarks from cheaper 1895-S and 1895-O *Dollars*. The 1895 Philadelphia *Dollar* is commonly called the "King of Morgan Dollars."

1913 LIBERTY NICKEL

Rare coins are art as much as oil paintings or antique furniture. To a collector and admirer of the rare and the beautiful, an exceedingly hard-to-find coin is as much a challenge to locate as is tracking down a precious marble sculpture or an exceptional manuscript.

Yet the *1913 Liberty Nickel* makes us feel a bit guilty as well as delighted when we're lucky enough to view one, because the five known specimens were all illegally struck at the Philadelphia Mint by Mint employee Samuel W. Brown. All five were acquired by Col. E.H.R. Green, the eccentric millionaire stamp and coin collector. After Green died, a St. Louis dealer, B.G. Johnson, bought the five *Nickels*, then sold them separately to different collectors. Coin collector James V. McDermott used to carry his *1913 Liberty Head Nickel* around in his pocket, and casually show it in bars to startled drinkers! This McDermott specimen, purchased at the ANA Convention auction by Omaha coin dealer Aubrey Bebee for a bid of $46,000, can now be seen in the ANA Museum in Colorado Springs, CO (see Chapter 19). A specimen of the *1913 Liberty Nickel* sold at the 1985 Buss Sale for $385,000.

1876 CARSON CITY 20¢ PIECE

The fabled Carson City, NV Branch Mint struck 10,000 of the *1876 Twenty-Cent Pieces* with CC mintmark (15,900 were struck in Philadelphia that year). But most of the Carson City specimens were melted before being released to the public, with the result that fewer than twenty pieces are known. The "CC" mintmark is on the reverse side, below the eagle, and *all genuine pieces* show a doubling of the word "LIBERTY" on the shield on the obverse. Beware of counterfeits and altered dates. An Uncirculated *1876-CC 20¢ Piece* sold for $69,300 in the 1987 Norweb Sale.

1907 EXTREMELY HIGH RELIEF DOUBLE EAGLE

Even higher in relief than the *"High Relief"* 1907 Double *Eagle* (selling for around $5,000 to $8,000 for "typical" specimens), the *1907 Extremely High Relief Double Eagle* ($20 gold piece) was struck in the quantity of only a couple of dozen pieces; the *Eliasberg* Proof specimen sold in 1982 for $242,000. Mint records show that 11,250 *"High Relief"* coins were struck in 1907, and these are the four-figure priced pieces usually offered for sale. Beware, of course, of counterfeits.

Production problems caused the Mint to lower the relief, and 361,667 *"Low Relief"* 1907 $20 gold *pieces* were coined; these with Arabic numerals instead of Roman numerals for the date (as were on all high relief coins). What is there to say except that the coin is beautiful?

1907 INDIAN HEAD DOUBLE EAGLE PATTERN

Unique (only one known) and in private hands, the *1907 Indian Head Double Eagle* was obviously a pattern, and exists in gorgeous Proof. It was sold in 1981 for $475,000, and again at the 1984 Paramount Auction for $467,500. Only one person in the world can own it at a time (unless you buy it in syndicate or partnership, as the "King of Siam Proof Set" was purchased in 1990).

1933 DOUBLE EAGLE

Although none was officially released by the Mint, 445,500 specimens of the *1933 Double Eagle* ($20 gold piece) were coined. Nevertheless, some escaped into private hands, as coins have a way of doing, and U.S. Treasury agents seized one out of a New York auction in 1944. Others have since been seized, and officially the coin doesn't exist. It is against the law to own it or sell it; undoubtedly a few still exist but are kept secret if the owners are aware of what they possess!

1964-D PEACE DOLLAR

The *1964 Denver Peace Dollar* was legally struck, to

the tune of 316,076 coins, but was never released legally. Officially called *"trial strikes,"* some probably escaped the Denver Mint in the pockets of Mint employees. The obverse is the same as the normal *Peace Dollars* of 1921-1935. It was decided to remelt them after they were struck because of (1) fears of hoarding of them by the public (who hoarded the *1964 Kennedy Halves* at time of issue), (2) the enormous amount of silver the *Dollars* would consume for the authorized mintage of 45 million, and (3) the coin shortage at that time prohibited the release of coins that might not circulate.

It is an interesting fact of petty (or grand) larceny on the part of some Mint employees, that the *1913 Liberty Nickel* was illegally struck by a Mint employee; and both the *1933 Double Eagle* (described above) and the *1964-D Peace Dollar* were remelted at *exactly the original minted weight for the total mintage*. This indicates that if any escaped the Mint (as they apparently did), it was due to their having been taken by Mint employees after a metal blank or other coin was substituted for the coveted contraband coin, so that the total melt weight would remain constant.

In 1973, the U.S. Department of the Treasury released a statement about the *1964-D Peace Dollars*, which included these words: "Should anyone have such trial Mint-struck pieces in his possession, they are the property of the United States which it is entitled to recover since the pieces were never issued." And yet, no such proclamation has been issued for the *1913 Liberty Head Nickel* (which is freely traded and exhibited), probably because the Mint has never acknowledged that this *Nickel* was officially struck (as the *1933 Double Eagles* and *1964-D Dollars* had been).

1943 COPPER LINCOLN CENT

No bronze (copper alloy) *Lincoln Cents* were officially minted in 1943, a year of critical copper shortage during World War II when copper was needed for munitions. However, a few *copper specimens of 1943 cents* were struck, possibly by accident as the "switchover" occurred, with a few copper planchets getting mixed in with the normal steel planchets for the production run. Several dozen pieces may exist. Outright counterfeits are the most dangerous because they may have proper weight and metal content. Many normal *1943 steel cents* have been electroplated with a copper coating to simulate the *1943 bronze* rarities, but such fraudulent specimens are attracted to a magnet, the first test for a faked *1943 copper cent*. Likewise, a few *1944 steel cents* are known, maybe produced under similar "mistaken" circumstances, and are also, as with the *1943 coppers*, extremely rare.

1974 ALUMINUM LINCOLN CENT

More than 1¹/₂ million "trial strikes" of *1974 Aluminum Lincoln Cents* were struck in 1973 (therefore, postdated) from normal *Lincoln Cent* dies. The aluminum cent was proposed because of the increasing market price of copper at that time, causing hoarding of cents by the public. All of the *1974 Aluminum Cents* were melted, except for ten to fourteen pieces that were not returned to the Mint by Congressmen to whom the coins were loaned for monetary committee consideration. Congress never authorized the circulation coinage of this *Aluminum Cent*. One coin exists in the Smithsonian's Collection, and all others are illegal to own, although several people undoubtedly have them, maybe even people whose reputations at the moment are spotless.

153.

154.

155.

157.

156.

158.

159.

160.

161.

162.

163.

164.

165.

166.

153. 1652 Massachusetts Bay Colony silver *Oak Tree Shilling*. Struck by John Hull some time in the 1660-1667 period, although all coins bear the 1652 date to evade English laws against local American Colonial coinage. Lot #1173 of the Bowers and Merena *Norweb* sale of October 13, 1987. The "Spiny Tree" variety, sometimes described as "the oak that got changed into a pine." Graded AU-50 in the catalog. Realized $18,700 (including 10% buyer's fee). Courtesy Bowers and Merena, Inc.

154. Reverse of the *Oak Tree Shilling* of the previous photo. Catalog description includes: "Possibly one of the finest known of the variety … Sharp and complete root structure. Finer than the Roper:17 specimen, itself an outstanding Extremely Fine coin. Purchased privately from Henry Chapman, date unrecorded." Courtesy Bowers and Merena, Inc.

155. 1652 Massachusetts Bay Colony silver *Pine Tree Shilling*. Lot #1196 of the Bowers and Merena *Norweb* sale of October 13, 1987. Catalog description includes: "MS-60, among the finest known … Obverse letters USE strangely elongated and soft, as on the Noe plate coin …" Realized $26,400 (including 10% buyer's fee). Courtesy Bowers and Merena, Inc.

156. Reverse of the *Pine Tree Shilling* of previous photo. Quality is not cheap; it's priceless! Or almost so. You can buy a lot of *Pine Tree Shillings*, but you won't find many of this quality. Purchased privately from New Netherlands Coin Company on July 31, 1956; earlier ex. Winsor:17, Mills:36, Ryder collections. Courtesy Bowers and Merena, Inc.

157. 1859 Transitional Pattern silver *Half Dime* in Proof. Lot #359 of the

Bowers and Merena *Norweb* sale of October 12, 1987. Catalog description includes: "Proof-63. Judd-232; Adams-Woodin 309. 1859 obverse and 1860 reverse. Interesting, in that the inscription UNITED STATES OF AMERICA does not appear on either obverse or reverse …" Realized $12,100 (including 10% buyer's fee). Courtesy Bowers and Merena, Inc.

158. Reverse of 1859 Transitional Pattern *Half Dime* from previous photo. Catalog description includes: "Toned blue and gold. An important and very rare coin. Only a few specimens are known to exist of the 1859 transitional … From the Palace Collection of King Farouk of Egypt, 1954." Courtesy Bowers and Merena, Inc.

159. 1875 Proof *$3 Gold Piece*, one of the great rarities in the U.S. gold series. Lot #721 of the Bowers and Merena *Norweb* sale of October 13, 1987. Catalog description includes: "Proof-63 or finer. Brilliant surfaces …" Mint records state that twenty examples were struck this year, but Breen and Akers have pointed out that more are known (perhaps thirty or so). Realized $110,000 (including 10% buyer's fee). Courtesy Bowers and Merena, Inc.

160. Reverse of the rare 1875 *$3 Gold Piece* from the previous photo. Passed from Henry Chapman to Albert Holden, circa 1908. Courtesy Bowers and Merena, Inc.

161. 1876 Carson City Mint *Twenty-Cent Piece*, silver. Mint records state that 10,000 were struck, but almost all were remelted, leaving about a dozen or so known today. The word "LIBERTY" is doubled on the obverse, characteristic of all genuine 1876-CC *Twenty-Cent Pieces*. Lot #691 of the Bowers and Merena *Norweb* sale of October 12, 1987. Catalog description includes: "MS-

64 to 65. Medium lilac and blue toning. Very sharply struck ..." Realized $69,300 (including 10% buyer's fee). Courtesy Bowers and Merena, Inc.

162. Reverse of rare 1876-CC *Twenty-Cent Piece* from previous photo. The auction catalog includes comments from Emery May Holden Norweb about this coin: "It is true that officially the branch mints did not make Proofs, but every so often one appears. Probably a workman standing talking rubbed a planchet back and forth on his apron before putting it in the machine, and a Proof surface turned out. This coin can be classed as a branch mint Proof ..." Courtesy Bowers and Merena, Inc.

163. 1899 Proof *Double Eagle ($20 Gold Piece)*. Lot #650 of the Bowers and Merena *Saccone* sale of November 6, 1989. Catalog description includes: "Proof-64/65. A glittering gem Proof specimen of this rare date. Just 84 Proofs were minted, and of that number fewer than half survived, only a small number of which could possibly match the quality of the coin offered here. A prize specimen which should attract enthusiastic bidding attention." Realized $33,000 (including 10% buyer's fee). Courtesy Bowers and Merena, Inc.

164. Reverse of the 1899 Proof *Double Eagle* of the previous photo. Proof U.S. gold coins, at least before the "modern" ones of 1984 to date, are the ultimate in beauty in the U.S. gold coinage series. Not cheap, but precious and of a rarity and sublimity that an equivalently-priced luxury new automobile can hardly imitate. Courtesy Bowers and Merena, Inc.

165. 1907 Roman Numerals High Relief *Double Eagle ($20 Gold Piece)*. Lot #668 of the Bowers and Merena *Saccone* sale of November 6, 1989. Catalog description includes: "MS-64/63. Pronounced high rim in areas. A superb specimen of one of the most desired of all American coins ..." Realized $12,100 (including 10% buyer's fee). Courtesy Bowers and Merena, Inc.

166. Reverse of the 1907 Roman Numerals High Relief *Double Eagle* of the previous photo. Designed by artist Augustus Saint-Gaudens on commission from President Theodore Roosevelt, this coin is beauty made metal. Also struck in extremely rare "Ultra High Relief" and in the "cheaper" low relief versions for circulation. Courtesy Bowers and Merena, Inc.

1

5

6

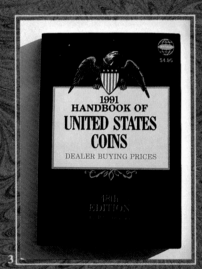

2

7

3

8

4

9

UNITED STATES WARTIME CENTS

STEEL

1943   1943D   1943S

SHELL CASE COPPER

1944   1944D   1944S   1945   1945D   1945S

13

10

14

11

15

12

16

17

BUFFALO NICKEL   *Photo-Certified Coin Institute*

1938-D/D   MS-60

18

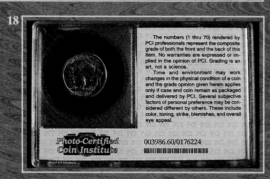

The numbers (1 thru 70) rendered by PCI professionals represent the composite grade of both the front and the back of this item. No warranties are expressed or implied in the opinion of PCI. Grading is an art, not a science.

Time and environment may work changes in the physical condition of a coin and the grade opinion given herein applies only if case and coin remain as packaged and delivered by PCI. Several subjective factors of personal preference may be considered different by others. These include color, toning, strike, blemishes, and overall eye appeal.

Photo-Certified Coin Institute   003986.60/0176224

19

20

21

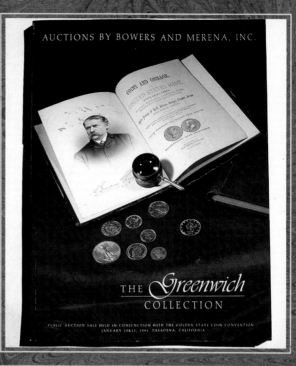

AUCTIONS BY BOWERS AND MERENA, INC.

THE *Greenwich* COLLECTION

PUBLIC AUCTION SALE HELD IN CONJUNCTION WITH THE GOLDEN STATE COIN CONVENTION
JANUARY 24&25, 1991 PASADENA, CALIFORNIA

22

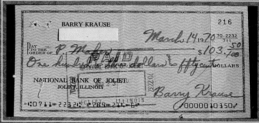

BARRY KRAUSE   216

March 14, 1970

PAY TO THE ORDER OF P. Mafor $103.50

One hundred three dollars & fifty cents DOLLARS

NATIONAL BANK OF JOLIET
JOLIET, ILLINOIS

Barry Krause

23

U.S. PROOF COINS 1957

24

25

29

26

30

31

27

28

32

33

37

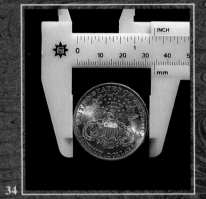

34

38

35

39

36

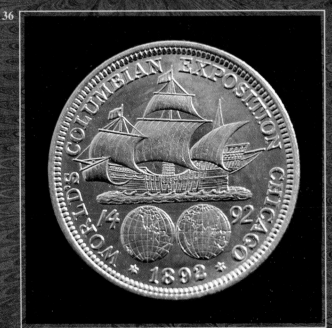

40

41

45

42

46

43

47

44

48

49

53

50

54

55

51

52

56

57

62

58

63

64

59

60 61

65

9

Popular Foreign Coins

Foreign coins may be collected by time period, some logical divisions being:

Ancient (with its subdivisions, e.g., Greek, Roman Republic, Roman Empire)—circa 7th century B.C. to 500 A.D.

Medieval—500 A.D. to 1400 A.D.

Renaissance—1400 A.D. to 1600 A.D.

Modern—1600 A.D. to 1900+ A.D.

"Current"—coins in use now.

Each of these time periods can be further subdivided to suit a collector's convenience. For example, you might decide to collect coins made during one monarch's reign, such as: Edward the Confessor (A.D. 1042-1066—Medieval) or George III (1760-1820—Modern) or Elizabeth II (1952 to date—Current), three of my favorite British monarchs (for their coins).

Or you could get into "topicals" (thematics), such as collecting animals on coins, for example: Australian kangaroos, Canadian geese, Congolese elephants, Bolivian llamas, and Chinese dragons.

You might specialize by metal type: just "minor base metal coinage" (copper, zinc, aluminum, tin) or precious metal coinage (silver, gold, platinum). You could, as many collectors do, specialize by size: small coins, those under the size of a U.S. *Half*

Dollar, or *Crown-size coins*—those about the size of an old U.S. *Silver Dollar*.

Like the collector of U.S. coins, the collector of foreign issues can concentrate on errors, patterns, overstrikes, counterstamps (merchant's guarantee marks), handstruck coins, machine-struck coins, commemoratives, medals, Proofs, war money, etc.

It may be necessary to learn a little foreign language vocabulary in order to translate the inscriptions on foreign coins. Coins of Ceylon and Egypt, which have had large illiterate populations, have been struck in shapes that weren't exactly round, hence the collecting of square, hexagonal, fluted edge coins, etc. Blind people appreciate coin denomination differences that can be felt; size alone or in combination with a reeded edge vs. smooth edge (as in U.S. coins) can help blind people sort out the different denominations. When I was in high school in my hometown of Joliet, Illinois, there was a blind man who sold candy and cigarettes in the main Post Office building (now in the National Register of Historic Places; it was finished in 1903) on Scott Street, and he made change by feeling the coins quickly. Of course, he trusted his customers to tell him what denomination of paper currency he was handling.

We discussed ancient coins in Chapter 1, so let's look at a few later examples of coinage of the world.

MEDIEVAL AND BYZANTINE COINS

The Byzantine Empire, with its capital at Constantinople (Istanbul), spans the Middle Ages — dates often cited for Byzantine coinage are 395 to 1453 A.D. References exist for both Byzantine and other Medieval coins, but because of their lack of popularity with most U.S. numismatists, Americans are generally ignorant of these coins. Thus, they are cheap to buy, unsupported by heavy U.S. collector demand, but not too cheap because affluent Europeans appreciate a nice *Crusader Penny* in unusually well-struck silver, or a rare "date" gold *solidus*, the standard Byzantine gold coin, which is for sale at a fraction of what an *aureus* of the Twelve Caesars would cost.

Early Medieval European coins, including Byzantine issues, are artistically poor, another reason helping to depress demand. The majority of the people in Medieval times lived on feudal manors where coins were unnecessary, even for those who could afford them. Some coins could always be secured from the royal or noble treasure box for external trade when needed. All Medieval coins were *hammered*, the term given to them by custom, meaning *hand-struck* individually, like the ancient coinage that predated them. Consequently, quality of Medieval coins varies considerably, even within one type or variety, so shop around before you spend a lot of money.

During the Middle Ages, Florence issued silver and gold *florins*, and Venice issued silver and gold *ducats*, all of which are eagerly sought by collectors. The silver *groschen*, introduced in 1300 by King Wenceslas II of Bohemia, was the leading silver coin in central Europe in the years following. The English gold *noble* was the standard English gold coin in the late Middle Ages (1344 on).

RENAISSANCE COINS

Coins were first dated in the 1400s according to the Western European calendar as we know it. The Gregorian Calendar, introduced by Pope Gregory XIII in 1582, was a corrected form of the Julian Calendar it replaced, and which we now use. *Renaissance Medals*, while not strictly coins because they weren't lawful money, are collected by knowledgeable (and rich!) numismatists as evolving examples of the "moneyer's art."

The French *écu d'or* was the standard French gold coin from 1385 to 1640. The English gold *sovereign* (still minted today, and a favorite of British spies like James Bond) was begun during the reign of Henry VII (1485-1509) and was equivalent to 20 silver *shillings*. A date run of British gold *sovereigns* in high grade condition is spectacular to see.

Origin of the Thalers

In 1486, the Tyrolean Archduke Sigismund minted a large silver coin known as the *guldengroschen*. Displaying an armed Medieval horseman, it was the first large silver coin of central Europe at that time. Early 16th century German emperors delighted at the large silver surfaces of these new *thalers*, and coinage artisans crowded the coins' designs with saints, lettering, and heraldry (another reason they're unpopular in the U.S.—Americans don't like crowding). In 1520 the counts of Schlick in Bohemia began minting silver *joachimsthalers*, named after their silver mines in the district of Joachimsthal. The name of these coins was shortened to *thaler* from which our *dollar* is derived both linguistically and numismatically (a large silver coin). Seventeenth century silver thalers (like the *John George thalers* of Saxony) were used to pay the troops during the Thirty Years War of 1618-1648.

Siege Coins

Due to the massive influx into Europe of gold and silver from Spanish colonies in the New World, the number of coins in circulation rose as their purchasing power declined, producing rampant inflation in the 16th century. The supply of coinage metal, however, permitted the striking of many wonderful coins for the enjoyment of later generations of coin collectors. Such were the *siege coins*, also known as "*money of necessity,*" produced in Europe during the 16th and 17th centuries when siege warfare was popular.

Encircled walled cities, under military siege and

cut off from external commerce, issued coins of their own for local use and/or in the anticipation of external trade when the siege would be lifted. For example, siege coins are well-known from Vienna (1529), Haarlem (1572), Leyden (1574), Magdeburg (1629), and Newark (1645-46). Sometimes the besieging forces had to make their own coins as well, such as M. de Turenne, who coined bullion from his own plate to pay his soldiers at St. Venant in Artois (1657).

MODERN EUROPEAN COINS

It would take a book much larger than this one to outline the mere basics of world coins dated 1600 to the present. The *Standard Catalog of World Coins* (see Bibliography) attempts to do just that, for world coins from 1801 to date, in nearly 2,000 telephone-book sized pages! So I'm going to give you a couple of numismatic highlights of the Modern Period, when machine-struck coins replaced the hand-hammered versions from ages past.

The brilliant engraving master Jean Varin engraved the dies for the baroque French *écu d'argent* (the first large French silver coin) and the *louis d'or* in gold, both with an exquisite bust of Louis XIII, and both coined on the new minting machinery at the Louvre, 1640. Both of these coins are popular with French collectors.

When Thomas Simon was replaced by the Flemish Jan Roettiers as engraver at the London Mint, Simon protested (in vain) by producing his famous silver "*Petition Crown*" for Charles II in 1663. A nice *Petition Crown* graces the cabinets of all serious collectors of British coinage of the 17th century.

Maria Theresa thalers are large silver coins, all dated 1780 regardless of when they were struck (as they have been from 1780 to this day). They all look "alike," and there is a *Proof* version available to collectors. Used for commerce by Europeans doing business in parts of Africa and the Middle East where native peoples refuse other coins, the *Maria Theresa thaler* basks in the distinction of being a circulating coin design for more than 200 years! Closely related to silver bullion value, you can buy these *thalers* at any coin dealer.

The Industrial Revolution brought the new steam coinage press to England in the late 18th century, and in 1797 Matthew Boulton, under government contract, struck the hefty copper *Two Penny pieces* for George III at Birmingham. You see these coins at every large coin show, usually dark brownish-black in color. Original Uncirculated specimens are worth hunting for; be careful of cleaning and "recoloring."

The Italian engraver Benedetto Pistrucci designed the timelessly sublime *St. George & Dragon* reverse of the British gold *sovereigns* and silver *crowns* of 1817-1818 and years following.

Decimalization of Currency

Decimalization of currency became widespread in the countries of the world, starting with the United States in 1792 (when one *dollar* became equal to 100 *cents*, etc.) and France in 1794 (when one *franc* became equal to 10 *décimes* or 100 *centimes*). Belgium, Italy, and Switzerland went decimal in their monetary units in 1865, followed by Germany in 1873 (when one *mark* was made equal to 100 *pfennigs*). Canada adopted the *dollar-cents* system, like the United States, in 1857—one of the many reasons (including similar language, common history, adjacent geography, etc.) that collectors on both sides of the U.S./Canadian border collect the coins of each other's nation. I admire Canadian bronze *Large Cents* of any date and Canadian 20th century *silver Dollars*.

Decimalization came to Scandinavia and the Netherlands in 1875, to the Austro-Hungarian Empire in 1892, and to Russia (as it was then called) in 1897. Great Britain went decimal in 1971 when the ancient *pound-shilling-pence* system was converted to base ten mathematical divisions (with 100 "*new pence*" equal to *one pound*).

The Swiss *20 centimes piece* of 1881 was the first coin to be made of pure nickel. Nickel is the best "white" metal substitute for silver, and after silver disappeared from the world's circulating coinage (including the United States') in the mid-1960s, nickel coins along with copper (or some alloy thereof) became the normal metals in circulating coinage. Gold disappeared from circulation in the 1920s and 1930s. Circulating money today in all countries is *fiat money*, backed by the psychological, economic, and military strength of the issuing nation. Money no longer has *intrinsic value*, as *specie* (coined precious metal) is no longer used for circulating coins. And countries that issue "collector" coins in gold or silver are careful to stamp a face value lower than bullion value of the coins, and these specially produced coins (in UNC *business strikes* and *Proof*) never circulate unless somebody raids a coin collection for quick spending cash!

CURRENT COINS

If your budget doesn't allow you to own the great rarities pictured and discussed in this book, how about collecting the current coinage of countries that you visit or read about? Mexico is a little more than 100 miles away from my home in Los Angeles. When I took a group of my students on a camping field trip to Mexico, we were excited to exchange our American *dollars* for Mexican *pesos*, and returned to Los Angeles with pockets full of Mexican coins that we received in change from buying bread, soft drinks, gasoline, etc., with our *pesos*. Some of these coins dated all the way back to the 1940s. (This trip was before recent devaluation inflation of Mexican currency.)

I know a group of people who went to the Soviet Union on a vacation and were astonished to find the Soviet citizens eager to exchange small denomination Soviet coins (in *Kopeks*) for U.S. *Lincoln Cents*. Little did Victor D. Brenner dream, in 1909 when he was finishing his design for the new *Lincoln Cent*, that long before the 20th century was over there would be people flying across the ocean in jet-propelled aircraft, with some recent vintage *Lincoln Cents* to trade for the coins of a foreign land, and considering their nearly worthless copper pocket change to be more interesting than the quasi-miraculous airplane trip!

Know anyone planning to travel to another country? Ask him or her to bring you some coins back as a souvenir for your collection. Or maybe you can find a "pen pal" in a foreign nation who will exchange current coins with you for U.S. coins. And if all else fails, and you've been bitten badly by the current coinage collecting bug, try your local coin dealer's shop or a bank or a "foreign exchange" currency dealer, found in most American big cities in the "downtown" districts (check the telephone book Yellow Pages under "Coin Dealers," "Coins for Collectors," "Foreign Exchange Brokers," etc.).

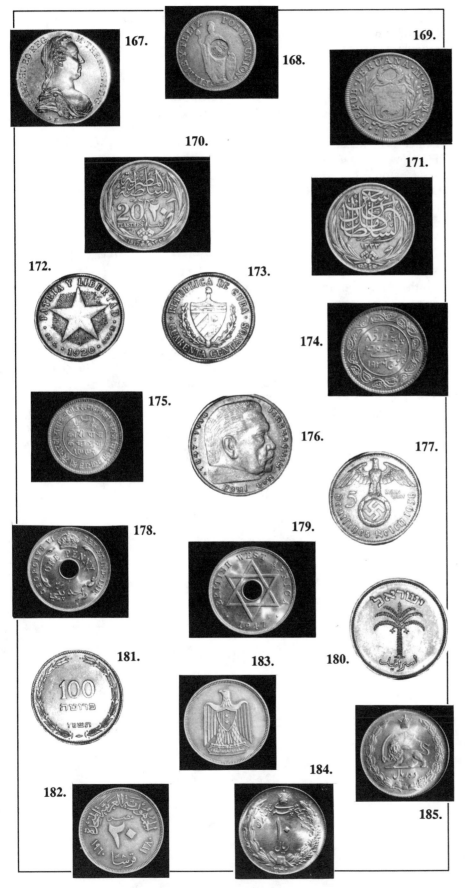

167. Austrian *Maria Theresa Thaler* of 1780, restrike in .833 fine silver, 28.0668 grams. An unofficial trade "dollar" that has been struck at various European mints from time to time until the present. Large silver coins are a popular collecting specialty, and you can concentrate on one country or collect the world. Author's collection.

168. 1832 Peru *8-Reales* piece, counterstamped with Fernando VII royal mark. Counterstamped coins are a subspecialty that provides many fascinating numismatic research avenues. Author's collection.

169. Reverse of the Peruvian *8-Reales* piece from the last photo. .903 fine silver, 27.07 grams. Monogram and "MM" mintmark indicate that this coin was struck in Lima. Author's collection.

170. Egypt *20-Piastres* silver piece issued under British Occupation, 1917. Circulated, original color coin, never been cleaned. Author's collection.

171. Reverse of the 1917 Egyptian *20-Piastres* piece from the previous photo. It is essential to get a copy of the *Standard Catalog of World Coins* by Krause and Mishler (see Bibliography) if you want to be a serious collector of foreign coins, 1801 to date, because the reference has more than 45,900 photos of coins like this one, for you to compare with your coins; especially useful if you don't read the foreign languages imprinted thereon. Author's collection.

172. Cuba 1920 *40-Centavos* piece, 10 grams, .900 fine silver. Circulated, original color coin, never been cleaned. Author's collection. Mintage 540,000.

173. Other side of Cuban 1920 silver *40-Centavos* piece. Also struck in

Proof, which is rare. Author's collection.

174. From Kutch, a native state of India in the northwest part of the country: *5-Kori* piece of 1936, struck in .937 fine silver, 13.87 grams, "Brilliant Uncirculated." Author's collection.

175. Reverse of the 1936 Kutch (Indian state) *5-Kori* piece. Uncirculated with pleasant surfaces. Author's collection.

176. Germany 1938 silver *5-Reichsmark* piece with portrait of deceased President Paul von Hindenburg. The tiny letter "A" behind the President's collar means the Berlin Mint. 13.88 grams, .900 fine silver. Mintage 8,430,000. Author's collection.

177. Reverse of the 1938 German silver *5-Reichsmark* piece showing the dreaded swastika of Chancellor Hitler's Nazi regime. We collect coins for the historical lessons they teach us, among other reasons, not to "honor" the people who issued

them. Otherwise, we would have to stop collecting ancient Roman coins, virtually every one of which portrays a dictator with some claim to mass brutality. Author's collection.

178. 1947 British West Africa *One Penny* piece struck in copper-nickel, "Brilliant Uncirculated." Little letter "H" below the central hole signifies the Heaton Mint at Birmingham, England. Issued under King George VI. 12,443,000 struck. Author's collection.

179. Reverse of 1947 British West Africa *One Penny* piece. Minted during the year that the author was born. A popular collecting specialty is coins made during your birth year, either of your own country or worldwide. Author's collection.

180. Israel 1955 copper-nickel *100-Prutot* piece, Uncirculated. 5,868,000 struck. Author's collection.

181. Reverse of 1955 Israeli *100-Prutot* piece; Uncirculated, although design "appears" to be weakly struck or worn at top. Author's collection.

182. Egypt (United Arab Republic) 1960 silver *20-Piastres* piece. Circulated, original color coin, never been cleaned. Tiny field scratches are more prominent in the photograph than they are when viewing the actual coin. Author's collection.

183. 1960 Egyptian *20-Piastres* piece from the previous photo. 14 grams, .720 fine silver. 400,000 minted. Circulated, original color coin. Author's collection.

184. Iran 1961 copper-nickel *10-Rials* dated SH1340, according to the solar Mohammedan calendar adopted by Iran in 1920; simply add 621 to the SH1340 date to get 1961 A.D. (one of the many reasons to refer to the *Standard Catalog of World Coins* by Krause and Mishler [see Bibliography]). "Brilliant Uncirculated." Author's collection.

185. 1961 Iranian copper-nickel *10-Rials* piece from the previous photo. 12 grams, mintage of 3,660,000. Uncirculated. Author's collection.

10

Medals and Tokens

When I was in fifth grade at Taft School, a public elementary school in my hometown of Joliet, Illinois, I used to wear a small religious medal on my chest under my shirt, supported by a thin chain around my neck. One day, when I lost it, my teacher announced: "This medal has been found. Whose is it? It must be somebody's medal!" I was a little embarrassed to walk up in front of the whole class and claim it (but I did, of course, because I wanted my medal back). I'm sure that nobody (besides me) who was there at that moment remembers it, including the teacher, but I remember it because it was *my medal*.

In the summer of 1970, I was backpacking with a friend through the hills and forests of southern Illinois, in my marathon cross-country hiking days, and we decided to give away a little present to anyone who was unusually helpful to us (like inviting us into their farmhouses for a cool drink). So I brought along a group of U.S. Mint 3-inch bronze *Presidential Inauguration medals* (restrikes) for Abraham Lincoln's Presidency—these cost $3 at that time; you can get the same medal today from the Mint for $21 by mail (see below). I can close my eyes and still see the surprised smiles on the faces of the rural inhabitants my friend and I encountered that summer,

as I handed them one of these heavy bronze medals (*Lincoln*—because of his Illinois background) as we were leaving their hospitality.

This chapter discusses *medals and tokens*, also collectively known as *exonumia*. As a collateral area of numismatics, it provides instruction and entertainment just as coins do. *Medals* are usually commemorative artistic creations, without any "practical" use. *Tokens* generally have a commercial use, such as bus tokens or metal dog tags. Military awards are classified under "*medals, orders, and decorations*" in numismatic talk. *Medals* and *tokens* are not legal tender; i.e., *medals* and *tokens* cannot be used indiscriminately as money, the principal difference between what is discussed in this chapter and official *coins*. Certain *tokens* (e.g., trade tokens, bus and subway tokens, encased postage stamps, etc.) have been used as money substitutes for limited "purchases."

ORIGINS OF MEDALS

Soon after coins were invented, medals were being conceived. Coins and medals are the two major branches of numismatics, and many collectors have both in their collections. In the 5th century B.C.,

Greek medals were apparently struck as athletic awards. In ancient Rome, medals were made to commemorate military campaigns and to honor the Emperor. Roman medals had the Emperor's portrait on the obverse side and symbols representing victory or health and prosperity on the reverse.

Medieval medals are generally of poor design and workmanship. Few medals of the Middle Ages have any artistic significance.

The Renaissance medals are a different story. Fifteenth century portrait painter Antonio Pisanello created a new art form: the medal. With molds lifted from wax models, Pisanello cast his medals in bronze, resulting in much better detail than could be found in earlier medals struck like coins. Pisanello created three dozen different medal design types between 1443 and 1455, and so "perfect" is his medallic art, few medal artists since Pisanello can claim to have approached his talent! Augustus Saint-Gaudens, who designed the *1907 U.S. Double Eagle* ($20 gold piece), was a devout admirer of the work of Pisanello.

TYPES OF MEDALS, BY SUBJECT

Here are some popular subject types of medals. Bear in mind that any medal may be made in a variety of metals—bronze, silver, gold, etc.—and that the market price of a medal when sold to informed collectors depends on rarity, demand, and metal type. A medal may be common in bronze but of the utmost rarity in gold. Other factors being equal, gold medals are more valuable than silver, which, in turn, costs more than bronze. The traditional metal for medals is bronze, due to its more durable nature than softer gold alloy, and because it is cheaper than gold or silver, which metals have often been used for special "presentation" versions of a common bronze design.

1. *Political medals* go all the way back to the ancient world. Made to honor a political ruler or royal family. The U.S. Mint strikes and sells medals honoring the U.S. Presidents, military heroes, historical events, etc. Write for a free illustrated price list of *Medals of the United States Mint*:

CUSTOMER SERVICE CENTER
U.S. Mint

10001 Aerospace Drive
Lanham, MD 20706
(301) 436-7400

2. *Historical medals* honor an event in history, such as the flight of the Wright Brothers or the discovery of gold in California. They are often issued on the anniversaries (50th, 100th, etc.) of such events.

3. *State medals* for some aspect of a U.S. state, such as a medal honoring the state's industries or anniversary of statehood. Notice how medal categories overlap: a medal may be state, historic, and political all at once! I used to have a huge collection of California medals before I sold it for spending money.

4. *War medals* are of several types: commemorative and hero-honoring medals, and those issued as military awards to soldiers. The combat medals (like the U.S. *Medal of Honor, Silver Star*, and *Bronze Star*) are especially sought after by military medal collectors. The *Purple Heart* is a wound medal that traces its origins back to the decorations George Washington gave his soldiers during the American Revolution.

5. *World's Fair medals* are forever popular among specialists in this field, particularly for older fairs, such as the World's Columbian Exposition held in Chicago in 1893.

6. *Topical medals* are like topical coins: medals with a specific theme such as those picturing animals or ships or railroad trains. I used to have a collection of medals and foreign coins picturing alligators and crocodiles, when I had a pet caiman (a type of South American crocodile).

7. *Medical medals* are actually a subtype of topical medals. Medical medals may honor doctors like Tom Dooley or Albert Schweitzer, medical pioneers like William Harvey (who discovered the circulation of the blood), or Edward Jenner (who "discovered" vaccination), or famous hospitals like Johns Hopkins Medical School or the Mayo Clinic. Related medals, like one honoring Wilhelm Roentgen (the discoverer of X-rays), also have a place in a "medical" exonumia cabinet. I once had a huge collection of medical medals when I used to teach high

school human anatomy and physiology. Occasionally I'd pass one around to show my students the portrait of some famous medical researcher, like Jonas Salk, who discovered the injectable polio vaccine.

8. *Infamous medals*, such as those produced by Nazi or Communist governments, honoring dictators, are collected by those who study the evil side of human nature.

9. *Space medals* are a popular topical medal specialty. You can collect medals praising U.S. astronauts and Soviet cosmonauts, rocket launches, space stations, moon landings, "robot" rocket flights to other planets, etc.

10. *City medals* (actually a subtype of U.S. state medals) honor a particular city, such as the 1960-dated medals commemorating the 350th anniversary of the founding of Santa Fe, New Mexico.

11. *Designer medals* may be collected in two ways: those medals that honor a medal artist, and those medals actually designed by that artist. Examples from American numismatic history: Victor D. Brenner (*Lincoln Cent*), Christian Gobrecht (*Liberty Seated* 19th century coinage), and Augustus Saint-Gaudens (*1907 $20 gold piece*).

12. *Memorial medals* include the likes of the *George Washington Funeral Medal* of 1800, struck in gold, copper, and bronze by Jacob Perkins of Boston. After Washington died at Mount Vernon on December 14, 1799, seemingly endless medals were struck to honor and mourn him. One of my favorites is the 28mm medal sculpted by William Kneass and struck by the U.S. Mint circa 1860, with a simple bust of Washington on the obverse and the reverse legend: "TIME INCREASES HIS FAME."

13. *Olympics Games medals*, both commemorative ones issued for collectors and the actual "awards" won in gold, silver, or bronze by the competing athletes. Even glory has its price, for some people anyway, because at the 1984 Summer Olympic Games in Los Angeles I noticed that some of the foreign athletes were selling their newly-won bronze medals near the Olympic Village dormitories at UCLA; presumably they wouldn't have sold their gold or silver winnings!

Other medal categories include private art medals, parade and celebration medals (like the *Mardi Gras*), coin club medals (usually struck annually), fraternal badges, religious medals, "so-called dollars" (silver dollar-sized U.S. historical medals), life-saving medals, municipal and military civilian citation medals, and sports medals. Go to any large coin show and you're going to see medals for sale, many in the $1 to $20 price range. See Chapter 14 for major coin show data, and Chapter 17 for numismatic periodicals that list upcoming coin shows around the country.

TOKENS

Tokens are small metal objects (usually circular like coins and most medals) that were issued for a specific commercial function. A token actually bridges the numismatic "gap" between medals and coins in the sense that medals tend to be purely commemorative and artistic, while coins are legal tender, money of the realm. Tokens are often issued by private business for specified trade with those businesses.

In no particular order, some examples of tokens that are collected are: bank and merchant storecards (called "cards" but actually these are metal and circular), bus and subway tokens, Latin American plantation tokens, prison tokens, Leper Colony coins (e.g., those minted at Manila in the Philippines between 1913 and 1927), apothecary weights, metal municipal dog tags, blood donor tags, military identification tags, parking lot tokens, encased postage stamps, government ration tokens, "wooden nickels," elongated coins, temperance (anti-alcohol) tokens, and "Hobo nickels" (*Indian Head-"Buffalo" Nickels* with the Indian Head carved into a caricature).

Of special interest (with dedicated collectors of each category—I once collected them all) are the following token specialties:

1. *Hard Times Tokens* were issued by private merchants and coiners in the 1834-44 period during economic turmoil in the United States. Many bear inscriptions regarding President Andrew Jackson's fight with the Bank of the United States, and political/economic slogans such as: "I TAKE THE RESPONSIBILITY" or "MILLIONS FOR DEFENSE,

NOT ONE CENT FOR TRIBUTE." Priced from $5 to $25 for circulated cheaper varieties. They were usually struck U.S. *Large Cent*-size in copper. Uncirculated specimens are desirable. Many *Hard Times Tokens* have been cleaned, destroying their value as far as purist collectors are concerned.

2. *Civil War Tokens* were privately issued (usually *Indian Head Cent*-sized) copper and brass pieces that served as "one cent" coins for small change during the coin hoarding days of the American Civil War. These tokens circulated heavily in 1862, 1863, and 1864. More than 10,000 different varieties are known from twenty-three states.

Many different merchants issued these tokens, including undertakers and taxidermists, who advertised their places of business on the token's inscription. Patriotic designs, such as flags, Washington or Lincoln, Liberty's head, shields, etc., appear on many of these tokens. Prices range from $5 to $10 for cheaper varieties, $50 to $100 or more for scarce specimens. Collect them in nice condition (AU to UNC) if possible, because they're available that way and look handsome in a coin holder or "album." Avoid cleaned tokens, as their market value has been irreparably damaged.

George and Melvin Fuld have published standard reference books on Civil War Tokens (see Bibliography). If you get serious about this token specialty, consider joining the *Civil War Token Society*, P.O. Box 330, Garnerville, NY 10923.

3. *Encased Postage Stamps.* By the summer of 1862, uncertainty as to the outcome of the Civil War made many citizens hoard American coins out of circulation, starting with gold and silver, and then copper. Small change became so scarce that unused postage stamps began circulating among the public as an emergency substitute for coins.

John Gault, a young Boston entrepreneur, patented his "Design for Postage Stamp Cases" with the U.S. Patent Office in July and August of 1862. Gault's invention was brilliantly simple: a small circular (like a coin) brass frame enclosed an unused postage stamp whose face was visible through a mica window. Sold to merchants at two cents over face value, these encased postage stamps saw limited but immediate circulation.

Businesses had their names and towns embos-

sed on the metal backs so that these encased stamps would carry their "advertising." Such commercial firms engraved as: "Drake's Plantation Bitters," "Ayers Cathartic Pills," and "Lord & Taylor, New York" are known to have sponsored a number of different stamp denominations in these encased postage contrivances. When Gault moved his business to New York City, it became known as Kirkpatrick and Gault, and encased postage stamps with the slogans "J. Gault" and "Kirkpatrick & Gault" were produced.

CAUTION: Dangerous fraud has been perpetrated on gullible collectors by crooks who manipulate encased postage stamps to:

(a) replace cracked or scratched mica with an undamaged substitute mica (pristine, flawless original mica is rare and commands a premium value);

(b) replace a low denomination stamp in the case with a higher denomination (30¢ to 90¢ values sell for thousands of dollars each);

(c) clean the whole case so it looks more or less Uncirculated, thus "meriting" a substantial market price.

Any expensive encased postage stamp purchase absolutely must come with an expertizing certificate of authenticity, either from the Philatelic Foundation (preferably) or the American Philatelic Society. These are the two most widely accepted authorities for expertizing U.S. stamps; write to them asking for a list of their latest expertizing fees and a submission form (be sure to enclose a stamped, self-addressed No. 10 envelope):

Encased Postage Stamp Expertizing Organizations

PHILATELIC FOUNDATION
21 East 40th Street
New York, NY 10016

AMERICAN PHILATELIC SOCIETY
   EXPERTIZING SERVICE
P.O. Box 8000
State College, PA 16803

Encased postage stamps bridge the collecting gap between numismatics (coins) and philately (stamps), and devotees of both disciplines collect these curious objects. Retail and auction prices for undamaged encased postage stamps of the U.S. Civil War (other countries have produced them also) run from $100 to $300 for the cheaper items, $500 to $2,000 and up for the rarer varieties (scarce business names and/or high denomination encased stamps). They aren't unobtainable, but their true rarity is shown by the fact that many coin and stamp dealers have no encased postage stamps in stock. Mandatory for collection of these items is getting and referring to the only reference book on this specialty: *The Standard Catalogue of Encased Postage Stamps* by Hodder and Bowers (see Bibliography).

4. *Love Tokens* are normal circulating coins (U.S. or foreign) that have been "countermarked" with privately hand-engraved initials, people's names, messages, and/or artistic designs as a "token" of affection (no numismatic pun intended) to be given as a present to another person.

Love Tokens were ubiquitously popular in the late 19th century, and many choice U.S. silver and gold coins have been, in one sense, numismatically "ruined" by such mutilations. But, in another sense, the Love Token-making craze created an amusing numismatic sideline (with an unmistakable human touch). Essentially unique, no two Love Tokens, like the human beings who fashioned them, are exactly alike.

Market prices for Love Tokens depend on the size of the coin used (the bigger or higher the denomination, the more expensive the Love Token), the degree of artistic skill and ornateness of the engraved design, and the emotional attraction of a collector to a given token: $5 for cheaper ones, $25 to $35 for the more expensive ones, not counting *Silver Dollars* and gold. I started a Love Token collection (as if I need any more things to collect!) during a visit to a Modesto, CA coin show to buy a few coins to photograph for this book. A dealer at the show had some nice ones at reasonable prices. If you are interested in this specialty, consider joining the Love Token Society, P.O. Box 1049, Huntingdon Valley, PA 19006.

5. *Presidential Campaign Buttons* are always in demand by political button collectors. Mostly 20th century, by virtue of their cost and availability, these buttons are the base-metal, colorfully-painted, circular (usually) "pin-back" ones that were worn to publicize candidacies during U.S. Presidential election campaigns. Earlier ones (pre-1920) are usually more expensive, as are popular Presidents, and extremely scarce buttons of both winners and (some) losers. Many fakes and facsimiles exist of U.S. Presidential campaign buttons, so be careful. Buy these buttons from reliable dealers who specialize in such.

And don't overpay for a John or Robert Kennedy button. Many of them (depending on the variety) were issued during their campaigns, and for all we know may *still* be manufactured by someone intent on cashing in on the mystique of these assassinated political folk heroes.

Price guides exist for political memorabilia, including campaign buttons. Try your local bookstore or coin shop, or write to a dealer who advertises to buy or sell such buttons (see Chapter 17, Numismatic Periodicals).

6. *Gambling Chips* are collected by a rapidly increasing number of collectors (including me). Gambling chips can roughly be broken down into three categories: old-time chips like 19th century ivory gambling counters and old-West poker chips; casino "chips" (called "checks" by casino personnel), both current and obsolete; and casino slot machine metal tokens, both current and obsolete. This is actually an inexpensive collecting field (as long as you don't start gambling with your collection!) for the beginning collector. Many tokens can be obtained at face value ($1 each) in the casinos themselves, and many varieties of obsolete (no longer redeemable for cash at the casino cashier's cage) chips are available for $3 to $10 each (at a discount off face value in some instances!). Antique gambling tokens and counters are the most expensive, running around $60 each for the cheapest ivory ones that are nice looking.

Some collectors go for the more "exotic" foreign chips from Asia (e.g., porcelain gaming counters of Siam), Monaco (Monte Carlo), Germany (Baden-Baden, etc.), England (the gaming clubs of London), or the Caribbean (Bahamas, Puerto Rico, etc.). Others look for gambling chips used on cruise ships offering casino entertainment.
Other collectors prefer American chips from gambling establishments in Atlantic City, NJ, Nevada, and/or local state-legalized card clubs (like in Gardena, CA or Deadwood, SD), or from illicit private gambling dives, obsolete or "current."

The ever-varying social stigma against gambling (becoming less so, with the introduction of state lotteries, legal horse racetracks, and "family-oriented" Las Vegas casinos like Circus-Circus and Excalibur) doesn't apply to collectors of gambling chips, any more than the justified antipathy towards dictators applies to collectors of coins showing dictators (otherwise, all collectors of ancient Roman coins would have to get rid of their collections in the hopes of regaining their societal respectability). See Chapter 18 for information on joining the Casino Chip and Gaming Token Collectors Club.

7. *Merchant's Tokens* are issued privately by businesses for self-publicity. Merchant "store cards" (actually circular metal tokens) became popular during the Civil War (see the Fuld book on the subject, mentioned in the Bibliography). Some merchant tokens circulated as money, either worth a cent or two, or with later ones (20th century) embossed with a specified value (e.g., "GOOD FOR 25¢ IN TRADE AT DELMONICO'S SALOON"). It is a challenge to research these tokens to discover where and why they were issued.

Subspecialties of merchant token collecting are: hometown businesses (what could be more numismatically "personal," unless you or someone in your family works for the U.S. Mint), "obsolete" trades (e.g., "CHALMER'S HORSESHOEING AND LIVERY SHOP"), department stores, gasoline stations, grocery stores, pharmacies and medical establishments, and saloons and houses of ill repute.

Merchant tokens are often cheap to buy today because of limited collector demand (how many collectors want a bakery shop token from an obscure country town in another state?). Typical retail price starts at about $2 each; $50 is an expensive one.

8. *Transportation Tokens*. With city bus and subway fares topping $1 a ride in many cities today, even adjusted for inflation it gets a little more expensive to collect municipal transportation line tokens than it did when I was a kid in the 1950s— when bus fare was 10¢, payable with a silver *Mercury Dime* if you wished. Still, huge collections of transit tokens are currently being assembled by collectors on a tight budget. You can find obsolete tokens in bulk or individually at a discount off "face" value in the token boxes at coin bourse dealers' tables. Whenever you're visiting a new city, get one of their transit tokens for your collection. And be choosy about condition: bright, shiny (uncleaned!), "Uncirculated" ones if possible!

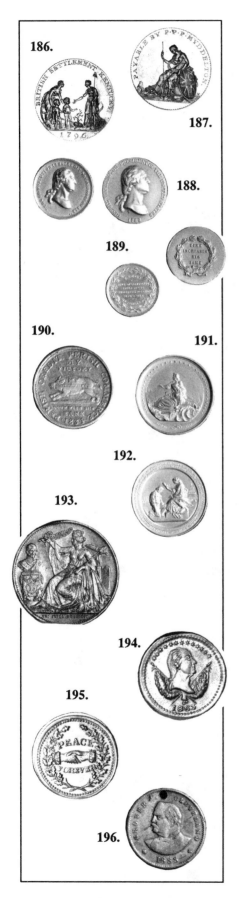

186.

187.

188.

189.

190.

191.

192.

193.

194.

195.

196.

186. 1796 *Myddelton Token* in copper. Lot #1401 of the Bowers and Merena *Norweb* sale of October 13, 1987. Catalog states, in part: "Proof-63 ... 173.1 grains. 28.7mm ... Rich, glossy deep brown, with mint red around the obverse and reverse peripheries. Flawless surfaces, sharp strike ...

"The Myddelton token dated 1796 was struck in Boulton and Watt's Soho Mint, intended for distribution by Philip Parry Price Myddelton, an entrepreneur who owned a large amount of land in Kentucky and who advertised in England for settlers to populate the land. The venture was never completed. The tokens, said to have been engraved by Conrad Kuchler ... probably never circulated.

"The obverse bears a representation of Britannia presenting two infants to Kentucky, who carries a staff surmounted by a liberty cap. Behind her is a cornucopia, while before is a victory wreath surrounding a young tree ..."

Considered one of the most beautiful tokens of this time period. Courtesy Bowers and Merena, Inc.

187. Reverse of the 1796 copper *Myddelton Token* from the previous photo. Catalog description states, in part: "The reverse depicts Britannia, downcast and defeated, her spear reversed. At her feet lie fallen scales of justice, fasces surmounted by a liberty cap, and an unsheathed sword. The symbolism of the reverse seems to reflect the British loss of the American colonies, or perhaps the loss of certain citizens who wished to emigrate to Kentucky." Realized $5,280 (including 10% buyer's fee) at the *Norweb* sale of October 13, 1987. Courtesy Bowers and Merena, Inc.

188. Two U.S. Mint *George Washington* medal restrikes in bronze. Left

medal's legend states: THE CONSTITUTION IS SACREDLY OBLIGATORY ON ALL (30mm diameter). Right medal's legend: GEORGE WASHINGTON PRESIDENT OF THE UNITED STATES 1789 (33mm). Author's collection.

189. Reverse of Washington bronze medals from previous photo. Left medal has a laurel wreath enclosing the words: U.S. MINT/OATH OF ALLEGIANCE/TAKEN BY THE/ OFFICERS AND WORKMEN/ SEPT. 2. 1861./JAS. POLLOCK DIR. Right medal shows a laurel wreath enclosing the words: TIME/ INCREASES/HIS/FAME. Author's collection.

190. *Hard Times Token*, struck in copper as usual, dated 1834. Such tokens, of many different designs, circulated as small change (being approximately the size of the contemporaneous U.S. *Large Cent*) in the 1834-1844 period, when coin hoarding existed. Legends on these tokens often deal with President Jackson's fight with the United States Bank. Author's collection.

191. U.S. Mint bronze restrike "Rescue Medal" dated July 26, 1866, with a man, woman, and sailing ship in the distance. 81mm bronze, weight 9 ounces (over ½ pound!). Author's collection.

192. Other side of "Rescue Medal" from previous photo. With the legend: BY JOINT RESOLUTION OF CONGRESS TO THE RESCUERS OF THE PASSENGERS OFFICERS AND MEN OF STEAM SHIP SAN FRANCISCO WRECKED DEC. 1853/TESTIMONIAL OF NATIONAL GRATITUDE FOR HIS GALLANT CONDUCT and design of man receiving laurel wreath on his head, with ship and Capitol building in background. Author's collection.

193. 1856 Belgium copper medallic issue honoring the 25th anniversary of the coronation of Leopold I (ruled 1831-1865). 10 grams, 28mm. In the exergue at bottom of medal are the letters: XXI JUILL.MDCC-CLVI (July 21, 1856). Dark chocolate brown on this side, lighter brown with much mint red on the other side (which has a simple laurel wreath enclosing the legend: XXV:/ANNIVERSAIRE/DE/ L'INAU-GURATION/DU ROI (25th anniversary of the inauguration of the king). A few surface marks, but virtually as struck. Author's collection.

194. *Civil War Token* struck in copper, with patriotic theme of George Washington's head, crossed flags, and thirteen stars. 19mm in diameter, the identical size of the then-current *Indian Head Cent*, this token was made to serve as small change during the coin hoarding by a public made nervous by Civil War uncertainties. About Uncirculated. Author's collection.

195. Reverse of U.S. *Civil War Token* of previous photo. Clean surfaces, rich light brown toning with traces of mint red all over, and conservatively graded by the author as About Uncirculated. 50,000,000 specimens of about 10,000 different designs of *Civil War Tokens* are estimated to have been privately issued, to fill the void as official U.S. Mint coinage disappeared from circulation. Author's collection.

196. Political medallion of Grover Cleveland, struck in brass, holed at the top for wearing. The author no longer owns this piece, so the weight and diameter are not available, but it was found in a dealer's "junk box" of miscellaneous coins and tokens. Cleveland lost the election of 1888 and was the only U.S. President to serve non-consecutive terms: 1885-1889 and 1893-1897. Author's former collection.

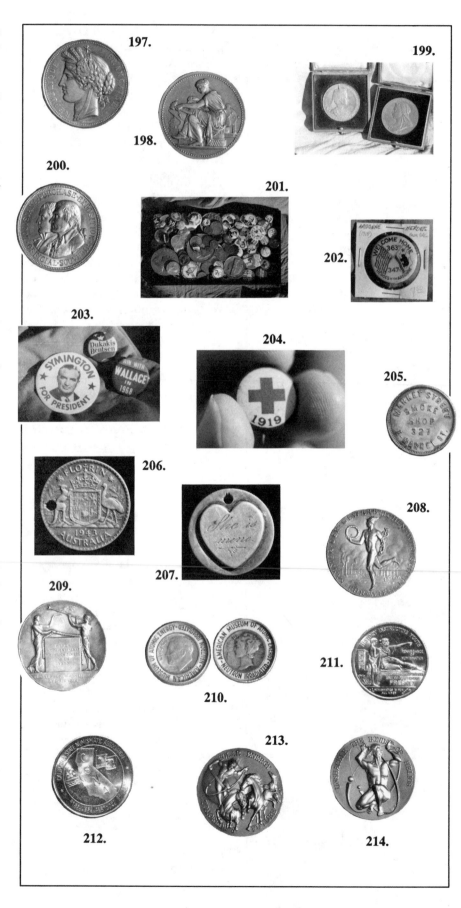

197.

198.

199.

200.

201.

202.

203.

204.

205.

206.

207.

208.

209.

210.

211.

212.

213.

214.

197. Large 19th century French medal, struck in bronze. Author's former collection.

198. Large 19th century French medal, struck in bronze. Author's former collection.

199. Turn of the century bronze British medals in their original presentation boxes. For the collector who appreciates British numismatics beyond mere coins. Author's collection.

200. *Louisiana Purchase Exposition* "so-called dollar" struck in yellow bronze, 34mm. Exceptional preservation, usually these are darkly tarnished. This specimen is original brilliant yellow metallic color on both sides *and* the edge. Reverse shows a map of Louisiana Territory. A souvenir from the Louisiana Purchase Exposition, held at St. Louis, MO from April 30 to December 1, 1904. Exposition medals are avidly collected. Author's collection.

201. What treasures lurk in this box of "exonumia"—medals, tokens, political buttons, etc.—that rests on a shelf in a coin shop, waiting for your inspection? Author's former collection.

202. World War I California regiment button, white with colored American and California flags, 33mm, with red, white, and blue ribbon attached behind, in its cardboard coin holder just as the author purchased it at a coin show, even showing the price paid!

203. Political campaign buttons for the U.S. Presidency; genuine. Beware of forgeries, especially for earlier and valuable ones. Author's collection. (Note: All of these candidates were losers. Perhaps you would rather collect the buttons of winners?)

204. Red Cross button from 1919. Red and black on white, with stick pin on backside. Author's collection.

205. Stockton, CA brass 30mm token. Other side has legend: GOOD FOR/50¢/IN MERCHANDISE. Author's collection.

206. This Australian silver *Florin* from 1943, actually minted in San Francisco as per the small "S" above the date, has a suspicious-looking hole at left. Author's collection. (See next photo.)

207. By turning it over, we see what the hole was for (previous photo): a chain or string for suspension as a "love token." The obverse of the *Florin* has been entirely shaved off and refashioned into a heart with the inscription "She is mine." U.S. coins made into love tokens are somewhat "common." It is a challenge to locate foreign coin love tokens of specific time periods and on specific types of coins. Author's collection.

208. Large base metal alloy Austrian medal of the Board of Industrial Trade for Vienna, dull gray color with darker gray toning. Struck in 1950. If it were made today, in an "anti-pollution" publicity era, the smoking smokestacks in the background would have to be modified. Author's former collection.

209. Reverse of the 1950 Austrian base metal medal, with inscription to a person honored "for extraordinary merit." Weight and diameter cannot be provided because this item is no longer in the author's possession. The author keeps a selection of foreign language dictionaries by his desk, just in case he needs to translate a foreign coin inscription. Author's former collection.

210. Two "encased" U.S. silver *Dimes* in plain circular aluminum cases with plastic "windows" on the front sides. Exonumia items add interest to a routine collection. Author's collection.

211. "HISTORY INSTRUCTING YOUTH" base metal medallion issued by the California State Numismatic Association (CSNA) for its 48th semi-annual convention, held in Fresno, CA on April 16-18, 1971. Design adapted from the *One Dollar Silver Certificate* of 1896, created by Will H. Low and engraved by Charles Schlecht. Author's collection.

212. "Reverse" of CSNA medallion from previous photo, bronze, 39mm, with a map of California, a ship at full sail to the left, and the California state flag to the right. The California State Numismatic Association was organized February 22, 1947 and incorporated June 2, 1961. Many states have regional and local numismatic societies that issue medals, either annually or otherwise. Author's collection.

213. "SOLAR ENERGY/TOMORROW'S FUTURE" 72mm bronze medal struck in ultra high relief, weighing a little over 7 ounces (almost ½ pound!). Edge inscription: © 1979 MEDALLIC ART CO.-DANBURY, CT.-BRONZE/THE SOCIETY OF MEDALISTS ISSUE #99 DONALD BORJA, SC. Author's collection.

214. Other side of Medallic Art Co. medal (from previous photo) with a representation of "Helios" (the Sun God in Greek mythology) with his wrists manacled to the electron orbits of a schematic atom, and the inscription: UNSHACKLE THE BONDS OF HELIOS. Bronze, struck in ultra high relief, for the collector of contemporary medallic art. Author's collection.

11

Buying Coins

I waited until this chapter to discuss buying coins because I wanted you to read the first ten chapters of this book before you run out and start buying coins for your collections, especially if you're a new or intermediate collector. If you haven't read them, take the time to read the previous chapters before your next visit to a coin shop or coin show — the money you may save can be properly diverted into the purchase of a coin that you will be proud to own. If you read this whole book, you'll be a minimally-informed coin consumer! Your next numismatic reading step, then, should be to hit the Bibliography books I suggest, maybe at your local public library if any of them are available there.

This chapter explains the ways to buy coins from retail coin dealers (fixed price lists, store stock, coin shows), from coin auctions, by mail, and directly from fellow collectors. See the end of Chapter 13 for a list and description of coin dealer organizations that help to monitor the business ethics of established coin dealers in the U.S. and elsewhere.

BUYING FROM RETAIL COIN DEALERS

Retail dealers are the source of most coins for collectors. There are several thousand retail coin dealers in the United States, including those with walk-in stores, mail order, and show circuit business. Some dealers are part-time, some are quite specialized (only *Morgan Dollars*, only circulated U.S. coins, only foreign gold, etc.), and some handle collecting supplies like albums and holders. But the essence of a retail dealer is to buy a coin wholesale (usually from a collector or an investor) and sell it retail.

When buying from any coin dealer ask yourself these questions: How long has the dealer been in business? Is he a member of standard dealers' coin societies (see Chapter 13)? Does the dealer openly state buy/sell prices or is everything "negotiable" depending on how rich the customer looks? Does the dealer buy back what he sells? Are the coins guaranteed genuine forever (can they be returned if later proven to be counterfeit)? Is there a prompt refund policy, even if coins are removed from the dealer's personal business holders? What do other dealers and collectors think of the dealer whose business you are considering?

Buying from Fixed Coin Price Lists

Many retail dealers sell from fixed price lists.

These are printed lists of coins arranged by country, date, mintmark, condition, and selling price. These lists are frequently updated, rendering older lists obsolete due to changes in price and stock. Fixed price lists are either printed in part or entirely in the national coin periodicals (see Chapter 17) or such lists are sent by mail to customers on the dealer's mailing list.

Advantages of buying from fixed price lists are (1) you can leisurely select coins for your collection without feeling pressured to "buy now," (2) you can "comparison shop" with price lists for similar coins from different dealers, (3) you know exactly what the coins will cost, and (4) you know what kinds of coins a particular dealer habitually carries in stock, so you can plan ahead—if you don't buy the coin this month, you are sure this dealer will have another one in stock next month or the month after that.

Disadvantages of fixed price lists are (1) you can't see the coin before you buy it (since most price lists aren't illustrated), (2) price-listed coins are notoriously misdescribed (e.g., scratches and rim nicks are often not mentioned), (3) a dealer may have more than one coin in stock that fits a particular description on the list, but if you're not one of that dealer's best customers, you may be sent the "worst" specimen of the lot, and (4) it is usually hard to bargain for a lower price because the dealer may want to see if anybody is willing to pay full list price first.

Buying from Coin Store Stock

Coin shops are so much fun to visit that if you live near one whose proprietor is friendly, you're going to spend more time and money there than might be good for you! Most coin store owners are eager to offer free advice and help to a customer, but courtesy dictates that you should try to make some kind of purchase (or sale) every time you go in the store so you don't waste the dealer's time and patience.

Advantages of buying coins in a store are (1) the dealer gets to know you and may save special items that he knows you want, (2) you see every coin before you purchase it, (3) you can examine a lot of coins close up before you decide which one to buy, (4) you can sell your surplus coins or even a whole

collection to the same store dealer when you need quick cash, and (5) you can chat with the dealer and other customers in the store, thereby acquiring, over time, invaluable numismatic knowledge from other people's experience.

Disadvantages to shopping in a coin store are (1) the shop may have little or nothing that you need in your collecting specialty, (2) you might buy a coin on impulse just because you see it and the dealer talks you into purchasing it, (3) the store may be out of the way, hard to get to, or have expensive parking, etc., (4) the lighting may be bad, so when you get a store-bought coin home you might start to hate its appearance when viewed under your bright desk lamp, and (5) by the very nature of coin store shopping etiquette, it is a little more embarrassing to drag a coin back to a store for a refund than to send it back through the mail to a mail order company, because it is assumed that once you examine a coin (in a store or elsewhere), your decision to buy or not to buy is more or less permanent. Of course, most dealers will refund a store-bought coin but will definitely get annoyed if you make a habit of returning items. For one thing, while you have the coin in your possession, the dealer can't sell it to anyone else, thus losing another potential sale and maybe even a customer as well!

Buying at Coin Shows

Buying coins at coin shows from retail dealers with tables there has many advantages: (1) at a show you can compare the stock and prices of many dealers all at once, and go back several times, if necessary, to the same dealers to reexamine a coin that will cost you a lot of money for your budget, (2) you benefit from the opinions and advice of many professional dealers all on the same day, so you can weigh the relative "logic" and market analysis that one dealer makes against that of another dealer, (3) a coin show, even a small one, will expose you to an enormous quantity of coins that you can see up close, thereby getting somewhat of a "refresher course" in your numismatic education from the sheer volume of material seen on the bourse floor, and (4) you may meet new dealers at shows, see stock you've never seen before, and make new dealer and collector contacts that may prove useful in the future.

There aren't many disadvantages to shows besides the debatable ones of (1) the fact that you might feel "poor" or intimidated if you're a new coin collector on a small budget and suddenly are overwhelmed with a million dollars' worth of rare coins in front of you, (2) you may overspend at a coin show from the sheer excitement and enormity of it, in much the same way that a casino visitor might bet recklessly when gambling in a lavish "money means nothing" atmosphere, and (3) you run the risk of spending your money on "sidelines" and new coin specialties to the detriment of your long-established collecting goals, just because if you're at all human, you're going to find a lot of interesting things at a coin show that you'll wish you owned in spite of your dwindling collecting budget due to show purchases! See Chapter 14 for major coin show locations.

Good coin show strategy is to make a quick circuit of the floor to get a general idea of what is available, spend time with your favorite dealers and those who seem to offer what you want to buy, then make your final buying decisions during your last hour or so at the show. And if you're going to sell as well as buy, you may decide to sell your material first to generate spending money for purchases of your own.

Important show advice: There will always be other shows in the future. Money is nice to have, too! Don't feel like you lost something if you walk out of a coin show without spending all the money you brought. Be selective and condition-conscious: if the coins are overpriced or in lousy condition, pass them up and take your money home.

BUYING FROM COIN AUCTIONS

While some coin dealers run auctions as well as handle retail trade, a coin auction company (however it is organized) offers great potential treasures for your growing collection. Retail and auction dealers are both listed in Chapter 13, but here are some quick tips on auction buying in general.

Auction buying advantages are (1) scarce coins that are rarely seen will periodically come up for sale at auction, (2) the best coins tend to be sold at auction (as opposed to retail price lists, for example), so you are more certain of getting quality merchandise, (3) prices realized tend to be an honest reflection of the current coin market, hence "fair" purchasing prices, (4) coins in an auction often come with "pedigrees" from famous collections, and (5) when you go to resell a coin bought at auction, you can say where it came from, e.g., "ex-the collection of somebody famous," which provenance will enhance the resale value of the coin.

Disadvantages of buying at auction are (1) you might overpay for a coin when swept up in feverish, foolish bidding during a hot floor auction battle, (2) most auctions won't allow you to return a coin that you've examined on the floor, or that you've bid on by mail and later decide that you don't like for reasons beyond auction catalog misdescriptions, (3) you might pay more for a coin at auction because of the prestige of the auction company with a huge mailing list of wealthy bidders. You don't always get things cheaply at auction. *Learn the current retail price of a coin (for comparable grade and quality) before you start bidding on it at auction.* Why pay more than it would cost you in a high class coin store or at a coin bourse?

BUYING COINS BY MAIL

Special precautions are necessary when buying coins by mail from dealers:

1. *Don't order the first time you see a dealer's advertisement.* If the company is successful, legitimate, and in business for the long haul rather than the short pull, you will see more of their ads as the months and years pass. I feel comfortable doing business with a company whose ads I've seen for a long time.

2. *Be extra cautious when sending money to post office boxes.* While some of the most reliable coin dealers in the world use post office boxes, so do fly-by-night crooks who open a box to hide their identity and true residence, then take your money and skip town without sending anything in return.

On March 14, 1970, when I still lived in Joliet, Illinois, I mailed my check for $103.50 in payment for a group of U.S. *Proof Sets* to a private dealer who had a post office box advertisement in the classified section of a Chicago newspaper. He cashed my check and never sent me any coins. My complaints to the newspaper and the U.S. Postal Inspectors in the Wisconsin town where this dealer had his box only brought me this notice: "Post office box closed. Occupant left no forwarding address." Obviously, he used a phony name, opened a box, cashed a bunch of checks from trusting coin collectors, then skipped town. Fresh out of college with education loans to pay off, $103.50 in 1970 dollars was a lot of money to me, and from this unpleasant experience I learned not to send money the first time I see a post office box ad.

3. *Send a small order first* to become acquainted with a mail order dealer's honesty and quality of service. If your trial order is satisfactory, wait a few months and try a larger order.

4. *If it looks too good to be true, it probably is*— permanent advice from the U.S. Postal Inspection Service, which forever fights, it seems to me, a losing battle against mail fraud. A first-time advertisement from an unknown dealer who offers for sale coins cheaper than the current market price for such material may or may not be legitimate. Greedy collectors looking for bargains are prime prey of coin companies who are outright criminals or practice questionable ethics like overgrading and not mentioning that a coin has been cleaned or damaged in the advertisement description.

5. *Check with somebody if you have doubts about a coin company's ad*. The publication in which the ad appears, the Better Business Bureau in the town where the company is located, and other coin dealers and coin societies should know something about this company if you plan to do serious business with it. Anyone can buy and sell coins, but a business reputation has to be earned in ways that go beyond mere dollars and cents!

6. *Don't hesitate to return coins for a refund* if you honestly don't like their quality relative to the price you paid. If a coin is advertised as Uncirculated, it had better not have wear on the high points of its design, because if it does, then it is not Uncirculated. An About Uncirculated coin should not have an ugly scratch across the numerals in the date, as a *1908-S Indian Cent* did when I received it from a mail order dealer who, of course, didn't mention the prominent scratch in his price list description.

Know, however, that if you continually return coins to a company, you will be dropped from their mailing list as a pest and impossible-to-please condition crank, whether or not you have valid reasons for disputing the company's coin descriptions. Of course, *price* has something to do with it also. A coin dealer expects a customer to be fussy about an expensive coin and will allow normal "returns" for such material due to the high price tag under negotiation. When you start returning and complaining about coins that retail for only a dollar or two each, you're history as far as that company is concerned.

7. *Wait a month after sending an order for coins before inquiring about what happened to it*. The company may be waiting for your check to clear. They may be temporarily out-of-stock of your coin but are expecting more any day. It takes time for mail to go both ways between you and a dealer. Registered mail (which is how most expensive coins are sent between people in distant cities) is particularly slow. I've waited five days to a full week for a registered first class parcel to make its trip in the U.S. mail. And maybe your order was lost in transit—don't assume that the dealer is a crook just because it takes a month to get a coin order. The company may be a small family or "one-man" operation, or the owner may be on vacation or traveling to coin shows when your order arrives.

8. *Type or hand print your order clearly*. This includes your name and mailing address. Make dates, mintmarks, and coin conditions crystal clear on your order sheet so the dealer knows exactly what you want.

9. *Send a bank or postal money order for faster service* when ordering coins by mail. Dealers are rightly suspicious of personal checks because they sometimes bounce. Some coin companies accept credit card payments, which usually allow your order to be processed more quickly, often the same day it is received.

10. *Phone ahead for confirmation on one-of-a-kind items, or list substitutes on your order form* if you want to avoid discouragement due to sold-out material. And if you're writing for any information before placing an order, always enclose a self-addressed stamped envelope (SASE), business-sized, No. 10, so that the dealer's stationery and price

lists/coin photos don't have to be squeezed into a tiny envelope.

BUYING FROM OTHER COLLECTORS

When buying coins from other collectors, you also have advantages and disadvantages, just as when you conduct business with professional dealers. Direct purchases from fellow collectors can be advantageous: (1) you make new coin collecting friends, (2) the prices may be cheaper than if you bought from a dealer, (3) a private collector may agree to a small dollar-value transaction and discuss it with you in more detail than a busy dealer could afford to do, (4) a fellow collector may also buy something that you want to sell, (5) a collector may agree to a coin trade more easily than a dealer would, and (6) you share numismatic knowledge with a collector who may have a different point of view than your usual dealer does.

Disadvantages of buying from collectors include: (1) they may not guarantee what they sell or give you a refund if you have second thoughts about the deal, (2) their knowledge may be more limited than a dealer's, to your subsequent detriment (an uninformed collector may innocently misattribute a coin or sell a counterfeit unknowingly), (3) a collector (like a dealer) may overgrade or overprice a coin out of greed, and (4) a collector-merchant who is not personally known to you may be an outright fraud. *Be especially careful when sending money to another collector who places a "first-time" classified ad.* You may never see anything for your money. Establish trust by correspondence, exchanging phone numbers or bank references, or by waiting a month or two before sending money through the mail to a new collector acquaintance.

Local coin clubs will introduce you to other collectors who are known to the membership. If the officers of the club tell you that a collector is honest, he probably is. Don't be overly paranoid about doing business with fellow collectors, but always remember that as the cash value of a transaction increases, so does the temptation for larceny in the minds of people who care more about money than about reputation.

COIN DEALER ORGANIZATIONS

See Chapter 13 for a list and description of coin dealer organizations that help to police the business ethics of established coin dealers in the U.S. and elsewhere. Membership in a dealers' organization doesn't guarantee the dealer will be fair and honest, and lack of membership doesn't automatically mean that the dealer is a crook. Maybe he disagrees with something about the organization, or prefers to be a "loner" in the coin business, or is a small-time dealer who thinks that buying a yearly membership for hundreds of dollars is a waste of money. *If a coin dealer has ever been expelled from a coin organization (dealer-oriented or otherwise), it would be helpful to know why.* The corresponding secretary of an organization will be happy to tell you whether a coin dealer is a "member in good standing" of that organization. There are a lot of coin dealers in the world. Why deal with one who has a questionable reputation?

215.

216.

218.

217.

219.

220.

221.

222.

215. 1904 Philippines silver *50-Centavos* piece, 13.4784 grams, .900 fine silver. Uncirculated, with die polish marks. Issued under United States administration. Author's collection.

216. Reverse of 1904 Philippines *50-Centavos* piece from previous photo. Issued under U.S. administration. Uncirculated with die polish marks. Only 11,000 business strikes issued. Author's collection.

217. 1980 People's Republic of China silver *30-Yuan* piece in Proof. 15 grams, .800 fine silver. 29,000 struck in Proof only. Author's collection.

218. Reverse of Proof silver 1980 People's Republic of China *30-Yuan* Olympics commemorative, honoring the Equestrian events. There are some collectors who refuse to buy current coins from countries whose politics they disagree with. The author bought this pre-Tian An Men massacre era coin specifically for photographing for this book.

219. Reverse of an *Indian Head Cent* showing definite evidence of moderate circulation. Learn how to grade the types of coins that you plan to buy, so that you get the grade for which you pay (see Chapter 6). Author's collection.

220. Iceland *500-Kronur* piece of 1974, Proof, 20 grams, struck in .925 fine silver. Commemorates the 1100th anniversary of the first settlement. A few scratches in the field, which probably won't be pointed out to you when you're buying the coin! Author's collection.

221. U.S.S.R. copper-nickel *1-Rouble* piece of 1967, Lettered Edge, Uncirculated. Handsome proof-like surfaces. Author's collection.

222. U.S.S.R. copper-nickel *1-Rouble* piece from previous photo, with Lenin portrayed on the reverse, issued in 1967 for the 50th anniversary of the 1917 Revolution. Uncirculated, with proof-like surfaces. Author's collection.

12

Selling Coins

If coins were never sold—or otherwise transferred in ownership—we would never be able to add choice specimens to our collections. And if we never sell any of our coins, we will never be able to enjoy cash profits derived therefrom, or have such suddenly released funds available to sink into another coin purchase, or have the money from our coin sales to be used for non-numismatic purchases!

This chapter explains how to sell your coins when that fateful day of mixed emotions arrives. Timing a coin sale, evaluating a collection, selecting the best market (outright sale to a dealer, private treaty, selling at auction, and selling to other collectors), and assorted miscellaneous selling tips are the highlights of the following pages. (See Chapter 11 when you're ready to buy coins again!)

REASONS FOR SELLING YOUR COINS

The decision to sell your coins will be based on one or more of the following factors. (1) You need cash. (2) You want to "weed out" the poorer specimens and replace them with better ones to upgrade your collection. (3) You have become bored with your coins and want to start a new specialty. (4) As a coin "investor," you want to take profits in a rising mar-

ket or cut losses in a falling market. (5) You have acquired duplicates or extraneous coins that don't fit your primary collections. (6) As a numismatic scholar/researcher, you have studied these coins and they are not needed for further research.

TIMING A SALE

A coin dealer advertises that "Now is the right time to sell," in the effort to convince you to sell your coins (he hopes, to him!). But no human being can foresee the future, and therefore nobody can honestly know whether the coin market will rise, crash, or remain "flat" for any given coin for the near or far future. It is sensible to take a profit when you can, if profits are a goal in your coin collecting. It also is logical to "ride out" a heavy paper loss during an abruptly falling market (like the slabbed U.S. *Silver Dollar* crash of October 1990) and wait until your coins are worth more before selling. On the other hand, seasons and holidays have nothing to do with obtaining the best prices for your coins. If your collection is worth substantial money, someone can be found to pay serious cash any day of the year. When bullion prices are high, sell your "bullion-tied" low grade silver or gold coins.

EVALUATING A COIN COLLECTION

The real price of anything is not what you can buy it for, but what you can sell it for. Many coin collectors live in dreamland regarding what they think their collections are worth. Coins are not necessarily worth full *Red Book* value and are almost never worth what you just paid for them (retail price) if you turn around immediately and try to sell them back to another dealer (wholesale price). The *Handbook of United States Coins (Blue Book)*®, available for $4.95 at any coin shop or in any public library, provides a rough guide to wholesale (dealer buying) prices, which you hope to receive from a dealer in an on-the-spot cash transaction.

Coin Collection Appraisals

Most dealers will do appraisals on coin collections, with the customer paying a pre-determined appraisal fee if the dealers don't subsequently get to buy the coins appraised. When you ask for an appraisal, specify the type of appraisal you want:

1. *Replacement value appraisals* summarize the current retail cost of replacing the coins in today's coin market. This type of appraisal is often used for insurance purposes (against theft, disasters, etc.).

2. *Sales value appraisal* is how much you can sell the coins for in today's market (wholesale, or "dealer's buying" price) or at auction. Also, most dealers will be happy to glance at a coin collection first in order to decide if it is worth appraising at all. It wouldn't make sense to spend $100 to have a collection worth $25 appraised!

PREPARING A COIN COLLECTION FOR SALE

To prepare a collection for sale, you must divide your coin groups into several arbitrary price categories, such as: (1) expensive coins, costing over $500 each at retail, (2) medium-priced coins, say from $50 to $500 each, (3) "cheap" coins, between $5 and $50 apiece, and (4) "inexpensive" coins at under $5 per coin. As a young collector on a tight budget, you may want to believe that coins you bought at 50¢ or $1 each are going to be fought over by every dealer in town when you give them an

opportunity to buy your "collection," but chances are that such dealers already have these relatively "worthless" coins in stock and don't need any more *unless* they handle bulk rolls of circulated *Indian Cents*, for example, or sell cheap foreign coins by the pound.

SELECTING A MARKET FOR SELLING COINS

Choose carefully where you sell your coins! Fit the coin to the dealer. The cheaper stuff should go to dealers who specialize in such material. Expensive coins should be sold to big-time dealers who can back up their purchases with real cash, *and* who will probably also have a ready market for reselling any expensive coins that they buy from you.

Study the coin company ads in the numismatic periodicals (see Chapter 17). "Buy ads" specifically state what a dealer is buying, maybe even down to prices and coin grades for individual coins. But don't overlook other dealers, especially those who habitually sell exactly the kind of material you want to get rid of. There are four main ways for a collector to sell coins: directly to a dealer, by private treaty, at auction, and to other collectors.

SELLING COINS TO A DEALER

The advantages of selling coins directly to a dealer include: (1) instant cash, as fast as you can walk in and out of a coin store, or wait for the mail to go both ways, (2) dealers keep up to date on the market values of coins, (3) you can sell small amounts, even a few dollars worth of coins, such as one $10 wholesale priced *proof set* or one circulated *Morgan Dollar*, and (4) you build up a working relationship with this dealer for future business, particularly if it is a neighborhood coin shop.

Disadvantages of direct sale to a dealer are (1) you may not get the best price because the dealer may be overstocked, undercapitalized, or short of "cash flow," or may be a borderline con artist, (2) you tend to accept almost any cash offer for small transactions, especially by mail, to avoid the hassles of offering your coins elsewhere, (3) if you are unfamiliar with the current market, you never know if the price offered for your coins is fair, and (4) the stress of a "forced sale" for desperately needed cash makes you vulnerable to any offer from the dealer. Distress sales are devastating to collector finances!

In general, for a collection worth a few hundred dollars, direct sale to a dealer is the selling method of choice.

SELLING COINS BY PRIVATE TREATY

Private treaty sales are conducted by dealers who take coins from a collector on consignment and offer them to the public at predetermined prices, with a predetermined dealer's commission (maybe 10 to 20%) to be deducted after the new customer buys the coins. It is a way for a cash-short dealer to do business, or for esoteric and "hard-to-sell" coins to wait around for the right buyer, or for a collector who can afford to wait for the money to realize a greater income from a collection.

Local coin shops tend to favor private treaties or store bid boards for cheaper coins. Big-time dealers who take out large display ads in the numismatic periodicals are, of course, the ones to approach for private treaty business with expensive coins, say $1,000 or more apiece.

Advantages of private treaty are (1) you, as the seller, can set your own price (with the dealer's advice) and wait until you get it, (2) you give business to a dealer, thus keeping you in his mind for future transactions, and (3) you can sell unusual items by waiting for an interested buyer to show up.

Disadvantages of private treaty are (1) you may wait seemingly "forever" for the sale to occur, (2) you have no guarantee that you wouldn't have gotten more at auction, and (3) the general risk of selecting the "wrong" dealer for private treaty selling of your coins, or of placing prices too high (which means they'll never sell) or too low (which means that, in effect, you will lose money in the current coin market). Substantial or famous collections are sometimes offered for sale by dealer advertising or even with their own exclusive private treaty sales catalogs.

SELLING COINS AT AUCTION

Coin auctions are the time-honored method for disposing of famous collections or of individual rarities of great cash value.

Advantages of selling at auction are (1) your coins will tend to bring current market prices, (2) the auctioneer's commission is only 10% (usually) of the hammer price (i.e., if a coin sells for $100 to a bidder, you receive $90, minus the lotting fee, if any), with the buyer, of course, paying another 10% commission, which only indirectly affects the seller collector, and (3) many bidders (including prominent collectors and dealers nationwide if not worldwide) will compete for your coins, thus assuring fair prices. It is a fact that auctions usually bring more money to a collector than outright sales to a dealer would.

Disadvantages of selling at auction are (1) unless you maintain a "reserve" price below which you will not let a coin be sold, you run the risk of cheap prices realized, to your financial detriment, in an unreserved public auction, (2) auction companies with limited advertising may not attract appropriate bidders, (3) you have to wait, maybe as much as six months before you see all of your money from an auction, although cash advances against prices realized are often given for large collections, and (4) your coins may be unsuitable for auction due to their cheap value per coin or generally inferior condition. Only the finest coins tend to be sold at auction, but you can find auction companies handling cheaper material.

SELLING COINS TO OTHER COIN COLLECTORS

If you have cheaper coins or personally know other coin collectors, you can always consider selling to them. Or you can take out a classified ad in one of the coin weeklies (see Chapter 17), offering your coins for sale at reasonable advertising expense. Some local coin clubs and national coin societies sponsor coin trading and sales by members.

Advantages of selling to other collectors are (1) you can sell cheap coins without feeling embarrassed in offering them to a professional dealer, (2) you build up friendships and acquaintances with fellow collectors who share your collecting interests, and (3) you can set your own selling prices with a courteous "take it or leave it" attitude.

The disadvantages of selling to other collectors

without using a dealer "middleman" are (1) you have to deal with collector whims like their asking for a refund later or complaining about the coins, (2) if selling to unknown collectors by mail you may have your coins stolen without payment being rendered, (3) private collectors rarely want everything you have to sell, whereas a dealer might offer a package price for your whole collection, and (4) for coins of substantial value you could be victimized by an armed robber when showing an unknown collector what you have for sale, in your home or at a pre-arranged location elsewhere.

SUMMARY OF COIN SELLING TACTICS

1. Sell expensive coins at auction.

2. Sell cheap coins either directly to a dealer who specializes in such material or directly to a fellow collector.

3. Don't be greedy.

4. Don't resent the economic necessity for a professional coin dealer to buy cheaper than he sells.

5. Don't expect a profit on every coin you sell.

6. Don't be afraid to reject an offer—shop around for another dealer's offers, if you don't like the first offer.

7. Be realistic about the wholesale or auction value of your collection in today's coin market.

Life is short. Peace of mind should be valued as highly as the monetary worth of your coins. When you decide to sell some of your coins, *sell them*, then move on to something else. Do you want to do serious business or do you want to play pointless games?

13

Coin Dealers

More than 750 coin dealers are listed in the *Coin Dealer Directory* (Western Publishing Co., Racine, WI, $4.95 current), which gives the name, address, coin specialty areas in which the dealer deals, and organizations to which the dealer belongs for every dealer in the book. It would take a volume far larger than the one you're holding just to begin to discuss the backgrounds and idiosyncrasies of a small fraction of these dealers. And I notice that a lot of local

dealers, especially those who have a mixed inventory of coins, stamps, and other collectibles, aren't even in the *Coin Dealer Directory*.

I've chosen to talk about only a few coin companies in this chapter, but the list includes some of the largest and most famous in the business. I've done business with most of them, but (of course) I have no financial interest in these or any other coin companies. Many, many outstanding coin dealers exist, and just because I don't mention them doesn't mean that their ethics and business practices aren't every bit equal to the dealers discussed below. Space limits prohibit praising everybody. The dealers that I list have long-standing reputations in the coin business; they are unlikely to have filed for bankruptcy, skipped town, or gone to jail when your order arrives. They do enough legitimate coin busi-

ness that they don't have to steal money to make a living. Plus, they value their reputations a lot more than making a fast buck—old-fashioned ethics that never go out of style! They also do so much business that they don't care if you buy or not when you're browsing through their coin stock. You never have a high-pressure salesman breathing down your neck when you decide to do business with these companies.

TO NAME A FEW

Bowers and Merena Galleries

BOWERS AND MERENA GALLERIES, INC.
Box 1224
Wolfeboro, NH 03894
(603) 569-5095

Bowers and Merena Galleries is one of America's leading rare coin firms, having been in business since 1953. By direct sales through catalogs, including the handsome periodically-issued retail-price catalog "Rare Coin Review," this firm offers its clients a wide variety of United States copper, nickel, silver, and gold coins, as well as Colonials, commemoratives, paper money, and other areas, plus an extensive selection of numismatic reference books. This company is the strongest believer (that I've seen in my thirty-five-plus years of coin collecting) in the time-proven advice: "Buy the book before the coin," and they back up their words with pages and pages devoted to describing the numismatic books they offer for sale, in each issue of "Rare Coin Review."

A division of this firm, Auctions by Bowers and Merena, Inc., conducts public auctions in New York City and other metropolitan areas, and over the years has handled a majority of the most valuable coin collections ever to come on the market, including the $25 million Garrett Collection sold for the Johns Hopkins University, the most valuable rare coin collection ever to cross the auction block. Other records held by the firm include the sale of the Norweb Collection at $20 million (the second most valuable coin collection ever auctioned), and the holding of eight of the top ten world's record individual prices for rare coins. Their auction catalogs, printed on quality paper and profusely illustrated with coin lot photographs, become reference works. Call or write for the sales date and price of their next auction catalog.

The president of the firm, Q. David Bowers, is the only person to have served as president of both leading numismatic organizations, the Professional Numismatists Guild (the leading organization of coin dealers) and the American Numismatic Association (the largest non-profit organization devoted to coin collecting). Bowers is also the author of many good coin books (see Bibliography), and his excellent, clear, and direct style of writing make *anything* that he writes worth reading. As far as popularizing the hobby through a prolific output of interesting books and articles, Bowers is to coin collecting what the venerable Herman Herst, Jr. is to stamp collecting!

Bowers and Merena Galleries has a staff of several dozen and services the needs of clients all over the world. Through a special offer for readers of this book, Mr. Bowers has given me permission to let you request a free sample copy of his latest retail price catalog, the "Rare Coin Review" (regularly $5 per copy). Write to the firm at their address above, and tell them that I sent you when you request a

free "Rare Coin Review." And in case you're curious, I get nothing from the firm for sending you there as a potential customer.

But I think one of the nicest things about Bowers and Merena Galleries is that you don't feel as if you have to spend a lot of money to be appreciated by them; they value a $20 order (and offer coins for sale that cheap and cheaper) and treat the $20 customer with as much care and courtesy as they do a $20,000 purchaser. And they buy the same coins that they sell, so the material in their stock consists of pieces worth buying, from either a collector's or a dealer's point of view. Anyway, I'd rather read the latest copy of their "Rare Coin Review" than eat, as this lavishly illustrated annotated coin price list is a small numismatic education in itself. I've been reading it on and off for twenty years, and when a new copy arrives I know I won't sleep that night because I can't put it down until I've studied the whole thing. It's the epitome of coin price lists.

Early American Numismatics

EARLY AMERICAN NUMISMATICS
P.O. Box 2442
La Jolla, CA 92038
(619) 273-3566

Early American Numismatics has one of the largest inventories of Colonial coins and Colonial currency in the United States. Dana Linett is the company president and has been a special ANACS consultant and *Red Book* contributor for years. His firm stands ready to service want lists for choice Colonials, as well as offering periodic fixed price lists and mail bid sales. Mr. Linett's mail bid sale catalogs are handsomely printed, with black-and-white photos, on slick paper of high quality. He also sells an assortment of reference books on Colonials.

Early American Numismatics buys and sells all Colonial coins, Colonial and Continental currency, pre-1800 U.S. bonds and fiscal paper, Colonial newspapers and lottery tickets, and encased postage stamps. This company recently released a photo-illustrated price list with ninety-five examples of *Fugio Cents*! A small amount of business is done with regular U.S. coins. Lovely, descriptive catalogs are issued from time to time, picturing choice Colonial coins with many in the $200 to $1,000 price range. Send for a free copy of the next catalog (to above address).

Jules J. Karp, Inc.

JULES J. KARP, INC.
P.O. Box 789, Wall Street Station
New York, NY 10268
(212) 279-0940

Jules J. Karp, Inc. sells circulated and uncirculated U.S. and foreign gold coins at prices near bullion value. Since the most recent retail prices of Karp are always a fair reflection of the current gold coin market, I always check his prices to see what gold coins are "really" worth in honest retail value. Sometimes you see companies offering to sell bullion gold coins at 25 to 50% above Karp's prices for, as far as I can see, identical quality.

Of course, when we get into distinguishing the different grades of Mint State (MS) gold coins, opinions fluctuate as much as the prices do, and buying uncertified uncirculated gold coins is always risky for the novice purchaser because one dealer's UNC may be another dealer's AU.

Jules J. Karp., Inc. will quote today's prices for generic (no choice of dates) U.S. gold *Liberty*, *Indian*, and *Saint-Gaudens* gold coins ($1 through $20 pieces, depending on the types that were made) as well as all foreign gold bullion coins such as English *sovereigns*, Canadian *Maple Leafs*, French and Swiss *20 Francs*, South African *Krugerrands*, etc., per piece or for quantities.

Numismatic Fine Arts

NUMISMATIC FINE ARTS
10100 Santa Monica Boulevard, 6th Floor
Los Angeles, CA 90067
(213) 278-1535

Numismatic Fine Arts specializes in auctions of top quality ancient coins. This company holds the world's record price for an ancient coin at auction: $605,000 for an ancient Roman *Brutus* "EID MAR" gold *aureus*. Call or write for information on their next catalog. A beginning collector of ancients, looking for bargains and cheap pieces to start a collection, would probably feel more comfortable doing business with a company that sells cheaper ancients. However, new collectors of ancient coins whom I have sent over to see material at Numismatic Fine Arts have told me that they've been treated with great courtesy and respect, even though they didn't buy anything.

Numismatic Fine Arts has auctioned off collections of ancient coins for the Santa Barbara (CA) museum (1975), the Boston Museum of Fine Arts (1980), and Johns Hopkins University (1984).

Rare Coins & Classical Arts Ltd.

RARE COINS & CLASSICAL ARTS LTD.
  (RCCA)
P.O. Box 374
South Orange, NJ 07079
(201) 761-0643
and
P.O. Box 699
Palm Desert, CA 92261
(619) 345-7161

Rare Coins & Classical Arts Ltd., operated by Dr. Arnold R. Saslow (Director and company President), buys and sells choice ancient Greek and Roman coins. Dr. Saslow has over thirty-two years of experience in the rare coin marketplace, was Overseas Director of Superior Stamp & Coin Company of Beverly Hills, CA from 1977 to 1980, and upon his return from London to the United States he started his own firm in 1980, the present RCCA. Dr. Saslow is recognized internationally as a specialist in classical ancient coins, and has attributed and appraised coins sold by the famous auction firms of Christie's and Sotheby's.

Rare Coins & Classical Arts Ltd. was initially located in New Jersey (where it still exists), and now has offices in Palm Desert, California and an associated office in London, England. RCCA is rated by Dun & Bradstreet as one of the top five firms specializing in ancient coins in the United States. RCCA attends about twenty-two of the largest coin shows in the United States, including the New York International and Chicago International coin shows, and is a featured attendee of the famous Long Beach tri-annual coin shows in California. RCCA is also a table holder at the London COINEX every fall.

Rare Coins & Classical Arts Ltd. doesn't publish a regular price list, but stands ready to buy or sell virtually any choice ancient coin, either at the coin shows that the company attends or by mail. When I recently talked with Dr. Saslow, both by phone and in person at a Long Beach coin show, he emphasized that the beginning collector of ancient coins should buy quality ("one nice coin rather than a half dozen low grade examples"). He pointed out that a nice collection of ancients can be assembled for $100 to $2,500 per coin, although he does sell cheaper coins for the collector on a tight budget, and more expensive coins for the affluent connoisseur (I photographed the choice ancient coins illustrated in the first chapter from Dr. Saslow's stock).

Collectors who are seriously interested in ancient coins may contact Dr. Saslow at above addresses for a free brochure explaining this collecting area. He specializes in buying and selling museum quality ancients in gold, silver, and bronze.

Silver Towne Coin Company

SILVER TOWNE COIN COMPANY
P.O. Box 424
Winchester, IN 47394
(317) 584-7481

Silver Towne was founded in Winchester, IN in 1949 by Leon E. Hendrickson, the company's proprietor to this day. From a humble beginning in a cigar box inside a restaurant owned by Mr. Hendrickson to the present ultramodern high security office complex that totals 12,000 square feet and employs about fifty people, the business has continued to grow. It also continues to amaze the world of big business that a company of this size would be content to be located in a small rural community of 5,000 in Indiana.

Silver Towne specializes in U.S. coins, bullion, and jewelry items. The volume of business jumped from $250,000 in 1966 to a whopping $300 million in 1980, according to Mr. Hendrickson. The company is a leader in the manufacturing of silver and gold medallions and bars, plus an assortment of jewelry. When facilities of Silver Towne were outgrown, the company purchased another large building for the smelting, manufacturing, and custom minting departments. Nearly 300 companies, organizations, and cities have used Silver Towne's products to publicize their products or events on custom-made art medallions.

The main emphasis at Silver Towne, however, has always been and continues to be coins for the collector. A large walk-in trade is always evident at Silver Towne in Winchester (about 70 miles east of Indianapolis by road), and the staff always seems as willing to help a young, budding numismatist with a $10 purchase as an investor who want to spend many thousands of dollars. The company has a large volume of coins for collectors to browse through on the premises; these coins range in price from $1 to hundreds of thousands of dollars each. In 1989 Silver Towne sold the highest priced single U.S. coin in auction history to that point—the *Dexter* specimen of the *1804 Silver Dollar*.

The retail store of Silver Towne is open during normal business hours five days a week, and also on Saturdays during November and December to serve collectors. Some of the staff attend about forty-five coin shows and conventions per year in the United States.

Besides a yearly catalog, which is printed every September, Silver Towne takes out full-page display ads every week in *Coin World* and *Numismatic News* (as well as in the monthly coin periodicals — see Chapter 17). The company does a large mail order business in many aspects of numismatics, from silver dollars to proof sets, and specializes in selling bullion and circulated coins in bulk at competitive prices. Look in any general coin publication for Silver Towne ads, or call or write for a price list. They don't mind doing business with a beginning collector on a tight budget.

Spink & Son Ltd.

SPINK & SON LTD.
5, 6, & 7 King Street, St. James's
London SW1Y 6QS England
(071) 930-7888

Spink & Son Ltd. bills itself as the "oldest established coin and medal business in the world." The company has evolved from a goldsmith business set up on Lombard Street in London by John Spink in 1666. Since the 1920s, Spink's has been at its present location on King Street.

Besides selling antiques in general, Spink and Son Ltd. has specialist departments including: English and Foreign Coins; Banknotes; Bullion; Orders, Decorations, and Medals; and Numismatic

Books. The company claims to have more in-house coin expertise than any other firm in London, with specialists in ancient, medieval, modern, and Islamic coinages working on the premises.

The Coin department of Spink's was established in 1830 and has the finest English and foreign coins for sale. The Coin department is located on the second floor and is open daily, Monday through Friday, from 9:30 A.M. to 5:30 P.M. London time. Spink's *Numismatic Circular* has been published since 1892 and offers numismatic items for sale, as well as printing scholarly articles (*not* light reading) such as "The Copper Coinage of the Visigoths of Spain: New Evidence" or "A Carolingian gold coin struck from a die of Chartres and found at Congham, Norfolk," which were published recently. Issued ten times a year, Spink's *Numismatic Circular* (on slick paper with black-and-white coin photos) is available for $45 (U.S.) per year for U.S. subscribers.

The Medals department on the third floor handles the sale of Orders, Decorations, and Campaign Medals and has designed and manufactured medals for more than sixty countries. Edward Joslin, the chief of the Medals department at Spink's, is considered the world's leading authority on military medal protocol. Mr. Joslin personally visited the Ugandan dictator Idi Amin at his Presidential Palace, where a huge order was negotiated for medals for the Ugandan army, police, and prison guard personnel.

Spink & Son, Ltd. conducts regular coin and medal auctions in London and elsewhere. You can get an upcoming auction catalog for $10 (U.S.), but write first to tell them what kinds of numismatic items interest you. The company publishes its own numismatic books and sells new and used coin books also.

Any coin collector visiting London should visit Spink's. They won't throw you out on the street if you don't buy anything, and you're welcome to come in to browse or chat with the salesmen. But don't take money in that you can't afford to spend. As for advice to serious collectors, Anthony Spink, one of the current directors of the company, says, "Buy what you can't afford" for the best chances for future value appreciation!

Stack's Coin Galleries

STACK'S COIN GALLERIES
123 West 57th Street
New York, NY 10019
(212) 582-2580

Stack's Coin Galleries bills itself as "America's Oldest and Largest Coin Dealer and Leading Coin Auctioneers for Over 56 Years." Stack's as a firm was established in 1858, dealing in all sorts of collectibles and antiques. By 1934 the family-run business had become limited to "Rare Coins and Postage Stamps." In 1934 they gave up the Postage Stamps division to concentrate on the "Rare Coin Business."

In 1935 Stack's introduced the "Public Coin Auction" into their business. In 1990 they celebrated their 55th anniversary of selling coins at public auction. During that period, Stack's auctioned more than 740,000 lots in over 500 separate catalogs.

Stack's sells coins in all series, from ancient times to modern, United States and foreign, in copper, silver, and gold. They specialize in United States coins, having built many of the noteworthy collections of these that have ever been assembled. Stack's maintains a small but elegant retail showroom at their address (above) in New York City, and has a staff of thirty people, of whom almost half are qualified numismatists. Their street window display is always impressive; when I was last there they had several hundred gold coins in the window, ranging from ancient Roman *aurei* to 20th century U.S. pieces. Showroom hours are Monday through Friday, 10:00 A.M. to 5:00 P.M.

Stack's regularly advertises their upcoming coin auctions in the numismatic press (see Chapter 17), and their auction sales generally include a wonderful selection of rare U.S. coins in choice condition. Send $10 for a copy of their next auction catalog, but write or telephone first to be sure that it will contain coins of interest to you.

Superior Stamp & Coin Company, Inc.

SUPERIOR STAMP & COIN COMPANY,
    INC.
9478 West Olympic Boulevard
Beverly Hills, CA 90212
(213) 203-9855

Superior Stamp & Coin Company was founded in 1930 in downtown Los Angeles. Through the years, they have followed the trend toward moving to the west side of Los Angeles, and today the company operates out of its own building in the heart of Beverly Hills.

Majority financial interest in the firm is held by Bruce McNall, owner of the Los Angeles Kings hockey team. The business is operated by Mark, Larry, and Ira Goldberg, who have been instrumental in bringing the firm from its infancy to its current status as one of the largest auction houses of rare coins in the world.

Superior Stamp & Coin Company maintains a huge inventory of rare stamps and coins and is the largest combined stamp and coin dealership in the western United States. Superior handles all types of coins: ancient through modern, U.S. and foreign, common and rare.

Superior has a retail department for mail orders or walk-in trade. Their building in Beverly Hills offers free parking underneath (enter from Olympic Boulevard), but I prefer to park on a side street when I visit there to avoid heavy Olympic Boulevard traffic during rush hour. The first floor showroom is devoted to coins and selected antiquities, which the company has also been famous for in the twenty years that I've lived in Los Angeles. Don't be intimidated by the armed guard and the plush showroom as you enter. Superior will do business with anyone who cares to buy or sell stamps or coins. They have a reputation for somewhat ignoring the "small" collector, but that's mainly because this company also caters to a more affluent clientele than many of the other stamp and coin stores in Los Angeles. I've made small purchases ($10 to $20) at their store without feeling that I was wasting their time. Once I wandered in and asked to see their AU Indian cents; a salesman patiently let me handle a selection of them on a felt pad, and I bought some nice ones at less than $10 each. Another time I asked to see some cheap medals, and they brought me a whole box of them from which I selected maybe fifty, and they let me have the lot for a couple of dollars per medal.

The auction catalogs of Superior become reference works in themselves; choice U.S. and foreign coins are always being auctioned off by them, either specialized collections like high grade U.S. *Large Cents* or a general group of U.S. or foreign coins in exceptional condition. Superior auctioned the legendary *King of Siam proof set* on the night of May 28, 1990 for a winning bid of $2.9 million, plus a 10% buyer's commission, for a total purchase price of $3.19 million. This set contains the finest known *1804 Silver Dollar*, graded MS-65 by PCGS before the sale! Coin broker Iraj "Roger" Sayah and private collector Terry Brand submitted the winning bid, and each assumed 50% ownership in the set. After the bidding, Sayah said he was willing to bid near $4 million and thought that the price he bought it for was cheap. For Superior's next coin auction catalog, call or write to find out what kinds of coins will be included, and the catalog's price (usually around $25).

Several times a year, Superior publishes an illustrated retail price list called "Money Talks," which offers interesting stamps and coins at fixed prices. I've made some great purchases out of this catalog, but things sell fast so phone your order in when you get the latest issue. Write for a free copy.

Superior's office and showroom hours are: Monday through Friday, 8:30 A.M. to 5:30 P.M. Saturday hours vary; sometimes they're open on Saturdays, sometimes not, so call to verify before a Saturday visit. You can park next to my car on a side street!

COIN DEALER ORGANIZATIONS

Most coin dealers are members of one or more of the following organizations. While organization membership, or lack of it, isn't the only way to judge a dealer's ethics, it is a fact that outright crooks tend to be expelled from professional organizations. So when you are considering doing business with a new coin dealer, ask him about his membership affiliations, then check with the organization to verify if the dealer is a member in good standing if you are suspicious about the dealer's ethics.

American Numismatic Association

AMERICAN NUMISMATIC ASSOCIATION
·(ANA)
818 North Cascade Avenue
Colorado Springs, CO 80903
(719) 632-2646

While the 30,000+ membership of the ANA consists mostly of coin collectors, many dealers and virtually all big-time dealers are also members. If a dealer has been expelled from the ANA, I would pick a different dealer for my business. Write or call the American Numismatic Association to verify whether a dealer is a member in good standing.

Professional Numismatists Guild

PROFESSIONAL NUMISMATISTS GUILD (PNG)
P.O. Box 430
Van Nuys, CA 91408
(818) 781-1764

The Professional Numismatists Guild is the largest coin dealer organization in the United States. Potential members are screened for financial and character reliability, and they must agree to a code of ethics by pledging to buy and sell at reasonable prices, to avoid false advertising, to refrain from knowingly dealing in stolen merchandise, to cooperate with governmental authorities in the prosecution of violators of laws involving numismatics, etc.

A free directory of PNG members is available by writing to the above address. Include postage when requesting free information from any coin organization. The PNG is non-profit and was incorporated in 1955. The *PNG Membership Directory* lists close to 500 members.

Canadian Association of Numismatic Dealers

CANADIAN ASSOCIATION OF NUMISMATIC DEALERS (CAND)
2525 Carling Avenue, Suite D4
Ottawa, Ontario K2B 7Z2 Canada
(613) 820-9204

The Canadian Association of Numismatic Dealers is an organization similar to the PNG (above). The CAND members are mostly dealers in Canada, but there are some U.S. dealers also. For a list of CAND members, contact the Executive Secretary of CAND.

Industry Council for Tangible Assets

INDUSTRY COUNCIL FOR TANGIBLE
ASSETS (ICTA)
666 Pennsylvania Avenue, SE
Suite 301
Washington, DC 20003
(202) 544-3531

The Industry Council for Tangible Assets is a trade association of more than 650 coin and bullion dealers, banks, brokerage houses, manufacturers, distributors, wholesalers, refiners, investment counselors, and others in the precious metals business. Not all coin dealers are members, but many who specialize in buying and selling precious metals (gold, silver, platinum, and palladium) *are* ICTA members. The ICTA formed in 1983.

The ICTA operates a "Coin and Bullion Dealer Accreditation Program" (CABDAP) whereby coin and precious metals dealers agree to abide by ethical standards and to provide information about their businesses to the CABDAP staff, which can investigate suspected violators and suspend or revoke their membership. A coin dealer may be a member of either the ICTA or CABDAP—or both or neither—and still be an honest dealer or a crook. It takes time for an organization to catch up with a dealer practicing questionable ethics; so, don't invest your life savings with any coin dealer in the first business transaction that you have with him.

The ICTA and CABDAP (both at the same address above) will be happy to tell you whether a coin dealer is a member in good standing. Also, the ICTA will send you free pamphlets about investing in precious metals. The one I like best is entitled "The Investor's Guide to Precious Metals." I disagree with their advice that sometimes it is OK to buy metals through a "storage program," whereby the dealer keeps the bullion on his premises or in his bank. If you buy anything, you should take immediate possession of it and store it safely where you can always get at it. In terms of coins and bullion, your own bank safe deposit box is hard to beat for security and peace of mind, especially if you also get an insurance policy on the coins and bullion stored in your bank box. Then you have nothing to worry about, barring bizarre freak occurrences like a bank vault burglary committed simultaneously with your insurance company going bankrupt, nuclear war, etc.!

British Numismatic Trade Association Ltd.

BRITISH NUMISMATIC TRADE
ASSOCIATION LTD. (BNTA)
P.O. Box 82
Coventry CV1 2SH England

The British Numismatic Trade Association was founded in 1973 by British coin dealers who were meeting regularly to discuss the implications of Great Britain's "Value Added Tax" (VAT), a type of national sales tax that no rational American would ever want to have introduced into the United States' Internal Revenue Service taxing system. The BNTA has grown into a group of nearly 100 numismatic dealers in England, Scotland, Wales, and Ireland.

The BNTA is a trade association only, and membership is open to any full-time coin dealer who is based in the British Isles and is registered for VAT. Applicants need to be sponsored by two existing members and have to agree to abide by a Code of Ethics. Each year memberships are reviewed to help keep the organization's standards for the benefit of dealers and collectors alike.

Not all coin dealers in Great Britain are BNTA members, but many are, and the Secretary of the BNTA (at the association's address above) will be happy to tell you whether a British coin dealer is a BNTA member in good standing. The BNTA also distributes a 35-page booklet listing current members.

It is a mark of great courtesy to enclose either the nation's mint stamps or some currency when requesting a reply by mail from an overseas organization. Most local stamp dealers can supply current British stamps (send about $1 U.S. in face value), or as a last resort, enclose an American dollar bill with your request and gamble that the recipient can convert it to local national currency.

International Association of Professional Numismatists

INTERNATIONAL ASSOCIATION OF
PROFESSIONAL NUMISMATISTS
(IAPN)
Löwenstrasse, 65
CH-8001 Zürich, Switzerland

The International Association of Professional Numismatists was founded in Geneva, Switzerland on May 12, 1951 with twenty-eight members. Membership is vested in numismatic firms, or in numismatic departments of other commercial institutions, and *not* in individuals. Today the IAPN has 110 member firms, in 22 countries on 5 continents.

In 1965 the IAPN held an international congress in Paris to consider the study of and defense against counterfeit coins, and in 1975 the IAPN established the International Bureau for the Suppression of Counterfeit Coins (IBSCC) in London. This Bureau maintains close links with mints, police forces, museums, dealers, and collectors, and publishes a semi-annual "Bulletin on Counterfeits" and specialized reports on counterfeits. IAPN members guarantee the authenticity of all the coins and medals they sell.

Membership in the IAPN is not easily acquired as applicants must (1) be sponsored by three present members, (2) have been established in business as numismatists for at least four years, (3) must be known to a number of members, (4) have carried on their business in an honorable manner, and (5) have a good general knowledge of numismatics as well as expertise in whatever field is their specialty.

The IAPN is a non-profit organization according to the Swiss Civil Code. A list of IAPN members (of which thirty-two are in the United States) can be obtained from the General Secretary at the address above.

14

Coin Shows

Just about every large U.S. city has coin shows every year. Even small cities may have local bourses. Technically, a *show* includes exhibits (competitive or otherwise) as well as dealer tables for buying and selling with visitors; the dealer table section is known as a *bourse*, a marketplace where buyers and sellers meet to do coin business. A lot of bourses are called shows, even though they have no exhibits.

One of the priceless advantages of subscribing to a weekly numismatic periodical (specifically *Coin World* or *Numismatic News*, see Chapter 17) is that they list in detail the upcoming coin shows throughout the United States, so that you can plan your trips and vacations around the coin show calendar. I like to visit faraway shows that attract different dealers than the ones in Los Angeles (where I live), so I can see new dealers' stocks of coins and chat with new faces!

The largest shows, discussed in this chapter, are truly impressive events. Besides having hundreds of dealer tables for you to browse over, the giant shows offer seminars, auctions, lectures and slide shows, and spectacular coin exhibits. The biggest names in the coin business turn up at the largest shows, and you can say "Hi" to the people you have read about in the coin magazines.

COIN SHOW "ETIQUETTE"

There are some established and unwritten rules to follow when visiting a coin show. Here they are, with my own opinions interjected:

1. *Don't steal.* Coin shows have both uniformed and plainclothes security walking around, and the inside of the local jail will look a lot more forlorn than the empty spaces in your coin albums, if you cross the line that separates coin thieves from honest collectors. Keep your hands on the table when you're handling a dealer's coins, and ask permission to take out some coins of your own to compare with the dealer's, so that there is no question about whose coins are whose. If you find a coin on the floor, turn it in to the front desk so you won't be accused of stealing it.

2. *Don't let anyone steal your coins.* Keep one eye on your bag of coin possessions at all times. Place your briefcase (if you bring one) between your feet when you sit in a chair. Protect your wallet from pickpockets. Patrons have been known to be robbed after they've left a big-time coin show. Don't advertise that you're carrying valuables as you walk and ride away, and beware of strangers suddenly approaching you and asking for directions, etc. Don't

leave valuables in an unattended car at or away from the show premises. If you think you're being followed, go to a public place and call the police. Don't be paranoid, but don't be vulnerable.

3. *Plan your coin show activities in advance.* Do you want to explore the bourse floor for a few hours first? Will you have enough time to see the exhibits? If you go with companions, set a time and place in the show to meet again if you become separated. Don't spend all your money with the first dealer. I like to look around for a while to compare prices and see what's available before I spend any of my money.

4. *Handle the coins of others with the utmost care, with more respect than if they were your own:*

(a) Always ask permission before you touch a dealer's coin including (and ESPECIALLY) taking it out of its holder.

(b) Handle coins slowly and firmly BY THEIR EDGES, not by their "flat" sides (obverse and reverse).

(c) Handle one coin at a time.

(d) Keep your own coins separated from the coins of others.

(e) Handle coins over the table (preferably on a felt pad) so that if you drop them they won't roll away or get scratched.

(f) Keep the dealer's coins in full view of the dealer at all times.

5. *Don't lean on glass display cases* that might break.

6. *Negotiation is acceptable* when buying or selling. Don't be embarrassed to ask for a small discount, but don't abuse the dealer's patience with petty bickering over a few cents' difference in price. Shop around when buying or selling coins at a show. Don't feel obligated to accept the first offer you get (or any offer).

7. *Time is money* to a busy dealer who has paid for a show table and maybe traveled a long distance to greet you at this show. It is considered bad manners to chat for an hour with a dealer, taking up chair-space at his table, then do no business with

him. Five or ten minutes is OK; an hour of financially unproductive "visiting" is not.

8. *Ask questions.* If you're curious about something, ask about it: "What's the price of that *Half Dollar*? Is that *Large Cent* originally toned? Do you have any more foreign *crowns* besides the ones in the case? Why is this *Dime* more expensive than that one? What is this little mark above the last numeral of the date? Can I look through your box of circulated *Morgans*?"

9. *Coin show food* is almost universally awful. It is generally tasteless or overpriced (or both). If you don't mind spending $5 to $10 of your coin budget for a show lunch counter meal of a stale hot dog, a tiny bag of potato chips, a donut, and a soft drink, then go ahead.

When I go to a coin show, I don't care what I eat because I go for the coins, not the cuisine. When I go with a companion, we sometimes plan ahead to have lunch or dinner away from the show at a place that serves real food. You can eat any time, but this show may be only once a year. On the other hand, I can't concentrate on coins when I'm really hungry. But I never eat or drink as I'm walking around the show; dealers don't like it when you spill your chili burger all over their displays of rare 19th century *Proof Patterns*!

10. *HAVE FUN AT THE SHOW!* This is the most important rule, and one that is too often neglected by people who know the price of everything but the value of nothing. If you're not enjoying yourself at a dealer's table, try another one. There are a lot of dealers at a big show!

It's not how much money you spend, or what kind of "bargains" you get, but how much fun you have that makes your coin show visit a success. Don't laugh at someone looking through a dealer's "junk box" of 10¢ foreign coins. And don't be overly awed by a well-dressed executive whose stack of hundred dollar bills may be just as tall as his numismatic knowledge and common courtesy may be short.

A Coin Show Incident

I didn't witness it, but a friend of mine told me of an incident he saw take place at a dealer's table at a big coin show. Two customers were seated at the table, one browsing through expensive coins, the other sorting through the foreign "junk" coins in the dealer's "10¢ box." Everybody was casually dressed.

The "rich" customer was about to conclude a big purchase from the dealer—they were counting out a large stack of $100 bills—when suddenly, for no special reason, the dealer joked about the "poor" customer's "cheap coins for a cheap man." Whereupon the rich man scooped up his money and announced loudly for all to hear:

Never criticize a collector by what kinds of coins he collects. This man next to me enjoys his 10¢ coins as much as I enjoy my $10,000 coins and, for all we know, he may even be a more competent numismatist than all of the rest of us put together! I will not buy any coins at this table because I prefer to do business with dealers who respect coin collectors!

And with that, he walked away.

Another Coin Show Story

I went to a big coin show to hunt for a few worn (Good condition) *Indian Head Cents* to give away as prizes to my students (when I used to teach junior high school science) for rewards in little contests and games that we would occasionally play in class. In fact, I took a few of these students with me to the coin show, on a voluntary Saturday "field trip."

The kids didn't have much money to spend, and when I noticed them chatting with what seemed to be a friendly dealer, I walked over to the dealer's table and listened in on their conversation. My students were courteously asking the dealer for a small discount off their cheap "*Buffalo Nickels*" and *Lincoln Cents*, which they had picked out from the dealer's stock, at prices (marked on the cardboard coin holders) of around 50¢ per coin, because, as they explained to the dealer, they only had a few dollars to spend at the coin show today. Without ever looking at me, the dealer then said to my students:

I was once a young coin collector just like you guys are. And a dealer back then gave me a real good deal that let me buy some nice coins on my small

allowance. Now I'm going to make a good deal for you—you may have the coins you picked out for free! Enjoy them, and remember to do something nice for young collectors when you grow up!

It was then that I introduced myself and decided to spend all of my money at this dealer's table, as he had rolls of cheap *Indian Cents* for sale, exactly what I came to the show looking for.

So you see, coin dealers are human. There are good dealers and bad ones. Give your business to the good ones, who, I think, outnumber the bad ones anyway!

THE BIGGEST U.S. COIN SHOWS

Four of the biggest coin shows every year are the ANA, the Central States, the FUN, and the Long Beach shows. People go to these shows to do business with top coin dealers and to take the pulse of the current coin market. If you've never been to a big coin show, you're in for a treat because it's a little overwhelming.

ANA Shows

The American Numismatic Association (ANA) coin shows are held twice a year: an early spring and an annual convention show. The ANA has been having annual conventions since 1891. The cities where they are held are determined when a local club makes a bid; then the ANA Board of Governors votes on the city proposal.

There are about 450 tables at the annual convention (anniversary) shows, where the dealer cost per table runs about $900, and visitor attendance averages 10,000 to 15,000. About 200 tables at $500 apiece grace the spring ANA show where attendance hits 5,000 to 8,000.

Exhibits, awards, and seminars are sponsored by the ANA at its shows. For information on the next ANA show, write:

AMERICAN NUMISMATIC ASSOCIATION
818 North Cascade Avenue
Colorado Springs, CO 80903

FUN Show

The Florida United Numismatists (FUN) coin

show is held in early January each year and is the show that "kicks off" the New Year season in the coin business. While the bourse may be the main reason most visitors attend, the show is also held expressly for the annual convention of the FUN state numismatic association.

Held since 1956 every year in Florida, the FUN show attracts over 500 dealer table sales and over 20,000 visitors. For information on next January's show, write:

FLORIDA UNITED NUMISMATISTS
P.O. Box 349
Gainesville, FL 32602

Central States Shows

The Central States Numismatic Society (CSNS) shows consist of a spring convention and fall shows every year in the central U.S. Since 1940 the CSNS has been holding annual conventions in different cities each year. The CSNS is a regional organization composed of thirteen states in the upper Midwest.

The spring convention is larger, with about 375 dealer tables at a cost of $375 per table. There is an auction in conjunction with, but separate from, the CSNS convention, and also educational seminars and competitive exhibits. The number of visitors varies with the location, but runs from 5,000 to 10,000 for the three-day spring convention. For information on the next CSNS show, write:

CENTRAL STATES NUMISMATIC
  SOCIETY
58 Devonwood Avenue S.W.
Cedar Rapids, IA 52404

Long Beach Shows

And then there's the Long Beach Numismatic, Philatelic and Baseball Card Exposition (as its evolving title currently is designated), held three times a year in February, June, and October. The Long Beach Exposition has the highest average attendance of any coin show in the world, drawing upwards of 20,000 collectors and dealers. The Long Beach Expo features 565 bourse tables, and there's a waiting list for renting a table at next year's shows. Table fees run $300 to $475, but that's irrelevant if you can't get one!

The Long Beach show is open only to dealers on Wednesday, then is available to public visitors for four days, Thursday through Sunday, but my experience is that a lot of dealers start packing up early on Sunday afternoon for their trip back home, so go to the show on Saturday at the latest, if possible (this applies to all coin shows). Admission is $2, less than the price of a movie, for what I think is the most spectacular coin bourse imaginable. Of course, the Los Angeles freeways are a show in themselves, but if you survive the freeway trip to the Long Beach Convention Center (where the show is always held), be prepared for a stiff parking lot fee. (The fee is almost worth paying for the security that it offers, but I prefer to park on a Long Beach side street and walk a few blocks to the Convention Center. The walk may be too long for you, though.)

Of special interest at the Long Beach show is the bourse section for dealers in ancient and foreign coins (100 booths), some flying in from overseas. At each show, auctions are held, as well as seminars and forums by nationally known numismatic organizations. The Long Beach Exposition proudly distributes a complete program guide at each show: this 80+ page book includes floor maps, dealer table directories, a schedule of events, feature articles, future show information, and dealer advertising.

And, like all coin shows but especially this one, the Long Beach show has a walk-in area near the show entrance, where plenty of free numismatic literature (magazines, brochures, newspapers) is offered. Billed as "The Show Often Imitated by Never Equaled!", the Long Beach Expo is run with care and success by Samuel Lopresto and Teresa Darling. The Long Beach Convention Center is a modern facility situated near the oceanfront in downtown Long Beach, and I suggest that you drive or take a taxi to cover the distance to a decent Long Beach restaurant (ask the people at the Long Beach Coin Club booth where they like to eat in town).

For information on the next show, see their full-page ads in *Coin World* and *Numismatic News* or write to Sam and Teresa at:

LONG BEACH EXPOSITION
112 East Broadway
Long Beach, CA 90802

223. 1805 Mexico City Mint *8-Reales* piece, silver, circulated. When you go to sell this coin, the buyer will be certain to notice its wear, "chop marks," and field scratches, and offer a lower price accordingly. Besides that, the coin has been cleaned! Author's collection.

224. Reverse of the 1805 *8-Reales* silver piece from the previous photo. The reverse is decidedly nicer than the obverse, but when you buy or sell a coin, you have to deal with the whole coin, including its edge, and adjust its market value accordingly. Author's collection.

225. Reverse of a San Francisco Mint *"Mercury" Dime*, Uncirculated, with extremely small surface marks (can you find them?). Also, the central horizontal "bands" are not completely split, which is OK, but prevents the coin from bringing top dollar when sold. Author's collection.

226. An active bourse floor at a major coin show. The people in the immediate foreground are inspecting numismatic exhibits displayed in locked glass cases on tables. The people visiting the dealers' booths in the background are buying, selling, and learning about coins as they chat with dealers and browse through dealers' stocks. Photo courtesy American Numismatic Association.

227. Dr. Arnold R. Saslow of Rare Coins & Classical Arts Ltd., arranging his stock of ancient Greek and Roman gold coins at a Long Beach, CA coin show. Author's photo, taken with Dr. Saslow's permission.

228. Dr. Arnold R. Saslow of Rare Coins & Classical Arts Ltd., writing out some information (which the author requested) on ancient coins, at his company's display tables at a Long Beach, CA coin show. When visiting a coin bourse like this one, do not lean or put heavy objects on the glass-topped display cases; ask permission before you handle a coin out of its holder; and feel free to ask questions without necessarily buying something. Author's photo, taken with Dr. Saslow's permission.

15

Coin Investing

Sometimes you have to wonder whether it is good or bad that we can't see into the future. There are many reasons to collect coins, and the prospect of financial gain from them is just one reason. If it were easy to make a lot of money, we would all be rich. Because the future is uncertain, and because so many factors (including uncontrollable ones) are involved in the market fluctuations of a freely traded commodity in a supply-and-demand economic system (which is what the coin business is), investment advice seems a little pretentious. If any so-called "investment advisor" *knew for a fact* which coins would make big profits in the next year or two, that advisor wouldn't be selling his advice, he'd be taking it himself. Remember that the next time somebody offers you a "sure thing" deal on coins that will "undoubtedly skyrocket in value in three months!"

Still, it is a challenge to buy coins with an informed eye toward future price appreciation, and that is the purpose of this chapter. Three factors determine a coin's market price: rarity, condition, and demand. Some coins are rare but have no collector/investor demand (certain "minors" of the Dark Ages). Other coins are rare in Uncirculated condition, but relatively "common" and cheap when found in a well-circulated state (many U.S. *Colonial*

coins). Still other coins are not rare, but their selling prices are astronomical because of the tremendous collector demand for them. The 1877 *Indian Cent*, struck in a total mintage of 852,500, is certainly not an impossibly "rare" coin, but sells for $200 for even a well-worn specimen. Compare it with the market prices of *Morgan Dollars* of similar mintages and similar grades.

I suggest that you be a collector first, a numismatist second, and an investor last. In other words: learn how to *collect* coins first. Then study them by reading about them, discussing them with dealers and other collectors, and by carefully looking at them (*numismatics*). Then, if you wish, think a little about *investing* a small portion of your funds in coins for possible long-term profits. Most experienced coin dealers agree that a nice meaningful coin collection, built up over a period of years, has a chance of becoming a wise investment.

FEDERAL TRADE COMMISSION "CONSUMER ALERT"

Before you invest a cent in rare coins, send right now for a free pamphlet from the Federal Trade Commission. The pamphlet is entitled "Consumer

Alert: Investing In Rare Coins" and is available by writing to:

FEDERAL TRADE COMMISSION
Pennsylvania Avenue at 6th Street N.W.
Washington, DC 20580
(202) 326-2180 (Public Affairs number)

Excerpts from this pamphlet are as follows: "Use common sense when evaluating your dealer's reputation and reliability before you send money or authorize a credit card transaction ... Comparison shop: visit several dealers before buying. Check prices in leading coin publications [see Chapter 17 of this book] to make sure you are not being overcharged ... (and) the dealer may be misrepresenting the quality or grade of the coin."

The pamphlet goes on to list some sales techniques commonly used by dishonest dealers:

(1) False Grading Claims ... False grading is the most common form of rare coin fraud.

(2) False Certification Claims ... Grading certificates can be misleading, outdated, or completely fraudulent.

(3) False Claims About Current Value ... Some dishonest sellers grade their coins accurately but overprice them. For example, they may charge $5,000 for an accurately graded $10 Indian gold piece, which has a current retail value of only $1,750.

(4) False Appreciation Claims ... There is no guarantee that any coin will appreciate in value.

(5) False Claims About Bullion Coins ... Fraudulent sellers of bullion coins often overprice their coins, or mislead consumers about the coins' bullion content or rarity ... study the bullion market before you buy, and choose your dealer carefully.

COIN ORGANIZATIONS

Most big-time coin dealers who supply "investment quality" coins are members of one or more of these organizations (write to see if the dealer is a member

in good standing; also, see Chapter 13 for descriptions of these organizations):

AMERICAN NUMISMATIC ASSOCIATION
(ANA)
818 North Cascade Avenue
Colorado Springs, CO 80903

PROFESSIONAL NUMISMATISTS GUILD
(PNG)
P.O. Box 430
Van Nuys, CA 91408

INDUSTRY COUNCIL FOR TANGIBLE
ASSETS (ICTA)
666 Pennsylvania Avenue, SE
Suite 301
Washington, DC 20003

And for a local coin store, check with the local Better Business Bureau or Chamber of Commerce to see how long the company has been in business, and if there are any unresolved complaints against it.

ADVANTAGES OF COIN INVESTMENT

Advantages of coin investment include:

1. *High liquidity*—Coins with recognized value are easy to sell, although you may have to shop around for the best price.

2. *Small storage space requirements*—Close your hand for a moment. You could be holding, within your closed hand, enough rare coins to purchase the building in which you are sitting now.

3. *Anonymity* — Coins bought or sold for cash amounts under $10,000 per transaction do not have to be reported to government authorities. Serious investment profits, however, are taxable income.

4. *Portability* — Coins may be transported with ease anywhere in the world. And dealers everywhere recognize the value in popular coins.

5. *Durability*—Within reason, coins are quite durable and may be stored for long periods of time without deterioration (if properly housed in holders, etc.). How durable is a race horse or fragile oil painting, not to mention their portability and "hideability"?

DISADVANTAGES OF COIN INVESTMENT

Realistic people have a balanced view of the world. Before you spend your life savings on rare coins, here are some possible disadvantages of coin investment:

1. *No regular interest income accrues from coins*, as happens with punctuality with bank savings accounts or "good" stock certificates. All "profits" from coins are strictly theoretical and "on paper only" until the coins are actually sold.

2. *Difficulty in buying premium quality cheaply.* Such premium quality (PQ) coins are defined as the best examples for their type and grade. But if they're such nice coins, nobody will sell them to you cheaply. So how can you turn a profit when you can't buy cheaply?

3. *Problems with coin grading and tampering.* If you think that the used car market is ripe with fraud, wait until you start exploring high-priced coins for possible "investment." Overgraded and cleaned coins are epidemic and have been for as long as I've been collecting coins (thirty-five years).

4. *Some coins are semi-liquid*; i.e., they may take a long time to sell for the best possible price. Examples: bizarre errors, esoteric foreign coins, "generic" junk, and "pedigreed" common coins whose major value lies in finding a buyer who appreciates the coins' previous owners.

5. *The impossibility of predicting market fluctuations* makes big money coin investing a little nerve-wracking. Should you sell or buy today? Sounds like the stock market, doesn't it?

SPECULATION VS. INVESTING

Speculation is short-term hoping to make a financial "killing" by buying and selling a freely traded commodity. *Investing* is long-term hoping to make a profit by buying and selling such commodities.

If you buy ten rolls of common date *Morgan Dollars* in UNC condition, and plan to hold them for six months in hopes of profit upon resale, that's speculation. If you carefully and over a period of time (say, a year or more), select one choice UNC example of each *Morgan Dollar* date and mintmark

(to the extent of your capital!), and hold this *Morgan Dollar* set for ten years to see what it will be worth then, that's investing.

Coin collecting history has shown that it is hard to "corner the market" by buying up and hoarding a particular type of coin in order to drive up prices. *Lincoln Cents* were "hot" in the early 1960s, *Morgan Dollars* in the 1980s, virtually "everything" in coins in the runaway inflation of the late 1970s. But what goes up can come down, a lesson to be learned from financial wheeling and dealing in a free market economy (which is what the coin business is).

1950-D Nickels were once driven up to $1,080 per roll of forty coins in choice UNC condition ($27 per coin) during the "coin roll craze" that started in the late 1950s, peaked in the early '60s, and crashed in the mid-'60s. Certified "slabbed" *Morgan Dollars* were feverishly overpromoted in the late 1980s, resulting in a shocking crash in the fall of 1990, which sent many *Morgan Dollar*-glutted dealerships toward the brink of financial disaster. In January 1991, I bought a *Morgan Dollar* that would have cost me triple what I paid for it if I had purchased it a year earlier.

"Cornering the market" has been attempted many times with varying degrees of success, but in the long run everything "evens out" because everybody knows what coins exist and who owns large quantities of them.

Speculation has temporarily run up the prices of numismatic items, but you have to ask yourself this question: Is the new higher price supported by collector demand? Collectors, not speculators ... not dealers ... not even "investors," are the ultimate consumers of rare coins. If broad masses of collectors aren't pushing the price up for a rapidly increasing coin market price, then it must be due to speculators and dealers buying and selling with each other, a perilous situation financially because when a few of these promoters panic and start "dumping" their "investments" on the market, the prices of these coins will crash as fast (if not faster!) than they once rose. Don't confuse *artificial scarcity* (caused by melting, hoarding, and overpromoting) with *real scarcity* (caused by a minuscule supply of a coin when compared with collector demand for it).

The coin investor, on the other hand, doesn't care about daily price fluctuations. The investor is in coins for the long haul, not the short pull. Most people who call themselves "investors" are really "speculators," and it is speculation that fits the impatient American personality well and helps to line the pockets and wallets of semi-larcenous businessmen who take advantage of people's obsession with "making money" by forever offering to sell overpriced, overpromoted merchandise.

OVERPROMOTED COINS

Coins available in quantity are promotable. Truly rare and nearly unique coins can't be found in large quantities to sell from slick brochures offering "investment quality" coins that in reality are as common as the day is long. So it stands to reason that what everybody's selling is not necessarily what you want to buy—that is, if you fancy yourself an "investor."

Most *Morgan Dollars, Liberty Walking Halves*, and a lot of *Double Eagles* ($20 gold pieces) were minted in the millions, so how can they be rare today? So what if it is the "finest known" of its kind if there were 12,760,000 minted (as in the case of the *1881-S Dollar*)? Is it worth a thousand times as much as the "second finest known"? And where are you going to sell a $10,000 coin that retails for $50 in "average" Uncirculated grades? You can buy a lot of nice coins for $10,000. Maybe even one that is really rare.

"Generic" Coins

In the overpromoted coin market of 1988-89, "generic" coins became defined as common date Uncirculated U.S. coins, usually "slabbed," and traded as a commodity like petroleum futures or sugar shares. Common date *Morgan* and *Peace Dollars, Saint-Gaudens Double Eagles*, late date *Liberty Walking Halves, Mercury Dimes*, and *Washington Quarters* were promoted as "investments." Generic coins aren't rare, even in UNC grades, although they may be promoted as such. This market crashed in 1990, as it should have, considering that, for practical purposes, virtually endless quantities of these generic coins exist. Where is the investment value in a coin that appears in dozens of large display advertisements in every coin magazine? If you're buying it for bullion potential price increase,

that's different, but don't call a common coin a rare coin.

Nobody "wholesales" large batches of "mark-free" AU *Barber Half Dollars*, because these coins don't exist in quantity. Pieces are bought and sold one at a time. Dealers have trouble finding choice Uncirculated *Half Cents, Bust* coinage, rare date gold, and *Colonial* coins, and have no trouble selling them once they get them in stock. Go to a large coin show (like the ones described in Chapter 14) and walk around for a couple of hours, looking at the dealer coin displays. The coins that you *don't* see are the ones that are probably rare!

COIN MARKET CYCLES

"Boom" and "Bust" cycles afflict the coin market with the regularity of day and night. Coins get overpromoted, overbought, overpraised, then a few "investors" get nervous and start to sell ... then "speculators" start to sell ... and then coin dealers get panicky and try to sell their "questionably valued" coins — and the market crashes. These coin market "dips" (or "corrections" as they are charitably called by eternal optimists) have occurred for a broad range of coins in 1937-38, 1945-46, 1950-51, 1957-58, 1966, 1976, 1981-82, and 1990. Investors get burned, speculators get discouraged, even some dealers go bankrupt, and the market stagnates.

Then a fascinating thing happens, as sure as the clockwork of a finely tuned timepiece. Somebody starts to buy again, then more people buy, then the prices of coins rise a bit and even more people get interested and buy. And we have the birth of at least a temporary "upswing" and maybe the ground floor of a new coin "boom market."

Bernard Baruch, the Wall Street wizard, had some excellent advice when asked how to make money in the stock market. He replied that his investment philosophy was to buy when others are selling, and sell when others are buying. By going against the trend of a changing market ("contrarian" investment strategy), you have a chance to get things at bargain prices and sell them at a nice profit when others are feverishly buying during a boom phase. Unfortunately, it takes nerves of steel to be alone in a crowd!

What will the coin market do during the next

twelve months? If I knew that, I wouldn't be a writer; I'd be rich (beyond any conceivable human lust for wealth). There are three main categories of coin markets: (1) an up and down "roller coaster ride" for speculated items, (2) a steady long-term price increase or decrease in an overall rising or falling market, and (3) a flat (no change) market for several years straight (for certain coins).

COIN INVESTMENT RACKETS

Beware of any "coin investment" promotions that promise:

❑ Guaranteed profits
❑ Priceless heirlooms
❑ Limited quantity (everything is limited, including the air we breathe and sand grains on the beach)
❑ Only five or ten per customer (why not 50 or 100?)
❑ Lowest price in the world
❑ Inside market reports—only $50 a month
❑ Limited time for this "sale"
❑ Guaranteed grading
❑ "Now is the only logical time to buy"

Overgrading and overpricing are the most dangerous traps that lurk for the coin investor to stumble into. "Third party" grading, such as slabbing and certification, helps, but learn how to grade your own coins (by reading and collecting and visiting a lot of coin dealers/shows) for the types of coins on which you plan to spend serious money.

While not illegal, I don't like dealers who advertise: "Any coin removed from its holder is considered sold." How can you examine the edge unless you pry the coin out of its holder? Of course, if you take a coin out of an expensive "slab," the original seller has a right to insist that you get it reslabbed before accepting it for a refund. I don't like *POR* ("Price on Request") in coin ads either; everything should be priced up-front so there's no mystery in the deal. I love coin dealers who put a price on every coin that they show me, *before I have to ask for it*. I avoid dealers who price their merchandise based on how much money they think they can get out of you.

Edge and rim nicks are often not mentioned in ads offering coins for sale. One coin in a group or roll may be "bad" when you spread the coins out, a common rip-off coin scam. They figure that you won't bother to return a whole group of coins if only one is substandard.

Crooked dealers (they exist) engage in outright lies, calling an AU coin UNC (or vice versa, depending on whether they're buying or selling). Crooked dealers use outdated catalogs, to show "low" buying prices, and overpriced retail lists, to show you how much you have to pay for a coin. And they vastly underpay when buying from a customer. Or they "cherry-pick," which means that they buy only coins they can "steal" at cheap prices, leaving you with your "worst" coins that may be hard to sell alone (without any "good" coins in the batch)!

Lee F. Hewitt, who published *The Numismatic Scrapbook Magazine*, used to say: "There is no Santa Claus in numismatics." Or as the U.S. Postal Inspection Service says: "If it sounds too good to be true, it probably is."

WHAT TO BUY

Now that I've scared you for your own protection (if you've been reading this chapter from the beginning), let's list some coins that might be worth buying for long-term investment, say ten years or more. This is provided, of course, that you buy them at a fair market price today, and you'll only know what that is if you shop around, get informed, and find out what coins are really worth in the legitimate coin market. I don't guarantee you'll make profits, but these are the coins that I would buy if I were a serious and sober coin investor.

1. Any 19th century *U.S. Proofs* in UNC grades.

2. *U.S. Half Cents* and *Large Cents* in UNC with original color, never been cleaned, no unsightly scratches or rim nicks.

3. *U.S. Bust* coins in high grades, especially scarce dates.

4. *Indian Head* and *Lincoln Cents* with low mintages, graded AU to UNC.

5. Ancient coins in silver and gold, EF to FDC (extremely fine to "Fleur-de-coin," i.e., UNC), well-centered and pleasingly toned (not tarnished),

costing $100 or more per coin. And stick with popular types, like Roman *denarii* or the coins of Athens, Corinth, and Syracuse (Greek).

6. Any 19th century European silver *crowns* or gold coins with small mintages, UNC and Proof.

7. *U.S. Patterns* purchased for "reasonable prices" (do your homework).

8. *U.S. Pioneer* gold coins in all grades. Not counterfeit or overpriced.

9. "Key Dates" in popular coin series, such as *1877 Indian Cent, 1909-S VDB Lincoln Cent, 1895 Morgan Dollar*—all grades, maybe bought at auction to limit the amount spent (research the market). Be sure they're genuine.

10. Perennially popular U.S. classics, such as: high relief *1907 $20 gold piece, Large Cents* in the $20,000 price range, U.S. *Commemorative Half Dollars, Liberty Seated*, and *Barber* coinage in scarce dates—all in high grades, preferably UNC and unblemished.

11. Scarce date 20th century coins like the *Liberty Walking Half Dollars* and *Mercury Dimes* (scarce dates only) in choice AU to UNC.

12. Whatever all of the coin dealers are forever advertising to buy; if the top dealers continually want it, it must be worth having. They've been in the coin business longer than you have and they know what's good!

COIN INVESTING TIPS

Here are some tips to make you a better investor:

1. Buy the book before the coin (see Bibliography).

2. Subscribe to and read the numismatic periodicals (Chapter 17).

3. Join some coin societies and read what they send you (Chapter 18).

4. Go to coin shows and find out what coins are really worth (Chapter 14).

5. Start slowly. There are a lot of coins in the world. You don't have to spend your life savings on coins today.

6. Buy quality rather than quantity (one coin for $100 rather than ten coins for $10 apiece).

7. Diversify your investment. Buy different types of coins to spread your risk.

8. Pay cash, no credit terms or interest charges.

9. Take immediate possession of your purchases, and hide them well at home or put them in a bank safe deposit box.

10. Keep records of what bought, date purchased, amount paid, where purchased, coin condition, etc.

11. Only invest a small portion of your total cash assets, say, about 10 to 20%. Remember, money in the bank is nice to have, too!

12. Study coin auction prices to keep current with the market.

13. Review your coin "portfolio" about twice a year to chart your paper profits and losses. You can deduct losses from profits when figuring gross capital gains income for the IRS, after the coins are sold.

14. Separate your coin investments from your idle coin "collection." It is OK to *collect* coins at a financial loss; it is not satisfying to *invest* at a net loss. Of course, the best investment may be a smart collection built up over the course of many years, as the leading coin dealers advise.

15. Get insurance for your collection when it grows to present an unacceptable risk for possible theft. The ANA offers low cost coin insurance for members (see ANA in Chapter 18). Insure coins when sending them by mail or private carrier.

SELLING YOUR COINS

The real value of anything is not what you can buy it for, but what you can sell it for. Arlyn Sieber, the Editor of *Coins* magazine, says that the most frequent complaint in mail that he receives from *Coins'* readers is the bad experience that collectors have when they try to sell their coins. Some tips for selling coins:

1. Be realistic. Ask for a strong *wholesale* price and expect one from a dealer. Sell at auction if your coins are worth $500 or more each.

2. Pick the market well. Dealers specialize. Don't offer Swedish copper to a *U.S. Silver Dollar* dealer. Go to a coin show and offer your coins with your "asking price" to several dealers to test the market.

3. Separate the better coins from the cheaper ones so they are easier to distinguish. Keep cleaned and questionable coins away from your gems.

4. Don't feel obligated to accept a dealer's offer for your coins. Once they're sold, they're sold!

5. Plan ahead, if possible, when selling coins. Distress sales for emergency money are almost always disastrous. Sell your second-rate coins first; keep the best ones for last.

6. Timing is important. Sell during times of high inflation and high gold/silver bullion prices. Don't sell when the coin market has just crashed!

7. Get a coin certified genuine and have it graded before you sell it, if it will help the sale price.

8. Be cautious when selling to strangers, either by mail or in person. Try a "small" deal first. Photograph your rare coins to make sure they aren't switched if the buyer returns them to you.

9. Don't be greedy. Take a moderate profit when you can. Sell at a loss if you have a coin that stagnates in value year after year, and put the money into something else. Limit your "downside" risk.

10. Talk with collectors and dealers. The more you know about coins, the better investor you'll be.

BULLION INVESTING

Gold and silver bullion are the two most commonly purchased metals for bullion investing/speculating. The *intrinsic value* is the melt worth of a coin, medal, or bar made from precious metal. The *melt point* is when the fluctuating free market price of precious metal in a coin equals the coin's face value. The melt point for pre-1965 U.S. silver coinage is $1.38, and this commodity market price was reached in 1977.

The Price of Silver

Long maintained at an "official" price of $1.2929 per ounce, the price of silver was allowed to float freely upward in the late 1960s and throughout most of the 1970s as demand outpaced supply. The Hunt brothers (Herbert and Nelson Bunker) of Texas tried to "corner" the silver market in the 1970s by buying up silver on the New York Commodity Exchange for a total of 50 million ounces (at a time when the U.S. Treasury had 117 million ounces). The price of silver on the Comex floor closed at $48.70 on January 17, 1980, its all-time high. People whose memories go back that far will recall the lines of customers waiting outside coin shops and bullion brokerages, waiting to sell their silver coins, sterling tableware, silver jewelry, etc., for what seemed like an ever-increasing silver market price based on "limitless" demand and speculation. Speculators with silver withheld it from the market to drive up the price further, leading many to believe that industrial and jewelry demand would push silver above $100 an ounce.

Then, of course, the market crashed, as markets have a way of doing when overspeculation creates an artificially contrived "demand" for anything! By March 27, 1980, barely nine weeks after its all-time high, silver had dropped to $10.80 per ounce, and "investors" holding large stocks of it were ruined financially. Just as much as people wanted to buy silver in early January 1980, now they wanted to dump it as fast as possible before the price sank even further. When nobody wants to buy something, the price crashes through the floor. I remember a lot of coin dealers who became wealthy overnight in the silver business, then suddenly chained their shop doors and filed for bankruptcy as their huge inventories of silver were rendered practically worthless.

Silver prices in the 1980s hovered mostly between $5 and $10 per ounce, then drifted lower, so that on December 14, 1990, silver dropped below $4.00 per ounce for the first time since February 9, 1976 when it closed at $3.96.

Thus, if you hoarded old "silver" *Dollars* and other pre-1965 U.S. silver coinage, and sold it for bullion value alone (ignoring any numismatic worth) at any time in the 1970s, you would have made a nice "profit" over your "buy-in" price of fa value. But if you were unlucky enough to buy s near its peak in late 1979, early 1980, then yo suffered a paper loss of awesome proportio real loss if you actually sold your sudden silver "investment."

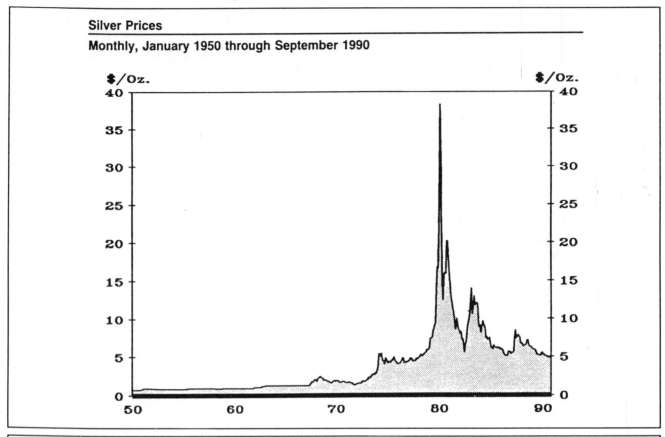

Silver Prices

Monthly, January 1950 through September 1990

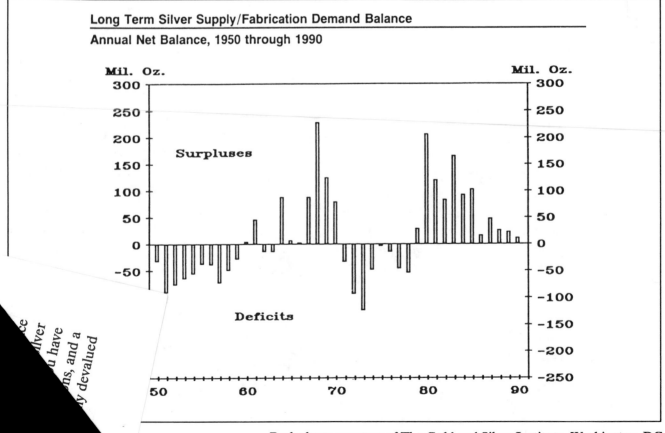

Long Term Silver Supply/Fabrication Demand Balance

Annual Net Balance, 1950 through 1990

Both charts courtesy of The Gold and Silver Institute, Washington, DC

The Price of Gold

Gold was freely traded at close to $20 per ounce during the California Gold Rush, hence the *$20 gold piece (Double Eagle)* of 1850, with .96750 ounce of pure gold content. Prospectors were "ripped off" left and right by unscrupulous merchants and upstart bankers who offered the Gold Rush miners $15 or less per ounce for their native gold dust and nuggets!

The United States was on the "gold standard" from 1900 to 1934, a time when paper currency was convertible to gold. President Franklin Roosevelt called in the gold that citizens held and paid them $20 per ounce for it. After the turn-in deadline, he raised the price of gold to $35 per ounce (January 31, 1934), and the government prohibited the private hoarding of gold bullion and gold coin—earning Roosevelt the eternal hatred of "hard money" advocates. After all, law-abiding citizens who dutifully turned in their gold coins, bullion, and gold certificates for $20 an ounce now wished they still had some gold, suddenly worth $35 an ounce.

In 1971, President Nixon stopped selling U.S. gold stocks in exchange for foreign-held American paper dollars, and on December 18, 1971, the official price of gold in the U.S. rose from $35 to $38 per ounce. The price of gold was allowed to float upward on private commodity markets and reached $61 per ounce in December 1972. *Double Eagles* were now worth $59 each for bullion value. In February 1973, the U.S. raised the official price of gold from $38 to $42.22.

President Ford lifted the ban on the private ownership of gold (in effect since 1934) and from December 31, 1974, U.S. citizens were once again allowed to buy and sell gold in any form. Gold stood at around $180 per ounce in the mid-1970s, then dropped to $107.75 on July 20, 1976, then climbed to an all-time high of $850 on January 21, 1980. Since then, it has fluctuated, mostly between $350 and $450.

Ways to Own Gold and Silver

Besides stock in gold mining companies (just like during the California Gold Rush), silver and gold futures, and bullion "storage" contracts, you can take possession of the actual bullion and store it yourself at home or (preferably) in a bank vault. I recommend that you *be very careful when buying gold or silver bullion because there have been many crooks in the business*. Be sure that you're getting what you're paying for. For big purchases, deal with long-established companies, either straight bullion brokerages (like Deak & Co.) or coin dealers who also do bullion business.

Here are some ways to own gold and silver:

1. *Bullion bars*, sold from one ounce up, stamped with the name of the "mint" that made them and usually the notation ".999 fine" (meaning 99.9% pure precious metal). Example: "Engelhard" silver bars, the 10 ounce and 100 ounce being most popular.

2. *Bullion coins*, minted by country governments to sell to collectors/investors. Generally containing one ounce of precious metal. Examples: Gold South African *Krugerrands*, Canadian *Maple Leafs*, Mexican *50 Pesos*, and American *Eagles*. One ounce silver "rounds" and "art bars" are collected numismatically (for reasons besides their silver content). Bullion bars and coins are bought by dealers at a slight percentage below "spot price" of bullion that day and sold by dealers at a slight premium over "spot." Shop around for the best deal if you're buying or selling huge quantities of gold or silver.

3. *Bullion-related coins* are "generic" coins traded for their bullion content, not usually their numismatic value. Examples: Worn U.S. coinage pre-1965 in silver or gold, *not* scarce dates or mintmarks, such as bags of circulated 90% silver coinage like *Franklin Halves* or *Washington Quarters, Silver Dollars*, and gold *Double Eagles* ($20 gold pieces) that are worn.

4. *"Raw" bullion* in unrefined dust, nuggets, or native mineral specimens. Be careful that you get what you pay for—study the market. These items can have collector value above bullion value. They can also be assayed out at much less than 100% purity!

5. *Gold and silver medallions*, "art bars," *jewelry*, and *trinkets*. Usually overpriced, much above bullion value, fun to own, but not the best bullion "investment."

Bullion Investing Information

Get the free pamphlets, "Your introduction to investing in gold" and "Your introduction to investing in silver," and publications list from:

THE GOLD AND SILVER INSTITUTE
1112 Sixteenth Street NW, Suite 240
Washington, DC 20036
(202) 835-0185

TELEMARKETING FRAUD

I don't buy anything over the telephone. The biggest consumer racket of the 1980s was telemarketing fraud. It works like this: a stranger with a tongue smoother than the field on a freshly-struck *Proof* coin will make an unsolicited telephone call to you and offer to sell you something "great" at a "bargain price" in "limited quantities" for a "very limited time"—it might be rare coins, it might be gold or silver bullion, it might be shares in a mining district where "everybody" is striking it rich. The con job may even include outright misrepresentation and lying, which you'll discover after you send them your money and receive shoddy merchandise in return. Don't give them your credit card number or the name of your bank.

Legitimate coin dealers and bullion brokers don't have to beg you to buy anything. They have enough business that they don't need yours, and if they want your business, they probably won't be making strange telephone calls to people they don't even know, offering a "once in a lifetime opportunity" to make a killing in the coin/bullion market. If it is that good a deal, tell the caller to buy it himself, then hang up and don't feel guilty about insulting a stranger who cares even less about your welfare. On the other hand, if your favorite coin dealer calls you at home, it is time to talk, but buy only after you've seen the goods and thought about the deal for a while.

"RED BOOK" COIN PRICES: 1961-1991

Since the first edition in 1947, the annual *A Guide Book of United States Coins®* (affectionately called the "*Red Book*"®) by R.S. Yeoman has been the standard U.S. coin catalog for determining (1) retail coin prices, (2) mintages, (3) "what" exists in major varieties, and (4) "what" is popular to collect. The *Guide Book* replaced the *Standard Catalogue of United States Coins and Tokens* (by Wayte Ray-

mond), which was popular in the 1930s and 1940s, as the "collector's bible" of collectible U.S. coins, classified by type and condition.

The *Guide Book* is published once a year, so naturally there is a time lag between a rapidly changing coin market (as sometimes happens) and the revision of market prices in the *Guide Book*. The *Guide Book* price quotes are *average retail coin prices*, supplied by a number of "contributors" (chiefly prominent dealers) several months before publication. A "dash" in a price column means that the coin is known in that grade, but its price cannot be determined. An *italicized* price means "unsettled value." *Lack of any price* in a column means that the coin is either unknown in that grade or is uncommonly traded in that grade.

The *Handbook of United States Coins®* (also known as the "*Blue Book*"®), by the same author and publisher, is the *wholesale* price guide to U.S. coins; i.e., the prices for which dealers will buy coins. My experience has been that a lot of dealers try hard to sell coins for about *Red Book®* prices, and will offer approximately *Blue Book®* prices when they buy coins from collectors. "Everybody" uses the *Red Book®*, and you see collectors carrying it around with them and referring to it, when they explore the bourse floor of a coin show.

How I Selected the Coins for the Price Chart

I chose the following coins, to chart their retail market prices for 1961 to 1991, because these coins are among the most popular and well-known U.S. coins (outside of the great rarities). These coins on my charts are instantly recognized by knowledgeable collectors and dealers. They are exactly the kinds of coins that intelligent collectors and investors buy (if they can afford them!) to complete their series (date and mintmark) sets or type sets, and for long-term investment potential. I didn't worry about whether or not the coin shows high or low price appreciation. I picked coins that "never go out of style"; coins that will always be "scarce" and desirable; coins that every collector would love to own, finances permitting.

Western Publishing Company, of Racine, WI, gave me specific permission to reprint in this book their *Red Book®* coin prices from their 1961, 1971, 1981, and 1991 editions:

RETAIL UNITED STATES COIN PRICES FROM *RED BOOK*® EDITIONS OF 1961, 1971, 1981, 1991					
Coin Type	Total Mintage	1961 Value	1971 Value	1981 Value	1991 Value
1652 Pine Tree Shilling, silver, large planchet, *Very Fine*	———	$85.00 Fine (unpriced VF)	$475.00	$1300.00	$2800.00
1793 "Chain" Large Cent, copper, *Fine*	36,103	215.00 to 250.00 (depending on the variety)	800.00 to 950.00	2500.00 to 2800.00	4750.00 to 5000.00
1856 Flying Eagle Cent, copper-nickel, *Proof*	1,000 (estimated)	840.00	2500.00	2750.00 (Proof-60)	4800.00 (Proof-63)
1877 Indian Head Cent, bronze, *Proof*	900+ (in Proof)	275.00	1100.00	1800.00 (Proof-60)	2750.00 (Proof-63)
1909-S V.D.B. Lincoln Cent, bronze, *Uncirculated*	484,000	97.50	200.00	400.00 (MS-60)	475.00 to 650.00 (MS-60 to MS-63)
1955 "Doubled Die" Lincoln Cent, bronze, *Uncirculated*	———	80.00	400.00	550.00 (MS-60)	675.00 to 1200.00 to 3000.00 (MS-60 to MS-63 to MS-65)
1937-D "3-legged Buffalo Nickel", copper-nickel, *Uncirculated*	———	50.00	220.00	550.00 (MS-60)	1800.00 (MS-63)
1916-D "Mercury Dime", silver, *Uncirculated*	264,000	360.00	675.00	2500.00 (MS-60)	3500.00 (MS-63)
1932-D Washington Quarter, silver, *Uncirculated*	436,800	90.00	250.00	700.00 to 3000.00 (MS-60 to MS-65)	900.00 to 5500.00 (MS-63 to MS-65)

Coin Type	Total Mintage	1961 Value	1971 Value	1981 Value	1991 Value
1921-D Liberty Walking Half Dollar, silver, *Uncirculated*	208,000	235.00	900.00	2600.00 (MS-60)	2200.00 (MS-60)
1936 Proof Set (U.S. Cent, "Nickel", Dime, Quarter, Half Dollar), *Proof*	3,837 (in Proof)	385.00	875.00	8750.00	5100.00
1985 "Morgan" Dollar, silver, *Proof*	880 (Proof only)	700.00	4750.00	20.000.00 (Proof-60)	19,000.00 (Proof-63)
1934-S "Peace" Dollar, silver, *Uncirculated*	1,011,000	60.00	275.00	2500.00 to 10,500.00 (MS-60 to MS-65)	1400.00 to 4800.00 (MS-60 to MS-63)
1848 $2.50 Gold Piece (Quarter Eagle) with "CAL." counter-mark, gold, *Uncirculated*	1,389 (with "CAL." countermark)	750.00	6000.00	30,000.00 (MS-60)	30,000.00 (MS-60)
1907 $20.00 Gold Piece (Double Eagle) Saint-Gaudens, High Relief, Roman Numerals, gold, *Uncirculated*	11,250 (in High Relief)	365.00	950.00	10,000.00 (MS-60)	8500.00 (MS-60)
1936 Gettysburg Commemorative Half Dollar, silver, *Uncirculated*	29,928	20.00	44.00	325.00 to 800.00 (MS-60 to MS-65)	250.00 to 300.00 to 1800.00 (MS-60 to MS-63 to MS-65)

Coin Type	Total Mintage	1961 Value	1971 Value	1981 Value	1991 Value
1900 Lafayette Dollar Commemorative, silver, *Uncirculated*	36,026	50.00	180.00	1900.00 to 7000.00 (MS-60 to MS-65)	800.00 to 2600.00 to 18,000.00 (MS-60 to MS-63 to MS-65)
1915-S Panama-Pacific $50 Gold Piece, Round, gold, *Uncirculated*	483	2500.00	5000.00	20,000.00 to 38,000.00 (MS-60 to MS-65)	32,000.00 to 46,000.00 to 115,000.00 (MS-60 to MS-63 to MS-65)
1849 $10 Gold Piece, Moffat & Co. (private California), gold, *Uncirculated*	——	250.00	—— (unpriced in UNC)	8000.00	13,000.00
1861 Confederate Half Dollar, Restrike, silver, *Uncirculated*	500 (for the "Restrike"—*not* the Scott Token)	475.00	675.00	1100.00	2750.00

From *A GUIDE BOOK OF UNITED STATES COINS*® by R.S. Yeoman, © 1961, 1971, 1981, & 1991 Western Publishing Company, Inc. Used by permission.

Why Coin Prices Rise

As you can see from the charts, the long-term trend is rising coin prices, except for some decreases from 1981 to 1991 due to changing coin grading standards for Uncirculated coins; the general "flat" coin market of the 1980s, after the "crash" from the boom period of 1979-81; and moderate (rather than runaway) inflation of the 1980s U.S. economy.

So, are coins a good investment? That depends on which coins you buy (partially luck), getting honest quality for your money, when you bought the coins (partially luck), and when you sell them (your choice, but no guarantee that you've picked the "right" time to sell). You would have profited handsomely if you bought a *1955 Doubled Die Cent* in pristine UNC condition in 1961 and sold it well-preserved in 1991. You would have lost money if you bought a *1936 Proof Set* in 1981 and sold it in 1991.

Coin prices rise for the following reasons:

1. Inflation in the general economy pushes the price of everything up over time.

2. The natural "attrition" and deterioration of the quality and quantity of coins over the years as coins are mishandled, lost, and age (with deleterious effects to their metal surfaces).

3. Increasing knowledge by collectors and dealers results in increased demand for "better" coins, the recognition of "sleepers," and the publicity of correctly perceived "condition census" scarcity.

4. Fads come and go with coin collecting, as with

other human endeavors. When a certain type of coin becomes the latest collecting fad, the market price skyrockets, and success builds on success, resulting in investors jumping in on the action and igniting a boom market.

5. Market promotion, justified or otherwise, by coin dealers can up the price of a type of coin. Prime example: *Morgan Dollars* in the 1980s weathered a roller coaster price ride up and down, as grading standards, encapsulation ("slabbing"), and overpromotion affected their sales.

6. Increasing numbers of collectors and increasing personal wealth of collectors push coin prices up.

And because the long-term trend of all six of the preceding factors is towards continuation and acceleration of them, *the long-term trend of coin prices is towards increases*.

THE COIN DEALER NEWSLETTER (CDN)

Published weekly since 1963, the *COIN DEALER Newsletter* (as the publication is titled)—also known as the "Greysheet" because of its color and by its *CDN* initials — reports the national, dealer-to-dealer, wholesale coin market, monitoring transactions and offers to buy and sell coins sight-seen. The *CDN* covers "Bid and Ask" prices for most commonly collected U.S. coin types and series. "Bid" price is what a dealer is willing to pay; "ask" price is what a dealer would like to get for a coin. Subscribers to the *CDN* also receive a free monthly supplement called the *Monthly Summary*, which carries a two-page small print analysis of the current coin market.

The same company also publishes the *CERTIFIED COIN DEALER Newsletter* (the "Bluesheet") —a weekly report on the highest known bids of actively traded PCGS, NGC, ANACS, and NCI coins certified by those grading services. It is also known as the *CCDN*.

Subscription rates for the *CDN* are: $50 for 6 months, $89 for 1 year, $147 for 2 years. The *CCDN* is $30 for 3 months, $56 for 6 months, $99 for 1 year. The price is not cheap, but the information is up to date, and the bigger U.S. coin dealers subscribe to these newsletters, as do serious investors; you don't have to be a dealer to subscribe.

Ron Downing, the President of the company, has told me that readers of this book may obtain a free sample copy of the *CDN* or *CCDN* upon sending a No. 10, business-sized, self-addressed stamped envelope to the company's headquarters:

COIN DEALER Newsletter
P.O. Box 11099
Torrance, CA 90510

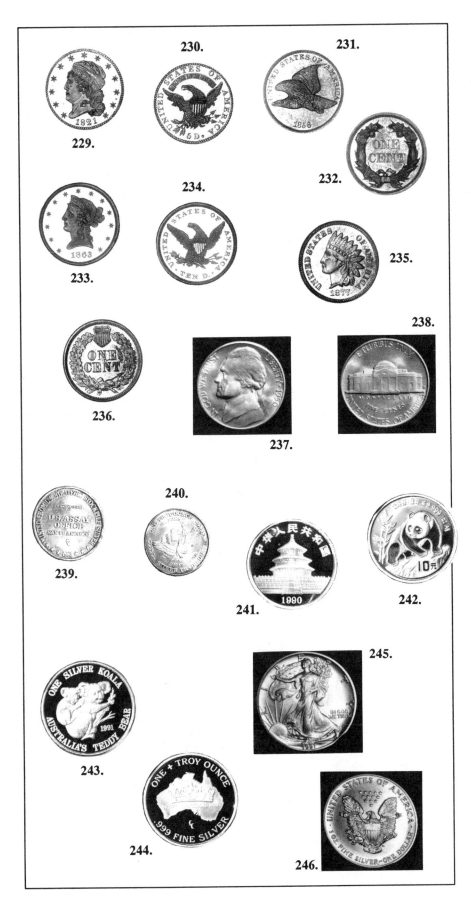

230.

231.

229.

234.

232.

233.

235.

238.

236.

237.

240.

239.

241.

242.

245.

243.

244.

246.

229. The only Proof 1821 *Half Eagle* (*$5 Gold Piece*) in private hands. Lot #773 of the Bowers and Merena *Norweb* sale of October 13, 1987. Catalog description states, in part: "Proof-63 to 64. A glittering, gorgeous specimen with rich golden coloration ... one of just two known to exist, the other being in the Smithsonian Institution." Realized $198,000 (including 10% buyer's fee). Courtesy Bowers and Merena, Inc.

230. Reverse of the 1821 Proof *Half Eagle* from the previous photo. Randall Lot #926 in 1885; ex: Col. E.H.R. Green; Lot #237 of the King Farouk sale of February 1954. Something for the serious coin investor. Courtesy Bowers and Merena, Inc.

231. 1856 *Flying Eagle Cent* in "Proof-65." Lot #25 of the Bowers and Merena *Saccone* sale of November 6, 1989. Designed by James B. Longacre, the 1856 *Flying Eagle Cent* is, by general consensus, a pattern of the "small cents" design that replaced the *Large Cents*, thus showing that the public was willing to accept a coin whose face value was less than its bullion value. The only regular U.S. coin with an eagle on the obverse. Always popular, always in demand; buy them with nice color and no problems. Realized $13,200 (including 10% buyer's fee). Courtesy Bowers and Merena, Inc.

232. Reverse of the 1856 Proof *Flying Eagle Cent* from the previous photo. It is a small coin (compared to a *Silver Dollar*, for example), so be sure to inspect it carefully before buying it. Any surface flaws or blemishes that you overlook will most definitely be found by your prospective buyer when you go to sell the coin. Courtesy Bowers and Merena, Inc.

233. 1863 Proof *Eagle ($10 Gold Piece)*. Lot #555 of the Bowers and Merena *Saccone* sale of November 6, 1989. Catalog states, in part: "Proof-64 to 65. A glittering gem specimen which ranks as one of the very finest of 10 or fewer estimated to exist today, at least two or three of which are impaired, and two of which are impounded in institutional collections (the American Numismatic Society and the Smithsonian Institution)." Realized $39,600 (including 10% buyer's fee). Courtesy Bowers and Merena, Inc.

234. Reverse of the 1863 Proof *Eagle* from the previous photo. Exquisite. Acquired by Ambassador and Mrs. R. Henry Norweb from the Hollinbeck Coin Company, June 1953. Proof 19th century U.S. gold coins have proven good *long-term* investments for astute (and lucky) buyers. Courtesy Bowers and Merena, Inc.

235. 1877 *Indian Head Cent*, Uncirculated business strike. Lot #170 of the Bowers and Merena *Norweb* sale of October 12, 1987. Catalog notations state, in part: "Although this issue does not have the lowest mintage (that honor lies with the 1909-S) it is the most highly sought after issue in the series. Even heavily worn issues command a premium. At the time of issue, the rarity of the 1877 cent was not recognized, and it was not until the turn of the century that people noticed how few were actually in circulation ..." 852,500 minted. MS-64 to 65, as per catalog. Realized $3,520 (including 10% buyer's fee). Courtesy Bowers and Merena, Inc.

236. Reverse of the 1877 *Indian Head Cent* from the previous photo.

Cleaned, scratched, unpleasantly colored, "carbon spotted," and weakly struck coins, *Indian Cents* or otherwise, are worth less than pristine original specimens. This is especially so with copper coins, which seem to absorb the ravages of time with the readiness that a sponge soaks up water. Beware of altered dates and outright counterfeits in 1877 *Cents*. Courtesy Bowers and Merena, Inc.

237. 1950 Denver Mint nickel *5¢ Piece*, commonly called the "*1950-D Jefferson Nickel.*" Speculation can run up the price of coins, and the 1950-D "*Nickel*" is a prime example. Its market price rose from 5¢ in 1950 when minted, to 15¢ in 1951, to $17 in the early 1960s when the roll craze was booming. Now you can buy a choice Uncirculated specimen, like this one, for $10 or less. COIN VALUES DON'T CONSTANTLY GO UP! Author's collection.

238. Reverse of the 1950-D *Jefferson* "*Nickel*" from the previous photo. Notice the mintmark "D" to the right of the Monticello building. "Full steps" in front of the building command a premium when the coin is sold. 2,630,030 minted—certainly not a "rare" coin by anybody's definition. Author's collection.

239. Exactly one troy ounce of pure silver (ignoring "wear" loss!) resides in this "silver round" minted from the U.S. Strategic Stockpile of silver, formerly stored at the U.S. Assay Office (now U.S. Mint), San Francisco. "Bullion" silver for the silver investor. Author's collection.

240. Other side of the "silver round" from the previous photo. Inscription reads: ONE TROY OUNCE/

31.1 GRAMS/.999 FINE SILVER/ SILVER TRADE UNIT, and the piece bears a rather hastily designed eagle and American flag. For the silver bullion investor. Author's collection.

241. People's Republic of China *10-Yuan* silver bullion Proof (commonly called a "Silver Panda") of 1990. Issued yearly with slight design changes. One troy ounce, .999 fine silver. For the silver bullion investor. Author's collection.

242. Reverse of the Chinese *10-Yuan* silver bullion coin from the last photo. The author did not buy Chinese bullion coins after the Tian An Men massacre and purchased this specimen only to photograph for this book. Politics can influence coin collecting; each collector is a free agent who must decide which coins to buy and which not to buy. Author's collection.

243. Australian "*One Silver Koala*" bullion issue of 1991. Australia's response to the worldwide demand from investors for silver bullion "rounds." Proof. Author's collection.

244. Reverse of Australian *One Silver Koala* from previous photo. New Queensland Mint. Proof. Author's collection.

245. U.S. *Silver Eagle* silver bullion coin of 1991. Issued yearly since 1986, with obverse being Adolph A. Weinman's *Walking Liberty Half Dollar* design. Author's collection.

246. U.S. *Silver Eagle* reverse. One troy ounce fine silver, $1 face value. Issued for the silver bullion market. Reverse designed by John Mercanti. Author's collection.

16

Forgeries, Fakes, and Errors

A coin may not be what it appears to be. It may have been cleaned by polishing, whizzing, dipping, washing, or rubbing. It may have faked toning, faked luster, and plugged holes or depressions. It may have a mintmark added, mintmark removed, altered date, or altered lettering. It may be re-engraved, electroplated, reprocessed, recolored, or made to look like a Proof. It may be an outright counterfeit, made by casting, electrotyping, or die-striking. And it may be an error, either genuine (from the Mint) or artificial (faked by a con artist).

You are not insulting the seller when you meticulously inspect an expensive coin before you buy it. Any dealer who values his reputation more than he needs to make a quick buck will be happy to have you submit an expensive coin to a third-party authentication and grading service (see Chapter 6 for addresses) *before* the sale is finalized.

This chapter will introduce you to the subject of altered and counterfeit coins, not make you an expert at detecting such. True authority in a hobby/collectible discipline like coin collecting comes from long experience in handling and studying the objects in question. You don't become an expert from reading a book chapter or listening to a quick lecture! By endlessly studying what genuine coins look like, we prepare ourselves for the unexpected intrusion of a faked piece while we're perusing a fresh selection of coins that we've never seen before. References do help, and the more numismatic books in your library (or better yet, in your head), the more likely you are to resist deception and attempted larceny by those who prey on the ill-informed.

In the article entitled "Some Observations upon the Counterfeiting of Coins and Medals" by Lyman Haynes Low, which originally appeared in the July 1895 issue of the *American Journal of Numismatics* of the American Numismatics Society (reprinted 1979 by Sanford J. Durst, New York, NY; reprinted here with permission of Durst Publications, Ltd.), Mr. Low explains:

When we have met a friend, and have become thoroughly familiar with his features, we are able to recognize the correctness of his likeness at sight, and to discover without an effort the slightest defect or departure from exactness. This habit of mind is equally applicable to every alteration of date, etc., upon coins, and a faithful observation is sure to result in the detection of any attempt to deceive. None of these are so perfect as to pass the careful scrutiny of a trained eye.

CLEANED COINS

Because untoned, brilliant shiny coins are preferred by most collectors (and almost all investors), coins are cleaned to defraud the unwary. You always see ads from dealers "begging" to buy ORIGINAL, PROBLEM-FREE COINS. These coins are always in demand because most coins have problems (or seem to acquire problems, if you look at them long enough!). "Original cabinet toning" means never having been cleaned; the toning may or may not be "pretty," and may or may not be worth buying. "Problem-free" means a coin with no damage or other distracting surface blemishes. A problem-free coin may be *any* grade. For example: a problem-free GOOD grade translates as "honest wear, design visible but well-worn, no distracting scratches or tarnish, definitely having no evidence of ever having been cleaned or artificially colored."

Washing

The most mild cleaning treatment for a coin is to wash it in distilled water or an inert neutral solvent. This usually results in no damage and may even remove surface dirt and oil. Adding soap to the water will increase its cleansing effectiveness, and freshly unearthed buried coin hoards are often given a soap washing. If the coin is scrubbed with a brush or harshly patted dry with a towel, some hairline surface scratches may become visible.

Dipping

Dipping usually refers to placing a coin momentarily in an acid bath to give it a false luster. Dipping removes some metal molecules every time the coin is dipped, resulting in loss of original *Mint bloom*. Dipped coins lack original toning and look "too new" for the coins' age. Many old U.S. coins (especially silver) were cleaned a long time ago and have since "retoned" so that they look almost original. Don't confuse acid dipping (which is harmful) with neutral solvent cleaning (which is usually harmless). Ancient silver coins have been successfully dipped to remove surface grime, an exception to the rule of no dipping. This is the source of all those shiny silver Roman *denarii* that were discovered by treasure hunters as clumps of encrusted metal. Acid is used to bring out the date in worn

Buffalo Nickels, but the coins' market value is destroyed.

Whizzing

Whizzing means scraping the coin with a wire brush on an electric tool. It leaves telltale hairline scratches all over a coin's surface, sometimes parallel to each other in one direction. From a distance the coin looks Uncirculated. Up close, maybe under magnification if necessary to detect an "expert" job, the coin looks "wrong." Whizzed copper coins look unnaturally orange.

Chemical Cleaning

Actually related to the narrowly-defined technique of "dipping," the chemical cleaning of coins generally includes semi-corrosive cleansing agents like baking soda or drain cleaner. Chemical cleaning with varying strengths of solution makes coins appear uniformly bright, unlike the variable toning shades on an original coin.

Rubbing

Copper and silver coins may be rubbed with a pencil eraser to remove surface tarnish. Rubbing leaves a disturbingly dull shine on the coin, and every knowledgeable collector will pass up a coin so treated. Try it on a *Lincoln Cent* that has turned brown (not a rare one!). Rubbing, like most coin cleaning, causes the coin to appear "too shiny" for its age and grade. A coin grading Very Good or Fine doesn't shine like an Uncirculated specimen.

PATINA (TONING)

Patina is the natural colored oxidation layer on the surface of a coin. Beautiful patina makes a coin valuable. Original patina is almost always preferable to shiny cleaned coins. Toning often begins at the coin's periphery and works its way inward over the years. This is especially true for coins that were housed in albums, with cardboard touching their edges. Patina is also called *toning*.

Genuine toning should exhibit gradual shade gradations, not abrupt changes from color to color, except for coins that were stored in such a manner that they were partially exposed to sulfur material (like coin folders or cloth coin bags). Just about any color is possible with toned coins, with silver specimens showing the most vivid shades. I like old silver coins with golden centers, changing to green, blue, or violet as you go towards the rims. The worst silver toning is splotchy gray/black, and don't let a dealer sell you a coin whose toning you don't like ("original" isn't always nice-looking).

Peace Dollars, for example, tend to have less colorful toning than *Morgan Dollars* because *Peace Dollars* are more recent and haven't been in the Mint bags as long. I like *Peace Dollars* with rich golden toning.

Buffalo Nickels tend towards steel blue-gray in tone, and some of the nicest ones are golden yellow or rainbow colored. Copper coins tend to tone brown, blue, and green. A nicely patinated ancient Roman bronze *sestertius* with lightly greened fields highlighted by dark brown portrait and lettering *should be left alone*; you'll never duplicate that 1,900-year-old toning once you start messing around with the coin by cleaning it in a mistaken attempt to "improve" its antique appearance!

Artificial Toning

Artificially toned coins often lack underlying Mint luster. They're colorful but "dull." Bright, gaudy, iridescent colors are always suspect on a coin. It may be natural toning, but then again, it may be a heat-treated or chemically altered coin. People stick coins in ovens, blow cigarette smoke on them, and bury them in the ground to create "instant toning." A high school chemistry lab has all kinds of metal toning reagents; I can verify that because I used to be a chemistry teacher.

Artificial toning may be used to hide coin defects like scratches, hairlines, altered mintmarks, repairs, altered dates, and light wear in AU coins that purport to be UNC. Artificial toning is epidemic on *Large Cents* and all U.S. *Silver Dollars* from *Bust* varieties through *Peace Dollars*. Faked toning often looks streaked and blotchy, not smooth and gradual in shades. Mint luster may be gone under artificial toning, a sure sign of tampering. What usually happens is that an ugly tarnished coin is cleaned, artificially toned, then pawned off as "Original Uncirculated."

ALTERED COINS

Altered coins are deliberate frauds. While it is legal to sell cleaned and retoned coins offered *for what they are*, coins whose designs are knowingly altered and then fictitiously sold as genuine rarities are criminal deceptions, worthy of a jail sentence.

Mintmark Removal (Etching)

Mintmark removal is one of the easiest coin alterations to make, although a good job requires skill. A 10-power or 30-power (ten to thirty times natural size) magnification lens of quality optics (color-corrected, non-distorting images) is needed for visual examination of coin details, like mintmarks. It is best to compare a suspected coin with a genuine one of the time period. There should be no evidence that a mintmark was ever there for a genuine *1895 Morgan Dollar* of which 880 *Proofs* were released to the public; the "O" or "S" may be removed from a New Orleans or San Francisco-dated *1895 Dollar*. The *1922 "Plain" Lincoln Cent* is often faked by removing the "D" from a Denver variety; get this coin authenticated.

Mintmark Adding (Adhesion and Chasing)

A mintmark may be soldered onto a coin to make it appear to be a valuable mintmarked variety. On genuine coins, look for smooth metal flow lines and clean junctures between the mintmark and field. The *1914-D Lincoln Cent, 1916-D Mercury Dime*, and *1932-D* and *S Washington Quarters* have been produced with mintmarks stuck onto plain Philadelphia versions. Get these coins authenticated.

"Chasing" is the delicate art of fashioning a mintmark (or whatever) by pushing metal across the coin's surface so that enough metal can be accumulated from which to engrave a mintmark. *Adhesion* means sticking a mintmark (or whatever) onto a coin, presumably by cutting it off a cheap coin. Beware of such work done a long time ago, and the coin "retoned."

Altered Dates

A scarce *1914-D Lincoln Cent* "look-alike"" can be produced by shaving down the first numeral "4" in the date of a *1944-D Cent* so that it resembles a "1"—distinguishing traits of this altered coin are (1) tool marks around the suspicious numeral 1, (2) uneven spacing between numerals, (3) the V.D.B. is on the shoulder of a genuine *1944-D Cent*, no V.D.B. at all on the *1914-D Cent*, and (4) the color is different due to slightly different alloy. A conscientious "coin doctor" will take pains to scrape off the shoulder V.D.B. and will try to recolor the contrived *1914-D Cent* so it looks authentic.

Assume that any rare date coin has been altered and inspect it well or get it certified when in doubt. Some commonly altered dates:

- ❑ *1856 Flying Eagle Cent* from an *1858 Large Letter Flying Eagle,* by cutting the last "8" into a "6".
- ❑ *1877 Indian Cent* from another *Cent* in the 1870s, with the last digit removed and replaced by a "7".
- ❑ *1909-S VDB Lincoln Cent* from soldered-on "S" mintmarks, etched VDB initials, etc., changed from other dates.
- ❑ *1909-S Cent* from a *1919-S Cent*.
- ❑ *1914-D Cent* from a shaved *1944-D Cent*.
- ❑ *1931-S Cent* from a *1936-S Cent*.
- ❑ *1916-D Dimes* from other dates, e.g., *1926-D*.
- ❑ *1923-S Liberty Standing Quarter* from a *1928-S Quarter*.
- ❑ *1893-S Morgan Dollar* from an *1898-S Dollar*.
- ❑ *1904-S Morgan Dollar* from a *1900-S* or *1901-S Dollar* with the last digit removed and a "4" transplanted. All genuine *1904-S Dollars* have a large "S".

Altered Devices

Beware of a faked *1937-D* "*3-legged Buffalo Nickel*" (or a *1936* "*3-legged*" for that matter!) made from a normal coin with the leg removed by acid action or etching. Get this coin authenticated.

The *1864* "*No L*" Bronze *Indian Head Cent* is shaved to mimic the pointed bust *1864-L* variety, and an "L" added at the bottom of the headdress.

The *1922 Grant Memorial* commemorative silver *Half Dollar* comes in two varieties: one with a little five-pointed "star" in the obverse field above the letter "N" of the word "GRANT" and the more common type lacking the star. In UNC grades, the "with star" variety sells for six times the price of the

"no star" coin, leading the very-industrious forger to punch in a star. The problem is compounded because the original starred variety has an *incuse* (depressed) star, which is a lot easier to fake than a *relief* (raised) star. Faked stars may be irregular in appearance, and the opposite side of the coin (reverse) *may* be a little flattened from the punching process on the altered coin.

Electroplating

Lead-based gold coin counterfeits are electroplated with gold to look like solid gold coins. Rusty *1943 steel Lincoln Cents* are surface stripped, then recolored by electroplating with fresh zinc. These *reprocessed* steel cents are usually brighter than the normal ones, and they often show wear and scratches partially covered over by the replating, a lot of work for a cheap coin.

Rare *1943 bronze cents* can be imitated by copper electroplating a *1943 steel cent*. The first test for a suspicious specimen is to use a magnet: steel cents "jump" towards the magnetic field; genuine solid "copper" ones are unaffected. More dangerous are cast and die-struck counterfeits of the *1943 bronze cent* — these are unaffected by magnets, just like genuine examples of this rarity. Get the coin authenticated before buying it.

FAKED PROOFS

Just because somebody says it is *Proof* doesn't necessarily mean it is. Genuine high grade *Proofs* must have original Mint luster on all parts of the coin design, including the letters and central devices for 19th century and early 20th century U.S. *Proofs*. Early 20th century U.S. *matte Proofs* are an exception, as these are derived from sandblasted dies without mirror surfaces. Even experts will debate whether or not a coin is in fact a *matte Proof*. Recent (post-1980) U.S. *Proof* coins tend to be heavily "frosted" in the devices because the devices aren't polished on the dies like the fields are.

Proofs often have higher rims and better all-over striking because of the care with which they were made. Polished business strikes may pretend to be *Proofs*, and for heavily "impaired" *Proofs*, it may be a bit difficult to distinguish the genuine "circulated" *Proof* coin from a "*Proof*-like" business strike.

RE-ENGRAVING, PLUGGING, ETC.

Worn and faint features of a coin may be fraudulently enhanced by re-engraving. Holes and defective depressions may be "plugged" with fresh metal filler. When a coin is advertised as "expertly repaired," it may be an honest compliment to the skill of the "coin doctor," or it may be a subtle insult to the assumed observation ability of the potential purchaser. A repaired coin is repaired; let the buyer decide just how "expertly" it was done. *It is not illegal to sell altered coins if they are accurately described with their alterations mentioned.* It is against the law to pass a coin off, knowing that its description is fraudulent. It is against the law to sell outright counterfeits or even to possess them.

COUNTERFEIT COINS

Counterfeiting began not long after the first coins were invented more than twenty-five centuries ago in ancient Lydia. The temptation to "get something for nothing" runs deeply in the souls of people who would rather cheat their neighbors than earn their wealth honestly. A counterfeit coin is totally spurious—it was made by a private individual, not by an "official" Mint (government or private). Counterfeit coins are of two categories: those made to pass as current circulating money of the realm, and those made for their numismatic value (usually copies of rare coins) to deceive coin collectors.

Penalties for Counterfeiting

In ancient Rome, counterfeiters were burned alive or fed to the animals in the arena. King Canute, an 11th century A.D. monarch of England, Denmark, and Norway, cut off the hands of counterfeiters (punishment one might receive in Saudi Arabia today). In the late 18th century, some authorities believe that two-thirds of the coins circulating in England were counterfeit. Paper money in Colonial America often bore the warning: "Tis Death to Counterfeit" although penalties weren't always capital upon conviction. Carl Wilhelm Becker (1772-1830) was a famous forger of ancient Greek and Roman coins, known as the "Becker forgeries" today, made for the growing collector interest in ancients at that time. Throughout the 19th century, many notable coin cabinets (collections) had unattributed counterfeits mixed with the genuine pieces, before further research and publication of how to detect such fakes was done.

United States Secret Service

Organized in 1865, the U.S. Secret Service (currently in the Department of the Treasury) is charged with, among other things (such as protecting the President and his family), the apprehending of U.S. residents suspected of counterfeiting. In response to my request for information on coin counterfeiting for use in this book, Robert R. Snow, Assistant Director, Office of Government Liaison and Public Affairs, U.S. Secret Service, sent me a letter in which he states:

> *It is not legal to possess counterfeit coins ... There is no such thing as a "replica" that is legal. Most of our coin cases involve alteration of genuine coins, i.e., removing mint marks, or changing dates. Actual counterfeiting of coins is usually done overseas and involves gold coins. They often have a higher gold content than the genuine but demand very high prices because of their numismatic value (if they were genuine).*

U.S. Counterfeiting Law

Mr. Snow was also kind enough to send me photocopies of the *U.S. Criminal Code* statutes that apply to counterfeiting: "Title 18, Section 485. Coins or bars" states:

> *Whoever falsely makes, forges, or counterfeits any coin or bar in resemblance or similitude of any coin of a denomination higher than 5 cents or any gold or silver bar coined or stamped at any mint or assay office of the United States, or in resemblance or similitude of any foreign gold or silver coin current in the United States or in actual use and circulation as money within the United States; or*

Whoever passes, utters, publishes, sells, possesses, or brings into the United States any false, forged, or counterfeit coin or bar, knowing the same to be false, forged, or counterfeit, with intent to defraud any body politic or corporate, or any person, or attempts the commission of any offense described in this paragraph—

Shall be fined not more than $5,000 or imprisoned not more than fifteen years or both.

U.S. Criminal Code Title 18, Section 487 prohibits making or possessing counterfeit dies or molds for U.S. coins; and Section 488 prohibits the same for foreign coins. Section 489 prohibits the making or possessing of U.S. or foreign coin "likenesses" (i.e., replicas or facsimiles), and Section 490 prohibits the counterfeiting of U.S. minor coins (1-cent and 5-cent pieces). Penalties vary for these other offenses. Section 492 requires the "Forfeiture of counterfeit paraphernalia"; that is, you must surrender counterfeit coins and devices to make such to an agent of the Treasury Department, or other proper officer, or "be fined not more than $100 or imprisoned not more than one year, or both." You get a receipt for the counterfeit coin, but you don't get the coin back unless it proves to be genuine. Other Sections of the *Code* apply to counterfeiting paper money, bonds, etc.

TYPES OF COUNTERFEIT COINS

There are three basic methods of making counterfeit coins: casting, electrotyping, and die-striking.

Cast Counterfeits

Cast counterfeits are made by producing two molds (obverse and reverse sides) and pouring molten metal of the proper alloy between the molds. The molds are taken off of a genuine coin, so all counterfeits subsequently cast from that coin's mold impressions will look alike, including any surface flaws in the original coin. *Replicas* (legal cast counterfeits) have been extensively made over the years for U.S. Colonial coins, and some of these replicas may bear the inscription "COPY" or "REPLICA" on the forgery. Crooks will file this inscription off, however.

"Quality" cast counterfeits are made by the lost wax process. Cast counterfeit coins may show remnants of a telltale "joint line" along the coins' edges —where the two molds were brought together—al-

though a good casting forger will carefully file away this line. Ancient coins may have such a line but be genuine.

Another feature present in some cast coins is a little "bubble" or "pimple"—either in relief or incuse —that formed when some foreign matter got between the mold and the coin. Microscopic examination may be required to detect these casting idiosyncrasies, which may be "constant varieties" if the flaw is in the mold.

Electrotype Counterfeits

Electrotypes are counterfeits that consist of two thin pieces of metal (the obverse and reverse sides) that are joined together, sandwiching a base metal "core" (often lead). Electrotypes are produced by taking wax impressions of each side of a coin, coating them with graphite, then suspending them in an electrolytic solution, which gradually deposits a thin metal "shell" on the graphite-coated wax, resulting in an obverse or reverse "face," which is then affixed to its opposite counterpart clamped on either side of the base metal core.

Early U.S. copper coins were electrotyped extensively, even by U.S. Mint employees in the 19th century for "honest" sale to collectors (who knew they were buying "copies" of real coins).

Electrotypes can be identified by the "line" along their edges, where the two mold halves came together. Also they may have a different specific gravity (weight) than genuine coins. The American Numismatic Society Museum in New York City (see Chapter 19) has an interesting collection of electrotypes.

Die-struck Counterfeits

Die-struck counterfeits are made from counterfeit dies. These counterfeits are potentially the most deceptive because they are made the same way that real coins are made. A die is prepared by machine-engraving from a genuine coin sample (similar to the Janvier reducing process) or by "impacting" by forcing a genuine coin under great pressure into a softened steel blank (which will be used as the counterfeit die).

Die-struck counterfeits will look much like genuine coins, including having the same alloy composition and many of the striking characteristics of real coins. Die-struck counterfeits, however, will have constant "flaws" that can be detected positively when compared with genuine die-struck examples in quantity.

Dangerous die-struck counterfeits are known of: the *1856 Flying Eagle Cent, 1909-S VDB Lincoln Cent, 1955 Doubled Die Lincoln Cent, 1937-D "3-Legged Buffalo Nickel"* (manufactured in Italy from spark-erosion dies), *1939-D* and *1950-D Jefferson Nickels* (made in quantity by a Dallas, Texas counterfeiter, since sentenced to fifteen years in prison), *1916-D Mercury Dime*, and many U.S. gold coins.

U.S. gold coins have been extensively counterfeited in places like Hong Kong, Iran, Italy, Lebanon, and Morocco. The *U.S. $3 gold pieces* of 1854-1889 have been so heavily counterfeited that many experts believe that more counterfeits may exist than genuine specimens! Gold coins are counterfeited for one of two reasons: low gold alloy content or underweight planchet (to sell for fraudulent intrinsic [bullion] value), or proper weight and gold content but of rare date or variety (to sell for fraudulent numismatic premium value). All U.S. gold coin series should be suspect for counterfeits, which generally show one or more of these traits: heavy die polish, constant "flaws," cracks, weak devices, wrong diameter, wrong weight, rough fields, surface "pimples," missing features, "fuzzy" junctures of relief design features where they meet the field.

"Safe" Detection Devices for Counterfeit Coins

1. Comparison with a known genuine specimen of the same type, date, and variety is the best way to start your "testing" of a questionable piece.

2. Microscopic examination, preferably under a 30-power three-dimensional dissecting microscope (like the ones used in biology labs).

3. Weighing the coin with a gram scale (either electronic or "balance" type) to compare against known weights.

4. Measuring the diameter and thickness with a caliper (or a millimeter ruler if that's all you have)—modern machine-struck coins have narrow dimensional tolerances.

5. Checking with a magnet to see if the coin is

magnetic—as pre-1982 Canadian "*Nickels*" should be—and as genuine *1943 U.S. bronze Lincoln Cents* should not be!

Avoid chemical tampering with a coin. And don't scratch it, even along the edge, to see if its metal is "pure."

COINAGE ERRORS

Coinage errors warrant a whole book in themselves (and several nice ones exist: see the Hudgeons, Margolis, Spadone, and Taxay books in the Bibliography). Some collectors find Mint-caused coin errors to be an intriguing specialty. Not all errors are of great value; indeed, many (such as recent off-struck *Lincoln Cents*) can be obtained for only a couple of dollars over face value. DON'T OVERPAY FOR A COIN ERROR. Find out what the error market says a particular coin should be worth. Get a copy of *Error Trends Coin Magazine* (see Chapter 17) to check latest coin error retail prices.

Examples of Coinage Errors

Here are examples of some of the more popularly collected coinage errors; i.e., "mistakes" that were produced at the Mint when the coins were being made:

ABNORMAL REEDING—Wrong number or wrong orientation of "grooves" on a coin's edge.

BROADSTRIKE—The "collar" didn't hold the "edges" of the coin's metal in place during striking. Ancient coins are normally broadstruck because they didn't use collars then.

BROCKAGE — Mis-struck coin showing obverse impression on the reverse, for example. Caused by a newly struck coin adhering to a die, then acting as a "die" itself when a fresh planchet is struck.

CLASHED DIES — When two dies hit each other without a planchet between them, resulting in die impressions being transferred between the dies, and then such impressions being struck on a planchet.

CLIPPED PLANCHET—Improperly punched planchet, usually showing a "piece" out of the resultant coin. Often faked.

DIE BREAK—When a whole piece of metal is

torn away from a die, resulting in an abnormal "raised" area on the coin struck from such a die.

DIE CRACK—A split in the die (with no loss of die metal), resulting in a coin with an irregular "raised" line that isn't part of the intended design.

DOUBLED DIE—A doubled impression in a die, resulting in a doubled expression on the coin. Caused when the hub is rotated between impressions when preparing a working die. Example: the *1955 Doubled Die Cent*. Not to be confused with Double Struck.

DOUBLE STRIKE—Coin produced from unaligned sequential die strikes, resulting in duplicated design images on the coin. This is a striking error, not a die error (as in Doubled Die coins).

EDGE ERRORS — Include wrong lettering, wrong reeding, smooth edge by error, edge strike (coin struck on edge by a non-edge die), split edge (planchet), jammed edge (weak strike or non-strike along the edge).

EXTRA METAL—Stray piece of metal adhering to planchet during striking. May appear as a "spur" along the edge of the resultant coin.

FILLED DIE—Portion of the die incuse engraving gets filled with foreign matter, resulting in that portion of the coin's design being weakly struck or nonexistent. A variety of the "struck through" family of errors. The *1922 "Plain" Lincoln Cent* is an example of a filled die coin—the mintmark "D" was filled on the working die, so coins struck from it have a faint or nonexistent "D".

INCOMPLETE DIE — A die that is not finished, but used to strike a coin.

LAMINATION—Splitting and flaking of metal off a coin or planchet. The split layers may still be visible on the finished coin, or may have been broken off.

MINTMARK ERRORS — Include double punched, missing mintmark, misaligned mintmark, over mintmark (punched over another mintmark, either the same or different).

MULE—Coin made from two dies that are not supposed to be used together, such as the obverse of a *Dime* and the reverse of a *Nickel*. Also called "mismatched dies."

MULTIPLE STRIKE — A coin that has been struck more than once, with at least two of the strikes out of alignment. Double and triple strikes are types of multiple strikes. Triple struck coins are rare.

NUMERAL ERRORS—Include missing numbers, wrong date, overdates, inverted numeral, misaligned numeral.

OFF-CENTER—Coin struck partly on, partly off the planchet, resulting in a blank area on part of the finished coin.

OVERDATE—Coin on which one or more of the numerals in the date is superimposed over another numeral (either the same or different), due to the numeral being punched over another numeral in the die.

OVER MINTMARK — One mintmark superimposed over another, the same or different. Example: D over S, written as D/S in shorthand.

OVERSTRIKE—A coin struck on a previously struck coin; may or may not be the same type of coin. Common with U.S. Colonials, which were struck on any available "planchet," including other coins. Sometimes used synonymously with "double strike."

PLANCHET IMPERFECTIONS—Evident before, during, and after striking. Common with ancient through Colonial coins because of poor quality control and lack of uniformity in planchet preparation. "Clipping" is a planchet imperfection.

RECUT DIE OR HUB—"Reentry" of an engraved portion of a die. Not strictly an error unless the recutting "overlap" inadvertently shows on the finished coin.

REPUNCHING—The same aspect of a coin's design is punched more than once into the die, resulting in overlapping due to misalignment of the punch between entries into the die. Examples: repunched dates, repunched mintmarks, repunched devices.

ROTATED DIE—Coin is struck from dies that are not normally oriented, resulting in the reverse not being in proper alignment with the obverse design. Normal on ancient coins.

STRUCK THROUGH — When some foreign object (including a piece of stray metal) gets between a die and the planchet during striking, resulting in the object's impression appearing on the finished coin.

UNIFACE STRIKE — A coin struck on only one side, caused by a planchet or other coin coming between the planchet and one of the dies. May be intentionally uniface as a non-error piece.

UNSTRUCK PLANCHET — A planchet that escaped the minting process without being struck at all. Also called a "blank."

WRONG DESIGN — Wrong lettering, wrong numerals, wrong date, wrong motto, etc.

WRONG METAL—May be one of several different categories: completely different type of metal, wrong alloy mixture, wrong "cladding," struck on a foreign coin planchet, false planchet (struck on a piece of metal that was never meant to be a coin). The *1943 bronze Lincoln Cent* is a wrong metal error.

247.

248.

249.

250.

251.

252.

253.

254.

247. Copy of 1652 *Pine Tree Shilling* (facsimile, not genuine). Crude and unlikely to fool anyone. Author's former "collection."

248. Reverse of 1652 *Pine Tree Shilling* copy (facsimile, not genuine) from previous photo. For genuine specimen, see photo in Chapter 2. Author's former "collection."

249. Copy of Bolivia (Potosi) *8-Reales* piece (facsimile, not genuine). Crude and unlikely to fool anyone. Author's former "collection."

250. Other side of Bolivian *8-Reales* piece facsimile (not genuine). Notice the word "COPY" in incuse lettering at lower right of coin. With "well-made" facsimile coins, a crook will sometimes obliterate the disclaiming word "COPY" or "FAC-SIMILE" and try to sell such pieces as genuine specimens to gullible buyers. Author's former "collection."

251. This 1861 New Orleans Mint silver *Half Dollar* has been "plugged" at the top of Liberty's head, not a very good job of workmanship, but obvious for the photo's purpose. So-called "expert plugging" consists of filling coin holes with a metal appearing similar to that which the coin was made of, and blending the plug's surface in with the rest of the coin's design. Heavy toning (artificial or otherwise) will sometimes mask plugs and other coin defects. Author's collection.

252. Reverse of plugged 1861-O *Half Dollar*. It is legal to buy or sell "doctored" coins, *provided* that the defects are pointed out to the potential buyer. The 1861-O *Half Dollar* is romantic because although all were struck at the New Orleans Mint, 330,000 were struck by the U.S. government, 1,240,000 under post-secession State of Louisiana, and 962,633 under Confederate authorities—but they all look alike and can't be differentiated from each other! Author's collection.

253. 1955 Doubled Die *Lincoln Cent*, the most famous *Cent* error in U.S. coinage history. Only the obverse is doubled. Beware of counterfeits. Lot #54 of the *Saccone* sale of November 6, 1989. Courtesy Bowers and Merena, Inc.

254. Reverse of 1955 Doubled Die *Lincoln Cent* from previous photo. Getting more expensive to buy in choice Uncirculated state. Courtesy Bowers and Merena, Inc.

17

Numismatic Periodicals

You have to read the weekly coin newspapers and the monthly coin magazines to know what is going on in the coin world. Most public libraries subscribe to one or more numismatic periodicals, but sooner or later, if you're getting serious about your coins, you will want to buy your own subscriptions so that (1) you can read and study the articles in the comfort of your home, (2) you can circle passages or coin prices or clip out articles for future reference, (3) you can file the entire issue away, to read at leisure at home or while traveling (like to a coin show!), (4) you can keep the printed dealer advertisements to compare with those of other dealers and to verify the accuracy of your orders when they arrive.

I've listed here the best known and the largest U.S. circulation coin periodicals covering "general" collecting topics and current numismatic news. (For specialty journals, see Chapter 18.) It's only my opinion but if I were a beginning coin collector, I would subscribe to these coin periodicals in this order:

LEADING PERIODICALS

Coin World

COIN WORLD, P.O. Box 150, Sidney, OH 45365. Published weekly, $26 per year for U.S. addresses, $66 per year for foreign subscribers. Published by Amos Press.

"Everybody" reads *Coin World*. This 11 x 15 inch weekly newspaper has a circulation of 74,000 and has more than 100 pages per issue. Much of the publication is devoted to current coin news and display ads of prominent coin dealers. Editorials, feature articles (like "Canadian silver dollars" or "Collector Profiles"), regular columns (including one by Q. David Bowers), letters to the editor, and a dozen pages of classified ads make each issue of *Coin World* eagerly anticipated. Weekly *Coin World* "Departments" that I always turn to are: "U.S. Auction Calendar" listing upcoming coin auctions; "U.S. Show Calendar" listing upcoming coin shows across the country by region; and "U.S. Trends," which summarizes current retail prices for most commonly collected U.S. coins by date, mintmark, and grade. Collecting coins without reading *Coin World* every week is like driving a car while wearing a blindfold.

Numismatic News

NUMISMATIC NEWS, 700 East State Street, Iola, WI 54990. Published weekly, $27.95 per year for U.S. addresses, $108.95 for foreign subscribers. Published by Krause Publications (no relation to this author), also the publisher of *Coins*, *Coin Prices*, and *World Coin News* (see following this periodical).

This 11 x 15 inch weekly newspaper (same size as *Coin World*) runs about eighty pages per issue. *Numismatic News* is slightly shorter in number of pages than *Coin World* but covers similar current coin news, show information, auction announcements, coin market fluctuations, etc. *Numismatic News* tends to be a little less "formal" in editorial and writing style than *Coin World*, but both are quality weeklies and many collectors subscribe to both, some just to one. There's always the chance that a news item or photograph of an error will appear in only one of these weeklies, so all serious coin collectors and dealers read both of them. Important departments with headings in *Numismatic News* are "Reader Reactions"—the letters to the editor; "Coin Market" by eternally optimistic long-time numismatic commentator Bob Wilhite with current retail prices of commonly collected U.S. coins listed by type, date, and grade; "Auction Calendar" with upcoming coin auctions; "Show Directory" listing upcoming coin shows by state (a little easier to find one than in *Coin World*'s "Show Calendar"); my favorite section, "Coin Clinic" by writer Alan Herbert, in which readers' questions on coins are answered, sometimes with closeup photos of the coins. Dealer display ads and a dozen or so pages of classified ads appear weekly in *Numismatic News*, and some dealers advertise only in either *Coin World* or *Numismatic News*, so if you subscribe to both publications, you'll see the ads of virtually all of the important coin dealers in the United States. The "Collectors Marketplace" section of *Numismatic News* has two or three pages of medium-sized display ads of dealers offering to sell specifically-priced coins, all of which are less than $100 each.

Coin World started in 1960, *Numismatic News* in 1950, and I've been reading both every week for years and will probably continue to do so even after I'm dead so that I don't miss anything in the latest coin news!

The Numismatist

THE NUMISMATIST, 818 North Cascade Avenue, Colorado Springs, CO 80903. Published monthly,

$28 per year ($26 to ANA members) for U.S. addresses, $33 for foreign subscribers ($28 for ANA members). Published by the American Numismatic Association.

While officially the "journal" of the ANA, a nonprofit society (see Chapter 18 for more information), and *not* a commercially privately owned publication like the others I've listed in this chapter, I decided to include *The Numismatist* here because (1) so many serious coin collectors are ANA members, (2) information on shows, auctions, and new coin books appears in *The Numismatist* just as in the other periodicals, and (3) many dealers of prominence have current ads in *The Numismatist*.

Furthermore, more than 31,000 ANA members receive *The Numismatist* in the mail each month, and it has been published continuously since 1888, so I figure that any coin publication that old and that popular should also keep company with the other coin monthlies and weeklies in this chapter.

Every serious coin collector and dealer in the United States who wants to keep up to date on what's happening in coin collecting reads *Coin World*, *Numismatic News*, and *The Numismatist*.

The Numismatist averages from 160 to 174 pages per issue, is about 7³/₈ by 9¹/₄ inches in page size, and has pages of clean white paper bound with a slick-surfaced stiffer cover. Copies of *The Numismatist* will stand upright on a book shelf, or they can be bound in hardcover yearly "volumes." I like this magazine's size because it is small and easy to read on an airplane or a bus, and its printing quality lends itself to permanent filing for future reference.

The Numismatist has feature articles of lasting value every month, on U.S. and foreign coins or medals, written by experts and serious students of numismatics, often with illustrative photographs and a list of references at the end of each article. "Departments" every month in *The Numismatist* include "Letters" (to the editor) wherein readers' comments and debates are aired; "Membership News"—a calendar of upcoming coin shows, club activities, and ANA membership data; "Consumer Alert" (one of my favorites) by Kenneth Bressett, who notifies readers of numismatic rip-off schemes, usually from advertisers in non-numismatic media; and wonderful regular monthly columns by top coin writers, including: "No Worse for Wear" by David

W. Lange and "Coins and Collectors" by Q. David Bowers.

The Numismatist has display ads, usually in understated good taste (ANA members are harder to fool!), of leading coin dealers, as well as a small classified ad section at the back of each issue. A new collector might be a little bored with some of the articles in *The Numismatist* and would probably be better off subscribing to *Coin World* or *Numismatic News* if funds are tight, but just about "everybody who's anybody" in the coin hobby (dealers, collectors, and scholars) in the United States is also a member of the ANA, and once you pass the preliminary stages of neophyte coin collecting, you're going to want to read *The Numismatist* so you can find out what everybody else is reading. Reports on counterfeit coins, with the genuine and counterfeit coins photographed side by side, are priceless bits of information that appear in *The Numismatist* from time to time.

Coins

COINS, 700 East State Street, Iola, WI 54990. Published monthly, $19.95 per year for U.S. addresses, $38.95 for Canada and Mexico, $35.20 for surface mail to foreign subscribers. Published by Krause Publications (no relation to this author).

I like *Coins* because it is a well-done magazine. With pages sized 8 x 10^7/$_8$ inches in typical magazine format, *Coins* is in many public libraries and on sale at newsstands. The first 34 pages of every 98 to 114 page issue are printed on slick paper, often with articles and ads picturing coins in gorgeous color. The rest of the magazine consists of modified newsprint-quality paper.

Besides feature articles on specific coins and the state of the market, *Coins* runs regular monthly columns such as: "Basics and Beyond" by B. Michael Thorne; "Collector Queries" by Alan Herbert — a question-and-answer column for readers' coin questions; and "Market Watch" by coin business observer Bob Wilhite.

"Departments" in every issue of *Coins* include: "Coin Value Guide" wherein commonly collected U.S. coins are priced with latest retail values and are listed by date, mintmark, and grade; "Calendar," which lists upcoming coin shows; and "Reader Forum"—the last page before the back cover—where an individual reader gets a whole page to expound on some aspect of coin collecting. It was with great pleasure that one of my former students, Matthew Wolfberg, had a "Reader Forum" page to himself in the June 1990 issue of *Coins*, in which he explained twenty-two collecting tips he had learned from experience in collecting ancient coins in his article "Advice to the new collector of ancient coins." Matthew used to be a high school student of mine, and I got him interested in ancient coins. He is majoring in Archaeology at the University of California at Santa Barbara, but he wrote this ancient coin lover's article when he was seventeen.

A lot of display and some classified ads appear from coin dealers in *Coins*. The ads have a *slight* tendency to lean toward the beginning collector, but many expensive coins are offered for sale also, with a large "middle range" of "collector" and "investor" coins for people with money to spend. Because of the longer lead time for a monthly publication like *Coins* (as opposed to the coin weeklies, *Coin World* and *Numismatic News*), there is a chance that in a rapidly changing market the prices quoted by a dealer's ad in *Coins* may have gone up or down by the moment you place your order, so if the order is important to you, confirm the price by mail or phone.

COINage

COINage, 2660 East Main Street, Ventura, CA 93003. Published monthly, $23 per year for U.S. addresses, $33 for all foreign subscribers. Published by Miller Magazines, continuously since 1964.

With pages measuring 8 x 10^3/$_4$ inches, this magazine format publication runs 130 to 138 pages for a typical issue. The first 34 pages of each issue are printed on slick paper, often with nice color photos of coins in articles or dealer ads. The rest of the magazine pages are black ink on modified "newsprint."

COINage has about a dozen feature articles per issue, which makes this magazine well worth reading. Some recent article titles are: "Mint Mistakes" by J.T. Stanton, "The Nazi Counterfeits" by Timothy B. Benford, "Gold and Silver Outlook" by Bob Wolenik, and "Coins of the Middle East" by David T. Alexander.

Columns appearing in *COINage* include: "In Error" — a coin errors column by Don Wallace; "Rogues, Rascals & Reformers" by Ed Rochette—

detailed articles on notable coin counterfeiters, etc.; and "Sleepers" by Paul M. Green—coins that are underpriced, in his opinion.

Plenty of large and small display ads give the coin shopper something to enjoy with *COINage*. For the money, it is a magazine worth reading, especially for the beginner or intermediate coin collector. On sale at many newsstands.

Coin Prices

COIN PRICES, 700 East State Street, Iola, WI 54990. Published once every two months, $15.95 per year for U.S. addresses, $20.95 for foreign subscribers. Published by Krause Publications (no relation to this author).

A retail price guide to every U.S. coin normally collected, listed by series, date, and mintmark, and priced by ANA grades ranging from Good-4 through Mint State-65 and Proof-65. Pricing pages are interspersed with dealer display ads with coins for sale.

Coin Prices is not an article magazine. You don't buy it to read coin articles, you buy it to check prices. It is kind of like a mini-*Red Book*® in magazine form, updated semi-monthly. More than a thousand prices change with every issue, and *Coin Prices'* editor is noted coin market analyst Bob Wilhite. All U.S. coins from 1792 to date are priced, including commemoratives, proof sets, and mint sets. Special issues of *Coin Prices* are run from time to time to include values for U.S. paper money, U.S. Colonial coins, and Canadian and Mexican coins. There are around 100 black-and-white 8 x 10⁷/₈ inch magazine-style pages per issue.

World Coin News

WORLD COIN NEWS, 700 East State Street, Iola, WI 54990. Published twice a month, $24.95 per year for U.S. addresses, $58.25 for foreign subscribers. Published by Krause Publications (no relation to this author).

World Coin News is an 11 by 14 inch biweekly newspaper covering old and modern world coins (no U.S. coins). Sixty pages is a typical issue size, and most of the dealers who advertise in *World Coin News* are U.S.-based. A lively "Letters" page prints reader opinions on collecting world coins; a recent

issue had twelve letters on the coin-slabbing controversy. A coin auction schedule and show calendar appear in every issue, as well as the "World Coin Roundup" page listing new coin types from the world's governments.

Excellent articles and columns by top coin writers appear in *World Coin News*. For example, the "World Coin Clinic" column by Alan Herbert—answering readers' questions about world coins; "Inside the Market" by Tom Michael — analyzing market prices for world coins; and "What's Old" by noted ancient coin dealer Harlan J. Berk — discussing ancient coins (a recent column of his was entitled "Your first 25 Greek gold and electrum coins").

You *don't have* to subscribe to *World Coin News* to collect coins of the world, but it sure helps. And the dealers' display and classified ads give current prices, so you can keep in touch with the world coin market.

Canadian Coin News

CANADIAN COIN NEWS, 103 Lakeshore Road, Suite 202, St. Catharines, Ontario L2N 2T6, Canada. Published every two weeks, $21.95 (Canadian dollars) per year to Canadian addresses, $24.00 (U.S. dollars) for U.S. residents, $36.95 (Canadian dollars) for foreign subscribers. Published by Trajan Publishing Corporation.

Canadian Coin News is an 11³/₄ by 17 inch (page size) newspaper printed on newsprint in black and white with a little color to highlight display ads. The magazine, intended for coin collectors in Canada and collectors of Canadian coins, has around twenty-eight pages per issue.

Coins of the world, as well as coins of Canada, are discussed in *Canadian Coin News*. Of special interest is the display advertising of dealers offering fixed price Canadian coins for sale—useful for taking the pulse of the Canadian coin market.

Canadian Coin News publishes a couple of letters to the editor per issue, has a list of coin shows upcoming in Canada, and has useful articles on all aspects of the coin market. Valuable for collectors of Canadian coins is the four-page "Trends" feature in every issue, which lists Canadian coins 1858 to date, and prices them by date and series in up to eleven different grades (ANA Good-4 through

Mint State-65). A few classified ads round out the publication.

I mention *Canadian Coin News* because a lot of collectors on both sides of the U.S./Canadian border collect the coins of each other's countries, and this newspaper is the most prominent Canadian coin newspaper published.

Error Trends Coin Magazine

ERROR TRENDS COIN MAGAZINE, P.O. Box 158, Oceanside, NY 11572. Published monthly, $15 per year for U.S. addresses. Foreign subscribers should write for specific subscription rate. Published by Arnold Margolis, noted error coin dealer.

Error Trends is a handy little 5³/₄ by 8¹/₂ inch black-and-white magazine printed on strong paper and running about 40 pages per issue. The enlarged photos of error coins are excellent. True, this magazine is written and published by a dealer, but Margolis does such a fine job of it that you have to tolerate the fact that he may have a slight conflict of interest in writing about a specific error, then maybe selling it in the same magazine.

Error Trends demystifies coin errors by explaining how they occur at the Mint. Margolis writes in an entertaining, easy to understand style, and if you are a serious collector of coin errors, you must subscribe to this magazine. Each issue also has display and classified advertising from people besides the publisher. The information in the articles in *Error Trends* is entirely unpretentious and straightforward.

18

National Coin Societies

Membership in a national coin society has benefits that far exceed the annual dues, which usually run between $10 and $25. A chance to meet other collectors who are also interested in your specialty area, trading privileges, current market analysis (what things are selling for), and a chance to read the latest published research and expert commentary are certainly worth a dollar or two a month! One fact learned from one issue of a society journal can repay your membership fee many times over.

Nobody will come to your home or beg for extra donations if you join a national coin society. Most guard their membership lists with special trust, and you may keep your address confidential if you wish. Membership in societies is good for references; a ten-year ANA or PNG member is looked upon as serious about coins and somewhat creditworthy.

Here are some of the more popular coin societies. Send a self-addressed stamped envelope for the latest information regarding membership requirements, benefits, annual dues, etc.

ACTIVE TOKEN COLLECTORS ORGANIZATION (ATCO)
P.O. Box 1573
Sioux Falls, SD 57101

For collectors of U.S. and foreign tokens. ATCO has more than 600 members, and publishes a sixty-page journal eleven times a year, with plenty of ads in each journal issue for buying, selling, and trading all types of tokens; each member can run a free ad (40 words or less) each month. Annual dues $20.

AMERICAN ISRAEL NUMISMATIC ASSOCIATION (AINA)
5150 West Copans Road, Suite 1193
Margate, FL 33063

Founded in 1967, the AINA is a cultural and educational organization for the study and collection of Israeli coins and related numismatica. Publishes a 40-page journal, *The Shekel*, six times a year. Annual conventions and numismatic study tours of Israel. Dues $15 per year.

AMERICAN MEDALLIC SCULPTURE ASSOCIATION (AMSA)
P.O. Box 6021
Long Island City, NY 11106

More than 200 members in the U.S. and abroad. For collectors and others interested in medals. Publishes a newsletter, *Members Exchange*, six times a year, an illustrated magazine, *Medallic Sculpture*, and a *Directory of Members*. Sponsors special events and exhibitions. Dues are $25 annually.

AMERICAN NUMISMATIC ASSOCIATION (ANA)

818 North Cascade Avenue
Colorado Springs, CO 80903
(719) 632-2646

"Everybody" is a member of the ANA, the largest numismatic organization in the United States (32,000). Founded in 1891 to advance and promote the study of coins, medals, tokens, and paper money. Membership benefits include: the handsome monthly 160 to 174 page journal, *The Numismatist,* a *Numismatic Resource Directory*, access to the world's largest lending library of numismatic references (more than 30,000 items), low cost coin insurance, a money museum, access to research services by ANA staff, and twice a year conventions held in changing cities across the country.

The ANA has sponsored "National Coin Week" since 1924. Currently held in April of each year, "National Coin Week" promotes numismatics with the general public and endeavors to spark interest in coin collecting. Like most coin organizations, the ANA is incorporated not for profit. The ANA no longer authenticates and grades coins, having sold that part of its operations to Amos Press of Sidney, OH in 1990 (see Chapter 6).

Annual ANA dues are $26, plus a one-time initiation fee of $6. Junior members (under age eighteen) pay $11 per year and receive a quarterly magazine, *First Strike*. You can be a coin collector without being an ANA member, but why would you want to?

AMERICAN NUMISMATIC SOCIETY (ANS)

Broadway at 155th Street
New York, NY 10032
(212) 234-3130

Not to be confused with the ANA (above), the ANS has some goals that are similar, but the ANS appeals directly to the advanced numismatist who visits the ANS building to do research. The ANS was founded in New York City in 1858, and sponsors

conferences, workshops, seminars, and public meetings. The ANS supports numismatic research, education, publication, and exhibition—and the exhibits complement the results of research.

In 1981 the ANS started the Society's computerized research, whereby visiting numismatic researchers are encouraged to add to the computer's data bank, with new input reviewed by a staff curator. Research is done by advance appointment.

The ANS has three vaults of coins, the collection being the only prominent numismatic collection that is private (not a "public" museum like the Smithsonian). The ANS collection has strong emphasis on ancients and U.S. coins, and most coins have been donated over the years.

The ANS Museum contains outstanding coins and medals, choice examples of which are always on exhibit, and the Museum staff assists researchers with numismatic studies. The ANS Museum houses one of the finest numismatic collections in the United States. Photographs and color slides of material in the ANS Museum can be ordered, and members receive a 10% discount.

The ANS Library is one of the world's most comprehensive collections of numismatic literature, with almost 100,000 items cataloged. The ANS Library maintains open stacks for the use of the visiting public; provides a reference service by mail or telephone; and allows people outside of New York to borrow books through inter-library loan via local public libraries.

ANS members receive the annual journal *ANS Museum Notes*, the quarterly *ANS Newsletter*, and the *Annual Report*. Members also receive discounts on all ANS publications and photographic services. For scholarly numismatists. Annual ANS dues are $30 ($20 for full-time students).

AMERICAN VECTURIST ASSOCIATION (AVA)

46 Fenwood Drive
Old Saybrook, CT 06475

The American Vecturist Association is a society of transportation token collectors. It publishes a monthly newsletter, *The Fare Box*, which has from 12 to 20 pages per issue. The AVA also publishes the *Atwood-Coffee Catalogue of United States & Canadian Transportation Tokens* in three large volumes; these are for sale to members at a discount. The word "vecturist" in the title of the Association is derived from the Latin *vectura*, which means "passage money" in the Roman vernacular. The AVA meets in annual convention each August in various cities throughout North America. Founded in 1948, dues are $15 per year, plus a one-time $1 initiation fee to pay for initial mailings.

BARBER COIN COLLECTORS' SOCIETY (BCCS)
P.O. Box 382246
Memphis, TN 38183

The Barber Coin Collectors' Society has more than 500 members (of whom this author is one of the Charter Members) who are interested in the U.S. coins designed by Charles E. Barber, Chief Engraver of the U.S. Mint from 1880 to 1917. The *"Barber" Liberty Head* type coins were minted from 1892 to 1916 and consist of the regular issue *Dimes*, *Quarters*, and *Halves* (see Chapter 7).

The BCCS publishes the *Journal of the Barber Coin Collectors' Society*, a quarterly publication of several dozen pages stapled in booklet form. Recent articles in the *Journal* include: "Original & Problem-Free Barbers," "Barber Quarters—A Date by Date Analysis," and "What Should You Pay For Those In-Between Grades." The *Journal* also contains dealer ads and classified ads from members. BCCS dues are $10 per year.

BUST HALF NUT CLUB (BHNC)
P.O. Box 4875
Margate, FL 33063

The Bust Half Nut Club is a society of serious collectors of U.S. *Bust Half Dollars* minted from 1807 to 1836. Membership is somewhat selective: prospective candidates must be sponsored by a current BHNC member, must *own* at least 100 different die marriages as attributed by Overton's 1970 revised book, must furnish a list of halves currently owned, etc. The group meets once a year, publishes a newsletter about every other month, and issues a census of each individual member's collection. Not for the beginning collector. Annual dues $15.

CASINO CHIP AND GAMING TOKEN COLLECTORS CLUB (CC&GTCC)
P.O. Box 63
Brick, NJ 08723

The Casino Chip & Gaming Token Collectors Club (of which this author is a Charter Member) is a society for collectors of gambling chips, "checks" (the casino term for table gambling chips), and tokens (like the slot machine $1 tokens). A rather hefty stapled quarterly newsletter, the *Casino Chip and Token News*, is published for members. Ads, auctions, and illustrated articles on gaming chips fill the pages of this interesting newsletter (of fifty pages or so). Emphasis is on past and present gambling chips and tokens of casinos in Nevada and Atlantic City, NJ, but other current and obsolete chips of U.S. and foreign casinos are discussed in the newsletter. CC&GTCC dues are $10 per year.

CENTRAL STATES NUMISMATIC SOCIETY (CSNS)
58 Devonwood Avenue S.W.
Cedar Rapids, IA 52404

The Central States Numismatic Society is a regional organization of collectors and dealers in thirteen states of the upper Midwest (IA, IL, IN, KS, KY, MI, MN, MO, ND, NE, OH, SD, WI). The CSNS sponsors a spring convention and a fall show each year in a different location. The CSNS spring convention attracts about 375 dealers to the bourse (see Chapter 14). The Society journal, *The Centinel*, contains several dozen pages of articles and ads. CSNS dues are $5 per year ($1 for collectors under age nineteen)!

CIVIL WAR TOKEN SOCIETY (CWTS)
P.O. Box 330
Garnerville, NY 10923

The Civil War Token Society was formed in 1967 for collectors of U.S. Civil War Tokens. The Society publishes a quarterly *Journal*, conducts token auctions for members, and has a library open to member use. One of the main benefits of the CWTS is the chance to meet and exchange information with other collectors of Civil War Tokens. (See Chapter 10 for discussion of these tokens.) Annual dues $7 ($3.50 for members under eighteen).

DEDICATED WOODEN MONEY COLLECTORS (DWMC)
5214 North Autumn Lane
McFarland, WI 53558

The Dedicated Wooden Money Collectors society was formed in 1976 and has more than 300 members at present. The society publication, *Timberlines*, is issued eleven times a year. Have you ever heard of wooden nickels? DWMC holds its annual meeting at the ANA Convention. A fun organization. Dues are $5 per year.

EARLY AMERICAN COPPERS INC. (EAC)
P.O. Box 15782
Cincinnati, OH 45215

Early American Coppers is a specialty society founded in 1967 for collectors of early U.S. copper coins: *Colonials*, *Half Cents*, *Large Cents*, and *Hard Times Tokens*. More than 1,200 current members throughout the United States. Publishes a magazine, *Penny-Wise*, six times a year; a swap and sale column is in each issue for member use. EAC holds several meetings a year in sites rotated around the country. Dues are $16 per year.

INTERNATIONAL NUMISMATIC SOCIETY (INS)
P.O. Box 66555
Washington, DC 20035

The International Numismatic Society is a non-profit educational and research organization. The INS staff will help numismatic researchers with their projects. The Society magazine is *Numorum* (begun in 1978) wherein articles by INS members and others are printed; featured articles include pieces on new forgeries and the detection of counterfeit and altered coins. The INS Authentication Bureau will authenticate and grade coins for set fees. Annual dues $18.

JOHN REICH COLLECTORS SOCIETY (JRCS)
P.O. Box 205
Ypsilanti, MI 48197

The John Reich Collectors Society is organized to encourage the study of numismatics, particularly United States silver and gold coins minted before the introduction of the *Seated Liberty* design. Publishes information on such coins in the three times a year *John Reich Journal* (recent articles include: "Those Darned Counterstamped Bust Quarters," "Pre-Turban Bust Dollars," and "Half Dime Collection Sold at Auction"). *Not* for the beginning coin collector. Annual dues $10.

LIBERTY SEATED COLLECTORS CLUB (LSCC)
P.O. Box 1062
Midland, MI 48641

The Liberty Seated Collectors Club is a society of collectors and students of the U.S. 19th century *Liberty Seated* coinage. The society's 52-page publication, *The Gobrecht Journal*, is sent to members three times a year. The Club President, John McCloskey, told me that "we try to publish original material on the silver *Liberty Seated* coinage of the 19th century. Much of what is published in the *Journal* is not available through any other publication." Recent articles in *The Gobrecht Journal* include: "Estimating Proof Mintages for Early Seated Dollars," "Liberty Seated Half Dollars of the Smithsonian Institution," and "A New Variety of the 1875-CC Twenty Cent Piece." *Not* for the beginning coin collector, but for those with a genuine interest in this series. The LSCC has more than 600 members (of whom this author is one). Annual dues $11.

LOVE TOKEN SOCIETY (LTS)
P.O. Box 1049
Huntingdon Valley, PA 19006

Founded in 1972, the Love Token Society was organized to promote interest in the privately-engraved coins known as Love Tokens. Publishes a newsletter called the "Love Letter" six times a year, in which stories, articles, member ads, and member activities are printed. Membership open to all persons twelve years of age or older. Society holds its annual meeting each year at the ANA annual convention. Annual dues $10.

NEW ENGLAND NUMISMATIC ASSOCIATION (NENA)

P.O. Box 383
Newtonville, MA 02160

The New England Numismatic Association is a regional society in New England. Founded in 1947, the NENA currently has about 400 members. Holds an annual conference, produces an annual medal, and publishes the *NENA News*, a quarterly news bulletin. Annual dues $5 ($3 for members under eighteen).

NUMISMATIC BIBLIOMANIA SOCIETY (NBS)

4223 Iroquois Avenue
Lakewood, CA 90713

The *Numismatic Bibliomania Society* is for collectors of numismatic literature, especially out of print and scarce reference works. The Society's quarterly journal, *The Asylum*, runs several dozen pages and has articles and ads about numismatic literature. *Not* for the beginning coin collector. Annual dues $15.

ORDERS AND MEDALS SOCIETY OF AMERICA (OMSA)

P.O. Box 484
Glassboro, NJ 08028

The Orders and Medals Society of America is for collectors of military medals, lifesaving awards, insignia of knighthood, honor citations, etc. Founded in 1951, the Society now has 1,200 members worldwide, with collecting specialties mainly in the U.S., British, and German areas. The OMSA journal, *The Medal Collector*, is published ten times yearly, and contains articles covering orders and medals, new book notices, buy-and-sell ads, etc. About 560 pages are published each year in the journal. A Society convention is held each year in August with presentations, exhibits, and dealing among members. Annual dues $20.

PACIFIC COAST NUMISMATIC SOCIETY (PCNS)

610 Arlington Avenue
Berkeley, CA 94707

The Pacific Coast Numismatic Society was founded in 1915 by Farran Zerbe, who came to San Francisco to supervise the U.S. Mint Exhibit at the Panama-Pacific International Exposition. The PCNS was the first organization established to serve coin collectors in the western United States. It remains a regional organization with emphasis on the San Francisco Bay area.

The PCNS holds regular meetings and publishes *The Journal*, with articles, comments, and a few ads. *The Journal* is issued quarterly and runs several dozen pages per issue. Annual dues $15.

SOCIETY FOR ANCIENT NUMISMATICS (SAN)

P.O. Box 2830
Los Angeles, CA 90078

This is a society for ancient coin specialists. Not really for the beginner, but for someone already interested in the serious collection of ancient coins. Publishes a quarterly journal called *SAN: Journal of the Society for Ancient Numismatics*. Some recent articles in this *Journal* were entitled: "Three Dimensional Graphics on Ancient Coins" and "Graeco-Roman Religion and Roman Policy on a Coin of Alexandria." Of practical use is the four-page centerfold insert in the *Journal*, with three dozen display ads and business cards of ancient coin dealers.

Annual membership dues are $10, and every back issue volume (yearly issues) of the *Journal* is available for $10 per year, for the last seventeen years, starting with Volume I, so if you wish, you may order every journal that this society has ever issued, for permanent reference.

SOCIETY OF PRIVATE AND PIONEER NUMISMATICS (SPPN)

P.O. Box 4423
Davis, CA 95617

The Society of Private and Pioneer Numismatics is a collector organization devoted to the study of private and pioneer gold coinage of the western and southeastern United States. The *Newsletter of the Society of Private and Pioneer Numismatics* is sent to all members; recent *Newsletter* articles include: "British Columbia Gold," "An Unlisted Variety of California Gold," and "Private & Pioneer Gold Literature (Part 2)." Society members also collect and study "fractional" gold coinage of California, gold souvenir tokens, and western mining or banking scrip. Not for the beginning coin collector. Annual dues $10 plus a one-time $5 initiation fee.

SOCIETY FOR U.S. COMMEMORATIVE COINS (SUSCC)
P.O. Box 302
Huntington Beach, CA 92648

The Society for U.S. Commemorative Coins promotes the collecting and study of such coins. The SUSCC gives slide shows and presentations on U.S. commemoratives at major coin shows in the U.S. The SUSCC quarterly newsletter, *The Commemorative Trail*, runs several dozen pages per issue and does *not* contain advertising. Recent newsletter articles include: "The Antietam Commemorative," "1946 Iowa Statehood Centennial Commemorative Half Dollar," and a piece on Trygve Rovelstad, the designer of the *Elgin, IL Commemorative Half Dollar*. Annual dues $15.

TOKEN AND MEDAL SOCIETY (TAMS)
P.O. Box 951988
Lake Mary, FL 32795

The Token and Medal Society has more than 2,000 members interested in "exonumia" — the branch of numismatics dealing with medals and tokens. Publishes a *Journal* six times a year, offers loan of its library volumes to members, has annual meetings and awards. The TAMS has published important exonumic books, such as *Medallic Portraits of Adolph Hitler* by Colbert and Hyder and *Arkansas Trade Tokens* by Robinson. The Society covers everything from "game counters and car wash tokens to American Legion and Presidential Inauguration medals." Annual dues $15.

FOREIGN NUMISMATIC SOCIETIES

Some important foreign-based English language numismatic societies are:

BRITISH NUMISMATIC SOCIETY (BNS)
c/o Royal Mint
Llantrisant, Pontyclun
Mid Glamorgan CF7 8YT Great Britain

The British Numismatic Society was founded in 1903 and encourages the study of British coinage struck or used in Great Britain and Ireland from the introduction of coinage into Britain in the first century B.C. down to modern times. The annual *British Numismatic Journal* is distributed clothbound to all members and contains scholarly numismatic research. The Society holds meetings and has a library for member use. Write for membership fees.

CANADIAN NUMISMATIC ASSOCIATION (CNA)
P.O. Box 226
Barrie, Ontario L4M 4T2 Canada

The Canadian Numismatic Association is a non-profit educational organization, incorporated by Dominion Charter in 1963. Bills itself as the "world's second largest numismatic association," presumably after the ANA's claim to be largest. Members mostly reside in Canada and the U.S. Holds an annual convention, maintains a lending library of books and slides, and publishes *The Canadian Numismatic Journal* eleven times per year; the *Journal* contains CNA news and articles on Canadian coins. Yearly dues, in both Canadian and U.S. dollars: $25 ($21.50 for applicants under twenty-one).

ROYAL NUMISMATIC SOCIETY (RNS) - LONDON
Department of Coins and Medals
British Museum
London WC1B 3DG England

The Royal Numismatic Society was founded in 1836 and received its present Royal Charter in 1904. The Society publishes an annual *Numismatic Chronicle* and occasional *Coin Hoards* journals. Members receive these journals and have access to the Society's Library at the Warburg Institute in London. Regular Society meetings occur throughout the year in the rooms of the Society of Antiquaries, Burlington House, Piccadilly, London. Members receive 25% discount on Society Special Publications. For membership application and current fees, write to the Society's Honorable Secretary at the above address.

ROYAL NUMISMATIC SOCIETY OF NEW
ZEALAND, INC. (RNSNZ)
P.O. Box 2023
Wellington 6000, New Zealand

For collectors of New Zealand coins. Annual dues $20 in U.S. dollars.

SOUTH AFRICAN NUMISMATIC
SOCIETY (SANS)
P.O. Box 1689
Cape Town 8000, South Africa

The oldest numismatic society in South Africa, with about 250 members of whom 10% reside overseas. Founded in 1941. Publishes a monthly newsletter. Specializes in the study of coins, medals, and banknotes of South Africa. Annual dues $25 in U.S. dollars.

255.

256.

257.

255. Exterior of The American Numismatic Society building, located at Audubon Terrace, Broadway at 155th Street, New York City. Founded in 1858, the present building of the ANS dates from 1905, with later expansions. The ANS is a research-oriented organization. Copyrighted photo, courtesy of The American Numismatic Society, New York City.

256. Curators' offices and coin study area of The American Numismatic Society, whose staff includes six curators, specialists in various numismatic areas. Visiting researchers, who are usually advanced numismatists who already have some knowledge about their area of specialty, are helped by the curators. The author was deeply impressed with the orderly arrangement of everything in the Society's buliding, when he made a "surprise" visit. Photo courtesy of The American Numismatic Society, New York City.

257. Roman curatorial and coin study area of The American Numismatic Society. When the author visited this room, he asked William E. Metcalf, Chief Curator, to show him some "Nero gold," whereupon Mr. Metcalf escorted the author into the vault off the picture to the left, and pulled out a large tray of coins from Nero's reign: fifty specimens of gold *aurei* neatly filed alongside many more silver *denarii*, and Mr. Metcalf pointed out that the reddish tinted coins were from Pompeii. Photo courtesy of The American Numismatic Society, New York City.

66

70

67

71

72

68

69

73

74

75

76

79

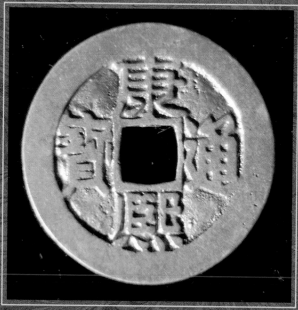

77

80

78

81

82

83

84

88

85

89

86

90

87

91

92

93

96

94

97

95

98

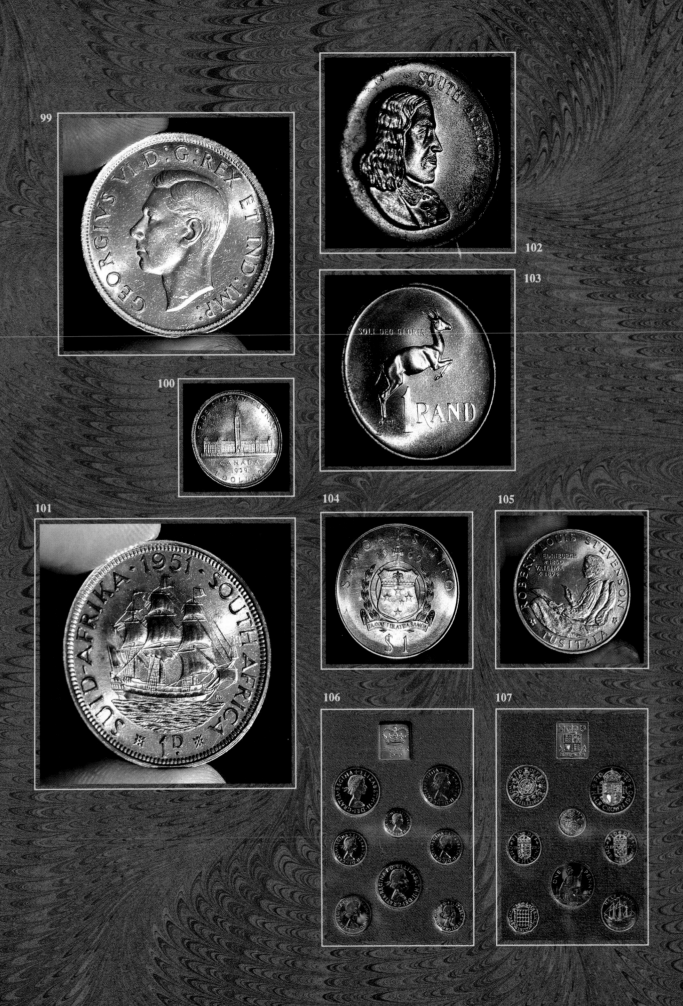

108

112

109

110

113

111

114

115

116

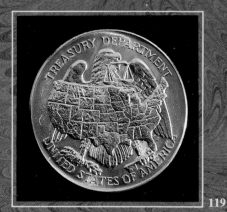

119

120

122

117

121

118

123

124

125

126

Museums

Here are some of the more important coin museums that have numismatic items on display. Call or write before traveling far to visit them, so you can be sure they will be open when you arrive.

Why go to a museum to see coins or medals? You'll see a lot more coins at a small coin show or even at a well-stocked coin shop than you'll ever see on display at the average museum with coin exhibits! You go to a museum to see choice numismatic specimens of historical importance ... for the explanatory exhibits and displays of historical artifacts that were fashioned contemporaneously when the coins were made ... for the "period" atmosphere of museum exhibition halls and galleries, which brings mere metal coins and medals to life in a way that a simple auction catalog or dealer's price list can't hope to accomplish.

Stand inside one of the basement vaults of the "Old Mint" building in San Francisco or touch the walls of the Carson City Mint building, and then tell me that you don't feel the presence of history fluttering through the corridors and coining rooms where glittering silver and gold bullion, fresh from the western mining camps, was once poured with pride and care into the shape of malleable ingots that were destined to be transformed into the pre-cious pocket money of the citizens of a great and growing nation!

Coin museums? You don't go to them to be overwhelmed with endless piles of little metal disks —you can see that at any coin show. You go to coin museums to experience, as well as you're able through time and space, a little of the human emotion and intellectual satisfaction that must have sprung forth in the eyes of those long ago engravers and mintmasters whose very hands created the coins and medals now displayed behind glass and plastic —metal ambassadors from a time and place when currency meant stacking a handful of gold or silver coins on a merchant's marble cash counter, not reaching for a brittle plastic credit card or a booklet of paper checks in an imitation leather cover!

CALIFORNIA

WELLS FARGO HISTORY MUSEUM
420 Montgomery Street
San Francisco, CA 94104
(415) 396-2619

Tormey Herold gave me a tour of this museum. He is a retired employee of Wells Fargo & Co. and now works three days a week here as Museum

Guide. He showed me a gorgeous polished metal gold scale made by Howard & Davis (Boston) and explained how fifteen people could ride on the authentic Concord stagecoach (nine passengers inside, six or more riders on top). Be sure to see the *Augustus Humbert Pioneer $10, $20*, and *$50 gold pieces* at this Museum, as well as the display of San Francisco minted coins. Also on exhibit here is the *Columbian Exposition Half Dollar* that was presented to James B. Hume (Wells Fargo's Chief Detective) at San Francisco, in its original company presentation card holder and envelope.

I was impressed with the exhibit of nice gold dust samples from many different California localities. Also, the "California Currency" display is worth seeing. The Museum traces the history and success of the Wells Fargo Express Company from its beginnings in 1852 in San Francisco.

As I was leaving the Wells Fargo History Museum, Mr. Herold asked me about the *Diamond Jubilee* coin that his father bought in 1925 and gave to him. (I told Mr. Herold that I was writing this coin collecting book, so he figured that I knew something about coins.) Finally I realized that he was talking about the *1925 California Commemorative Half Dollar*. I explained to him that his coin is worth $50 if worn, $100 and up if in nice condition.

The San Francisco Wells Fargo History Museum is open Monday through Friday, 9 A.M. to 5 P.M. with free admission.

MUSEUM OF MONEY OF THE AMERICAN WEST
Bank of California
400 California Street
San Francisco, CA 94104
(415) 765-0400

This Museum is around the corner and a quick walk from the Wells Fargo Museum (above). The Museum is one small but fascinating room devoted to Private gold coins and ingots of the Gold Rush era. If you're addicted to Pioneer Gold coins, you'll be in heaven for every minute you spend in their presence in this room. The Museum is in the basement of the Bank of California headquarters building.

Highlights of this Museum are: an extensive showing of California gold coins and ingots, speci-

mens of native gold, Utah and Colorado gold coins, and the unique original steel hub used to make the dies for the California Octagonal $50 slugs of 1851-1852 (hand cut by Charles Cushing Wright of New York City, October-November 1850). I kind of like the Museum's proof *U.S. Assay $20 piece*, as well as the three types of rare ingots on display: *specie*, "*conversion*," and *transport ingots*. Don't miss the 53.85 ounce transport gold ingot: large, brilliant, and handsome. The Museum display caption for the transport ingots states: "Since all these ingots were destined to be melted down at a mint, any that are extant were most likely robbed from a stage and buried, never reclaimed, and accidentally discovered years later."

Museum hours are Monday through Friday, 10 A.M. to 4 P.M. with free admission. Walk to Chinatown for dinner afterwards.

OLD MINT MUSEUM
5th and Mission Streets
San Francisco, CA 94103
(415) 744-6830

No trip to San Francisco is complete for a coin collector without a visit to the Old Mint, first opened in 1874, surviving the 1906 San Francisco earthquake, and now a Museum open free of charge to the public, Monday through Friday (except holidays), 10 A.M. to 4 P.M.

On display in a security room at the Old Mint is a pyramid of twenty-eight gold bars weighing a total of 10,642.90 troy ounces; also a selection of gold coins; Commemorative silver coins; a large collection of California tokens (Hotel, Saloon, Banks); a copper framed *Panama-Pacific* gold set (1915); original Mint equipment, including impressive scales for weighing bullion; and many, many medals in exhibit cases.

Tim Morgan of the U.S. Treasury Department gave me a tour of the Old Mint. He said that no robbery attempt was ever made in the sixty-three years of Mint operation (1874-1937) because of obvious heavy security. He pointed out several original Mint coin-counting tables covered with green felt, as we walked toward the coinage press room where he let me strike my own souvenir Mint medal on an 1869 coinage press. As I was walking out, I asked Mr. Morgan, "How long have you been giving tours of the Old Mint?" He smiled and replied, "Over a century, I think."

COLORADO

AMERICAN NUMISMATIC ASSOCIATION MUSEUM (ANA MUSEUM)

818 North Cascade Avenue
Colorado Springs, CO 80903
(719) 632-2646

This Museum is open 8:30 A.M. to 4:00 P.M., Monday through Friday; and the same hours on Saturday between Memorial Day and Labor Day. Admission is free to ANA members and to children under 10; 50¢ for those 10 to 17; $1 for non-members 18 and older.

Located on the campus of Colorado College at the foot of Pike's Peak in Colorado Springs, the ANA Museum is one of the largest museums in the world for coins, medals, and paper money. The Museum's holdings range from ancient coins to current pocket change, from primitive barter "money" to modern medals and badges.

Of special importance at the ANA Museum are: the Kenneth Keith Collection of Mexican coins, the Norman H. Liebman Collection of paper money related to Abraham Lincoln, and the Robert T. Herdegen and Richard W. Lloyd Memorial Collections of worldwide coins. The Museum has had a permanent building since 1967, and its collections, of which a tiny portion is exhibited, have grown tremendously from the donations of hundreds of individuals.

The ANA Museum has eight galleries of exhibits, some permanent, some changing periodically. Permanent exhibit areas include: the Hall of Nations, Colorado Gallery, Modern Medallic Hall, Hall of Presidents (with the Elliott Markoff Collection of American presidential numismatic memorabilia), the Americana I Gallery (with pre-1792 coins used in America), and the Americana II Gallery (with a panorama of all United States coinages following the establishment of the Philadelphia Mint in 1792).

The ANA Museum has on exhibit the McDermott specimen of the *1913 Liberty Head nickel* and the *Idler-Haseltine* specimen of the *1804 Silver Dollar*, valued at $1 million each, both donated to the Museum by Aubrey and Adeline Bebee of Omaha, Nebraska. Veteran numismatic dealer Bebee has also generously given the Museum a collection of U.S. paper money, assembled over a period of forty years and valued at $2 million. Choice examples of these notes are on prominent display at the Museum.

The American Numismatic Association Museum is in Colorado Springs, CO about sixty miles south of Denver off U.S. Interstate Highway 25.

GEORGIA

DAHLONEGA COURTHOUSE GOLD MUSEUM

Public Square, Box 2042
Dahlonega, GA 30533
(404) 864-2257

This Museum is housed in what was the old Lumpkin County Courthouse, built in 1836. It operates under the Georgia Department of Natural Resources, Parks and Historic Sites Division. Open every day of the year: Monday through Saturday, 9:00 A.M. to 5:00 P.M.; on Sunday, from November through April, 10:00 A.M. to 5:00 P.M.; on Sunday, from May through October, 10:00 A.M. to 6:00 P.M. Admission is $1.50 for ages 19 or older, 75¢ for ages 6 to 18, free for children under 6. Dahlonega is about fifty miles north of Atlanta on U.S. Highway 19.

The Dahlonega Courthouse Gold Museum tells the story of Georgia's gold mining history, which began in 1828 (twenty years before the California Gold Rush), when gold was discovered by Benjamin Parks in this area while he was out hunting deer. The Dahlonega Mint opened in 1838 (see Chapter 2) to strike coins from deposited bullion.

This Museum is a handsome old building with solid brick exterior walls 22^1/$_2$ inches thick and interior brick walls 12 inches thick. The bricks and mud mortar between them all reveal traces of gold from the clay of Cane Creek (about a mile away) from which they were made. This Museum has several rooms of exhibits relating to methods of mining, some mining equipment and artifacts, as well as an exhibit safe with samples of ore, nuggets, and a set of Dahlonega-minted gold coins. Be sure to see the film "Gold Fever" when you visit the Museum.

PRICE MEMORIAL HALL
("site" of Dahlonega Mint)
North Georgia College
Dahlonega, GA 30597

On a knoll a couple of blocks south of the Dahlonega Courthouse Gold Museum (described above) stands a building with a gold leaf spire. It is Price Memorial Hall, the administration building of North Georgia College, built on the foundations of the Dahlonega Branch Mint (which burned down in 1878). On display in this building is a set of fifty-nine Dahlonega gold coins. The building is open to the public Monday through Friday, 8:00 A.M. to 5:00 P.M., and anyone may go in to view the set of coins without charge.

MISSOURI

MERCANTILE MONEY MUSEUM
Mercantile Tower
7th & Washington
St. Louis, MO 63101
(314) 421-1819

"Money makes the world go 'round," so you will enjoy seeing old and new money at the Mercantile Money Museum. On display is the Eric P. Newman Collection of coins and currency, a wealth of U.S. coins, foreign coins, and paper money. Newman founded the Museum, which is a cooperative undertaking of the Mercantile Bank and the Eric P. Newman Numismatic Education Society.

In addition to many changing exhibits, which represent over eighty countries' numismatic material, the Museum features two audiovisual mannequins (perfect for kids visiting the Museum)—Benjamin Franklin and a counterfeiter. Franklin expounds on money matters and the world scene, peppering his remarks with many witticisms. The counterfeiter, in prison garb, ruefully explains his predicament and the penalties for counterfeiting. A charming Victorian library houses the "Newman Collection of Numismatic Literature" and is available by appointment to serious numismatic students and scholars.

In St. Louis for a day or two? Go see the Money Museum! Open 9:00 A.M. to 4:00 P.M. every day of the year. Free admission.

NEVADA

NEVADA STATE MUSEUM
600 North Carson Street
Carson City, NV 89710
(702) 885-4810

This Museum is housed in the Old Carson City Mint building where coins were minted from 1870-1893. It includes exhibits of Carson City mint-marked coins and coinage equipment, including a coin press. While you're there, go into the other rooms of this Museum and look at the taxidermy displays, archaeological artifacts, and mineral specimens. Then, for memory's sake, you may want to review the minting exhibits again—showing the whole coinage process from bullion depositing through ingot melting, rolling, and annealing, to blanking, washing, weighing, and coin striking! In its twenty-three years of operation, this Mint made $49.2 million from 56.6 million coins.

Currently being reinforced because of its purported vulnerability to earthquake hazard, the Museum building should be open again by the time you get around to visiting it. Hours: 8:30 A.M. to 4:30 P.M. every day of the year except major holidays. Admission $1.50 for adults, free to children under 18. Free parking on nearby streets in a driver's paradise and my favorite Nevada city: Carson City. And should gambling fever hit, I offer you no advice for your encounter with the gambling casinos down the street!

NEW JERSEY

THE NEWARK MUSEUM
49 Washington Street
Newark, NJ 07101
(201) 596-6550

The "Numismatic Collection" of the Newark Museum was begun in 1909, the year of the Museum's founding. Internationally recognized, this is the only public comprehensive numismatic collection active within the state of New Jersey. In storage and on exhibit are coins, tokens, and paper currency; and other objects related to finance, such as lottery tickets, checks, bonds, and bullion; and exonumia like medals, plaques, badges, decorations, and good luck pieces. The collection currently numbers more than 28,000 items and continues to grow through gift and purchase.

Highlights of the collection include the Dr. William S. Disbrow Collection of over 3,300 specimens of coins, tokens, and paper currency of the world (purchased by the Museum in 1919) and the Frank I. Liveright Collection of 6,500 items including over 400 "siege pieces" and nearly 1,800 U.S. coins (donated in 1925). In offering his magnificent collection as a gift to the Museum, Mr. Liveright wrote: "I have come to believe that my collection has assumed such proportions that it should be devoted to public use."

Gallery hours are: Tuesday through Sunday, 12:00 noon to 5:00 P.M. (closed Mondays and major holidays). Free admission but donations are welcome. Parking is available at the adjacent Penny Lane lot on the corner of Central and University Avenues—have the parking ticket stamped at the Museum's Information Desk.

NEW YORK

AMERICAN NUMISMATIC SOCIETY MUSEUM (ANS MUSEUM)
Broadway at 155th Street
New York, NY 10032
(212) 234-3130

The first museum in the world to exhibit only numismatic items. Nearly one million specimens are in this Museum, and it has the world's most comprehensive library of numismatic literature. It is operated under the auspices of the American Numismatic Society (founded in 1858), not to be confused with the ANA Museum (see COLORADO listing in this chapter).

The ANS Museum has many important collections, only parts of which can be exhibited at any given time. More than 87,000 pieces in the Edward T. Newell Collection of ancient Greek, Roman, and Byzantine coins reside in this Museum. The George H. Clapp Collection of U.S. *Large Cents* and the Edward Groh Collection of *Hard Times* and *Civil War Tokens* are impressive.

The ANS Museum contains one of the four known *Confederate Half Dollars* and the coinage press of Augustus Bechtler of North Carolina. The Museum has one of the world's best collections of

Islamic and Far East coins. In 1987, the Museum took possession of the private medal Collection of Victor D. Brenner (who designed the *Lincoln Cent*). Many important Medieval and Modern world coin collections are in the Museum, as well as a pageant of United States coins of all time periods.

Advanced exhibition techniques are used in the ANS Museum display halls, which explain as well as show the sample specimens from the Museum's vast stock of numismatic treasures.

The American Numismatic Society regular publication series includes: *ANS Museum Notes*, *Numismatic Notes and Monographs*, *Numismatic Studies*, and *Ancient Coins in North American Collections*. Over the last twenty-five years, the ANS photography staff has photographed nearly a quarter of a million objects from the ANS Museum and other collections for use in research and publication. The ANS Library has almost 100,000 items.

Of special interest in the Museum's galleries is the "World of Coins" exhibition of the history of money.

Museum hours are Tuesday through Saturday from 9:00 A.M. to 4:30 P.M.; and Sunday from 1:00 P.M. to 4:00 P.M. The Library section is closed on Sundays. Closed on national holidays. Free admission. There are many things to see in New York City, but if you're a coin collector, this Museum should be first on your list.

NORTH CAROLINA

MINT MUSEUM OF ART
2730 Randolph Road
Charlotte, NC 28207
(704) 337-2000

This building was originally built in 1836 in uptown Charlotte as the first Branch of the United States Mint. It produced *$5 gold coins* prior to the outbreak of the Civil War. Later it was used as a Confederate Headquarters, as a hospital, and as an assay office. Moved in 1933 to its present site, the Mint Museum of Art opened in 1936 as the first art museum in North Carolina.

Besides fine arts from around the world of various time periods, the Museum displays coins. In December 1990, the Museum opened its new exhibit on its collection of Charlotte Mint coins and history of the Charlotte Mint. The exhibit is composed of the finest known set of Charlotte-minted gold coins (fifty pieces) and artifacts pertaining to the gold rush in the North Carolina Piedmont region, and history of the Mint operation (1838-1861) and Assay Office (1867-1913). The Museum also has a collection of Bechtler Mint gold coins from Rutherford County, North Carolina, the region that was the main source of the country's gold supply from 1790 to 1840; Spanish Colonial gold and silver coins; and several U.S. type sets.

The Museum galleries are open on Tuesdays from 10:00 A.M. to 10:00 P.M.; Wednesday through Saturday from 10:00 A.M. to 5:00 P.M.; and Sundays from 1:00 P.M. to 6:00 P.M. Closed Mondays and some holidays. Admission is $2 for anyone 13 or older, $1 for children aged 4 to 12, and free on Tuesday evenings after 5:00 P.M. and also on the second Sunday of each month. Free parking on the Museum grounds.

OHIO

CLEVELAND MUSEUM OF ART
11150 East Boulevard at University Circle
Cleveland, OH 44106
(216) 421-7340

Most big city art museums have some coins and/or medals on exhibit, and the Cleveland Museum of Art is a good example. They don't have the largest coin collection in the world, but they do have some ancient Greek and Byzantine specimens and European and American medals of the past several hundred years. The R. Henry Norweb Collection of British gold coins is here, and the visitor can see gold coins of the British Isles that date from pre-Roman times to the 20th century.

Museum hours are: Tuesday, Thursday, and Friday, 10:00 A.M. to 5:45 P.M.; Wednesday, 10:00 A.M. to 9:45 P.M.; Saturday, 9:00 A.M. to 4:45 P.M.; and Sunday, 1:00 P.M. to 5:45 P.M. Closed Mondays and major holidays. And, unlike most art museums, photography is permitted here, without flash or tripod (but not allowed in special exhibitions or for certain copyrighted 20th century artworks). Free admission.

RHODE ISLAND

MUSEUM OF ART
Rhode Island School of Design
224 Benefit Street
Providence, RI 02903
(401) 331-3511, ext. 360

This Museum's numismatic collection is strongest in ancient Greek coins, of which they have a major group, and in 19th and 20th century medals, especially American.

Museum hours: Tuesday, Wednesday, Friday, and Saturday, 10:30 A.M. to 5:00 P.M.; Thursday, 12:00 noon to 8:00 P.M.; Sunday and holidays 2:00 P.M. to 5:00 P.M. Summer hours (June 16 to August 31) are Wednesday through Saturday, 12:00 noon to 5:00 P.M. Admission fees are $2 for adults 19 and older, 50¢ for visitors 5 to 18, free to children under 5, 50¢ for college students, $1 for senior citizens.

VIRGINIA

MONEY MUSEUM
Federal Reserve Bank of Richmond
701 East Byrd Street
Richmond, VA 23219
(804) 697-8148

About 575 specimens are on display, representing 350 kinds of money—primitive monies, ancient coins, Colonial commodity money, Colonial and Continental coins and paper money, U.S. coins and paper money, Confederate currency, early paper money of Virginia, and U.S. Commemorative coins. On exhibit at this modern Museum are: a Franklin Printing Press, a Production Balance Beam (on which coin blanks and coins were weighed at the third U.S. Mint), a Cannonball Safe (once used by banks and merchants to store money), and barter money (like wampum and tobacco).

Be certain to see the gold bar weighing 401.75 troy ounces (999.8 fine) and the silver bar at 1061.16 troy ounces (999.75 fine), as well as the $500, $1,000, $5,000, and $10,000 Federal Reserve Notes, and an uncut sheet of twelve $100,000 gold certificates. The oldest coin in the Museum is a silver *stater* of Croesus (c. 561-546 B.C.).

Any coin collector who visits Richmond and

doesn't see this Museum hasn't been to Richmond! Hours: Monday through Friday, 9:30 A.M. to 3:30 P.M. Free admission.

VIRGINIA MUSEUM OF FINE ART
Boulevard and Grove Avenue
Richmond, VA 23221
(804) 367-0844

The coin display at this Museum is a representative selection of ancient Greek and Roman pieces in gold, silver, and bronze. Highlights of the Greek series are a *dekadrachm* of Syracuse, a gold *octadrachm* of Queen Arsinoe of Egypt, and a gold *stater* of Alexander the Great. Significant Roman coins include a *denarius* of Julius Caesar plus a number of choice Imperial pieces in both gold and silver.

The coin gallery has just been remodeled. Museum hours: Tuesday through Saturday, 11:00 A.M. to 5:00 P.M.; Sunday, 1:00 P.M. to 5:00 P.M. Closed on major holidays. Admission is free, but a $2 donation is requested.

WASHINGTON, DC

NATIONAL NUMISMATIC COLLECTION
National Museum of American History
Smithsonian Institution
Constitution Avenue at 14th Street, NW
Washington, DC 20560
(202) 357-1300

Of course, there's always the Smithsonian! The Hall of Monetary History and Medallic Art is on the third floor and exhibits a breathtaking array of U.S. and foreign coins, tokens, medals, and paper money. About 900,000 specimens reside in the National Numismatic Collection, and obviously only a small fraction of them can be displayed at any given time. My feeling is that they show too many specimens in too small a space, but what do you expect when you're faced with the problem of exhibiting the best coin collection in the United States, if not the world?

The National Numismatic Collection had its origins in the mid-19th century, shortly after the Smithsonian was founded in 1846. Various numismatic collections were acquired by the Museum in the 19th century. In 1923, the fabulous U.S. Mint collection (totalling 18,291 specimens) was transferred from the Philadelphia Mint to the Smithsonian, much to the alarm of Philadelphia citizens and Mint sympathizers who stated that the Mint collection, begun in 1792 when the Mint was established, was one of the finest coin and medal collections in the world and should stay in Philadelphia. The Mint collection included choice examples of U.S. coins that were struck each year at the Mint, as well as foreign pieces that the Mint acquired over the years. Thus, the Smithsonian now has, for instance, the only known *1849 $20 gold piece* of the U.S.

So many famous collections have been donated to the Smithsonian that to single out one of them would be a disservice to the honor of the others! About forty years ago, the Museum took possession of the Paul Straub Collection of more than 5,000 gold and silver coins. In 1968, the Museum acquired the 6,125 specimens of the Josiah K. Lilly estate: all gold coins, many of exquisite condition and rarity. In 1978, the Smithsonian acquired the famous Chase Manhattan Bank Money Museum's collection of coins, medals, tokens, and paper currency. Also in 1978, Mr. and Mrs. R. Henry Norweb donated a *1913 Liberty Head "Nickel"* to the Museum; only five such pieces are known, another one being given by Aubrey and Adeline Bebee to the ANA Museum in Colorado Springs.

I once spent a day in the Smithsonian, intending to see something in every hall, and I ended up spending all of my time gazing at the stamp and coin exhibits. If the Smithsonian's National Numismatic Collection makes you feel that your personal coin collection is worthless after you get home and start mentally comparing them with each other, there is some consolation. The National Collection was built up over two centuries, much of it was donated, sections of it were accumulated by individual wealthy men over a lifetime of serious spending, and after all, it belongs to all Americans, just like all the artifacts in the Smithsonian! Wear comfortable shoes and allow plenty of time when you go to see the National Numismatic Collection.

The Museum is open every day of the year except Christmas: 10:00 A.M. to 5:30 P.M. in the winter; 10:00 A.M. to 7:30 P.M. from April to the beginning of September. Someone once said that the best things in life are free—definitely applicable to the Smithsonian, which charges no admission fee.

CANADA

BANK OF CANADA CURRENCY
    MUSEUM
245 Sparks Street
Ottawa, Ontario K1A 0G9 Canada
(613) 782-8914

The National Currency Collection of more than 100,000 items is at this Museum; about 10% of the collection is on permanent display.

The Currency Museum consists of eight galleries. Gallery 1 features objects that were used as money prior to the introduction of coinage. Gallery 2 traces the development of currency from ancient to modern times. Galleries 3-6 present the evolution of the use of money in Canada. Gallery 7 has temporary exhibits. Gallery 8 is called "Collector's Corner" and features a reference collection (one of each date) of Canadian decimal coinage as well as the tokens that formed the essence of Canadian collecting in the late 19th and early 20th centuries. Additional examples of ancient and medieval coinage and world coinage of the 20th century round out the exhibits.

Great rarities are on exhibit, such as the *1911 Canadian Silver Dollar* pattern of which two are known, one here and one sold at auction in 1979 for $160,000 U.S.; and the *1936 "Dot"* silver *Ten Cent Piece* of which four are known to exist. There is also a chance to see a full run of Canadian decimal coinage from pre-Confederation period to date.

The Currency Museum has a 7,500-volume library open to the public during business hours.

Museum hours: Tuesday through Saturday, 10:30 A.M. to 5:00 P.M.; Sunday 1:00 P.M. to 5:00 P.M. Closed Mondays and holidays, but open Mondays from May to Labor Day. Free admission.

GREAT BRITAIN

DEPARTMENT OF COINS AND MEDALS
The British Museum
Great Russell Street
London WC1B 3DG England
(071) 636-1555

If the Smithsonian doesn't have enough coins for you, you can always hop over to England and give the British Museum a numismatic whirl. The Department of Coins and Medals holds upwards of 600,000 specimens of money of the world of all time periods. Besides donations, the British Museum has been fortunate in being able to make purchased acquisitions. The Department of Coins and Medals has been able to buy gold or silver objects that have been declared "Treasure Trove," and the vast majority of these are coins. In this way, important hoards of coins, buried during the many periods of crisis and instability throughout Britain's history, have entered the permanent collections of the British Museum.

The British Museum has one of the finest collections of ancient Roman coins in the world. The financial systems of Europe of the Middle Ages are well represented, as is the coinage of Asia through the ages. The oldest medal in the Museum is a piece struck to celebrate the capture of Padua in 1390. Other medals from the Italian Renaissance and later ones of French, Dutch, Swiss, and Scandinavian origin are in the medal collection. The Museum has one of the best collections of paper money in the world.

Hours: Monday through Friday, 2:00 P.M. to 4:30 P.M.; Saturday, 10:00 A.M. to 12:30 P.M. Free admission. See, having fun in London is not so expensive after all!

258. Entrance of the Wells Fargo History Museum at 420 Montgomery Street, San Francisco, near Chinatown. Other Wells Fargo Museums at: 444 South Flower, Los Angeles, and 1000 Second Street, Old Sacramento, CA. Author's photo.

259. An original Concord Stagecoach, built in the 1860s, of the type that carried passengers and gold and silver shipments. Could carry 15 passengers: 9 inside and 6 more on top! $300 was the fare from St. Joseph, MO to Sacramento, CA — more than an advance purchase airplane ticket might be today, and that doesn't consider inflation! Author's photo, Wells Fargo History Museum, San Francisco.

260. Portraits of Henry Wells and William G. Fargo, founders of Wells, Fargo & Company, which opened its doors in San Francisco on July 13, 1852, providing banking, express, and mail delivery service to merchants and miners within — and to and from — the California gold fields. The company's stagecoach empire reached its peak between 1866 and 1869 when it virtually controlled the overland mail and the land transportation in western United States (and adjacent "territories"). A Wells Fargo superintendent wrote to one of the company's

gold country agents: "Pay no more for gold dust than it is worth, nor pay any less. This is the only true motto to do any kind of business on." Author's photo, Wells Fargo History Museum, San Francisco. Reflections in the paintings are Museum exhibits across the room.

261. Exhibit of "California's Varied Money," displaying gold dust, private mint gold coins, U.S. gold coins, early paper money, and even foreign coins, which circulated in California during the Gold Rush period and after. Author's photo, Wells Fargo History Museum, San Francisco.

262. Closeup of specimens in "California's Varied Money" exhibit (from previous photo). Central three coins are a *$50* octagonal "*slug*" of Augustus Humbert, and *$10* and *$20 Gold Pieces* of his U.S. Assay Office in San Francisco. Author's photo, Wells Fargo History Museum, San Francisco.

263. 1892 silver *Columbian Half Dollar* commemorative coin — the very one presented to James B. Hume, Wells Fargo's chief detective at San Francisco — in its original company presentation card holder and paper envelope. On display at the Wells Fargo History Museum, San Francisco. Author's photo.

258.

259.

260.

261.

262.

263.

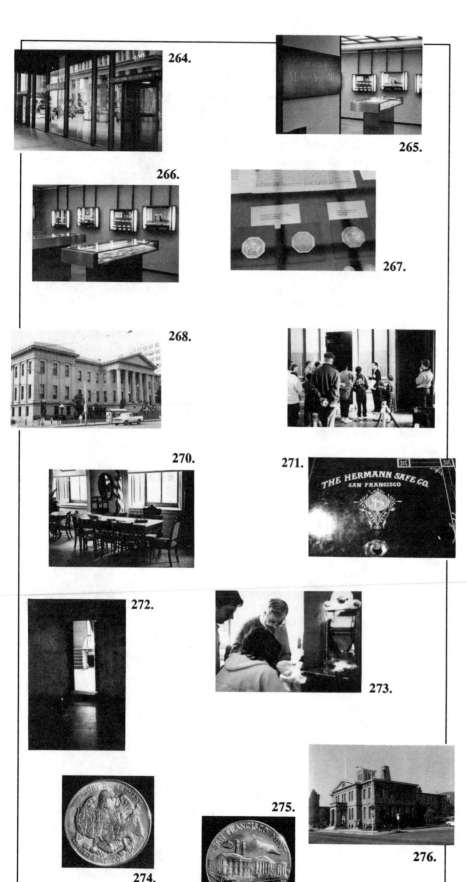

264.

265.

266.

267.

268.

270.

271.

272.

273.

274.

275.

276.

264. The Bank of California head-quarters at 400 California Street, San Francisco, has a small Museum of Money of the American West in its basement. Walk through the ornate bank lobby to reach the stairs to the basement museum. Author's photo, Bank of California, San Francisco.

265. Entrance to the Bank of California's Museum of Money of the American West in San Francisco. Consists of one small but fascinating room, which you enter through opened bronze "barred" doors that make you feel as though you're about to go someplace special! And indeed you are, if you love Pioneer gold coins and their romantic history. Author's photo, Bank of California, San Francisco.

266. The visitor to the Bank of California's Museum of Money of the American West is greeted by a gold-colored rug on the floor, excellent lighting, and understatedly enchanting display cases containing glittering specimens of California, Colorado, and Utah Pioneer gold coins! Highlights of the collection include an 1853 Proof U.S. Assay Office *$20 Gold Piece,* extremely rare western assay ingots, an 1867 gold monetary ingot (stamped 5 oz., $102.00) of the Bank of California, Gold Hill, NV, and three display cases of native gold. Author's photo, Bank of California, San Francisco.

268. *$50 Gold "Slugs"* produced by Augustus Humbert, U.S. Assayer in San Francisco, dated 1851, at the Bank of California's Museum of Money of the American West in San Francisco. A few of the coins in the Museum are not in the best available condition, but all are genuine as far as the author could tell. Exceedingly rare pieces that are seldom seen make a visit to the Museum worthwhile, for those who love to stand in the presence of Pio-

neer gold coins. Author's photo, Bank of California, San Francisco.

268. The "Old Mint" in San Francisco, on 5th and Mission Streets, now a Museum and National Historic Landmark. The first San Francisco Mint opened in 1854 on Commercial Street. The second Mint building, the one pictured, was planned just after the great California earthquake of 1868, and built between 1869 and 1874 at a cost of $2 million. Opened in the summer of 1874, this building is one of the finest examples of Federal classic revival architecture in the West. It was designed to withstand earthquake shocks, with stone walls 2 feet thick with a metal skeleton—one of the few structures in the business district to survive the San Francisco earthquake of 1906! Author's photo, Old Mint, San Francisco.

269. Tours of the Old Mint at San Francisco are conducted Monday through Friday (except holidays) by U.S. Treasury Department guides. Allot a couple of hours to wandering around the building on your own to see the exhibits of coins, medals, original Mint bullion scales, coinage presses, vaults, and assorted tools and machines, such as the automatic coin weigher and electrolytic gold and silver analyzer. When the author visited, his tour guide stated that in the sixty-three years of Mint operation in this building (1874-1937), no robbery attempt was ever made, due to the heavy security. Author's photo of Old Mint tour, San Francisco.

270. A coin viewing table, covered with green felt, in the Old Mint at San Francisco. Every five years the rugs were burned to recover $20,000 worth of bullion at a time, from gold

and silver dust that settled into the rugs during working operations at the Mint! Before you leave the building, be sure to see the display of twenty-eight gold bars of total weight of 10,642.90 troy ounces of .9999 fine gold (since tours of Fort Knox are forbidden). Author's photo, Old Mint, San Francisco.

271. One of the vault doors in the basement of the Old Mint building, San Francisco. Viewing the vaults and the huge granite blocks of the building's walls makes a basement detour well worth your time. Author's photo, Old Mint, San Francisco.

272. To the author, the most impressive vault in the basement of the Old Mint at San Francisco is the empty one in which he was standing when he took this photograph, looking out the vault's doorway toward the staircase leading to the main floor. Pause inside this cool vault, surrounded by riveted metal plate, and in the still atmosphere and dim fluorescent vault lighting maybe you can feel the ghosts of history hauling in cartloads of gold and silver bullion fresh from the Western mining camps, and hauling out bags of newly minted coins for distribution to San Francisco citizens, who were impatiently waiting in the public counting rooms upstairs, for their gold *Double Eagles* and silver *Dollars* proudly emblazoned with the tiny letter "S" denoting "minted at San Francisco." Author's photo, Old Mint, San Francisco.

273. At the Old Mint Museum in San Francisco you can buy a bronze (copper and tin alloy) blank for $1 and strike your own souvenir medal on an 1869 coinage press (visible at right) manufactured by Morgan &

Orr Builders of Philadelphia. You press a button on the end of an electric cord and the loud coinage press stamps out your medal, much like the one that the Mint employee is admiring with two visitors who have just "struck" this specimen as a souvenir of their Mint visit. Author's photo, Old Mint, San Francisco.

274. The bronze medal the author "struck" when he visited the Old Mint in San Francisco (see previous photo). Ninety tons of pressure on the coinage dies made this souvenir medal, which now resides in the author's collection. Author's photo.

275. Other side of the souvenir bronze medal struck by the author when he visited the Old Mint in San Francisco. In 1937, the third and last San Francisco Mint building (called the "New Mint" by San Franciscans) opened for business on Duboce Street, a bit out of the downtown area; and the Old Mint building (pictured here) was used for government offices until 1968, and on June 16, 1973 the Old Mint was opened as a public Museum and Mint facility. Author's photo and collection.

276. Carson City Mint in Carson City, NV, where coins were struck from 1870 to 1893. Now the Nevada State Museum. Built of sandstone in the late 1860s, the Carson City Mint received local bullion, especially Comstock Lode silver, for conversion into coins. The Museum has many taxidermy, archaeological, and mineral exhibits as well as its numismatic displays. Has the original Carson City *Dollar* press in operating condition, and CC-mintmarked coins for visitors' examination. Official photograph, courtesy Nevada State Museum, Carson City, NV.

Glossary

This is a glossary of some common coin terms and their recognized abbreviations, as used in standard catalogs and reference books, numismatic periodicals, dealer price lists, auction descriptions, and at coin exhibitions. See Chapter 16 for COIN ERROR definitions.

Also, to simplify everything, I use the word "coin" where a more complete definition would include "medals, tokens, etc."

ADJUSTMENT MARKS — File marks on a planchet that was overweight; common on 18th and early 19th century coins.

ALLOY — A mixture of several different metals. Named with the most common metal ingredient first; e.g., Copper alloy or Silver alloy.

ANNEAL—To soften metal by heating. Commonly done with blanks for coinage. Heating, followed by slow cooling, results in hardened metal. Fast cooling will result in brittle metal.

ASSAY — Analytic test to determine purity of a metal sample (ore, refined bullion, coin, etc.). An Assay Office returns deposited metal in bar form; a Mint returns metal in coin form.

ATTRIBUTION—Identifying a coin; i.e., when it was made, who is the ruler portrayed, which Mint it came from, etc. Commonly used in ancient coin collecting.

AUREUS—Standard gold coin of ancient Rome.

AUTHENTICATION—Declaring a coin genuine. Usually done by a certifying "authority" such as a grading service, coin society authentication service, etc.

BAG MARKS — Marks on Uncirculated coins, caused by contact with other coins in Mint bags. Synonymous with CONTACT MARKS.

BASE METAL—Non-precious metal, such as copper, nickel, tin, etc.

BIT—A "piece-of-pie"-like section cut from a *Spanish Milled Dollar*. A BIT is an eighth of a "Piece of Eight." Worth 12 ½ cents at the time.

BLANK—Circular metal disk from which a coin will be made. Also called FLAN or PLANCHET.

BLANKING—Stamping out BLANKS from metal strips, in the planchet preparation process.

BOURSE—A place dealers and collectors gather to buy and sell coins.

BRASS—Alloy of copper and zinc.

BRILLIANT UNCIRCULATED (BU) — New, shiny coin. Highly lustrous.

BRONZE—Alloy of copper and tin.

BULLION—Precious metal, usually in ingot form. Sometimes refers to coins of high metal purity, traded for their BULLION value. BULLION is refined purified metal in standard-sized bars.

BURNISHING—To polish to a shiny surface.

BUSINESS STRIKE—A coin made for circulation; as opposed to a PROOF or PATTERN or TRIAL STRIKE, etc.

CABINET—The connoisseur's term for a coin collection. Derived from the pre-20th century custom of storing coin collections in trays in wooden CABINETS.

CABINET FRICTION—Tiny scratches or wear on a coin due to its rubbing against its album parts or storage tray; called so regardless of actual cause.

CARTWHEEL—Slang for U.S. *Silver Dollar*. Also, a *George III 2-Pence* copper piece of Great Britain. Also, synonymous with a highly reflective surface of a coin (e.g., "CARTWHEEL luster").

CASH—Old Chinese coin, usually brass, with a central "square" hole for stringing. Also, synonymous with MONEY.

CHERRY PICK — Buying only the best coins at prices often less than they're really worth, often from an owner who doesn't know the coins' actual value. Derogatory term, implying greed and possible dishonesty.

CIVIL WAR TOKEN—Small, usually base-metal (such as brass or bronze) TOKEN that circulated as small change during the American Civil War.

COB — Roughly-cut Spanish-American Colonial coin, in silver or gold.

COIN—Small, usually circular, piece of metal made for use as money.

COLLAR—The restraining metal ring that holds a blank in place while it is being struck by the obverse and reverse dies.

COLLAR DIE—A collar made to form an edge pattern on the coin; e.g., reeding, lettered edge, etc.

COMMEMORATIVE — Coin or medal issued to honor a person, a place, or an event, often on its anniversary. May or may not be legal tender.

CONDITION—Grade of a coin; i.e., a measure of its accumulated wear and surface marks.

CONDITION CENSUS—Finest known specimen of a coin, and average condition of the next five finest known.

CONTACT MARKS — Minor scratches on Uncirculated coins due to the coins hitting each other inside Mint bags. Uncirculated coins may have numerous CONTACT MARKS but no wear. Synonymous with BAG MARKS.

CONSTELLATION—A group of stars on a coin.

COPY—A coin reproduction, often made obviously so (e.g., with the word "COPY" on it).

COUNTERFEIT — Imitation coin, made with intent to deceive, either to pass as money or for the numismatic trade.

COUNTERMARK — A punch mark on a coin. For example, to indicate change of value, special circumstances of coinage (such as the "CAL." countermark on some U.S. 1848 *$2¹/₂ gold pieces*).

COUNTERSTAMP—A punch mark on a coin, indicating a non-issuing agent's guarantee of value. For example: "Chop Marks" counterstamped by Oriental merchants on U.S. *Trade Dollars*. Defined loosely, a COUNTERSTAMP is a type of COUNTERMARK. Defined narrowly, COUNTERMARKS are official, COUNTERSTAMPS are unofficial (i.e., placed by an authority that didn't issue the coin).

CROWN—*Silver Dollar*-sized coin of Great Britain. Also refers to any large foreign silver coin.

DEBASE—To reduce the precious metal content in circulating coinage; done under government authorization.

DECADRACHM (or DEKADRACHM) — Large ancient Greek coin, equivalent to 10 *Drachms*.

DENARIUS — Standard silver coin of ancient Rome.

DENOMINATION—Face value of a coin.

DEVICE—Main design on a coin, such as royal portraits, coats of arms, allegorical figures (like Liberty or Athena), politicians' busts, etc.

DIE—A hardened piece of metal from which a coin is struck. Obverse and reverse dies strike the front and back sides (respectively) of a coin.

DIPPING—Immersing a coin in a mild acid bath to create artificial luster; actually destroys the genuine Mint luster.

DOLLAR—Standard monetary unit of the United States. Equivalent to 100 cents. Often used to refer to a U.S. *Silver Dollar* or other Dollar-like coin.

DOUBLE EAGLE—U.S. *$20 gold piece.*

DOUBLOON—Old Spanish-American gold coin, officially called an *8-Escudos piece.*

DRACHM—Ancient Greek silver coin, roughly the diameter of a U.S. *Dime*, but much thicker.

EAGLE—U.S. *$10 gold piece.* Also, a bird commonly seen on coin designs, such as the reverses of U.S. coinage.

EDGE—Narrow curved surface perpendicular to the obverse and reverse "flat" sides of a coin. The EDGE may be plain, reeded, or lettered. Sometimes confused with RIM.

ELECTROTYPE—Copy of a coin, made by electroplating. Common in 19th century U.S. coins.

ELECTRUM—A natural alloy of gold and silver. Used for the first coins ever made—those of Asia Minor and the Greek world.

ENCASED POSTAGE STAMP—Postage stamp enclosed in a metal holder, appearing much like a coin, with a "window" on its obverse to show the stamp. Circulated as small change during the U.S. Civil War. Made by other countries also.

ERROR—Coin production defect. May not be valuable; don't overpay just because it is an error.

EXERGUE—Area of a coin below the devices, often used for the date, separated by a line from the rest of the coin's design.

EXONUMIA—Collecting coin-like objects such as medals, tokens, badges, and political pins (buttons).

EXPRESSION—A "positive" (or normal) image of a coin's design, usually in relief as appearing on a finished coin. Opposite of IMPRESSION.

FACE — Coin surface, usually the obverse, but sometimes refers to the reverse.

FACE VALUE — The denomination that is stamped on a coin.

FIAT MONEY—Money not backed by bullion. For example: modern U.S. paper money; having no intrinsic (bullion) value.

FIELD—"Flat" areas on the obverse and reverse of a coin; the areas without devices, inscription, etc.

FILLER—Low-grade coins purchased to complete a collection. Also called HOLE FILLER or SPACE FILLER. Generally not recommended except by those who are selling such.

FINENESS—Purity of a precious metal sample, either in coin or bullion form. Example: ".999 fine AU" means "99.9% pure gold." Don't assume that all that are so marked are in fact what they purport to be. A lead bar can be gold-plated, etc.

FLAN—Piece of metal that becomes a coin. Also called BLANK or PLANCHET.

FLEUR-DE-COIN (FDC) — Means Uncirculated when referring to unworn foreign or (especially) ancient coins. Synonymous with MINT STATE in foreign coin catalogs.

FLIP—Soft plastic coin holder.

FLOW LINES—Microscopic lines on a coin's surface, caused when the flan's metal is squeezed under the pressure of striking.

FROST — "Whitish" effect on a coin from sandblasted dies; often used to describe the devices of Proofs. Sometimes used synonymously with LUSTER or MINT BLOOM.

GRADE — Condition of a coin, which can be

bated not only for the lifetime of a collector, but for as long as the coin exists.

HAIRLINES—Tiny scratches on a coin's surface, caused after being struck. HAIRLINES are *below* the coin's surface as struck, whereas minute PIE CRACKS are *above* (in relief) the coin's surface.

HALF EAGLE—U.S. *$5 gold piece.*

HARD TIMES TOKEN—Large Cent-sized copper token used as small change during the 1833-1843 period of financial turmoil in the United States.

HOARD—A secretly hidden group of coins, often from ancient times, found by accident in modern times.

HUB—A piece of metal with a "positive" (or relief) expression of a coin's design; used to produce the Working Dies. The HUB has the same design orientation (*not* a "reversed" image) as finished coins.

IMPAIRED — Damaged coin; usually refers to Proofs that have "escaped" into circulation, resulting in wear.

IMPRESSION—Reverse image of a coin's final design, as stamped or engraved into a metal die (made by stamping soft steel with the hub's "positive" expression). Opposite of EXPRESSION.

INCUSE—"Sunken" part of a coin's design; the part below the surface. Also called INTAGLIO or RECESSED. May be on the coin itself or on a die. Opposite of RELIEF.

INGOT—A bar of metal, either pure or alloyed. Ingots intended for coins are rolled into *strip*, and then the strip is punched into *blanks*. Ingots may be fraudulent; e.g., gold-plated lead bars.

INSCRIPTION—Lettering on a coin. Also called LEGEND.

INTRINSIC—Metal (bullion) value of a coin, as distinguished from face value and collector value. Currently made U.S. circulating coins have no intrinsic value.

KEY COIN—Rarest coin in a series, usually the one with the lowest mintage. Examples: *1877*

Indian Cent, 1916-D "Mercury" Dime, and *1895 Morgan Dollar;* all three of these have been counterfeited or produced from altered coins.

LEGAL TENDER—Coin or currency proclaimed by the government to be lawful money.

LEGEND—Lettering on a coin. Also called INSCRIPTION.

LETTERED EDGE—Letters on a coin's edge, either incused (intaglio) or relief (raised).

LIBERTY—The allegorical female representation on early U.S. coins. Also refers to the lettering "LIBERTY" on any U.S. coins.

LOVE TOKEN—Coin that has been altered by the engraving or punching in of initials, people's names, and/or artistic designs, etc.

LUSTER—The natural "sheen" or reflectivity of a coin, as minted. Also called FROST or BLOOM on an Uncirculated coin's surface. Gradually lost as a coin circulates. Instantly lost with the heavy cleaning of a coin.

MASTER DIE—Metal impression of a coin's design, used to make a *hub*, which, in turn, is used to make *working dies*. In modern times, MASTER DIES are never employed in striking coins directly.

MATTE PROOF — Proof coin with finely granulated surface. Commonly made during early 20th century for U.S. coins.

MEDAL—Piece of metal, usually circular, made to commemorate a person, a place, or an event. *Not* legal tender, hence not a coin.

MELT POINT—When the fluctuating free market price of precious metal in a coin equals the coin's face value.

MILLING—Machine-struck coin; or the edge design imprinted on coins before the introduction of collar dies. For technical reasons, don't call a reeded edge a milled edge. See REEDED EDGE.

MINOR COINAGE—Coins not of precious metal. Examples: base metal coins of the U.S.; e.g., $1/2$¢, 1¢, 2¢, 3¢, and 5¢ pieces. Also refers to a silver coin smaller than a CROWN.

MINT LUSTER — Natural "shine" of an Uncirculated coin.

MINT MARK (also spelled MINTMARK)—Symbol, usually one or more letters, indicating where the coin was minted.

MINT SET—One of each denomination coin for a given year for a given country. Usually refers to Uncirculated business strikes of these coins. Also called YEAR SET.

MINT STATE (MS) — Uncirculated. Often misgraded, deliberately or by ignorance. The most debated grading issue during the 1980s.

MISSTRIKE—A coin that is off-center, caused by the planchet failing to align properly with the dies during striking.

MODEL — Plaster relief artist's preparation of a coin design. The model is usually a much-enlarged version of the anticipated coin.

MOTTO — Patriotic and/or religious slogan on a coin. Examples: "IN GOD WE TRUST," "E PLURIBUS UNUM," "REX DEI GRATIA" ("King by the Grace of God").

MULE—A coin whose obverse doesn't match with its authorized reverse.

NUMISMATICS—The study of coins, medals, tokens, and related objects. A *numismatist* is a student of such.

OBVERSE (OBV)—Front or "face" of a coin. Also called "heads" side. The side of the coin bearing the main design, often a ruler's portrait. Opposite of REVERSE.

OVERDATE (OD)—Date numerals punched in over other numerals, either the same or different. Common in early 19th century U.S. coins.

OVERGRADING—Describing a coin as having a better condition than it does. The most common crime in coin dealing (by dealers or collectors) along with overpricing.

OVERMINTMARK — A mintmark punched in over another mintmark, either the same or different.

PATINA—Natural color on a coin, caused by aging (usually oxidation and associated chemical reactions). Can be faked somewhat to simulate genuine old color. Colorful genuine PATINA is prized by knowledgeable numismatists and poorly appreciated by beginners. Also called TONING.

PATTERN—Proposed coin design, struck for deliberation purposes. May be in same or different metals as ultimately intended for business strikes if adopted. An experimental coin as a trial design.

PENNY (d.) — British bronze coin. Also called a "Pence." Not to be used for an American "Cent."

PIECE OF EIGHT — *Spanish Milled Dollar* (8-Reales piece).

PLANCHET—Piece of metal, usually circular, from which a coin is struck. Also called FLAN or BLANK.

POUND (£)—British monetary unit. Equivalent to 20 Shillings or 240 Old Pence or 100 New Pence (starting in 1971).

PREMIUM QUALITY (PQ) — An outstanding coin for its grade. Overused by liberal graders who also happen to be selling the coin.

PROOF (PR or PF or PRF)—Coin made from specially prepared dies, resulting in a sharply struck specimen, usually with mirror fields, often with frosted devices. Struck usually for collectors or government officials. Not a grade; PROOF is a method of coin manufacture.

PROOF-LIKE (PL)—Coin similar in appearance to a proof strike, but from business working dies.

PROOF SET—One coin of each denomination in a given year, all struck in proof, usually expressly for sale to coin collectors. May or may not be in original packaging from the Mint.

PROVENANCE—The "pedigree" (ownership history) of a coin. A listing of auction appearances, private sales by dealers and collectors, and famous collections in which the coin has resided.

QUARTER EAGLE—*U.S. $2¹/₂ gold piece.*

"RAW" — "Unslabbed" coin, i.e., a coin without a

sealed holder. Slang term developed in the late 1980s; used derogatorily by those who like slabbed coins; used proudly by those who hate slabbed coins.

REAL—Spanish-American silver coin unit. Eight REALES were equivalent to one Dollar.

RECUT—An attempt to strengthen a weak impression on a die by reentering the design, often by repunching (as in the case of numerals). RECUTTING is detectable by a "doubling" of the design part. Not "complete" enough for a DOUBLED DIE definition. Not to be confused with DOUBLE IMPRESSION (see Chapter 16).

REDUCING MACHINE — Machine allowing a large plaster model to be duplicated on a small metal die. The Janvier transfer lathe, currently used to make U.S. coin design reductions, is in reality a type of reducing machine when the definition is used loosely.

REEDED EDGE—The "grooves" in a coin's edge running parallel to each other but perpendicular to the obverse and reverse planes. Current U.S. 10¢, 25¢, 50¢, and $1 coins have reeded edges. Impressed with a collar die during striking. Often confused with, or used synonymously for, MILLED EDGE.

RELIEF—Portion of a coin's design that is raised above the flat field surface. Opposite of INCUSE.

REPLICA—Copy of a coin, usually a crude and obvious facsimile (as contrasted with a dangerous authentic-looking "quality" counterfeit). Often states "REPLICA" or "COPY" or "FACSIMILE" somewhere on the coin, but these words may be filed off by the unscrupulous.

RESTRIKE—Coin produced from original dies at a later date than the date on the coin. May be officially (legally) or unofficially (illegally) produced. *All* 1804-dated U.S. *Silver Dollars* are RESTRIKES. Most 1780 *Maria Theresa Thalers* are RESTRIKES.

REVERSE (REV)—"Back" of a coin, the "tails" side. Opposite of the OBVERSE. The side usually without a portrait; often with a coat of arms. U.S. coins of higher denominations have traditionally had an eagle on their REVERSES.

RIM—The slightly raised border around the outermost limits of the field. Sometimes confused with EDGE. May be prominent as in *Wire RIM*.

ROLL—A standard "stack" of coins of a given denomination and type. What you get in a bank. Examples: 50 *Cents* or 40 *Nickels* to a ROLL. A standard Bag contains 100 ROLLS of a given coin.

SEIGNIORAGE—The difference between the face value of a coin and what it costs to make it. Sometimes defined as "the official monetary value of a coin minus its intrinsic (bullion) value at the time of manufacture." Carried on the books of the government as a "profit" to the U.S. Treasury. Alexander Hamilton, the first Secretary of the Treasury, was against SEIGNIORAGE on the grounds that it would promote counterfeiting. Since the removal of silver in circulating U.S. coins dated 1965 and later, the SEIGNIORAGE profit to the U.S. Treasury has been substantial: $467 million in Fiscal Year 1988, $594 million in Fiscal Year 1989, etc.

SEMI-KEY—Scarce coin in a series; not as rare as KEY coins but scarcer than common dates. Examples: 1931-S *Lincoln Cent*, some Carson City Minted *Morgan Dollars*.

SERIES—All of the coins with every possible combination of year date and mintmarks. Example: the *Lincoln Cent* SERIES from 1909 to present. Often collected as such.

SESTERTIUS—Large bronze ancient Roman coin. Avidly sought in high grades, uncleaned.

SHEKEL—Silver coin of ancient Judea.

SHILLING ("/" or "Sh") — British monetary unit, equivalent to 12 Old Pence or 5 New Pence (starting in 1971).

SIEGE PIECE—Coin made during a military siege. Also called *Obsidional* or *Money of Necessity*. Usually pre-20th century.

"SLAB" — Slang term for the plastic sealed ("encapsulated") coin holders produced by grading services; became popular in the late 1980s.

SLEEPER—An underpriced coin, not selling for its potential market value.

SLIDER—A coin just below its purported grade. Example: AU coin sold as UNC. "Honestly" used when stated as such. Or a derogatory term referring to overgraded coins priced such by greedy dealers.

SLUG—A *$50 gold piece*, produced during the early 1850s by private California mints. Or the *$50 1915-S Panama-Pacific Exposition gold pieces*. Or any *$50 gold piece*. Or a "fake coin" used in vending machines, either legally or illegally.

"SO-CALLED DOLLAR" — A commemorative medal approximately the size of an old U.S. *Silver Dollar*. Cataloged in the book *So-Called Dollars* by Harold E. Hibler and Charles V. Kappen, New York: The Coin and Currency Institute, 1963.

SOLIDUS — Ancient Roman gold coin that replaced the *aureus*. Tends to be less expensive and less desirable than the *aureus*.

SOVEREIGN—English gold coin, introduced by Henry VII.

SPECIAL MINT SET (SMS)—Produced in 1965, 1966, and 1967 by the U.S. Mint in San Francisco, when Proof Sets were not made by the U.S. Containing the 1¢, 5¢, 10¢, 25¢, and 50¢ coins of that year. Coins are unmintmarked.

SPECIE — Circulated coinage, especially coins of precious metal. Opposite of FIAT MONEY.

SPECIFIC GRAVITY (SP. GR.)—The weight of a substance compared to the weight of an equal volume of water. For example, pure gold has a SPECIFIC GRAVITY of 19.3. Used as a non-invasive test for a coin's authenticity. Archimedes used specific gravity principles when he determined that the crown of Hieron II, 3rd century B.C. King of Syracuse, was *not* pure gold.

SPECIMEN — Any numismatic item: coin, token, medal, etc.

STATER—Ancient Greek gold or silver coin.

STELLA — U.S. *$4 gold piece*. All are patterns, struck in 1879-1880.

STERLING SILVER — An alloy of .925 (92.5%) silver and .075 (7.5%) copper (usually). From the British *pound sterling*. Purer than 90% silver coins such as the ones minted pre-1965 in the U.S.; less pure than .999 fine silver bars, as silver bullion is commonly sold.

STORE CARD—A merchant's token, used as small change or for exchange for goods. Common in the U.S. during the Civil War and the first half of the 20th century.

STRIKE—The act of making a coin from the effect of the dies on a planchet. Also, the quality of the detail on a coin.

TETRADRACHM — Ancient Greek silver coin, equivalent to 4 *Drachms*. Very roughly the diameter of a U.S. *Quarter Dollar*, but much thicker.

THALER—Silver "Dollar" of Germanic states. The origin of our word *Dollar*.

TOKEN—A coin-like item, usually circular and of metal, used (usually) in place of money for some specific business transaction or for advertising purposes. Examples: bus and subway tokens, "Good For" tokens, souvenir tourist tokens, etc.

TONING—The natural oxidation of a coin's surface, resulting in color changes. If it looks "pretty," it is called TONING. If the discoloration is unattractive, it is called *tarnish*. TONING is extensively faked and is underappreciated by beginning collectors. Also called PATINA.

TRADE DOLLAR—A U.S. *Silver Dollar* produced for the trade with Asia. Minted from 1873 to 1885. TRADE DOLLARS are somewhat more expensive than *Morgan Dollars* due to (a) generally lower mintages of TRADE DOLLARS, (b) greater attrition of TRADE DOLLARS (which actually "circulated" overseas), and (c) the huge number of TRADE DOLLARS that were counterstamped with "chop marks," rendering them less desirable in the numismatic market, and thus raising the market values of unblemished specimens.

TRIAL PIECE — Coin struck during die preparation; not intended for circulation.

TRIME — U.S. silver *3-Cent Piece*, minted from 1851 to 1877. Actually a slang name for such.

TYPE—A "main" coin design, usually given major catalog status. Example: Wheat-backed and Memorial-backed *Lincoln Cents*.

TYPE SET—One coin of each type in a series or time period. Example: the simplest TYPE SET of U.S. 20th century *Quarter Dollars* would include a *Barber Quarter*, a *Liberty Standing Quarter*, and a *Washington Quarter*. Collectors collect by TYPE (a) because of mild interest in the whole series, (b) because they can't afford a date run in the series, or (c) for investment diversification.

UNCIRCULATED (UNC) — Mint State, a new coin. May have many *Bag Marks* or heavy *Toning*, but shows no wear on the high points of the design. UNCIRCULATED doesn't mean "never been handled" as virtually all coins are handled after their manufacture. UNCIRCULATED means *not worn*. IMPORTANT: A clean, unmarked, pleasantly toned "ALMOST UNCIRCULATED" (AU) coin may be worth more than a heavily marked ugly toned UNCIRCULATED (UNC) coin of the same type, date, etc.—a fact rarely advertised by dealers peddling "beat-up," awful-looking "UNC" coins!

UNDERGRADING—Assigning a lower grade to a coin than it deserves. Deliberately done by the unscrupulous when buying someone else's coins. Rarely done in retail sales. Accidentally done by the ignorant, to their financial benefit or detriment, depending on which way the transaction is directed!

UNIQUE—Only one known. Example: the *1849 Double Eagle* ($20 gold piece) in the Smithsonian's collection. Erroneously used in hyperbolic advertising; e.g., "semi-unique." A coin is either UNIQUE or it isn't.

UPGRADING — Replacing inferior coins with higher graded ones to improve the quality of a collection. Done by all smart collectors.

VARIETY — Same coin design, different distinguishable die impression. Example: different VARIETIES of the *1909 Lincoln Cent* ("Plain" ... "S" ..."SVDB"). Constant VARIETIES (more than one coin known of that variation) are avidly sought by specialists (e.g., *Large Cent* or *Bust Half Dollar* collectors).

VECTURISM — The study of transportation tokens.

WHIZZING—Removal of a thin layer of surface metal of a coin by brushing, buffing, burnishing, or polishing to make the coin look shiny. Done often to AU coins to pass them off as UNC. *Always* hurts the coin's market value in the eyes of knowledgeable buyers. Has been somewhat replaced by *dipping* as a faked luster enhancer.

WIRE RIM—Flange along the border of a coin, often seen in Proofs due to heavy striking pressure. The collar die squeezes metal up along the sides of the obverse and reverse dies. Erroneously termed "wire edge."

WORKING DIE—Die used to strike coins. Has a reversed image ("negative") of the final coin, and is usually impressed ("incuse") as opposed to the "expressed positive relief" image on the finished coin. Many working dies are used for large mintages.

WORKING HUB—A "transfer die" from which the working dies are made. The WORKING HUB has a positive expressed image (just like the finished coin), which is impressed into the working die.

YEAR SET—One coin of each denomination for a given year for a given country. Also called DATE SET. Usually includes all possible mintmarks to be complete. *Not* a Proof Set. Not usually packaged by the Mint (in which case, it would be called a MINT SET). Often used synonymously and/or erroneously for MINT SET.

Bibliography

Knowledge is power. Every responsible coin dealer will not hesitate to advise: "BUY THE BOOK BEFORE THE COIN." An informed collector is a smart collector, someone who is a pleasure to do business with, someone who appreciates rarity and quality when it is offered for examination or sale. First, read every coin collecting book in your local public library (filed under "737" call numbers in the Dewey Decimal System). Then visit your local coin shop to see what books your coin dealer has to offer. The "supplies and accessories" sections of the classified ads of the coin periodicals (see Chapter 17) have ads offering coin books for sale.

For scarce and out-of-print numismatic literature, try these dealers who specialize in such, at fixed prices or by mail bid sale:

NUMISMATIC LITERATURE DEALERS

CHARLES DAVIS
P.O. Box 1412
Morristown, NJ 07962
(201) 993-4431

SANFORD J. DURST
29-28 41st Avenue
Long Island City, NY 11101

(718) 706-0303

Orville J. Grady
6602 Military Avenue
Omaha, NE 68104
(402) 558-6782

George Frederick Kolbe
P.O. Drawer 3100
Crestline, CA 92325
(714) 338-6527

Numismatic Arts of Santa Fe
P.O. Box 9712
Santa Fe, NM 87504
(505) 982-8792

SELECTED NUMISMATIC BOOKS

Here are a few books of lasting value in numismatics, something for the beginner through the specialist, with emphasis on U.S. coins. Most have been written by recognized authorities. Most are still in print. I've included some standard handbooks and price guide catalogs also. I have no financial interest in any of these books or in the businesses of the preceding literature dealers.

Adams, Edgar H. *Private Gold Coinage of California, 1849-55, Its History and Its Issues.* Brooklyn, NY: Edgar H. Adams, 1913, reprinted by Stackpole Numismatic Books. 110 pages, plus black-and-white illustrative plates, hardbound. Adams' early 20th century research into California gold coins is summarized in this timeless book. Not for the casual reader, but for the serious student of these coins. Bowers says that nothing like this book has been seen in this numismatic specialty either before or after its publication.

Alexander, David T. et al. (editors). *Coin World Comprehensive Catalog & Encyclopedia of United States Coins.* New York: World Almanac, 1990. 456 pages, listing all major varieties of U.S. coins, including Colonials, Pioneer Gold, and a wonderful section on U.S. Patterns (lacking in the *Red Book*). A great companion volume to the *Red Book*. Hardcover $35. Softcover $19.95. Current. I like my hardcover version because it gets a lot of use. More than 800 black-and-white photos of coins actual size. Has a lot of information that the *Red Book* lacks.

ANA Staff. *ANA 1990-1991 Resource Directory.* Colorado Springs, CO: American Numismatic Association, 1990. 240-page softcover reference guide to ANA services, ANA member clubs, and ANA dealers. Clubs and dealers are conveniently listed by both geography and specialty. Useful for locating coin dealers and clubs in your state. $9.50 current.

Bowers, Q. David. *A Buyer's Guide to the Rare Coin Market.* Wolfeboro, NH: Bowers and Merena Galleries, 1990. 370 softbound pages with a gold mine of coin information. Useful "buying" recommendations for three categories of collectors—those on a tight budget, the "Connoisseur," and the "Elite"—for each coin series discussed. $14.95 current.

————. *Adventures with Rare Coins.* Los Angeles: Bowers & Ruddy Galleries, 1979, 1980 (3rd printing). Coins and history intertwined in a handsomely illustrated 305-page treat. Great bedtime reading. Great gift book for any coin collector. The lavish photographs alone are worth the price of the book. $24.95 current. *Anything* ever written by Bowers is worth reading. He's the best coin dealer-writer alive, and Walter Breen is the best numismatic scholar (for U.S. coins).

————. *Coins and Collectors.* Wolfeboro, NH: Bowers and Merena Galleries, 1988 Reprint. Originally published in 1964, this was Bowers' first book. 214 wonderful pages, softbound. The photographs alone of all the old coin dealer advertisements make great bedtime reading. $9.95 current.

————. *Commemorative Coins of the United States: A Complete Encyclopedia.* Wolfeboro, NH: Bowers and Merena Galleries, 1991. Impressive volume covering all U.S. commemorative coins, with historical backgrounds, design and distribution information, mintages, market price history, grading, and buying tips. 600 pages, over 300 photographs. Walter Breen says of this book: "If more history texts were as fascinating as Dave's, few kids would drop out of class." Current at $34.95 softbound, $44.95 hardbound. Good companion to Swiatek and Breen's reference.

————. *United States Coins by Design Types.* Wolfeboro, NH: Bowers and Merena Galleries, 1986, 1989 (2nd edition). 255 softbound pages guiding the U.S. "type set" collector. Tips, information, and opinions. $9.95 current.

————. *United States Copper Coins: An Action Guide for the Collector and Investor.* Wolfeboro, NH: Bowers and Merena Galleries, 1984, 1990 (4th printing, with corrections). Illustrated guide to collecting *Half Cents, Large Cents, Flying Eagle Cents, Indian Head Cents, Lincoln Cents,* and *2-Cent Pieces.* Stories behind the coins. 175 softbound pages. $9.95 current.

Breen, Walter. *Walter Breen's Complete Encyclopedia of U.S. and Colonial Coins.* New York: Doubleday, 1988. 754 hardbound pages, written by the foremost U.S. coin historian alive. Not a price catalog, but a description of die varieties and the history behind the coins. Over 4,000 black-and-white coin photographs. For the serious student of U.S. coinage. Mr. Breen is a numismatic consultant to the Smithsonian Institution, and his name is synonymous with U.S. coin knowledge. Not an inexpensive book, but I like the hardcover durability of it. $100 current.

————. *Walter Breen's Encyclopedia of U.S. and Colonial Proof Coins: 1722-1989.* Wolfeboro, NH: Bowers and Merena Galleries, Inc., 1989, Revised Edition (originally published 1977 by First Coinvestors, Inc. of Albertson, NY). 338 softbound pages. The definitive work on the history of U.S. Proof coinage. Not for the beginning coin collector, but for the serious student of the subject, this book is a logical companion reference to Mr. Breen's *Complete Encyclopedia* (see previous book listing). I wish that this book were hardbound for permanent reference durability, but it was brought out in softcover for wider distribution at a cheaper price. $29.95 current.

Bressett, Kenneth R. *A Guide Book of English Coins.* Racine, WI: Whitman Coin Products, Western Publishing Co., 1975 (8th edition). 144 slick-paper hardbound illustrated pages. Gives mintages and market prices (in 1975) of virtually all 19th and 20th century English coins (Great Britain). Out of print, but I like this book because it is small and easy to use, like the *Red Book* for U.S. coins.

Bressett, Ken and Abe Kosoff. *The Official American Numismatic Association Grading Standards for United States Coins.* Racine, WI: Western Publishing Co. (Whitman) in conjunction with American Numismatic Association, Colorado Springs, CO, 1977. 352 pages hardbound. Black-and-white drawings of commonly collected U.S. coins, arranged by series, with criteria for the ANA "Sheldon-style" grades AG-3 through MS-70. Out of print in hardcover but worth tracking down. In print in softcover at $10.95 current.

Brown, Martin R. and John W. Dunn. *A Guide to the Grading of United States Coins.* Racine, WI: Western Publishing Co. (Whitman Hobby Division), 1958, 1969 (5th edition). The first of the illustrated grading books, and maybe the best still, at least in its simplicity and ease of use. Commonly-collected U.S. coins are shown with black-and-white drawings and criteria for the "old-fashioned" grades of Fair through About Uncirculated. Out of print but worth tracking down.

Clain-Sefanelli, Elvira Eliza. *Numismatics—an Ancient Science; A Survey of its History.* Washington, DC: U.S. Government Printing Office, 1965. This is Bulletin 229, Paper 32 of *Contributions from the Museum of History and Technology*, Smithsonian Institution. 102 pages, softbound, black-and-white illustrations. An impressive history of numismatic scholarship through the ages. Material not easily found elsewhere. Out of print but in some public libraries. Worth tracking down for numismatic historical research. Not a book for the beginning coin collector.

Cohen, Annette R. and Ray M. Druley. *The Buffalo Nickel.* Arlington, VA: Potomac Enterprises, 1979 (4th printing). Mostly a price guide but valuable information also for the specialist in these coins. 130 softbound pages. $9.95 current.

Cross, W.K., editor. *The Charlton Standard Catalogue of Canadian Coins.* Toronto: The Charlton Press, 1991 (45th edition). The standard reference for collectors of all Canadian coins. 235 pages, softbound. Plenty of black-and-white coin illustrations. Coins are priced in a variety of grades. Much data about the coin's background and design. Essential for the collector of Canadian coins. $9.50 current.

Doty, Richard G. *The Macmillan Encyclopedic Dictionary of Numismatics.* New York: Macmillan Publishing Co., 1982. 355 hardbound pages. One of the nicest coin "dictionaries" in the ease of use and the clarity and readability of definitions. Hundreds of terms beautifully explained. Black-and-white photos, however, are not of the best quality. Doty was the Curator of Modern Coins and Paper Money at the American Numismatic Society in New York City when he wrote this book. Out of print but in some public libraries.

Dushnick, Stephan E. *Silver and Nickel Dollars of Canada: 1911 to Date.* Hicksville, NY: The Brooks Publishing Co., 1978. 171 hardbound pages of slick paper, profusely illustrated, explaining the Canadian dollar coins to the year 1978 when the book was issued. $10 current.

Fuld, George and Melvin Fuld. *Patriotic Civil War Tokens.* Lawrence, MA: Quarterman Publications, n.d. (a facsimile reproduction of the Third Revised Edition published in 1965 by Whitman Publishing Co., Racine, WI). 77 softbound pages. A standard reference in this field, has been supplemented with other works, but get this edition for its reference value and its simplicity. Also the authors of *U.S. Civil War Store Cards.*

Ganz, David L. *The World of Coins and Coin Collecting.* New York: Charles Scribner's Sons, 1980, 1985. 280 black-and-white photo-illustrated pages, hardbound. This book covers the history, collecting, and investment aspects of American coins. The author is a Manhattan lawyer specializing in numismatic matters, the Legislative Counsel to the ANA, and a *Coin World* columnist. $22.50 cover price. In many public libraries.

Halperin, James L. *N.C.I. Grading Guide.* Dallas, Ivy Press, 1986. Written when Mr. Halperin was just thirty-four years old. Copyrighted by the Numismatic Certification Institute of Dallas, this book attempts to explain the grading of Uncirculated and Proof U.S. coins, using words and illustrations. For the student of coin grading theory, circa 1986.

Hancock, Virgil and Larry Spanbauer. *Standard Catalog of Counterfeit and Altered United States Coins* (title page wording). New York: Sanford J. Durst, 1979. Outstanding reference on how to recognize counterfeit U.S. coins. Words and pictures show what to look for when analyzing specific coin fakes. 221 pages, hardbound. Entertaining and beautifully written in plain language. $30 current.

Heaton, Augustus G. *Mint Marks.* Wolfeboro, NH: Bowers and Merena Galleries, 1987 Reprint (originally published as *A Treatise on the Coinage of the United States Branch Mints,* Washington, DC, 1893). This book started the custom of collecting coins by mintmark; at the time of original publication in 1893, few coin collectors collected by mintmark. $6.95 current for the reprint.

Herbert, Alan. *The Official Identification and Price Guide to Minting Varieties and Errors.* New York: House of Collectibles, 1991 (5th edition). 412 softbound pages. Over 250 photos illustrating the minting process and coinage errors and varieties. This book is a useful companion to the Margolis and Spadone books. $12.95 current.

Hickox, John H. *An Historical Account of American Coinage.* Wolfeboro, NH: Bowers and Merena Galleries, 1988 Reprint (originally published by Joel Munsell, Albany, NY, 1858). The first significant book about U.S. and Colonial coins published in America. Not easy reading; for the numismatic historian. 156 softbound pages. $9.95 current for the reprint.

Hodder, Michael J. and Q. David Bowers. *The Standard Catalogue of Encased Postage Stamps.* Wolfeboro, NH: Bowers and Merena Galleries, 1989. From our sister hobby of philately, encased postage stamps bridge the collecting span between stamp and coin collectors. 191 pages, thoroughly illustrated with varieties of the U.S. encased stamps from the Civil War, priced in grades from Fine through Uncirculated (numismatic terms). Current $19.95 softbound, $27.95 hardbound.

Hudgeons, Mark. *The Official Guide to Detecting Altered & Counterfeit U.S. Coins & Currency.* Orlando, FL: The House of Collectibles, 1985 (2nd edition). Excellent reference to detecting altered and counterfeit U.S. money. 210 softbound pages of closely-spaced print, illustrated. $7.95 current.

Judd, J. Hewitt. *United States Pattern, Experimental and Trial Pieces.* Racine, WI: Western Publishing Co., 1959, 1977 (6th edition). The definitive reference on U.S. pattern coins, 1792 to date, with emphasis on 19th century pieces. 276 hardbound pages with photo-illustrations on slick paper. The market prices that are quoted are dated, but the coin descriptions and rarity data are valuable. Not for the beginner, but for the serious student of U.S. pattern coinage. Out of print.

Kerrigan, Evans E. *American War Medals and Decorations*. New York: The Viking Press, 1964. Excellent book for collectors of 20th century U.S. military medals (the kind that are pinned on uniforms). Divided into three sections: Decorations, Service Medals, and Civilian Awards. Interesting facts about each medal, and black-and-white sketches of most medal obverses. 149 pages, hardcover. $6.50 original cover price, out of print. In many public libraries. Worth tracking down.

Krause, Chester L. and Clifford Mishler (edited by Colin R. Bruce II). *Standard Catalog of World Coins*. Iola, WI: Krause Publications, 1992 (18th edition). 1,968 paperbound pages of the size and consistency of a telephone book. Over 45,900 black-and-white photos of world coins in all metals from 1801 to present. The standard world coin price reference for the 19th and 20th centuries. Essential to collectors of these coins. Coins are priced in F, VF, XF, and UNC grades and mintages are cited if known. $39.95 current.

See the *Standard Catalog of World Gold Coins* by the same authors for 704 paperbound pages pricing world coins made of gold, platinum, or palladium from 1601 to present. $45 current. Imagine writing these two books from scratch!

Leach, Frank A. *Recollections Of a Mint Director*. Wolfeboro, NH: Bowers and Merena Galleries, 1987 Reprint (from Leach, Frank A., *Recollections of a Newspaperman*. Samuel Levinson, San Francisco, CA, 1917, pages 289-406). Leach was Superintendent of the U.S. Mint in San Francisco during the 1906 earthquake and describes such in this book. Eyewitness Mint history. $9.95 current.

Lindheim, Leon. *Facts & Fictions about Coins*. Cleveland: The World Publishing Co., 1967. 280 pages in question-and-answer format, covering fascinating facts and stories about famous U.S. and foreign coins. Lindheim wrote the column "Coin-Wise" for Cleveland's *The Plain Dealer*. Impossible to put down if you have any curiosity about coins. Hardcover, out of print, $6.50

original price. In many public libraries.

Margolis, Arnold. *The Error Coin Encyclopedia*. Oceanside, NY: Arnold Margolis, 1991. 372 softbound pages, covering detailed descriptions of how normal coins are made, and of how many types of error coins occur. By the publisher and editor of *Error Trends Coin Magazine* (see Chapter 17). Indispensable for the serious student of U.S. coinage errors. $21.95 current. Good companion volume to the Herbert and Spadone books.

Overton, Al C. *Early Half Dollar Die Varieties, 1794-1836*. Escondido, CA: Donald L. Parsley, 1990 (3rd edition), first published 1967. A monumental study of 676 pages, hardbound; the standard reference for these *Half Dollars*. For the specialist. $59.95 current.

Porteous, John. *Coins*. New York: G.P. Putnam's Sons, 1964. 128 pages, well illustrated with black-and-white and color photos. Good outline of European coinage history from ancient times through the 19th century. Out of print. In many public libraries.

Reed, P. Bradley and *Coin World* staff. *Coin World Almanac*. Sidney, OH: Amos Press and New York: World Almanac, Pharos Books, 1990 (6th edition). 743 pages of facts about numismatics covering coin law, the U.S. Mint, U.S. and world coins, errors, coin collecting tips, and information on many coin organizations. $15.95 softcover, $29.95 hardbound, current.

Ruddy, James F. *Photograde*. Wolfeboro, NH: Bowers and Merena Galleries, 1970, 1988 (17th edition). Essential reference for grading U.S. coins below UNC. Designated an official grading guide to U.S. coins by the ANA in 1972. 202 pages with black-and-white photos of U.S. coins commonly collected, in grades AG to AU. Softbound, $9.95 current. Also a hardcover edition.

Sear, David R. *Roman Coins and Their Values*. London, England: B.A. Seaby Ltd., Fourth Revised Edition, 1988. The standard one-volume price guide to Republican and Imperial Roman coinage. 388 hardbound pages, plus black-and-white photos of coin photos. Prices quoted are retail in British pounds for coins generally grading Very Fine. Essential reference for the beginning collector of ancient Roman coins, despite its cost of $70 current (if your public library doesn't have a copy, it should). Not comprehensive, but representative by design types, this catalog lists current retail prices of ancient Roman gold, silver, and bronze coins. For more detail on Roman silver, for example, see the five-volume Seaby series on *Roman Silver Coins*, divided chronologically from the Republic to Romulus Augustus, and costing $35 per hardbound volume, current.

Also by the same author and publisher are the following retail price guide catalogs, which are considered the basic beginning references for collectors of such coins (all are hardbound, illustrated with coin photos, and all book prices are current): *Greek Coins and Their Values*, Volume I: Europe, 317 pages, $50. *Greek Coins and Their Values*, Volume II: Asia and Africa, 762 pages, $50. *Greek Imperial Coins and Their Values* (local coinage of the Roman Empire), 636 pages, $80. *Byzantine Coins and Their Values*, Second Revised Edition, 526 pages, $100.

Slabaugh, Arlie R. *United States Commemorative Coins* (spelled "Coinage" on the front cover and spine). Racine, WI: Whitman Coin Products, Western Publishing Co., 1975 (2nd edition). 160 hardbound pages of pure information about U.S. commemorative silver and gold coins. I like this book because it is small and easy to read on an airplane or a bus. Good companion volume to Swiatek and Breen's reference. Out of print, but available from literature dealers.

Spadone, Frank G. *Major Variety and Oddity Guide to United States Coins*. Orlando, FL: The House of Collectibles, 1981 (8th edition). 150 softbound pages illustrating and pricing many major and minor varieties. Good reference for the specialist. Good companion volume to the more "wordy" books of Herbert and Margolis. $4.95 current.

Swiatek, Anthony and Walter Breen. *The Encyclopedia of United States Silver & Gold Commemorative Coins, 1892-1954*. New York: F.C.I. Press,

Arco Publishing, 1981. 362 hardbound pages well illustrated with black-and-white photos of the coins themselves and collateral material (like original shipping packages, historical letters, etc.). Swiatek is an expert on U.S. commemorative coinage, and Breen is an expert on everything that he chooses to write about. $35 original cover price; has been reissued in softcover for $29.95, but I like the hardcover durability. Softcover current. In some public libraries.

Taxay, Don. *Counterfeit, Mis-Struck, and Unofficial U.S. Coins*. New York: Arco Publishing Co., 1963, 1976 (4th printing). 221 softbound pages. More "formal" in tone, but an excellent companion volume to Hancock and Spanbauer's book. Out of print.

Taylor, Sol. *The Standard Guide to the Lincoln Cent*. North Hollywood, CA: Sol Taylor, 1983, 1988 (2nd edition). The title explains the book. 172 pages. Essential for the serious student of this coin. $14.95 current.

Travers, Scott A. *The Coin Collector's Survival Manual*. New York: Prentice-Hall Press, 1988 (first edition 1984 by Arco Publishing). Guide to grading, buying, and selling coins in the volatile 1980s market. Useful analysis of coin grading circa 1988. $12.95 current, softcover.

U.S. Mint Staff. *Medals of the United States Mint*. Washington, DC: U.S. Government Printing Office, 1969, 1972 (revised printing). 312 pages, softcover. Catalog of bronze medals for sale by the U.S. Mint (at time of publication, and at *prices then*). Every medal's obverse and reverse are illustrated in black-and-white photos. Including brief Presidential biographies, this book is a history lesson via medal numismatics. $12 current. In most public libraries.

Van Meter, David. *The Coins Of The Twelve Caesars: A Numismatic History Of Rome In The Imperatorial And Early Imperial Eras*. Nashua, NH: Laurion Numismatics, 1990. This book combines careful history and biographical insights to explore the significance of the Roman coins of the reigns of Julius Caesar through Domitian. 176 pages softbound, plus 20 plates of over 200 black-and-white photos of coins. An excellent explanatory volume for some of the emperors in a standard catalog such as Sear's *Roman Coins and Their Values*. Van Meter's book is $19.95 current.

Welter, Gerhard. *Cleaning and Preservation of Coins and Medals*. New York: Sanford J. Durst, 1976, 1987 (4th printing), originally written in German, entitled *Die Reinigung und Erhaltung von Munzen und Medaillen*. While it is a "rule" in numismatics that you should not clean coins, this book gives technical methods for such, for those with steady nerves. 117 pages hardbound. $13 current. Not for the beginner.

White, Weimar W. *The Liberty Seated Dollar, 1840-1873*. Long Island City, NY: Sanford J. Durst, 1985. The only book to date that deals exclusively with these dollars. 83 softbound pages. For the specialist. $10 current.

Whitman Coin Products Editors. *Official Whitman Coin Dealer Directory*. Racine, WI: Western Publishing Co., 1990 (3rd edition). 184 pages, softcover. A guide to the major coin dealers in the U.S., listing their business and personal names, addresses, phone numbers, and specialty areas. Listed by state and specialty. Good for when you're traveling cross-country and want to visit some new dealers. $4.95 current.

Yeoman, R.S. *A Guide Book of United States Coins*. Racine, WI: Whitman Coin Products, Western Publishing Co., 1991 copyright (1992, 45th edition). Also titled *The Official Red Book of United States Coins*. Published since 1947, this book is the standard retail price guide for U.S. coins. The first book to buy when you begin collecting, because "everybody" uses the *Red Book*. 288 hardbound pages of solid information. In every U.S. public library. $8.95 current.

————. *1992 Handbook of United States Coins*. Racine, WI: Whitman Coin Products, Western Publishing Co., 1991 copyright (1992, 49th edition). Also called the *Official Blue Book of United States Coins*. 190 softbound pages, listing wholesale (dealer's buying) prices. Companion volume to the *Red Book*, which lists retail prices (see above). In reality, most collectors are content with just the *Red Book*. The *Blue Book* is $4.95 current.

ABOUT THE COLOR PHOTOGRAPHS

All color photographs are by the author, and coins illustrated are in his collection.

1. The desk of a coin collector is where coins are examined under artificial (usually incandescent) light and with magnifying lenses.

2. *A Guide Book of United States Coins*® by R.S. Yeoman (also called the *Red Book*®) is the first book to buy for serious collecting of U.S. coins. Published annually since 1947, the *Red Book* lists retail prices of all commonly collected U.S. coins by date, mintmark, and grade (and quantities minted, when known). Used by "everyone" in the U.S. coin business. Copyright Western Publishing Co., Racine, WI.

3. *Handbook of United States Coins*® by R.S. Yeoman (also called the *Blue Book*®) lists wholesale prices for U.S. coins; i.e., typical prices paid by dealers for commonly collected U.S. coins. Not as popular or as often quoted as the *Red Book*, but the *Blue Book* will give you an idea of what you can realistically get in cash for an immediate over-the-counter sale of U.S. coins to a dealer. Copyright Western Publishing Co., Racine, WI.

4. A box of U.S. *Cents* as they come from a Federal Reserve Bank to your local bank, and a bundle of cent-rolling papers, both color-coded in *red*, which means packaged "cents" in banking symbolism. Notice that they are erroneously still called "pennies" by long-established slang custom; there is no such coin as a circulating *Penny* in America—the proper name is *Cent*.

5. Exactly $100.00 face value (10,000 coins) in current U.S. *Cents* is visible here contained in a pair of 1-gallon pickle jars ($50 worth per gallon). The much-maligned and low purchasing powered contemporary U.S. *Cent* still serves a monetary function in daily commerce, as small change for "odd" amounts in purchase prices. Many coin collectors begin their hobby as "accumulators" of coins, perhaps by tossing *Cents* into a jar at home. Author's "collection."

6. Coins just purchased from dealers at a coin bourse (show), in their dealer-prepared soft plastic "flips" and cardboard coin holders—the way that coins are commonly sold. Notice the identifying data (possibly including the selling price, which may be a bit negotiable) that each dealer has written on the holders. Some of the author's purchases at a recent coin show. *Be extra careful when removing coins from stapled cardboard holders*: first remove all staples so they don't scratch the coin as you slide it out.

7. Coins may be stored in special albums, soft or hard plastic coin holders ("snap-lock" type is illustrated), and in hard plastic transparent coin tubes with screw caps. In this photo a "coin wallet," capable of holding several coins on plastic "pages," is partially covering a pair of cotton gloves of the kind used for the safe handling of choice Uncirculated or Proof coins, to prevent fingerprints from getting on immaculate coin surfaces. All for sale at your local coin shop.

8. A page of a coin album for U.S. *Morgan Silver Dollars*, with spaces for each date and mintmark. Choice specimens might be more safely stored in inert plastic coin holders, as some albums may chemically tarnish a coin kept a long time therein. *Be careful not to scratch a coin when sliding the album's plastic "window" panel over a freshly-inserted coin.*

9. The proper way to hold a coin: BY ITS EDGE, NOT BY THE OBVERSE AND REVERSE "FLAT" SURFACES. Notice the "lettered edge" on this coin, a *5-Shillings* copper-nickel Great Britain Queen Elizabeth Coronation piece of 1953.

10. Closeup of the lettered edge of the coin in the previous photo. Current U.S. *Cents* and *Five-Cent Pieces* have plain (smooth) edges, while current *Dimes, Quarters, Halves,* and *Dollar* coins have reeded ("serrated") edges.

11. The proper way to hold a choice Proof coin: by its edges using special cotton gloves, so that fingerprints don't accidentally mar the coin's pristine surfaces. Don't breathe on the coin or drop it; hold it over a soft surface, preferably a felt jeweler's pad enclosed in a retaining box. This coin is a *$5 Cayman Islands Proof* piece of 1975. Photo shot with a handheld camera in the author's right hand, of the coin being grasped by the author's left hand. All of the author's photos in this book are "hand-held"—the author doesn't own a tripod or copy stand, preferring handheld spontaneity in his photographs, an unconventional way of shooting small objects.

12. The reverse of the coin in the previous photo, photographed on purple velvet jeweler's felt.

13. During World War II a shortage of copper due to military needs necessitated the striking of U.S. *Cents* in zinc-coated steel in 1943. Bronze 1943 *Cents* are great

rarities, as only a few were inadvertently made, and they are often faked. Munition cartridge cases were salvaged and used for *Cent* coins for 1944-1946, although this collector's plastic display case only has room for 1944 and 1945 *Cents* of all mintmarks (P, D, and S).

14. The reverses of the *Cents* in the previous photo. One advantage of hard plastic display cases is that you can "handle" the coins without fear of them getting scratched or tarnished. Be cautious when buying hard plastic-enclosed coins. It is sometimes difficult to determine whether a visible scratch is on the coin or on the "inside" of the plastic case itself, and it is usually impossible to examine a coin's edge without removing it from the case.

15. A 1922 Philadelphia Mint "*Peace*" type *Silver Dollar*, in a PCGS (Professional Coin Grading Service®) sealed plastic holder stating its grade as "M64" (Mint State-64— see Chapter 6). The author purchased this coin specifically for photographing for this book, because he liked its lightly golden toning, most prominent in Liberty's hair behind the eye. *Peace Dollars* are plentiful in circulated condition, including AU grades, but well-struck, mark-free Uncirculated specimens are scarce.

16. The reverse of the coin in the previous photo. The dealer who sold this coin to the author had labeled it "GOLD TONING, PQ" (for "Premium Quality"—a coin market term meaning better than average for the grade), and the author agrees with the dealer's assessment. *Peace Dollars* are often more affordable than the more glamorous, heavily-promoted *Morgan Dollars*, but *Peace Dollars* are notorious for weak strikes (shallow detail) and heavy bag marks (tiny scratches all over). Pristine *Peace Dollars* will cost steep prices.

17. 1938-D/D "*Buffalo Nickel*" overmintmark. Certified genuine and M60 Uncirculated by Photo-Certified Coin Institute®. Unlisted in *Red Book* or several other catalogs. Undoubtedly caused by double punching of the mintmark into the die.

18. Reverse of "slab" described in the previous photo.

19. Membership in a national numismatic society has benefits that far exceed the value of the annual dues, which usually run between $10 and $30 per year. See Chapter 18 for information on some of the more popular societies.

20. Besides membership cards, buttons, medallions, journals, voluntary meetings, trading opportunities, and authoritative publications, numismatic societies sometimes offer "fun" items such as this embroidered cloth patch,

suitable for sewing on your jacket or cap. The author is a charter member of this organization.

21. An auction catalog of a major numismatic collection becomes a reference work in itself, long after the last coin in the sale is hammered down to the lucky bidder. Bidding at auction isn't for beginners, but serious collectors eventually dabble in auctions for buying or selling choice coins. Catalog courtesy Bowers and Merena, Inc.

22. In 1970 the author mailed this check to order some U.S. Proof Sets from a post office box coin dealer who advertised once in a Chicago newspaper. The check was cashed and the "dealer" apparently skipped town, as the box was closed when the author inquired about the matter with Postal authorities. Don't send money to a post office box if you aren't sure that the dealer is legitimate. (The author's signature has "changed" slightly since 1970, and he no longer lives in Illinois.) The "dealer's" name on this check was obviously an alias.

23. A 1957 U.S. Proof Set in a protective hard plastic holder. This set is not expensive, but for expensive coins you *must* insist on seeing the coins outside of "non-certified" coin holders, because coins often have edge damage that is impossible to examine while the coins are in holders.

24. The reverse of the 1957 U.S. Proof Set illustrated in the previous photo. Make sure that dust and scratches are on the plastic case, not on the coins. Proof Sets with "spots" of corrosion or ugly toning command cheaper prices than pristine sets without visible flaws.

25. The *California Diamond Jubilee* commemorative silver *Half Dollar* of 1925, the 75th anniversary of California statehood. Obverse features a kneeling prospector with a gold pan. 86,394 minted (distributed). Designed by California artist Jo Mora.

26. The reverse of the *California* commemorative *Half Dollar*, with a grizzly bear, symbolic of the California "Bear Flag" Republic, and prominent on the current California flag. Notice the little "S" at the bottom of the coin, indicating "San Francisco" where all of these coins were minted.

27. The *Indian Head Cent* was designed by James B. Longacre and represents a distinctly American theme in coinage design. The Indian Princess portrait, capped with a headdress of feathers, was used for the coin's obverse from 1859 to 1909.

28. The reverse of the *Indian Head Cent* shown in the

previous photo. Original color, undamaged *Indian Cents*, in either Uncirculated business strikes or choice Proof, are always in demand by collectors and dealers.

29. The first *Lincoln Cent*, issued 1909 for the 100th anniversary of Abraham Lincoln's birth. The obverse has remained basically the same since 1909. This is a Philadelphia strike, without a mintmark.

30. The reverse of the 1909 *Lincoln Cent* pictured in the previous photo. Get out a magnifying glass and notice the little letters "V.D.B." at the bottom of the coin—the initials of its designer, Victor D. Brenner. Such initials are currently at the bottom of Lincoln's shoulder, not on the reverse of present-day *Cents*, a situation unchanged since 1918. Choice original color early *Lincoln Cents* of scarce dates and mintmarks command high prices.

31. "Part" of the author's collection of hand-poured 20th century silver bars. These generally pre-date the silver price run-ups and melting frenzy of 1979-1980. Something different, for the collector/investor bored with the "usual" bullion bars that all look alike. Nineteenth century private mint U.S. silver and gold bars are great rarities and justly earn astronomical prices on the numismatic market.

32. A 1904 Philadelphia Mint *Double Eagle ($20 Gold Piece),* the most common date/mintmark in the series, with 6,256,797 minted. Common date U.S. gold coins tend to retail at a little over current gold bullion value, except for Proofs, of course, and high grade Uncirculated business strikes.

33. The reverse of the 1904 *Double Eagle* from the previous photo. Highly lustrous, "un-bag-marked" gold coins with no wear are premium quality collector coins. Beware of AU coins being sold as "Uncirculated."

34. A plastic caliper measuring a U.S. *Double Eagle's* diameter at 34 millimeters, the exact dimension for a genuine coin. U.S. gold coins have been extensively counterfeited. Weighing and measuring diameters are the first tests to be done for ascertaining the genuineness of a suspected coin. The physical characteristics of most coins are well-known and are listed in the standard catalogs.

35. The *Columbian Exposition* silver commemorative *Half Dollar* of 1892 (same type for 1893). Sold for $1 each at the World's Columbian Exposition held at Chicago during the summer of 1893. About 2½ million total mintage of both dates combined means that circulated examples are common and cheap. Flawless Uncirculated specimens bring hefty prices. Beware of

cleaned and overgraded *Columbian Half Dollars*.

36. The reverse of the *Columbian Half Dollar* pictured in the previous photo. The reverse features the *Santa Maria*, Columbus' flagship, sailing above the Western and Eastern Hemispheres of the Earth. Issued for 400th anniversary of the "discovery" of America by Columbus.

37. Part of the author's "grading set" of *Columbian Half Dollars*. From left to right, shall we grade these: Poor, Good, Extremely Fine, About Uncirculated? Although we don't know exactly what Columbus looked like (some records claim he had red hair and blue eyes) because no contemporary portrait of him has ever been found, U.S. Mint Chief Engraver Charles E. Barber adapted the coin's bust of Columbus from a work by Olin W. Warner.

38. The reverses of the *Columbian Half Dollar* "grading set." Designed by George T. Morgan, the designer of the *Morgan Silver Dollar* of 1878-1921.

39. *Eisenhower Bicentennial Dollar*. Struck in 1975 and 1976, although all are "dual dated" 1776-1976. Struck in both copper-nickel clad and silver clad Proofs and business strikes. Obverse designed by Frank Gasparro.

40. Reverse of *Eisenhower Bicentennial Dollar*. Designed by Dennis R. Williams, the winner of an open contest sponsored by the U.S. Treasury Department for creating the reverse design: "Liberty Bell and Moon" was Williams' successful entry. Photo shows Type II, with thin lettering. More than 240 million of all varieties were minted.

41. 1826 U.S. silver *Half Dollar*, circulated but pleasantly toned with stars, date, and bust highlighted against gray fields. Mint records show more than 4 million were minted that year, but that may include a few "restrikes" of earlier dated dies.

42. Reverse of 1826 *Half Dollar* illustrated in the previous photo. *Bust Half Dollars*, for many dates, exist in quantity in high grade circulated specimens, because they were stored and saved in banks at the time of issue, hence are relatively easy to locate today. Pristine Uncirculated examples will cost four-figure prices.

43. An 1878 San Francisco Mint *Morgan Silver Dollar*, the first year of issue, with 9,774,000 struck (at San Francisco). Produced with the prodding of the Bland-Allison Act of 1878. Designed by George T. Morgan. The author has owned this coin for so long that he has forgotten where he got it.

44. Reverse of 1878 San Francisco *Morgan Dollar*, the obverse of which is shown in the previous photo. Notice the little "S" under the wreath at the coin's bottom, designating the San Francisco Mint. *Morgan Dollars* were overpromoted by coin dealers in the 1980s, with a resultant market price crash in 1990. More than 27,000 M65 1881-S *Morgan Dollars*, for example, have been slabbed by the grading services, so how can common dates of this coin be rare?

45. The lower part of the reverse of a "slabbed" *Morgan Dollar*, showing detail of the coin's design, including a San Francisco mintmark. In general, Carson City mint-marked coins are the most desirable in their series. Beware of faked mintmarks: soldered on, altered, or removed.

46. Part of the author's "grading set" of *Morgan Dollars*. Get out a magnifying glass and examine their detail. The first coin in the upper line might grade Fair. The last coin in the lower line seems to be Uncirculated. How would you grade the others?

47. Reverses of the *Morgan Dollars,* the obverses of which are shown in the previous photo. The *Morgan Dollar* and the *Lincoln Cent* are the most popularly collected U.S. coins. Study them well before you sink a lot of money into either *Lincolns* or *Morgans*!

48. *Morgan Dollars* show wear first on their highest design points, generally: the hair above the eye and above the ear are the easiest places to see slight wear on the obverse; on the reverse, wear usually shows first on the breast feathers of the eagle, sometimes also on the wing tips and the head. Weakly struck dollars may be mistaken for worn ones, however, and some *Morgan Dollar* dates/mintmarks are notorious for weak strikes. This dollar is Uncirculated, but it is full of bag marks due to hitting other dollars inside coin storage bags. Bag marks (also called "contact marks") are especially undesirable when appearing on Liberty's cheeks or in the "middle" of the fields.

49. A *"Buffalo Nickel"* (officially called an *"Indian Head Five-Cent Piece"*) with delicate pleasantly mottled rainbow toning all over. Just what constitutes "nice" versus "ugly" toning is subject to endless numismatic debate, but toning that appeals to coin connoisseurs will also make them open their wallets generously to acquire handsomely toned specimens.

50. The reverse of the *"Buffalo Nickel,"* the obverse of which is shown in the previous photo. Pink and green toning predominate, and unfortunately the photo

doesn't do it justice—it is breathtaking in real life. The *Buffalo Nickel* was designed by Felix Schlag, who won a $1,000 prize for the winning design.

51. The reverse of a heavily toned *Jefferson "Nickel"*. Bluish-gray fields encircle a pink-accented Monticello building. Often weakly struck on the reverse, *Jefferson Nickels* command a premium when the "steps" in front of the building are clearly defined. Underappreciated for its occasional spectacular toning, the *Jefferson Nickel* is the only U.S. coin from the 1940s that can still be found in circulation. Designed by Felix Schlag, who won a $1,000 prize for the winning design, which has been continuously struck from 1938 to date.

52. The delicate crescent of multi-colored toning along the obverse rim attracted the author to this silver 1963 Denver Mint *Washington Quarter Dollar* lying on a dealer's table at a coin show. Originally intended as a one-year "commemorative" coin struck for the 200th anniversary of George Washington's birth, this coin, designed by New York artist John Flanagan, is presently our "work-horse" coin in its current copper-nickel clad circulation variety. First minted in 1932.

53. The reverse of the *Washington Quarter Dollar*, the obverse of which is illustrated in the previous photo, exhibiting a riot of color all over the design, such that it almost looks a little faked. Coin "doctors" do their larcenous best to fake toning, among other things.

54. Two 1964 Denver Mint *Lincoln Cents*. The coin on the left has been "whizzed" to make it appear Uncirculated. Notice the parallel striations, evidence of wire brushing — these are much more obvious than they would be in a well-done job. The coin on the right has normal surfaces and color. Tampering with copper coins to "improve" their appearance and hence their market value is, has been, and probably always will be, epidemic. Discriminating collectors try not to buy "cleaned" coins, and dealers are even less likely to purchase them.

55. A Proof 1957 *Lincoln Cent*. Look at the immaculate satiny field surrounding the word "LIBERTY" — a "matched" set of similar-appearing (color, luster, etc.) Proof *Lincoln Cents*, for the years in which they were made from 1936 to date, is an attainable goal at moderate cost. Buy them without "carbon spots" or other obvious flaws.

56. The reverse of the 1957 Proof *Lincoln Cent*, the obverse of which is shown in the previous photo. This is what a nice "Wheat Reverse" *Lincoln Cent* should look like. The only irritating defect is a tiny discoloration spot

between the "T" of the word "CENT" and the wheat ear on the right. Handle Proof coins as the author is holding this one: by the edges and with care.

57. A Proof 1964 *Jefferson Nickel* that has toned while still within its original soft plastic Mint-produced packaging. The scratches are on the plastic, not on the coin, as can be proven by gently sliding the coin around inside the plastic and watching whether a particular scratch "moves."

58. The reverse of the 1964 Proof *Jefferson Nickel*, the obverse of which is in the previous photo. Notice how several scratches extend over and outside of the coin, evidence that the scratches are on the plastic, not on the coin. Heavily toned specimen. When a packaged Mint-sealed Proof Set has distracting "spots" or "tarnish" (ugly toning) on any of the coins, its market price drops. Always inspect carefully and slowly both sides of every coin in a Proof Set before you buy it. It is amazing how many flaws you find on your coins when you get them home that you didn't see when you were buying the coins at the dealer's table!

59. An 1883 "without CENTS" *Liberty "Nickel" (Liberty Head Five-Cent Piece*, technically) that has been gold-plated. Such gilded coins were fraudulently passed as *$5 Gold Pieces* during the year of issue, prompting the Mint to add the word "CENTS" to the reverse, later in 1883. Also known as "racketeer nickels." Similar gold-plating can be done at the present time, so these pieces have no special value.

60. A 1942 *Liberty Walking Half Dollar*. Issued from 1916 through 1947, it is a popular coin among collectors and investors, especially in choice Uncirculated condition. Obverse shows a flag-draped Goddess of Liberty striding confidently forward toward the rising sun of a new day. Her right arm is extended in anticipation of the future, while she holds in her left arm branches of laurel (symbolic of honor) and oak (representing strength). Designed by Adolph A. Weinman, the *Walking Liberty Half Dollar* is considered to be one of the most beautiful American coins.

61. Reverse of the Philadelphia Mint *Liberty Walking Half Dollar*, the obverse of which is depicted in the previous photo. The reverse shows an eagle, proud and defiant, perched on a mountain ledge from which a pine branch grows, symbolizing protection over the growing United States. The fearless eagle represents America's willingness to defend itself in war, but the propitiating Liberty on the obverse means that America prefers peace. Often found toned or poorly struck. Beware of

overgraded and overpriced specimens. Be selective in buying these coins; they are not the rarest coins in the world.

62. 1904 Philippines *50-Centavos* piece, large size variety, silver in Uncirculated condition (the photo doesn't show its exquisite luster and well-struck details). Issued under U.S. sovereignty. Listed in the *Red Book*.

63. The "reverse" (because the "portrait" is on the other side, even though the date is on this side) of the 1904 Philippines *50-Centavos* piece, the obverse of which is displayed in the previous photo. From 1903 through 1919, U.S. sovereignty Philippines coins were struck at San Francisco and Philadelphia. This coin is Uncirculated: notice the streak of reflectivity extending from the "E" of "UNITED" through the "ER" of "AMERICA"—a "cartwheel" effect that is characteristic of lustrous silver and gold Uncirculated coins.

64. A 1964 U.S. Proof Set in its original soft plastic mint-sealed package. The 1964 Proof *Kennedy Half Dollar* is the only 90% silver Proof *Kennedy Half*. Struck at the Philadelphia Mint, where records show that 3,950,762 of these sets were produced in 1964. Buy Proof Sets like this one: without any distracting "spots" or ugly toning, especially on the *Cent* and *Half Dollar*, which are the most avidly collected coins when a Mint-sealed U.S. Proof Set is broken up.

65. The *Lincoln Cent*, still sealed in the 1964 U.S. Proof Set shown in the previous photo. All scratches are on the plastic, not the coin, which can be verified by gently sliding the coin around inside the soft plastic packaging to see whether a particular scratch "moves." Notice the richly colored copper surface of the field around the word "LIBERTY" and notice also the detail in Lincoln's bow tie (which should be expected in recent date Proof *Cents*).

66. A group of business strike *Lincoln Cents* from the 1930s, 1940s, and 1950s. Notice the subtle color variations, which are typical of a random selection of Uncirculated copper *Cents*. None of these coins appears to have been cleaned; they all exhibit color from natural aging.

67. This *Indian Head Cent* has not only been cleaned, it also has a "permanent" corrosive discoloration at the top of the obverse. Such coins do not belong in a serious collection, even for a beginner on a low budget.

68. Nineteenth century U.S. copper coins are notorious for being cleaned, which is unfortunate, considering that the cleaning almost always severely reduces the legitimate

market value. U.S. *Half Cents*, *Large Cents*, and *Indian Head Cents* are constantly being tampered with, in a larcenous effort to make them appear to have more luster and higher grade. This 1887 *Indian Cent* exhibits the typical dull, pale color of a cleaned copper coin. It would be impossible for a heavily worn coin such as this (which grades Good for surface wear) to have the "shiny" appearance that it has; worn *Indian Cents* that have seen extensive circulation are brown to black, sometimes with green copper oxides evident also.

69. This *Indian Head Cent* is heavily corroded and has turned grayish-black in color. Avoid these coins completely, even for rare dates—they are quite difficult to sell. A candidate for a cleaning laboratory, perhaps to be dipped in acid by a coin "doctor"?

70. Ugly brown toning on a 1963 *Washington Quarter Dollar*. Such mottled toning on a late-date coin is objectively unpleasant and therefore destroys the coin's market value.

71. 1920 San Francisco Mint *Standing Liberty Quarter Dollar*. Look with a magnifying glass just to the upper left of the date to find the "S" mintmark. Look to the upper right of the date to find the letter "M"—the initial of designer Hermon A. MacNeil. Several varieties, minted from 1916 through 1930. Liberty's left arm holds a shield from which the cover is being removed, symbolic of war and protection. Her right hand offers an olive branch, symbolic of peace. *Standing Liberty Quarters* before 1925 had dates in relatively high relief, and they wore off rapidly, so that many heavily circulated coins have no dates visible at all. Coins minted from 1925 to 1930 have their date region recessed, so that their dates are readable even with extensive wear.

72. The reverse of the *Standing Liberty Quarter*, the obverse of which is the subject of the previous photo. The reverse features an eagle in flight over three stars (Variety 2). "Routine" Uncirculated pieces are available, but pristine specimens with well-struck heads of Liberty and full shield details are elusive. Beware of altered dates, altered mintmarks, and artificial toning made to hide defects.

73. 1881 Philadelphia Mint *Half Eagle ($5 Gold Piece)* in AU condition (a little wear on the high points). This coin exhibits normal bag marks and typical toning found on 19th century U.S. gold coins. 5,708,802 specimens were struck in this year and mintmark.

74. Reverse of the 1881 *Half Eagle*, the obverse of which is illustrated in the previous photo. U.S. gold coins have

been extensively counterfeited, so be extra cautious when buying scarce varieties. Nice-looking AU coins are often sold as Uncirculated by the unscrupulous element of fast buck artists who give the coin dealer profession a bad reputation.

75. A silver *Ducaton* of United Netherlands, dated 1711 (on the reverse). A "sea-salvage" coin discovered from sunken treasure. The ocean is not very kind to copper and silver coins, but gold coins are often brought up to appear just about as nice as the day they went down to their temporary watery tomb.

76. The reverse of the *Ducaton* of the previous photo. The date "1711" is vaguely discernible inside an oval just above the lettering along the lower rim. Notice the subtle toning, typical of many sea-salvaged silver coins.

77. Chinese "*Cash*"—a bronze or brass coin made in seemingly endless quantities for hundreds of years by various Chinese mints. This particular specimen has been cleaned, making it easier to photograph in color, which is why the author bought it at a coin show, specifically for this book's illustrations. Attributed to the reign of the Emperor K'ang-Hsi (1662-1722) of the Ch'ing Dynasty.

78. The reverse of the Chinese "*Cash*" from the previous photo. From Shantung Mint. Counterfeits from this period of Chinese numismatics are prevalent. "*Cash*" is a general term referring to old Chinese coins with square "holes" in their centers, used for conveniently carrying them on a string. Most varieties are not expensive. Most show evidence of heavy circulation.

79. A *2-Reales* silver coin from Spain, struck during the reign of Ferdinand VI in 1759. The "whitish" areas in relief are nicely contrasted by the uniformly gray fields. Spanish coins have many devotees, both within and outside Spain, and because Spain was once a prime maritime world power (Spain financed the 1492 expedition of Columbus), the coins of this country have much history and romance to make them interesting to the collector.

80. The reverse of the Spanish *2-Reales* piece illustrated in the previous photo. The reverse features the royal coat of arms and crown and the Latin legend: "FERDINANDUS° VI° D° G," which translates as: "Ferdinand the Sixth, by the Grace of God" (Dei Gratia). Latin has been used on coins since ancient Rome. Modern United States coins bear the motto "E PLURIBUS UNUM" (One out of many).

81. A restrike of the famous silver Austrian *Maria*

Theresa Thaler. All are dated 1780, but they have been struck at many world mints up to the present day. Contains approximately ³/₄ ounce of pure silver. Struck in Proof and Uncirculated for the numismatic trade.

82. Reverse of the *Maria Theresa Thaler*, the obverse of which is shown in the previous photo. Reverse depicts the Austrian coat of arms. These coins continued to be minted for the trade with local populations of north and east Africa, who refused to accept other silver coinage in commerce.

83. 1795 Spanish silver *8-Reales* piece, a direct descendant of the *Spanish Milled Dollar* (also called a *Pillar Dollar* or *Piece of Eight*). Spanish *8-Reales* were the most commonly circulated large silver coin in early America in Colonial times and even into the first years of the young United States. This specimen, showing an armored bust of Charles IIII, has "chopmarks" counterstamped thereon, indicating Asian merchants' guarantee of value.

84. Reverse of the *8-Reales* piece from the previous photo. Specimens were struck in Latin American Spanish Colonial mints, from silver mined in the New World.

85. 1832 *8-Reales* piece from Peru (date on reverse). These large silver coins are direct descendants of the *Spanish Milled Dollars* of the 18th century. Counterstamped "F.7.º" for "Fernando Septimo" (Ferdinand VII, who ruled Spain from 1808 to 1833, although in exile until 1814).

86. Copper "Bank of Upper Canada" *Half Penny* "Token" of 1857. For the specialist in local pre-decimal Canadian coinage.

87. Reverse of *Half Penny* "Token" of the previous photo. Has been cleaned.

88. French silver *5-Francs* piece of 1874. Showing natural toning. Inscription translates as "Liberty, Equality, Fraternity."

89. French *5-Francs* piece, showing the reverse of the specimen in the previous photo. Notice the natural toning of the silver surfaces.

90. 1885 Philippines *50-Centimos* piece in silver with the portrait of Alfonso XII of Spain. Spain regained the Philippines at the Treaty of Paris, 1763, and held the islands until they were ceded to the United States in 1898 as a result of the Spanish-American War. Natural rainbow toning.

91. Reverse of the 1885 Philippines *50-Centimos* piece from the previous photo, showing the Spanish coat of arms. Notice the delicate natural toning, typical of older silver coins.

92. Prussia *3-Mark* silver piece, 1913, inscribed "DEUTSCHES REICH" (German Empire). Issued in both "business strikes" (of which this is an example) and Proof.

93. Reverse of the Prussian *3-Mark* piece from the previous photo. Issued in commemoration of the 100th anniversary of the defeat of Napoleon. Germany and France were traditional enemies through World War II, and their coinage and medallic issues often have emphasized their historical enmity.

94. Egypt silver *20-Piastres* piece of 1917 (AH 1335). 840,000 minted. Original color circulated coin; has never been cleaned.

95. The reverse of the Egyptian *20-Piastres* coin of the previous photo. 28 grams, .833 fine silver.

96. The reverse of a Canadian 1917 *One Cent* piece, showing evidence of cleaning. Notice the dull "orangish" unnatural color typical of cleaned copper coins. The author has included designated cleaned coins in this book so that collectors who are beginners can learn to identify them. 11,899,254 minted.

97. Although it has some bag marks, this 1936 Canadian *Silver Dollar* is still nice-looking, with lots of original luster. The second year of Canadian King George V (of Britain) *Dollars*, this coin was minted in a quantity of about a third of a million. Portrait designed by Sir E.B. MacKennal. 80% silver, 20% copper (.800 fine). 36mm, 23.327 grams as minted.

98. The reverse of the 1936 Canadian *Silver Dollar* from the previous photo. This "Voyageur Reverse" was continued into the 1980s on Canadian *Dollars*. The scene, created by artist Emanuel Hahn, is of a Canadian Indian and a Voyageur (agent for a French-Canadian fur trading company) paddling a canoe past an islet on which two windswept trees are growing. The bundle in the canoe just behind the Indian has tiny letters "HB" for Hudson's Bay Company. The semi-vertical lines in the background field are the northern lights. Can you imagine a more beautiful reverse for a Canadian coin? This specimen is Uncirculated with natural color.

99. Obverse of a 1939 Canadian *Silver Dollar*, with the portrait of Britain's King George VI designed by artist T.H. Paget. 80% silver, 20% copper (.800 fine). With

light golden toning along the right rim.

100. Reverse of the 1939 Canadian *Silver Dollar*, reverse designed by Emanuel Hahn, with a one-year commemorative motif for the Royal Visit of George VI and Queen Elizabeth to Canada. Featured are the Parliament buildings in Ottawa and the Latin inscription "FIDE SVORVM REGNAT" (He rules by the faith of the people). Lovely natural golden toning along the rim, "continued" from the obverse.

101. The reverse side of a 1951 South African *One Penny* piece, bronze, with darkly toned devices and lettering, which contrast nicely with the lighter fields. 3,787,000 struck for circulation, and 2,000 Proofs.

102. 1965 South African silver *Rand* with English legend, .800 fine silver. Natural golden yellow toning along the rims, with unappealing mottled brown toning interspersed.

103. Reverse of the 1965 South African *Rand* from the previous photo. Rather handsome delicate rainbow toning over much of the coin's surface. Toning greatly affects the desirability and therefore the market price of a coin. The quality of the toning visible here is often underappreciated by beginning collectors, who seem to think that bright, shiny, untoned "BU" coins are the only ones worth serious money, hence the epidemic of cleaning and passing off artificially polished AU coins as "Uncirculated."

104. Western Samoa *$1 (One Tala)* copper-nickel business strike of 1969. Just 25,000 struck, along with 1,500 Proofs. Western Samoa is an independent state (since January 1, 1962) in the Pacific Ocean 1,600 miles northeast of New Zealand.

105. Reverse of the Western Samoa *$1 (One Tala)* coin from the previous photo. One year commemorative reverse for the 75th anniversary of the death of Robert Louis Stevenson. Looked down upon by many wealthy collectors who dabble in classical rare coins, modern "topicals" such as this one actually introduce the numismatic hobby to many people. A numismatist should be judged by the amount of his knowledge, not the depth of his wallet. The author collects "alligator and crocodile" topicals, on coins and medals.

106. A 1970 Great Britain Proof Set of eight coins plus the seal of the Royal Mint, in its original hard plastic government holder. This was the last year of British non-decimal coinage. 750,000 Proof Sets were made in 1970.

107. The reverses of the 1970 Great Britain Proof Set. Take out a magnifying glass and look at the detail of these well-struck coins and the handsome surfaces of the *One Penny* piece. Inspect *every* coin, both obverse and reverse, of a Proof Set before buying it: distracting "spots" and unappealing tarnish lower the whole set's market value.

108. A Proof Great Britain 1970 *One Penny* piece of Queen Elizabeth II, the reigning monarch since 1953. Proof coins are made from specially polished dies and blanks and are usually struck under more pressure (and often with multiple striking blows of the coinage press) than are business strikes, hence the well struck-up detail and mirror surfaces of Proofs.

109. The reverse of the 1970 Great Britain *One Penny* piece in Proof, showing "Britannia" as she has appeared on British coins since early in the 19th century. As you can see, this coin has some hairline scratches; handle choice Proofs with great care, by their edges, to avoid marring their beautiful surfaces.

110. Sudan 1971 Proof *20-Ghirsh* coin in copper-nickel, dated 1391 of the Mohammedan Era (AH). Just 1,772 minted. Natural toning with surface marks.

111. The reverses of the coins in the 1971 Panamanian Proof Set of the following photo. The author has not priced the coins in this book that are illustrated in color, nor even many of the black-and-white coin photos, because he believes that market price is only one aspect of numismatics (and such prices fluctuate anyway, so that a published price may very well be obsolete by the time it is read). All the coins illustrated in color are from the author's own collection, and while none is a great rarity, all have a story to tell.

112. A 1971 Panama Proof Set in a hard plastic display holder containing six coins. This set was minted in the quantity of 10,696. Modern foreign Proof Sets are often beautifully struck, of moderate cost, and offer the collector an alternative to routine U.S. Proof Sets ... or to merely accumulating business strikes of foreign coinage, either by "type" or by date runs.

113. A Cayman Islands Proof Set of 1975, in its original government display case, issued in a quantity of just 1,785 sets. Notice the immaculately smooth fields (with an occasional speck of dust drifting across them) and the frosted "cameo" devices. Quality Proofs of the mint-master's art.

114. The reverses of the 1975 Cayman Islands Proof Set

of the previous photo. The Cayman Islands are a British dependency south of Cuba and northwest of Jamaica. Look at the coins' detail with a magnifying glass: the animals and ship designs make nice topical coins for the collector of such. The only reason low-mintage foreign Proof Sets (compared to U.S. sets) are so cheap is low collector demand; if collectors in the United States suddenly wanted to buy foreign Proof Sets with the enthusiasm that they purchase U.S. sets, the market prices of low mintage foreign sets would go through the roof.

115. The reverse of the *$5* piece of the 1975 Cayman Islands Proof Set pictured in the previous photo, featuring the country's coat of arms. The author photographed this coin so that the field would not reflect light into the camera's lens, therefore sharply delineating the frosty white devices. The coin is resting on a pad of dark purple velvet.

116. A Great Britain "*New Penny*" piece of 1979, bronze, with electric coppery toning. Britain adopted the decimal coinage system in 1971, replacing the ancient *PoundShillingPence* system with *100 New Pence* to the *Pound* (5 *New Pence* equal 1 *Shilling*; 25 *New Pence* equal 1 *Crown*). An "older-appearing" portrait of Queen Elizabeth.

117. The reverse of the 1979 Great Britain "*New Penny*" of the previous photo, exhibiting rich natural toning colors. The author purchased this coin at a coin show, specifically for photographing for this book.

118. A selection of casino gambling checks (chips) from both current and obsolete casinos. A popular specialty of exonumia (tokens, medals, etc.) in the last several years has been an explosive growth in the collecting of gambling chips, colorful and historical little items for the hobbyist who wants to branch out from "mere" coins and medals. Prices vary considerably from dealer to dealer; be careful that you don't overpay for a common gambling chip.

119. A copper U.S. Mint medallion, struck by the author on a 19th century coinage press when he visited the Old Mint building in San Francisco. For a fee of $1, visitors are permitted to press a button that strikes this medallion.

120. The reverse of the U.S. Mint medallion that the author struck when he visited the Old Mint building in San Francisco, showing the years of operation of the minting facilities in this building.

121. A double-struck off-center casino gambling token in base metal, very rare and extremely difficult to photo

graph because it is "three-dimensional"—the author has reflected sunlight on the flange at right, which would otherwise not show its detail well. The author used only natural sunlight in all of his photographs in this book (which are his, unless otherwise credited) of coins from his own collection.

122. The other side of the double-struck off-center metal slot machine token pictured in the previous photo. Error *coins* are a popular numismatic collecting specialty, but you'll have to hunt a long time to locate collectors who own a substantial showing of error *tokens* or *medals*.

123. A *Silver Star*, awarded for bravery by the U.S. military. In its original box, as shipped to the recipient. Military combat medals are a specialized branch of exonumia, the part of numismatics that deals with "non-coin" (not legal tender) items. U.S. combat medals have been extensively faked; beware of cheap imitations.

124. A Great Britain World War I *Campaign Medal* with its accompanying ribbon (original or otherwise!). Inscribed along its edge: "515525 Private Arthur William Lord," who served in the 14th (County of London) Regiment (London Scottish). He was born and enlisted in his home in Leicester, and the author's research reveals that he was killed in action in French Flanders, November 24, 1917. Precious history to hold in your hands, a treat that serious numismatists experience when they delve into the backgrounds of their numismatic acquisitions.

125. The reverse of the World War I British *Campaign Medal* shown in the previous photo.

126. *Woman Giving Money to a Serving Woman with a Child* by Pieter de Hooch, painted circa 1668-1672, oil on canvas, 73.0cm x 66.0cm, Los Angeles County Museum of Art, Mr. & Mrs. Allan C. Balch Collection. Reproduced with permission of the Museum.

A contemporary of Vermeer of the "Delft school" style, de Hooch's paintings often depict the quiet virtues of daily life in 17th century middle class Dutch domestic interiors. In this scene, the house mistress has just removed a coin from her purse and is offering it to a servant girl. The fleeting reflections in the mirror above the affluent woman's head and in the glass decanter and goblet on the Oriental carpet-covered table suggest the vanity of worldly efforts and the transitory nature of material possessions. An innocent child, tugging at the servant's dress and with free hand gesturing away from the scene of the picture, reinforces the warning against preoccupation with temporal things.

Index

Intrinsic value, 13, 100
Investing, 137-50
    advantages of, 138
    coin investment rackets, 141
    disadvantages of, 139
    in bullion, 143, 145-6
    tips, 142
Investor, 49
"Investor's Guide to Precious Metals, The," 129

J

J.W. Scott & Co., 91
Jackson, Andrew, 28, 105
Janvier transfer lathe, 42
Jefferson, Thomas, 25
Jefferson "Nickels," 32, 76
Joachimsthalers, 98
John George thalers, 98
John Reich Collectors Society (JRCS), 172
John Reich Journal, 172
Johnson, B.G., 92
Joslin, Edward, 127
Journal of the Barber Coin Collectors' Society, 171
Judean shekels, 17
Jules J. Karp, Inc., 125
Julius Caesar, 16, 17

K

Kellogg & Co., 29
Kennedy Half Dollars, 32, 47, 86
    1976, photos, 86
"Key Dates," 142
King of Siam Proof Set, 89
Kirkpatrick and Gault, 106
Kneass, William, 105
Kossoff, Abe, 64

L

Lange, David W., 165
Large Cents, 15, 26, 27, 28, 29, 42, 64, 73-4, 99, 141, 155
    Canadian, 99
Latin, use on coins, 16
Legal tender, 13
Lepton, 17
Liberty Head Silver Dollars, 31
Liberty Seated coins, 30, 77, 78, 85
Liberty Seated Collectors Club (LSCC), 172
Liberty Seated Dime, 1843, photos, 85
Liberty Seated Silver Dollars, 30, 78
Liberty Standing Quarter Dollars, 32, 76
Liberty Walking Half Dollars, 32, 77
Lincoln Cent, 1943 steel, photos, 35
Lincoln Cents, 32, 52, 75-6, 86, 93, 141
    1909-SVDB, 32, 75
    1914-D, 32, 75, 76

Lincoln Cents, cont.
    1922-"plain," 32, 75, 76
    1943, 76
    1943 Copper, 93
    1943 copper errors, 32
    1943 steel, 32
    1955 Doubled Die, 32, 75, 76, 86
    1974 Aluminum, 93
    varieties, 32
Linett, Dana, 124
Lives of the Twelve Caesars, The, 16
London Mint, 99
Long Beach Exposition, 134
Long Term Silver Supply/Fabrication Demand Balance, chart, 144
Longacre, James B., 74
Lopresto, Samuel, 134
Louis d'or, 99
Louisiana Purchase Exposition medal, photo, 110
Love Token Society (LTS), 107, 172
Love tokens, 107, 110
    photos, 110
Lovett, Robert, 91
Low, Lyman Haynes, 153
Luster, 68

M

M. Junius Brutus, 16
Machine-struck coins, 18
Marcy, William L., 90
Margolis, Arnold, 167
Maria Theresa thalers, photos, 20, 99, 101
Marshall, James, 28
Mason, R.B., 90
McCloskey, John, 172
McDermott, James V., 92
McNall, Bruce, 128
Medal Collector, The, 173
Medal of Honor, 104
Medallic Portraits of Adolph Hitler, 174
Medallic Sculpture, 170
Medals, 54, 103-5, 109, 110
    city, 105
    designer, 105
    historical, 104
    infamous, 105
    medical, 104-5
    memorial, 105
    Olympic Games, 105
    origins, 103-4
    photos, 54, 109, 110
    political, 104
    space, 105
    state, 104

1991 *Silver Eagle* one troy ounce bullion coin with a face value of $1 (on reverse). Issued by the U.S. Mint from 1986 to date, the obverse employs the *Walking Liberty* design created by Adolph A. Weinman for the U.S. *Half Dollar* current from 1916 through 1947. The *Silver Eagle* is minted at Philadelphia and San Francisco in a total mintage of more or less 6 million per year to supply the bullion and collector trade: Weight 31.101 grams, Diameter 40.6mm, Composition 99.93% silver, .07% copper, 1 Troy Ounce fine silver. Author's collection.